The People

Also by Selina Todd

Young Women, Work, and Family in England, 1918–1950

The People

The Rise and Fall of the Working Class,
1910–2010

SELINA TODD

JOHN MURRAY

First published in Great Britain in 2014 by John Murray (Publishers)
An Hachette UK Company

I

© Selina Todd 2014

The right of Selina Todd to be identified as the Author
of the Work has been asserted by her in accordance with the
Copyright, Designs and Patents Act 1988.

A CIP catalogue record for this title is
available from the British Library

ISBN 978-1-84854-881-7
Ebook ISBN 978-1-84854-883-1

Typeset in Bembo Std by Palimpsest Book Production Limited,
Falkirk, Stirlingshire
Printed and bound by Clays Ltd, St Ives plc

John Murray policy is to use papers that are natural, renewable
and recyclable products and made from wood grown in sustainable
forests. The logging and manufacturing processes are expected to
conform to the environmental regulations of the country of origin.

John Murray (Publishers)
338 Euston Road
London NW1 3BH

www.johnmurray.co.uk

Dedicated to Andrew Davies

And in memory of Jack Hirst, 1936–2012

Contents

Introduction

CLASS HAS UNITED and divided Britain since the Industrial Revolution. United, because class is widely accepted as a quint-essentially British fact of life, a heritage and language that we can all share. Divided, because class is no romantic tradition or amusing idiosyncrasy, but is produced by exploitation in a country where a tiny elite has possessed the majority of the wealth. The so-called 'traditional' working class – everyone who worked with their hands – constituted the vast majority of Britons in 1910, when this book begins, and although that was no longer the case a century later, most people still claimed to belong to the working class in 2010. Here, I tell their story.

The years between 1910 and 2010 were the working-class century. During the Industrial Revolution the working class 'was present at its own making', in the words of historian E.P. Thompson: colliers and craftsmen banded together to advance their own interests and challenge those of their employers.[1] But it was in the twentieth century that most Britons came to understand themselves to be working class and to be treated as such by politicians and the press. It was in this century, too – and specifically during and after the Second World War – that the working class became 'the people', whose interests were synonymous with those of Britain itself.

This working class was composed largely of manual workers and their families – miners, dockers and steelworkers, and also domestic servants – and lower grade clerical workers like typists, secretaries, office boys and messengers. They constituted more than three-quarters of the British people until 1950, and more than half as late as 1991. Then there were the large number of non-manual workers – nurses, technicians and higher grade clerical workers – who chose to identify themselves as working class by virtue of their family background and because they believed that working for a living meant they had more in common with other wage-earners than with employers or political leaders. Working-class people, therefore, formed the majority of British society throughout the twentieth century and into the twenty-first. By contrast, employers constituted just 3 per cent of the workforce in the 1900s, and only 4 per cent at the millennium.[2] This book is about how that unequal state of affairs affected people's lives, and how ordinary people adapted to, resisted and modified the circumstances in which they found themselves.

The People uncovers a huge, hidden swathe of Britain's past, but it is also an intimate history. It began as my attempt to find out about the history of one family – my own. My mother, Ruth, was one of six children born in Leeds in the 1940s. Her father, Fred Hirst, was a welder and her mother, Jean, had left the dole queues of inter-war Scotland with her best friend Nancy for the high life of shop work in Woolworths in Leeds. The Hirsts lived in Hunslet, the same industrial district from which Richard Hoggart, author of *The Uses of Literacy*, hailed. But their experience didn't reflect the romantic idyll of respectability described by Hoggart, nor the stable society of *Downton Abbey*. The story I heard was one about the increasing economic and political clout of the working class – especially during and after the Second World War, when factory workers and soldiers became 'the people', and increasingly central to political debate and British culture. But it was also a story about fighting for everything you got, whether by escaping from domestic service in the 1920s; making sure you were in a reserved occupation so you didn't have to fight 'their' war in the 1940s; or throwing orange peel and jeering at Winston Churchill when he appeared on cinema screens in the early 1950s, because it was Labour who had ensured that the 'people's war' brought about a 'people's peace' of welfare and full employment. Despite the post-war reforms, theirs was also a story of anger, that made clear that class inequality – and the indignities it caused – was never eradicated, and came back with a vengeance after 1979.

My father, Nigel, has a different story, but one that has also been missed from the history books. He grew up in Kent as an only child.

Following the early death of his mother, when Nigel was eight, his father suffered a mental breakdown and was institutionalized for the rest of his life. Nigel was taken into care. The post-war welfare state meant that a professional social worker was assigned to his case. But the welfare reforms brought about by the 1945 Labour government were still in their earliest years, and most children in Nigel's position relied on relatives to take them in – or were consigned to the children's homes run by voluntary organizations like Barnado's. Nigel was fortunate that his social worker was determined that he would escape that fate. She made arrangements for him to stay at a local cottage hospital, just a few years after health care had been made freely available to all in 1948, thanks to Labour's National Health Service Act. Nigel eventually found a home with his grandparents, and later an aunt and uncle. Their shared love of financial speculation, whether gambling (his granddad died with a bookie's slip in his back pocket) or get-rich-quick business schemes, spoke of fantasies of a different, better kind of life that no political party ever delivered.

Like most children in the so-called post-war 'golden age' of social mobility, Nigel failed his eleven-plus examination and attended a secondary modern school until the age of fifteen. He and my mother owed their education to routes other than those provided by the state. In my father's case, this was the labour movement: in his late teens he became a clerk for the Workers' Educational Association, an adult education organization founded by trade unionists and socialists in 1903. The WEA sent him to Ruskin College, a trade-union-funded adult education college in Oxford, where he met my mother. After leaving school at sixteen, disillusioned with what her grammar school had to offer, Ruth had become a clerk at Leeds' Family Service Unit (FSU) – a social work organization that aimed to improve the lives of those in need, rather than blame them for their plight. Her work there, and her involvement in the local Labour Party in the early 1960s, also led her to Ruskin. Neither of my parents aspired to climb the social ladder into the middle class: they wanted everyone's opportunities to be improved, and hoped to see Britain become a more equal society, in which working-class culture and life would not automatically be considered inferior. But they never idealized working-class life, for both did want to escape the poverty and uncertainty of their childhood.

I looked in vain for my family's story when I went to university to read history, and continued to search for it fruitlessly throughout the next decade. Eventually I realized that I would have to write this history myself. What began as the history of one family became a story about modern Britain, one based on the stories of scores of ordinary people.[3] They include women as well as men, and they talk of childhood experience as well as adult life – for class, as a relationship based on inequalities of power, affected life beyond the factory and the office. Winifred Foley, a trade unionist's daughter born in 1914, knew she was working class because she had to leave home for domestic service at the age of fourteen. Frank Gogerty, born in Warwickshire in 1918, is one of many people in this book whose life changed radically across the century: homeless at sixteen, he was a prospering car mechanic by 1940. He shared a widely held fear that the Second World War would destroy everything he'd worked for, but came home to relish the 'people's peace'. Prosperous in post-war Coventry, he nevertheless continued to identify as working class because he had to work for a living. Betty Ennis grew up in Iran and came to Britain in 1945; proud of her new council house in the 1950s, she saw her estate become a centre of deprivation by the 1970s, and at the millennium she remained a tireless campaigner for its residents.

Those who came of age after the war had more pleasure and independence when they were young, but found their freedom curtailed by rising unemployment and insecurity in the late 1960s. Teddy Boy Terry Rimmer, born in 1937, had exchanged rock and roll for rebellion on the picket lines of the Ford Motor Company by 1968. Jiving Judy Walker escaped Coventry for adventure in South Africa in the swinging sixties, only to return to a council flat in the 1970s and life as a community campaigner.

Other voices remind us that there was never a golden age of social mobility, and that fighting one's way up the social ladder was never easy or even pleasant. They include Bill Rainford, who thought he had a job for life in 1969, only to find himself made redundant thirty years later, and Paul Baker, the milkman's son who became a financial manager but sometimes wondered if his success was worth the sacrifices it took to leave his working-class background. We hear from all these people and hundreds more about how they made a life for themselves, often struggling in circumstances that, given the chance, they would never have chosen.

Too often, such personal accounts are dismissed as 'nostalgia'; sometimes by historians who are quite willing to use the reminiscences of politicians or aristocrats. It is certainly true that the stories people offer us about the past are framed by the context in which they are told. Most of the personal testimonies I draw on were narrated in the years after 1979 by people who were conscious of living in Thatcher's Britain, or with the legacy of the 1980s: namely the end of full employment and much post-war welfare provision. This certainly shapes their stories, as they compare what they had in the past with what they had after 1979. But even those who excuse themselves for having 'a bad memory' or being 'poorly educated' demonstrate a rich capacity to remember how life felt back then, as well as how they might judge those past experiences now, with the benefit (or otherwise) of hindsight.

Their stories prove that working-class people didn't always accept the views of politicians or employers. In fact, throughout the twentieth century the middle and upper classes were more likely to indulge in overly nostalgic reminiscences of the past than working-class people ever were: from the employers of servants harking back to halcyon days when everyone 'knew their place' to twenty-first-century condemnations of – in the words of the writer Andrew O'Hagan – a 'working class [who] were no longer a working class . . . people who craved not values but designer labels and satellite dishes' and formed 'the most conservative force in Britain'. According to this argument the age of the 'respectable' working class had ended in the 1960s; by the 1980s people had been made lazy by welfare, greedy by consumerism or arrogant by trade unionism, depending on the perspective of the writer.[4] But the stories of ordinary people remind us it was never quite like that: there was no golden age.

They also remind us that the working class was never entirely homogeneous. If gender and generation made a difference, so too did place. 'As you travel northward,' said George Orwell in his *Road to Wigan Pier* of 1937, 'your eye, accustomed to the South or East, does not notice much difference until you are beyond Birmingham. In Coventry you might as well be in Finsbury Park . . . and between all the towns of the Midlands there stretches a villa-civilization indistinguishable from that of the South.'[5] People had begun to move to Coventry from the north in search of work – a trend that was to continue after the Second World War, when migrants from Asia and the Caribbean would join the Welsh, the Irish and the Geordies in the city's increasingly expansive suburbs. 'My city is supersonic,' wrote Mr J. McHugh to the *Daily Mirror* when, in 1968, they asked readers to nominate Britain's 'Boom City'. 'New precincts to shop in. New art galleries . . . New flats and flyovers . . . At the moment our car industry is in the doldrums, but watch us zoom out of this, too.'[6] Alas, by 1981 when the Coventry-born band The Specials released their single 'Ghost Town', their lyrical account of the decimation of deindustrialization resonated in their home town. It is an image that today's residents feel sums up the city's problems, but says nothing about the spirit of its people.

Back in 1933, Liverpool was poorer and darker than Coventry, 'like a city in a rather gloomy Victorian novel', according to the writer J.B. Priestley. The city's working class was crowded into 'slum tenements . . . Faces that had shone for a season in brothels in Victoria's time now peered and mumbled at us. Port Said and Bombay, Zanzibar and Hongkong had called here. The babies told the tale plainly enough.'[7]

In Liverpool, as in many port towns and cities, working-class residents were never exclusively white or British-born. Throughout this book we shall see that there was never a homogeneous 'white working class' whose interests and identity can be distinguished from that of black Britons or recent migrants.

By the 1950s Liverpool was no longer such a popular place to settle, as increasing numbers of people looked to the prosperous south and Midlands for a living. In the 1960s the city became the home of Merseybeat, a centre of the swinging sixties founded on the fortunes of the Beatles, four 'ordinary lads' from Liverpool; but poverty never disappeared, for the city never benefited from the new manufacturing industries proliferating closer to London. 'Liverpool does not suffer from historical amnesia,' the journalist John Pilger pointed out when he visited the city in the 1990s. 'Although its pantheons of the slave trade and the industrial age have been made fit for tourists, the cobbles restored and swept litter free, the past remains defiantly the present. As a keeper of the sweat, blood and tears of ordinary people, Liverpool has few equals.'[8]

The differences between Liverpool and Coventry highlight the diversity of working-class life in twentieth-century Britain. Class is a relationship defined by unequal power, rather than a way of life or an unchanging culture. There can be no 'ideal' or 'traditional' working class. Instead there are individuals who are brought together by shared circumstances and experiences. It is their stories that *The People* sets out to tell.

This book begins in 1910 and ends in 2010. Between these dates, working-class people experienced a massive social and political trans-formation. In 1910 they had few rights and opportunities. They relied on themselves and their families, in an era of scant state social welfare provision and high unemployment. Until the 1940s, the history of the working class was largely one of people fighting for the most basic regulation of their working lives, often fruitlessly.

There were two major turning points for the working class in the twentieth century. The first was the Second World War. The dire need for people's labour in order to win the war gave the working class a new importance. The people themselves ensured that this endured into peacetime by voting in 1945 for a Labour government that left the important legacy of a National Health Service, free education, comprehensive social security and full employment. By 1950 the sons and daughters of servants were almost exclusively factory workers or clerks, most of them trade unionists, and all guaranteed 'cradle to grave' welfare provision and job security.

Important though these post-war years were – and they marked the apogee of working-class people's political and economic power – they were not ones of equality. After 1945, successive governments presented Britain as a meritocracy, in which anyone could climb the social ladder with hard work and talent. But only a few could attain 'success'. Far from being a 'meritocracy', in which anyone could succeed if they worked hard, post-war Britain remained a society where birth mattered more than effort.

But the years between 1940 and the mid-1970s were a period of relative prosperity and promise, especially given what came afterwards. For the second turning point came in 1979, with the election of Margaret Thatcher's Conservative government. As we shall see, the seeds of the particular brand of individualism that she nurtured were planted long before her election victory. From the late 1960s the international economic situation became increasingly uncertain, particularly after the oil crisis of 1973. Both Labour and Conservative governments found it more and more difficult to reconcile the demands of employers for constantly rising profits with those of working-class people who wanted decent housing, adequate wages and, as time went by, some participation in the way their workplaces and communities were managed. In the 1970s successive governments came down on the side of the employers. Yet although this pre-history to Thatcherism is important, 1979 was a watershed when, for the first time in forty years, the gap between the richest and the poorest began to widen rapidly, and Britain witnessed the fall of the working class as an economic and political force.

Most of the people in this book never became rich or famous. There is one exception: Viv Nicholson, whose story is told in 'interludes' throughout the book. In 1961 Vivian Nicholson's husband scooped the largest-ever win on the football pools. Viv famously declared that she would 'spend, spend, spend' their winnings; she did, and was broke by the mid-1970s. I have included Viv's story because it is so markedly different from the archetypal narrative of the 'trad-itional' working class, striving for either respectability or revolution. In this book I ask what happens to our understanding of the twentieth century if we place other groups into this story: domestic servants, schoolchildren, Tory voters and migrants. It is not a romantic or triumphalist account. We don't need working-class people to be revolutionary heroes or helpful neighbours in order to make the point that inequality is damaging and wrong. I began this book because I couldn't find the history of these working-class people in the established record of the twentieth century – and I also couldn't discover it in any of the romanticized myths of the working class promoted by left-wing politicians and academics or by sympathetic charity workers. The people I write about were not helpless victims of poverty who needed others to speak for them. Like Viv, they had minds and tongues of their own.

I have called these fragments of Viv's life 'interludes' in order to distinguish them in form and content from the more substantive chapters. They are drawn from Viv's autobiography and from press reports, supported by other personal testimonies and sources that link Viv's story back to the bigger themes of the book.[9] They weave the broader, public story that I tell into a more private and personal experience that shows that class is as much about personal feelings as it is about public action.

Viv's life offers, in magnified and glamorized form, a version of what happened to the working class. Between 1910 and 1945 the working class transformed themselves from the poor into the people. They did not all want to become respectable as middle-class social investigators fondly hoped: many wanted freedom from want and from anxiety, and took advantage of a bit of security or financial credit to have a good time when they could. They hankered for the good things in life, and after the Second World War they were encouraged to do so. Yet even when they managed to get holidays and houses they remained at the bottom of the political and economic pile. Inherited wealth, education and networks remained important and influential; sudden wage rises, a minimum wage, or even a windfall on the pools could not close this gap. In the 1980s the good times came to an end. The government accused people of causing their own return to poverty through greed or fecklessness. But like Viv, who as a pensioner defiantly claims to have 'no regrets', many of these people refuse to eschew their working-class identity.

I have sought to write a hopeful history. A majority of British people continue to identify themselves as working class today. In the middle of a major recession, most people, regardless of whether they identify themselves as working class, are acutely aware that economics matters: that who holds economic power, and what they do with it, makes a profound difference to the quality of all our lives. As we shall see, many people question the notion that individual interests reign supreme; that anyone can get on with hard work and effort;

and that this society is as good as it gets. Those who won wars, who got an education against the odds, who fought for better rights at work, and who worked hard to give their children the best possible start only to see them joining dole queues emphasize that life has not always been thus, and that it can change again.

PART I

Servants, 1910–39

I

Defiance Below Stairs

'ON OR ABOUT December, 1910,' wrote Virginia Woolf in 1923, 'human character changed.' This transformation was personi-fied 'in the character of one's cook. The Victorian cook lived like a leviathan in the lower depths, formidable, silent, obscure, inscrutable; the Georgian cook is a creature of sunshine and fresh air; in and out of the drawing-room, now to borrow the *Daily Herald*, now to ask advice about a hat.'[1]

Woolf was not alone in considering 1910 a watershed: the *Manchester Guardian* considered it 'a unique year' of political and social turbulence, and in many ways the year marked the emergence of the modern working class.[2] January began with a general election. The Liberal government called this in the hope of overturning the House of Lords' rejection of David Lloyd George's 1909 'People's Budget'. This Budget, which promised more state welfare assistance, proved popular with voters. The Liberals were returned to government, though with a massively reduced majority. Keir Hardie's ten-year-old Labour Party increased its MPs from twenty-eight to forty – largely due to voters in industrial districts – and now held the balance of power. Meanwhile, the political power of Britain's aristocracy was seriously undermined.

In May, Edward VII's sudden death encouraged the belief that the stability of the Edwardian era was at an end. Debate raged over how post-Edwardian Britain should be governed, and in whose interests. In July 10,000 suffragists offered one response, when they rallied in Trafalgar Square to demand votes for women. That autumn, working men and women added their voices to the call for reform. *The Times* lamented the 'strikes of an almost unexampled character' that broke out across the country, as men and women, old and young, demanded better wages and working conditions.[3] In August women chain makers in Cradley Heath in the Black Country struck for a minimum wage and a ten-hour day; in October their employer acquiesced, marking an important victory for the labour movement and for women. In November a strike of 30,000 miners in the South Wales valleys culminated in battles between workers and the British Army, after Home Secretary Winston Churchill ordered armed troops into the town of Tonypandy. On 18 November – 'Black Friday' – more than 300 suffragettes clashed with police outside parliament, leading to a six-hour riot in which 115 women were arrested and many more assaulted.

Meanwhile, Parliamentary debate about the power of the House of Lords reached an impasse, and in December the government called a second general election. Voting began on 3 December and did not conclude until 19 December, adding to an impression that Britain was politically volatile, if not unstable. The Liberals – who stood on a promise to abolish the House of Lords' right to veto legislation and to implement Irish Home Rule – were returned to government, and Labour gained two more seats.

In 1910 class relations changed for ever. Looking back on the year, a conservative *Times* editorial concluded that 'democracy, in the arrogance of its newly-asserted power, appears to believe that it can dispense with everything that in the past has made the real greatness and the enduring prosperity of nations'.[4] Whether democracy could or should survive was uncertain. On one side were those who agreed with *The Times* that Britain was better off with a strong aristocracy and a disenfranchised working class. On the other were working people like the miners of Tonypandy and the chain makers of Cradley Heath, who argued that ordinary workers should have more say over welfare, work and pay, both through the ballot box and in negotiation with their employers.

Woolf was right to see servants as barometers of social change. In 1910 – and in 1923 – domestic servants constituted the largest single group of working people in Britain.[5] Servants' relations with their employers were widely viewed as British society in microcosm. According to Ramsay MacDonald, speaking as Labour's first Prime Minister in 1924: 'The true separation in society is the moral and economic line of division between the producer and the non-producer, between *those who possess without serving and those who serve* [my emphasis].'⁶ And in the years after 1910, servants were central to the modern working class that was emerging. During the nineteenth century only skilled workers had had the bargaining tools to fight successfully for a modicum of power. Armed with a trade, their threats to strike or desert their post had far more impact than those of unskilled labourers; and unlike servants they worked alongside tens or hundreds of other wage-earners, with whom they could forge ties of friendship and solidarity. It was they who formed trade unions, and practised collective self-help in friendly societies. But by 1910 unskilled workers were increasingly making their voices heard, and their demands were increasingly hard to ignore.

The Edwardian years are often recalled as a 'long garden party on a golden afternoon' – at least for the wealthy – in which everyone knew their place and was fairly content with it.⁷ The reality was more unstable, uncertain and changeable. In 1900 the formation of the Labour Party testified to the rising significance of industrial workers as a political force. The Trades Union Congress was already thirty-two years old, but the establishment of the Labour Party marked a major advance for the unions.

Labour's success in the 1906 general election – it returned twenty-nine MPs – had an immediate effect. Worried about the threat of a Labour majority, or, worse, mass strikes, Herbert Asquith's Liberal government quickly introduced a series of welfare reforms. These gave the state greater responsibility for people's social conditions than ever before. The 1906 Trade Disputes Act ruled that unions were not liable for any damages incurred as a result of strikes; in the same year, the Workers' Compensation Act offered remuneration to people injured at work. In 1908 the miners – a strongly unionized workforce – won an eight-hour working day, and the government introduced an Old Age Pensions Act, which offered a non-contributory state pension to people aged over seventy who earned less than £31 a year. Flora Thompson, the oldest daughter of an Oxfordshire stonemason and a former nursemaid, was a thirty-two-year-old post office clerk in Bournemouth when the pension was introduced. She recalled the impact of the new arrangements in *Lark Rise to Candleford*: 'At first when they went to the Post Office . . . tears of gratitude would run down the cheeks of some, and they would say as they picked up their money, "God bless that Lord George [Lloyd George]" . . . and "God bless you, Miss!" and there were flowers from their gardens and apples from their trees for the girl who merely handed them the money.'[8]

In 1911 the Liberals introduced a National Insurance Act, which provided insurance against sickness and unemployment for manual workers and those earning less than £160 per year. The government had constructed a basic safety net, which covered not only the poorest, but all those who had to work for a living. In doing so, the Liberals established a foundation for the welfare state. They also acknowledged the labour movement's central claim: that those who had to work for their living had specific interests and needs that the government must address. The Liberals hoped their legislation would prevent popular protest, but in order to do so, their policies had to acknowledge that the working class was a distinct social and political group.

These reforms did not go far enough for many working-class people. Between 1910 and 1914 strikers and suffragettes attracted reams of newsprint in the British press. Labour activists and feminists made increasingly vociferous protests that all adult men and women be granted the right to vote. They argued that it was unjust to exclude 5 million men simply because they didn't own sufficient property, and that women's exclusion on the grounds of sex was ridiculous in a world where women's labour – as workers and as mothers – was so essential. In 1913 the suffragettes of the Women's Social and Political Union (WSPU), led by Emmeline Pankhurst, intensified their campaign to destroy public and private property, hoping that the resulting mayhem would force the government to take them seriously. Like most of the major social and political movements of the twentieth century, the WSPU's membership crossed class lines. Many of the leaders, including the Pankhursts, were from the middle class. In June 1913 Emily Davidson, a graduate of London and Oxford Universities, was killed at the Epsom Derby, when she stepped in front of the king's horse with a banner demanding votes for women. But suffragettes also included working-class women like Hannah Mitchell, a Lancashire milliner, who had come to the conclusion that 'without us having the vote, no one would ever put paid to the life of drudgery that trying to make ends meet caused us'.[9]

Women like Hannah Mitchell, who came to the suffrage campaign from the labour movement, argued that economic injustice was as great an evil as sexual inequality. In 1910, frustrated with the Liberal government's reluctance to commit funds to medical care, Labour women opened London's first child welfare clinic. Many middle-class nineteenth-century reformers like Helen Bosanquet had argued that the high death rate among working-class mothers and their children was due to poor parenting and sanitation. Against this, these Labour women stressed that poverty was to blame, and campaigned for the state to provide better food, housing and medical care.[10] In the same year, the Women's Co-operative Guild – which represented more than 27,000 women – called on the government to enfranchise all adult women, to allow them to serve on juries and to become barristers, to establish school clinics and to make divorce cheaper 'so as to be within reach of the poor'.[11] Their calls fell on deaf ears.

Meanwhile, thousands of factory workers were joining the picket lines. On Clydeside, in Scotland's industrial heartland, the number of working days lost to strikes between 1910 and 1914 was four times greater than the level recorded for the preceding decade. The strikers – many of them unskilled workers – demanded higher wages and shorter working hours, but also more negotiation over working conditions.[12] These protesters were particularly concerned about their employers' opportunistic tendency to define workers as 'unskilled' if they were involved in any procedure involving machinery, thereby justifying the payment of very low wages. This definition of 'skill' as non-mechanized artisanship was becoming redundant by 1910, as factories made increasing use of automated belts and industrial machines. Workers pointed out that operating machinery demanded skills such as speed, dexterity and strength. As Alice Foley discovered when she began work at a Lancashire mill aged fourteen, even the most menial job demanded 'nimble fingers' if she was to avoid serious injury. Her work left her 'so exhausted that I frequently fell asleep over tea or supper', yet she was paid a pittance as an 'unskilled' young woman.[13]

Fourteen-year-old Alice joined a strike instigated by weavers, who were concerned about automation in Lancashire's mills: 'in return for this technical innovation management claimed a substantial reduction in wage rates'. Strikers like Alice Foley challenged their employers' assumption that 'unskilled' women and young people were content, apathetic or entirely powerless. The 'long and exhausting' dispute in which she took part ended in almost complete failure, with the mill's owner making just a few grudging concessions. The same was true of most strikes at this time. Nevertheless, the protesters showed a determination and commitment to their cause that surprised many employers, politicians and journalists. In 1912 Dundee's jute workers – many of them women, most of them young – struck for higher wages. After three weeks, the *Scotsman* was amazed to find that 'nearly 30,000 workers' remained on strike, despite 'the distress which prevails in the homes of the poor people' – a reminder that many working-class families relied on women's earnings as well as men's.[14] This strike also ended in almost complete defeat. Yet as Alice Foley later wrote, the militancy of these years was 'a first shot in the human struggle to retain traditional methods of production against those fierce on-coming thrusts of technocracy and auto-mation which were to harass and bedevil the cotton industry for the next half-century.'[15] The actions of people like her did help to establish a modicum of negotiation with their employers and ensured that industrial workers were not forced into the deferential role demanded of domestic servants, who lacked any collective bargaining rights.

On the eve of the First World War, however, employers refused to grant their workers many rights at all. Unemployment was high, and their government favoured the harsh repression of industrial militancy; the mill owners and manufacturers of Britain could defy the strikers with the support of ministers of state. Less than a month after the Dundee jute strike of 1912 had failed, the socialist trade union activist Tom Mann was charged in Manchester with inciting mutiny. Mann, the son of a domestic servant and a miner, had helped to organize the great London Dock Strike of 1889, one of the first mass mobilizations of unskilled industrial workers staged in Britain.

In 1911 he had headed the committee that organized a huge strike of Liverpool's transport workers, a dispute that became infamous for the brutality shown by police towards peaceful demonstrators on 'bloody Sunday' – 13 August 1911. The Home Office and the police had been trying to bring Mann to court for his political activities ever since, and the decision to try him for sedition – on flimsy evidence – was taken at ministerial level. Mann received a six-month jail sentence of which he served seven weeks. After his release, the irrepressible Mann actively supported strikers in Britain and France in the years leading up to the First World War.[16]

The Liberal government's harsh reaction to industrial militancy was entirely in keeping with ministers' attitude to the working class more generally. Their welfare reforms were intended as a panacea that would undermine the labour movement, not meant to narrow the gap between rich and poor. The Workers' Compensation Act and the National Insurance Act replicated benefits that were already offered by trade unions and friendly societies. Those who were too poor to contribute to the existing insurance schemes found that the Liberal reforms offered very little. At 5s per week, the old age pension of 1908 could not keep people out of poverty (in 1901 the social reformer B.S. Rowntree had estimated that it cost a person 7s per week to live at a bare minimum, and Rowntree's minimum was very frugal).[17] The government had no interest in ending poverty, but only in doing the minimum required to pacify the public.

The strikers of Bolton, Clydeside, Dundee and Liverpool therefore had good reason to be angry. The government's promises of help raised their expectations – but the meagre assistance that the reforms delivered provoked bitter frustration. In 1913 a study undertaken by the Fabian Women's Group (allied to the thirteen-year-old Labour Party) indicated that poverty was a fact of life for many thousands of ordinary families. *Round about a Pound a Week* was the brainchild of Maud Pember Reeves, a founding member of the group. In 1909 she had persuaded participants to undertake a study of family life in Lambeth. Her introduction to their book indicates how intimidating the well-heeled reformer initially found the district she had chosen to investigate:

> Take a tram from Victoria to Vauxhall Station. Get out under the railway arch which faces Vauxhall Bridge, and there you will find

Kennington Lane. The railway arch roofs in a din which reduces the roar of trains continually passing overhead to a vibrating, muffled rumble. From either end of the arch comes a close procession of trams, motor-buses, brewers-drays, coal-lorries, carts filled with unspeakable material for glue factory and tannery, motor-cars, coster-barrows, and people . . . Such is the western gateway to the district stretching north to Lambeth Road, south to Lansdowne Road, and east to Walworth Road, where live the people whose lives form the subject of this book.[18]

Between 1909, when Pember Reeves and her collaborators first stepped under the railway arch, and 1913 they visited forty-two Lambeth families twice a week.

The Fabian women deliberately chose to study a group who were 'not the poorest people of the district. Far from it!'[19] Pember Reeves and her team were keen to show that hawkers, street entertainers and beggars were not the only ones who struggled to make ends meet. They revealed that a huge number of workers, including shop assistants, fish-fryers, seamstresses and factory hands, earning wages between 18s and 30s per week, also struggled to feed and clothe their families. As the Liberal weekly journal, the *Nation*, put it: 'If anyone wants to know how the poor live today, he will find it in Mrs Pember Reeves' little book . . . It is not outcast London that we are shown, but ordinary London, resolutely respectable; not "the submerged Tenth," but somewhere about the half.'[20]

Pember Reeves's most radical conclusion was that poverty was not confined to a tiny number of feckless people. The Fabian women challenged the assumption that the poor were to blame for their hardship – a judgement characteristic of Conservative and Liberal politicians and many of their middle-class voters. Under the terms of the nineteenth-century Poor Law, those who could not afford to keep themselves, whether because of low wages, sickness, unemployment or old age, had to turn to their local Board of Guardians for support. This committee of local ratepayers – usually including municipal councillors, a clergyman and an assortment of Liberal and Conservative voices – determined whether applicants deserved help, how much assistance to give them, and whether such help was offered in cash or in the form of food or clothing.

In 1904 thirty-three-year-old Hannah Mitchell, a member of the Independent Labour Party (ILP), witnessed how callous the Guardians could be. Hannah, the daughter of an agricultural worker, had left home at fourteen to become a servant. She had hated this work, particularly after her employer's son attempted to rape her. She managed to save up enough money to escape to lodgings in a Derbyshire village, where she found work as a shop assistant and involved herself in the trade union movement. She then became a seamstress, married a tailor whom she met at socialist meetings, and in 1904 was elected to Ashton-under-Lyne's Board of Guardians. Hannah was disgusted to discover that, with the exception of Labour representatives, all the other Guardians 'regarded the recipients of relief as ungrateful oafs battening on charity'.[21] This hadn't changed ten years later when the Fabian women published their findings. They demonstrated that Britain's labour market and welfare system ensured that the majority of working people lived in, or close to, poverty. This was a damning indictment of Britain's governance, especially after the era of Liberal 'reform'.

Meanwhile, the growth of an assertive working class was provoking fear among Britain's middle and upper classes. The 'servant problem' – defined by the *Concise Oxford Dictionary* in 1911 as the difficulty 'of getting and controlling servants' – attracted even more press attention than the strikers.[22] Employers' complaints of the trouble in finding 'reliable' servants were as old as the occupation itself. Yet in the years preceding the Great War, employers' anger and anxiety grew, because servants were increasingly behaving like industrial workers – as if they were, in fact, a working class, with shared interests that could conflict with those of their employers. This was particularly worrying since servants were meant to be pliable: most of them were young women in their teens, who left their family home at the age of twelve or fourteen to work and lodge in the home of their employer.

Between 1911 and 1914 the 'servant problem' became a focus for broader middle- and upper-class concerns about the increasingly assertive working class.[23] As long as they behaved in a subservient manner, employers could believe that the social order was stable; but a sly look or a barely disguised sneer were, in an era of welfare reform, strikes and suffragism, seized upon as yet another sign of class war. Masters and mistresses from the upper and middle classes alike bemoaned the loss of 'deference'. Lady Muriel Beckwith, the daughter of the seventh Duke of Richmond, characterized this relationship as 'a curiously close and unwritten law of obligation and affection . . . [and] dependence one on the other'.[24] Many employers argued that servants' conduct made them unfit for social freedoms, let alone the vote. 'Motoring at night, I hear, is one of the latest amusements,' claimed an anonymous employer of servants, who signed herself 'HMT' in a letter to the *Scotsman*. This anonymous writer argued that servants were regularly picked up by young men for evenings of racing around country lanes, leaving their posts deserted, 'and the old lady . . . is left in the empty house with door unlocked'.[25]

These employers' anger was exacerbated by the debate over national insurance. In 1908, when the Liberal government initially proposed introducing this, Asquith's Cabinet made clear that they intended to include servants in their sickness insurance scheme. This would require male servants to pay 4d per week, female servants 3d per week – and their employer 3d per week. They were to make these payments at the post office in return for stamps, which either employer or servant would keep in a book. Then, in times of illness, the payments entitled a male servant to 10s per week and a woman to 7s 6d per week, although nothing was paid for the first three days' sickness in order to prevent 'malingering'.[26] The National Insurance Act was to become law in 1911.

Some servants bitterly resented this proposed drain on their low wages, but the most vehement opponents were their employers. 'A rampageous campaign of "ninepence for fourpence" and "no stamp-licking" was launched on the country by irate mistresses and shocked respectability,' recalled Alice Foley, then a young cotton worker and trade unionist.[27] The Act, wrote one mistress to *The Times*, did 'not sufficiently differentiate the domestic servant boarded in the house from the trade employé for profit'.[28] The private home, such employers suggested, must remain beyond government interference.

These employers portrayed service as being distinct from other forms of wage labour, though, in reality, servants entered the labour market for the same reason as all other workers: they needed the money. In 1911 *The Times* published a flurry of letters opposing the Act, penned by such dignitaries as Lady Portsmouth, Lady Stanley and Sir William and Lady Bull. They declared that national insurance would 'weaken the kindly ties between masters and servants'; yet also that the Act would 'place . . . a premium on malingering'. They suggested that 'the splendid record of health and reluctance to give in which our maidservants have established' was only down to their harsh working conditions and lack of benefits. Give these young working women any licence, and they were likely to become feckless and irresponsible, a drain on society.[29] This argument against welfare provision would endure throughout the twentieth century and beyond.

Opponents of the Act worried that insurance would change the relationship between employers and servants into one in which the latter had a modicum more control. Until 1911 the law agreed that employers' needs should come first: the only legal obligations that a servant's employer had to fulfil were the provision 'of necessary food, clothing' and 'lodging'; they were also prohibited from inflicting 'any bodily harm' on servants sufficient to endanger their life or permanently damage their health.[30] Servants' working hours and conditions were unregulated; many endured twelve-hour days and few holidays (typically a Sunday once a week, a half day once a fortnight, and a week's unpaid annual leave).

The 1911 National Insurance Act did not, in fact, threaten this situation. The inclusion of servants made sense to the Liberal government as a means of protecting the occupation from decline, at a time when job opportunities in factories and shops were slowly expanding. The Liberals considered that the Act would offer a minimal degree of protection to all workers, while inculcating thrift by encouraging wage-earners to contribute towards their future welfare.[31] That the scheme was based on contributions, rather than on a redistributive tax, only reinforced the inequality between the richest and the poorest; it was, in George Bernard Shaw's words, 'a wholesale attack on the manifestly insufficient subsistence of the poor to save the visibly overflowing pockets of the rich'.[32] But the employers of domestic servants saw only a threat to their long-established right to treat their servants as possessions.

23

An investigation into the unpopularity of domestic service found that 'servants often speak sadly of themselves as a class apart'. The Women's Industrial Council derived their conclusions from question-naires filled in by more than 700 employers and over 500 servants in 1914. The latter's responses testified to servants' loneliness and discontent with their long hours and poor conditions. These were women like Margaret Morris, born in an Oxfordshire hamlet in 1900, who entered service with a farming family shortly before her fourteenth birthday. 'They fetched me in a pony and trap and that night I felt rather homesick . . . the next morning, after I'd had my breakfast, I was given a dustpan and brush and told to sweep out the dining room . . . I had my dinner on my own in the kitchen.' On her fourteenth birthday, a cold wintry day, 'I had to pluck this duck; I wasn't allowed to do it in the kitchen so I sat in a big chair in the yard. I didn't know how to set about it – oh! I was so unhappy. And then the postman came and brought me my birthday cards, and that cheered me up . . . but the lady wasn't too happy about it.' On one occasion when Margaret timidly asked if she could stay out until 9 p.m. on her weekly half day – the only time she could see her family – her mistress refused: '"No, we're not going to pay a maid and make our own supper," she said; "you'll be back here at 8 o'clock as usual." That's what they could get away with with country girls.'[33]

But although many servants hailed from rural backgrounds, the Women's Industrial Council revealed that 'they are by no means cut off from the remainder of the industrial community. The fathers and brothers of many of them have been on strike in recent years, and they have read the newspapers. Industrial unrest and the waves of the suffrage agitation have reached the minds of those servants who think, and have helped to focus the resentment of those who have only room in their minds for their own grievances.'[34] Servants, far from being either stupid or feckless, were knowledgeable about other occupations. They knew about the benefits that trade unions, wage regulation and reductions in working hours had brought to friends and relatives, and were frus-trated not to experience these.

At a time when other workers were gaining the right to negotiate collectively with their employers, servants were expected to be entirely subordinate to their masters and mistresses. They were obliged to be neither seen nor heard when cleaning, except when performing tasks of obsequious servility. In 1905 fifteen-year-old Edith Green of Keighley, West Yorkshire, began working for a coal merchant's family in Barnsley. When her employer returned home from work each evening, 'I even had to take his shoes off and put . . . his slippers on. And I thought that was a dreadful thing to do.'[35] Some employers changed their servants' names if they felt their workers' parents had made too 'uppity' a choice.[36] Edith Lockwood was twelve when she entered service in 1899. This was her first time away from home, and she was lonely and missed her mother. Nothing was familiar, not even her name, for her mistress 'didn't call me Edith . . . because she had a friend called Edith so she called me [my middle name] Annie'.[37] In 1914 Catherine Bairnson, just past her twelfth birthday, left her home in the Shetland Isles to become a maid in a middle-class Edinburgh household. Her mistress 'would inspect my room . . . she would look in my drawers when I was out.' This young maid quickly learned that, in the eyes of the wealthy and privileged, 'you weren't to be trusted.'[38] These rules, regulations and petty indignities taught servants to know their place: they were lowlier than their employers, and would remain so however hard they worked.

But many servants refused to accept that this *was* their place. It is a mark of just how authoritarian many employers were that servants' behaviour caused so much anger, for although defiance was not unknown, it was certainly muted. Trade unionists expressed frustration at the difficulty of organizing maids, but many servants couldn't see what a union would do for them, living as they did in houses that usually employed just one or two people. Still, despite their lack of union representation and their heavy dependence on their employers for bed and board, many refused to adopt the subservience demanded of them. Mrs Myers, who as a young woman entered service in Leicestershire, was among them. When her employer showed her the required uniform, Mrs Myers told her that 'I wouldn't wear [a cap] . . . cos I don't like the stuff on my hair.' She also refused to wear 'one of the aprons crossed over at the back with lace'.[39] Caps and aprons were deeply unpopular signs of servants' difference from most other waged workers, and a mark of an employer's control over their employee's body as well as their time.

Still more servants kept to themselves; the silence that their employers hoped was deferential was often a mark of dissent in a job where their privacy was constantly invaded. In her mid-teens Margaret Morris left the farming family she served to take up work in north Oxford's middle-class households. While Virginia Woolf believed that maids were becoming more assertive in treating their employers like equals by bouncing into the drawing room to 'ask advice about a hat', many servants saw this as a means of pacifying mistresses who were instrusive to the point of nosiness. 'They used to pass an opinion sometimes, if they liked a hat,' recalled Margaret Morris. 'In those days everyone wore hats, so if you had a nice one, you might say something to them about it, or ask them about it. So sometimes I used to volunteer information, but not very often.' Behind this apparently open relationship, Margaret was able to carve out a slim social life for herself. 'If we were supposed to go to church and we didn't want to go, we didn't. If we were going out with a boyfriend, we didn't tell them [her mistresses].'[40]

Many servants simply made the best they could of their job. Some enjoyed a warm relationship with their employers, like Kate Edwards, who worked as a companion to a middle-class woman in the 1900s and described her as 'a real friend', suggesting a relationship that was affectionate rather than deferential.[41] Others took pride in their skills, however poorly remunerated these were. Florence Thompson, born in 1893, had enjoyed domestic science at school: 'the cooking and all that sort of thing attracted me,' and this encouraged her to enter domestic service.[42] Her pride in her skills challenged employers' low value of domestic work that could be remunerated in meagre wages. Those servants lucky enough to be in larger, wealthy households might relish the food or warm clothing with which they were provided. Bessie Allan worked at New College, Oxford, in the 1910s. She came from a poor home in East Oxford – 'I'd never been in a posh house, let alone a college, before!' – and enjoyed the lavish breakfasts of 'porridge, toast and kedgeree'.[43] Like many servants in institutions, she derived her pleasure from these material benefits rather than from her relationship with her employer.

Some servants emulated their employers' lifestyles. In 1913 twelve-year-old Lily Blenkin, a carpenter's daughter from Easington, County Durham, became a maid in an upper-middle-class household. She believed that she learned a lot from her employers' lifestyle, which she judged 'better than mine'.[44] But Lily Blenkin's attitude towards her employers was not as straightforwardly deferential as this comment suggests. 'If I'd been better at school,' she said, 'I might have gone in for something more than domestic service.'[45] Many maids compensated for their thwarted aspirations by taking a vicarious pleasure in their employers' lives, valuing the proximity that their posts afforded them to smart dinners and fashionable parties.

There was a thin line between emulation and overstepping the mark. Maids who resented their employers might gossip about them, or wear their mistresses' clothes.[46] Mrs Bairnson recalled that on those occasions when her Edinburgh mistress went out, 'I'd never have had the nerve then to do it on my own but the other two servants said "come on" . . . We went upstairs and had tea in the drawing room. Well it was the only way to – to get above it.'[47] Even Lily Blenkin transgressed her allotted role, for in claiming that 'being in service taught me how to make things nice when I got married', she asserted her right and ability to live like her employers, as far as her limited resources allowed. She refused to accept that her role in life was primarily to serve her social superiors. And that refusal seemed radical and dangerous to many servants' employers in 1914. It denied the service relationship on which the British social hierarchy had been based for so long.

The changing attitudes of servants that Virginia Woolf discerned had brought them few tangible results by 1914. Despite the growth in factory work, many thousands of people had to rely on domestic service for employment, and couldn't easily afford to lose their job by openly defying an employer. Nevertheless, their aspirations to escape service for something better caused their masters and mistresses increasing anxiety, as factory jobs became available and as the insurance debate intimated that servants were workers, too. Employers were acutely aware that the radical strikers of the industrial picket lines had representatives stationed in their parlours and kitchens. Here was a sign that a modern working class was emerging, a shared identity that bound together unskilled workers and artisans, maids and miners, in frustration and anger at how little life offered them.

If the relationship between strikers and servants caused the country's masters and mistresses some consternation, so too did the realization that their servants would gladly desert their posts for something else. Before 1914, that 'something else' usually meant marriage. Despite being fond of her mistress, Kate Edwards said, 'if a gel got a good chance of a nice steady man what 'ould provide her with a home and a roof over her head, she took it.'[48] Marriage provided freedoms that service could never offer, and maids tended to marry earlier than factory workers or clerks.[49] When the chance came to leave, even those who professed to enjoy their work, or to have affection for their mistress, packed up and moved on without a backward glance. Margaret Morris stayed in service until she married at the age of thirty-four. She was so happy at her final workplace that she returned there frequently once she was a married woman 'to make jam and bottle fruit'. But it was her companions in servitude she missed, not her mistress. And like many servants, Margaret was determined that her children should not follow in her footsteps: 'I wouldn't want any girl of mine to go into service – it was such a hard life . . . I would have loved to have done office work.'[50] Servants like Margaret Morris made the best of their situation, but their view of the world differed from that of their employers, who believed that it was the job of the working class to serve them.

Britain in 1914 was not a peaceful place. In the years preceding the Great War, the modern working class had begun to emerge. Unskilled workers, including servants, began to assert their independence from their employers with increasing vociferousness. The occasional strikes and riots of the late nineteenth century were replaced with a concerted wave of industrial militancy. The 'servant problem' reached new heights, as maids took the anger expressed by their fathers and brothers on the picket lines into their employers' kitchens and parlours. The labour movement was beginning to make an impact on British political life. The successes of the new Labour Party provoked reforms that did not ameliorate poverty but did question the older division between those who served and those who were served. The Liberal welfare reforms acknowledged that the interests of these two groups were not mutually complementary; that workers' welfare was not adequately served by the existing social and political arrangements; and – in the debate over national insurance – that paid workers, whether in private houses or in factories, had some important interests in common.

Nevertheless, the position of these workers remained weak. '[W]e were a cowed and passive community,' judged Alice Foley in later years; 'fear of the sack or victimisation' prevented anything else. 'We might, at off moments, have had mild yearnings for a more gracious existence, but they were nebulous urges rather than dynamic thrusts.'[51] She was a millworker; servants had even less power. They did, however, have examples of 'gracious existence' in front of them on every working day, in the form of their wealthier employers. Living in the dark corners of comfortable houses, servants were constantly able to contrast their own living conditions with those of their masters and mistresses. At the same time, they could compare their lack of bargaining power with the limited, but growing rights of fathers, brothers and sisters engaged in the factories. In 1914 they were rich only in hopes and dreams. War, and its aftermath, would give them the ability to realize a few of these.

2

Bobbed–Haired Belligerents

O N 4 AUGUST 1914 the British government declared war on
Germany. The Great War – allegedly the war to end all wars
– had begun. Within months, servants had virtually disappeared from
middle- and upper-class households, as young women flocked to the
munitions factories. Fifteen-year-old Robert Roberts, an engineering
apprentice in Salford, observed that the exodus from service was due
to young women's desire for 'freedom – above all, freedom to meet
men easily'. This freedom was granted by the proliferation of mill
and shop jobs as men went off to fight, and by the nation's need
for munitions, which greatly expanded the number of factory jobs
available.[1] These posts offered shorter working hours and better wages
than servants received and, crucially, the chance of an independent
life. In 1919 the War Cabinet Committee on Women in Industry
discovered that young, working-class women were reluctant to return
'to living-in service, except as a last resort. They want more freedom
and limited hours of work.'[2] By 1921 there were 1,335,389 servants
– a million fewer than in 1911.[3]

The First World War dramatically challenged class relations in
Britain. The conflict brought thousands more people – including
servants – into industry, and these workers won new economic and
political rights. Before the war, those who endured poor pay and
long working hours had had two options: find a better job (not
always possible) or go on strike (which might lead to the sack).
During the war, employers and government needed the workers –
not only skilled artisans, but the unskilled labourers and former
servants who staffed the munitions factories. At least 1 million women
joined the workforce during the conflict. Labour leaders were able
to strike new bargains over wages and working hours with employers

and the government – and to establish a permanent place at the national negotiating table. In 1914, 437,000 women and 3,708,000 men had belonged to trade unions. By 1920 over 1 million women and 7 million men were union members.[4]

But if the shared experience of war work was important in the rise of the modern working class, so too was the aftermath of war. The post-war coalition government of Conservatives and Liberals reneged on wartime promises to provide peacetime employment and 'homes for heroes'. The government coerced many women into returning to the hated domestic service. The combination of raised expectations, as a result of war work, and resentment at the post-war shortage of housing and jobs fuelled ordinary people's desire for regulated industrial work, leisure time and serious political consideration. Employers' attempts to clamp down on new signs of independence among their workers – personified by the fashionably bobbed-haired maid – only exacerbated the tension.

Factory and shop workers did well out of the war. In 1916 the government reached an agreement with the trade unions, whereby the right to strike was curtailed for the duration of the conflict in return for greater negotiating rights. Workers benefited from better pay and shorter working hours. The Andrews family of Bristol were among them. In 1914 Mr Andrews struggled to find work, relying on casual labouring in the city's docks and railway yards to feed his seven children. Nellie, his fourteen-year-old daughter, looked forward with both eagerness and dread to the day she could leave school in 1916: eagerness, because she would be able to contribute to the family coffers, but dread because the only available work was domestic service. Yet by 1915 her family's circumstances had changed; her parents' 'best days were in the war'. Bristol's port was bustling with business, the railways were busier, and the city's factories were looking for new labour as men went off to the front. 'My father had work and my mother had . . . a little job herself.' Nellie's own prospects improved. She was able to get a job at the Wills tobacco factory in Bedminster, south Bristol's largest employer and one of the city's best: as well as paying reasonable wages and providing paid holidays and a pension, the Wills family had equipped their factory with electric lighting, modern machinery, proper bathrooms and a workers' canteen. By 1917 the Andrews family had 'three of us at Wills'. With five regular earners, '[w]e had more food for the little ones, a bit more money'.[5]

Working at Wills was far preferable to being a maid – or a 'skivvy' as factory workers scornfully called them. In 1920 servants were paid between 4s and 18s per week, but in a shop or factory a woman could earn 28s; their weekly wage had doubled since 1914.[6] Factory and shop workers were employed for a forty-eight-hour week, whereas servants were at their employer's beck and call twenty-four hours a day.[7] The war generation had new experiences by which to judge service – and find it wanting. 'Since I came into service I have had to give up all my church work and musical education,' complained a young woman who worked as a cook in 1919 and had begun her working life as a munitions worker. 'A girl in a shop or factory can take up any social work and also improve her education.'[8]

Many middle- and upper-class observers feared that working-class women's rejection of 'skivvying' heralded a wider, radical social transformation. In 1918 the Representation of the People Act granted universal male enfranchisement for men aged over twenty-one; previously, property qualifications had barred 40 per cent of them from voting in national elections. Female householders aged over thirty were also granted the vote, though this left women without property (including most domestic servants) and those in their twenties disenfranchised. These were important victories for the labour and suffrage movements, won from a government that fearfully hoped for a more stable transition to peace than the revolution and revolt seen in Russia and Germany. The 1918 Education Act raised the school leaving age from twelve to fourteen, a goal that had been passionately pursued by a generation of trade unionists in the cotton towns of Lancashire, where mill owners used children as cheap labour. In 1919 the government passed the Housing and Town Planning Act, which required local authorities to house all who needed accommodation. The Housing (Additional Powers) Acts of the same year offered financial incentives to private builders willing to construct houses for sale.

These measures did not, however, stem the flow of support for the labour movement. In 1918 the Labour Party adopted a new constitution, which committed it to the redistribution of wealth. Labour MPs won sixty-three seats in the general election that year, a pronounced shift in working-class allegiance from the Liberals.

Trade union membership had risen during the war, as the unions gained greater power and credibility.[9] But those who supported Labour were also disillusioned with Lloyd George's coalition government. It had won the 1918 election promising a land fit for heroes who voters were assured would return to steady jobs and better homes. Yet by 1919 dole queues were rising, as British industry struggled to convert back to a peacetime economy. The government did nothing to help. Dole payments remained meagre for the thousands of men and women who found themselves out of work. The Fourth Reform Act enfranchised just 40 per cent of women. The coalition government was persuaded by textile manufacturers to delay the implementation of the 1918 Education Act until 1921. Millions of people continued to live in overcrowded slums in Britain's cities. Five hundred thousand families badly needed new houses at the end of the war, but the government did not follow up its legislation with any direct support for local authorities and by 1921 only 214,000 houses had been built.[10]

Rebellion was the immediate consequence. In 1919 riots broke out in most major towns and cities. The police and the army struggled to quell protests in places as disparate as Glasgow and Luton. On 31 January hundreds of striking workers campaigning for a forty-hour week clashed with police at Glasgow's George Square. Among those convicted was the labour activist Emanuel Shinwell. He received five months' imprisonment for incitement to riot. William Gallacher served three months on the same charge. Gallacher, who was later to become a prominent Communist MP, was one of the 'Red Clydesiders' who had first come to the attention of police and politicians in 1915, when these shipbuilding workers and their wives organized rent strikes and walkouts in the shipyards. Those involved were incensed by the behaviour of local landlords and employers, who had used the arrival of hundreds of war workers in the city to raise rents and reduce wages.

The riots of 1919 were triggered by deep resentment at the coalition government's call for a 'national' effort to win the war which, in reality, seemed to cost ordinary workers far more dearly than industrialists and property magnates. The treatment of Shinwell, Gallacher and their fellow rioters fuelled the protesters' sense of injustice. Antagonism and mutual suspicion shaped relations between employers and workers on Clydeside into the mid-1920s, which settled into a vicious cycle of wage cuts, walkouts, and lay-offs.

The Clydeside protesters also included older people, the unemployed, children and women who didn't work, all of whom joined the rent strikes of the post-war years. In Glasgow as elsewhere, many people viewed landlords with at least as much bitterness as employers. Sometimes they were the same people, and often they had a finger in many pies; some came from landowning families, others had got rich as industrialists. In small towns residents could easily trace the connections between landowning gentry, industrialists and landlords, who were often members of the same family. Percy Wiblin grew up in Abingdon, Oxfordshire. His childhood home was an overcrowded house in a medieval courtyard; the decrepit houses were let out by the owner of the clothing factory that took up one side of the court. When Percy married in 1930, he and his wife Lil rented 'a little house . . . full of bloody bugs and fleas' from another local factory owner, Bill Brind. 'People in them days never had a say in nothing,' Percy recalled. 'If someone like the Morland family [local brewery owners and landlords] or the Saxby family came along and said something, what they said went and that's that. That's how the town was run and they had people on the council, well-to-do people, belonging to [these families]. They were the controllers of Abingdon.'[11] While reform of the House of Lords had curtailed some of the aristocracy's political ambitions, their power endured, as many families remained significant landlords, and some adapted to the new challenges of post-war Britain by becoming manufacturers or press magnates. The connection between inherited wealth, industrialists and the political elite was never entirely broken.

By the summer of 1919 frustration at the government's hypocrisy had provoked riots elsewhere. One of the most uproarious was in Luton, where local politics was run along similar lines to those described by Percy Wiblin. Unemployed ex-servicemen were angered by the local council's extravagant victory celebrations. On 19 July they joined the official victory parade and heckled the mayor's proclamation of peace. The crowd then surged forward, causing the mayor and municipal councillors to retreat ignominiously into the town hall pursued by hundreds of protesters. At the subsequent trial of those arrested during the disorder, prosecutors attempted to identify 'ringleaders', but the conflicting reports suggested that the riot was entirely spontaneous. Forty-year-old Maud Kitchener admitted that she had 'urged the crowd to attack the police'. She told a packed courtroom at her trial that she had been 'wearing a soldier's coat for fun', feeling that as a working woman she had more affinity with the soldiers than many of the local dignitaries did.[12] Joseph Pursey, 'wearing three wound stripes', was accused of shouting, 'The mayor and town clerk are in here, boys. Let's fetch them out!'[13] Shops were raided – one group of rioters looted three pianos from a music shop – and the Food Office attacked. The mayor spent the evening hiding in his darkened parlour rather than enjoying the sumptuous banquet the council had planned. In the early hours of the morning he was smuggled out of town disguised as a special constable.

Fear was the most significant result of the riots: fear of the working class and of what they were capable. In Luton, the mayor retired from political life, the council organized a banquet for workhouse residents, and the rioters received light sentences, reflecting the authorities' fear of repercussions. In Glasgow the Red Clydesiders did not achieve all they hoped for but their actions checked the avaricious ambitions of their employers and landlords. In this climate many politicians cast uneasy glances at Russia, where war had resulted in revolution, and at Germany and Italy where revolution was only narrowly averted. Fear of working-class people's collective power was to shape relations between parliament and the labour movement and, no less significantly, between employers and workers for the next decade.

In October 1922 the Conservative Party decided to end their post-war coalition government with the Liberals. Lloyd George resigned as Prime Minister, to be replaced by the Conservative leader Andew Bonar Law. A month later, Bonar Law called a general election which saw his party returned to government. The Conservatives won primarily with middle-class votes, but they also attracted some of the new working-class voters, having assiduously targeted newly enfranchised working men since 1918. Party political affiliations had never been divided entirely along the lines of social class, but the rise of the Labour Party provoked anxiety among some Conservatives and Liberals that the working class might now unite to oust them from power. After 1918 both Liberals and Conservatives worked hard to forge mutually beneficial alliances in English, Welsh and Scottish municipal politics. These alliances were, as the historian James Smyth points out, 'always for one purpose – to keep Labour out of office'. They did so primarily by courting the vote of those electors who swelled the ranks of organizations like the Middle Class Union, and whose anxieties about taxation and working-class independence most Liberal and Conservative politicians shared. But these parties also offered a negative appeal to working-class voters, by promoting an anti-socialist message that stressed its links to 'foreign' Bolshevism, violence, tyranny and economic instability. Voting Conservative was, for some working-class men, a vote that marked them out as patriots; it also seemed to guarantee some degree of political and economic certainty and, particularly in some rural constituencies, a vote for one's landlord or employer.[14]

The Conservatives continued the strategy set by the coalition it replaced, by introducing policies that deliberately sought to limit the economic and political power of the majority of the electorate. In the month between the fall of Lloyd George's post-war coalition and the general election, Bonar Law appointed Arthur Griffith-Boscawen, the fifty-seven-year-old son of a Denbighshire landowner, as Minister of Health. His brief included that nagging post-war problem: housing. When Boscawen took up his post, overcrowding – defined as more than two people occupying a room – was experienced by millions of people who lived in cottages, terraced houses or – particularly in Scottish cities – tenement flats.

Life was hard in such conditions, particularly for the women who struggled to keep their homes clean. Winifred Foley grew up in a 'two-up, two-down' miner's cottage in the Forest of Dean, which housed her family of six until Winifred left to enter service in 1928.

In her village, as in many others, overcrowding was made worse by the fact that there were 'no drains and no dustmen' and no electricity. Winifred Foley's home relied on paraffin lamps which were expensive to run and smoky, creating yet more dirt.[15] In their tiny living room-cum-kitchen her mother sought to dry clothes around the fire and cook, while five or six young children played at her feet. Far from being an idyllic existence, rural life was often hard, cramped and claustrophobic.

Boscawen was faced with ameliorating these problems. He was an experienced Conservative politician, well respected in the senior ranks of his party. He had served as Minister of Pensions in the wartime coalition, and then as Minister of Agriculture in the post-war government. Yet he began his new role by refusing to honour the promise of the wartime coalition to build more houses. Boscawen dismissed the notion that working-class voters required better housing, and advised young couples to continue sharing their parents' cottages and tenements, rather than seeking a home of their own: 'In China and the East generally,' he declared, 'they continue to live under the parental roof quite contentedly.' Boscawen's comments illuminated just how remote the working-class voter was from his party's interests. His suggestion that working-class Britons had less in common with the middle and upper classes of the country than with the native peoples of China and Asia − at this point still widely regarded as socially and biologically inferior to Britons − was highly revealing.[16]

Unfortunately for Boscawen, many of his voters disagreed with his assessment. In the general election of November 1922 he lost his seat, after just one month in post. Sadly for the voters, however, the Conservatives held to his determination to limit expenditure on public housing. The housing problem was not solved during the 1920s because private builders constructed very few houses for rent, local authorities were not given the money or incentive to build many council houses, and those that were built had rents that were beyond the reach of poorer families. 'In practice,' the historian John Burnett writes, 'council houses went to . . . small clerks and tradesmen, artisans and the better-off semi-skilled workers with average-sized families and safe jobs.'[17] Demand fell woefully short of need.

The government's unemployment policies focused not on creating jobs, but on coercing women into domestic service. The right-wing press supported its stance. Their 'life of idleness' thundered a *Times* editorial, 'ought not to be paid out of the public purse'.[18] Lord Beaverbrook's *Daily Express* lamented the 'abuse of the dole' by women 'for whom domestic service is obviously a suitable employment'.[19] Viscount Rothermere's *Daily Mail* ran a successful scaremongering campaign about unemployed women's 'abuse' of the dole. Following this press onslaught, Bonar Law's Conservative government announced in 1922 that unmarried women's unemployment benefit would be stopped if they refused to take up domestic service – even if taking a job meant moving away from their family's home.

Yet this policy did nothing to help those adult men who made up the majority of Britain's unemployed. Unemployment reached a peak in 1921, when 11 per cent of insured workers were out of work, plus uncounted thousands who did not have insurance.[20] The unemployed had worked in those industries that had over-produced goods in the final years of the war or the early post-war years – like shipbuilding – or that faced stiff competition from overseas. With the exception of textile manufacture, which employed thousands of women in north-west England, these industries overwhelmingly employed skilled men. Miners, steelworkers and construction workers were badly hit, with unemployment reaching more than 20 per cent in each of their industries.[21]

That men were turned out of their jobs by women was a myth – but a very powerful one. The Conservatives were not alone in blaming male unemployment on women workers. In 1920 Manchester's first Labour Lord Mayor, Tom Fox, declared that '"pin money" girls – those who were merely working to provide themselves with pocket money – would have to leave the Town Hall departments so that their places could be filled by ex-service men.'[22] However, a subsequent enquiry discovered that the increase in women's employment in the town hall 'is due mainly to the extended work of the departments' rather than to women replacing men.[23]

These politicians ignored the part that employers and government played in causing male unemployment, which was not due to women taking men's jobs, but to the rapid decline of heavy industry. The light industries that were beginning to replace it specialized in the mass, mechanized manufacture of clothes, food and furniture; employers adopted assembly-line production to enable them to employ unskilled, young and women workers, who were cheaper than skilled, adult men.[24] Government, implacably on the side of the employers, refused to interfere in such recruitment policies – or to take any responsibility for finding work for the thousands of men who found themselves on the dole.

Increasing the supply of domestic servants was not only a means of diverting attention from government ministers' laissez-faire approach to industrial work, but a means of fostering support among the middle-class voters on whose support the Conservatives relied. Young working-class women's 'restless desire for independence, which is a legacy of the war' – in the words of a *Daily Mail* editorial – threatened their employers' way of life.[25] In 1920 George Askwith – in his biographer's words, a 'trenchant and egocentric' civil servant who had been the wartime government's leading adviser on industrial relations – founded the Middle Class Union. This was the first of a number of ratepayers' associations and groups – among the others was the Anti-Waste League – formed in reaction to what Askwith saw as the threat posed by trade unions and welfare expenditure to the living conditions of middle-class ratepayers.[26] The Union, like other ratepayer associations, proved popular among angry householders incensed at government spending on the unemployed.

Middle-class writers and politicians portrayed maids as symbols of a newly independent, potentially insurrectionary working class. Some represented the demands of modern workers for greater independence as unpatriotic. In 1919 Lady Askwith, George Askwith's wife, wrote a pamphlet arguing that domestic service must be reinvigorated in order to secure the future of the British race. The government's Ministry of Reconstruction published this in a short series of pamphlets designed to ease the transition back to civilian life. Middle-class women's 'health and prosperity', concluded Ellen Askwith, 'is of more vital importance to the future of the race than satisfying the demands of a single body of workers'.[27] Despite the fact that the vast majority of Britons were working class, this writer, and most of the government, presented their interests as marginal and insignificant; it was the middle class whose needs were of 'vital importance'.

The increase in factory and shop work, and the 1918 Education Act, fuelled antagonism and anxiety towards an increasingly politically and socially autonomous working class. Reporting on a government enquiry into the shortage of servants in 1923, the *Daily Mirror* noted disapprovingly that 'the "improved standard of education" has (as usual) resulted in a general sense of superiority to home-keeping tasks'.[28] A large number of middle-class commentators believed that the slightest improvement in workers' living conditions was highly threatening to the country's social stability – and their own privileges.

Those women who found themselves forced back into domestic service bitterly resented it. Before the war, few other opportunities had presented themselves. But the experience of war work – either their own, or that of older sisters or friends – broadened the post-war horizons of young wage-earners. In 1922 fourteen-year-old Emily Cleary left school. She lived in a village on the outskirts of Manchester, and she had high hopes of getting skilled work as a confectioner. The war, she said, 'made all the difference in the world – you see there was nothing much for girls before – girls of my class I mean – girls – country girls like that, there was nothing for them except service.'[29] Emily realized her goal but her training made her ill. When she recovered, her mother told her she was leaving home to enter domestic service. 'There was nothing then . . . my mother was desperately poor, and in those days, it was usual to do as you were told.'[30]

Although the number of domestic servants actually increased between 1921 and 1931, men and women in the towns and cities were increasingly able to find factory work. After a slow post-war start, manufacturing began to expand. Older industries like steel had relied on smaller numbers of skilled workers, but the new manufacturing employers chose to concentrate on consumer goods – tinned foods, fashionable clothes and electrical appliances – produced cheaply and uniformly by using as much mechanization as possible. They didn't need workers who had served a lengthy apprenticeship, but they did need large numbers of employees to staff their production lines, and young wage-earners, who were cheaper to employ than adults, were suddenly in demand.

Those women who did enter domestic service could constantly compare their own employment experience with that of their counterparts in factories and shops. Ellen Gibb was a teenager when she left her home in an isolated hamlet in Leicestershire to work as the single maid in a middle-class household in a village on the outskirts of Leicester. But by the time she began work, the girls who lived in her employer's village were benefiting from a regular bus service into the city, where they found work in the expanding textile and clothing factories. At six o'clock each evening, while she was busy cleaning her employer's house, 'I used to see the girls come off the bus, and I used to think their lives were indeed free.'[31] But young women's opportunities remained limited outside the biggest towns and cities.

The conspicuous numbers of factory and shop workers able to enjoy their independence meant that domestic service was increasingly seen as menial work, only undertaken by children from the poorest families and the most rural backwaters. Like most men and women who entered service after the First World War, Edith Edwards felt that there was 'always a stigma about' her work.[32] Edith, who grew up in Macclesfield, aspired to become a clerk, but 'we were very, very poor'.[33] Her father was dead; her family relied on the pittance her mother earned from multiple cleaning jobs. Becoming a clerk meant a typing or book-keeping course, or at least the expense of a white blouse. So she became a servant, a job that was increasingly associated with poverty, lack of liberty and the broken promises of the Great War.

That these women wished to leave service for industrial or retail work gives us a sense of how degrading thousands felt domestic work to be, for factories and shops were not congenial places to work. In 1928 the London Advisory Council for Juvenile Employment noted that 'the average factory worker is either a machine minder or feeder or is engaged in parcelling, filling, wrapping or some form or another of packing, and it is mainly in this latter kind of work that women, girls and boys are employed.'[34] Their work was boring and the hours were long. Conditions were often atrocious. As late as the mid-1930s, thousands of industrial workers in London's East End, Birmingham and Manchester were employed in small, cramped, ill-lit workshops reminiscent of the nineteenth century, which evaded the detection of the Factory Inspectorate and were 'a positive menace . . . to the health of the worker'.[35] At the Ferranti factory where fourteen-year-old Lucy Lees was employed in Lancashire, the roof was so dilapidated that bird droppings fell on the workers below.[36]

Householders responded to their young servants' grievances with antagonism. Petty victimization and bullying were the lot of many maids. In 1923 fifteen-year-old Nora Sandys left her home in a Lancashire village to become the sole maid of a large Victorian rectory a few miles distant. Her typical day began at six o'clock, when she had to rise in a poky, unheated bedroom and dress quickly before beginning her work 'collecting the shoes, going downstairs, taking them back, cleaning out the grate, lighting the fire, filling the scuttle, laying the table for the master's breakfast, going into the lounge, tidying that up . . . taking the mistress's breakfast up on a tray to bed'. By this stage, Nora had been on her feet for more than two hours. If she was lucky, she would have time to snatch a cup of tea and a slice of bread and butter for her breakfast, before she had to 'bring out the dustpan and brush and do the carpet and dust all the furniture which was very heavy mahogany carved furniture . . . Then the hall, and washing up, and then the main bedroom, my bedroom, landing and bathroom.'

Nora had to work quickly, for all these chores must be completed by noon if she was to prepare lunch punctually. The vicar and his wife demanded a hot lunch each day, so she had to find time to prepare the meat or fish earlier in the morning, and then, at midday, 'cook the vegetables and change from my morning uniform into my afternoon uniform by one o'clock and the lunch table had to be laid'. After eating her lunch alone in the unheated kitchen, Nora had a full afternoon's work to get through, without any companionship. 'I was very strong, I was very healthy and by this time [my mistress] had broken my spirit completely so I just became very obedient,' she recalled. 'I didn't question anything.'[37]

Nora Sandys's workload wasn't unusual; few servants in the 1920s had any companion to help them with the chores and cooking. Middle-class families could rarely afford, or accommodate, more than one 'maid-of-all-work'. The stately homes of Britain, with their large numbers of footmen, maids and kitchen staff, had only ever provided employment for a tiny minority of servants, and by the 1920s they were fewer in number and sparser in wealth, as cheap exports eroded the value of agriculture and aristocratic families sold off some of their land. By the 1920s, over 70 per cent of households that employed servants had just one, usually a young woman, who was expected to shoulder all the domestic work and often look after their employers' children as well.[38]

These middle-class householders did not need to employ maids; their modern, inter-war houses were smaller, brighter and easier to clean than Edwardian villas or Georgian townhouses, and there were new ways of cleaning them. As early as 1919, Baxendales, one of Manchester's largest department stores, declared on its advertisements that 'Vacuum cleaners will solve the Servant problem'.[39] By the 1930s, most salaried professionals could afford the new vacuum cleaners, fridges and cookers – yet potential customers remained reluctant to buy. They preferred, in the words of Winifred Foley, who entered service at the age of fourteen, 'a creature that would run on very little fuel and would not question her lot'.[40] For this calculation to work, servants had to cost less than the time and money a middle-class woman would have to invest in domestic appliances. And so middle-class households employed a maid-of-all-work for a pittance.

Faced with such unremitting drudgery, it is unsurprising that some servants, like Nora Sandys, became resigned and despairing. But other post-war servants channelled their hopes for a better sort of life into their limited leisure time and embraced the new world emerging outside their attics and basements. In larger towns and cities the cinema was beginning to gain popularity; by 1916 Britain already boasted 5,000 purpose-built picture houses.[41] Nevertheless, before the advent of the 'talkies' in the late 1920s, dancing was an even more popular pastime. Between 1918 and 1925, 1,100 dance halls opened across the country, catering for a predominantly working-class clientele.[42] The Saturday night dance 'was an escape from reality for thousands of shop assistants, factory workers and employees who could afford to go out only once a week', recalled one man. He was a regular of Brighton's Regent dance hall, which opened in 1923 and accommodated 1,500 dancers on peak nights.[43]

Servants had too little leisure time to indulge in these treats on a regular basis. But what their employers found so infuriating was that, however much their liberty was constrained, their maids flaunted signs of new independence in the heart of middle- and upper-class households. 'The old-fashioned maid knew her place,' bemoaned one correspondent in the letters page of the *Manchester Guardian* in 1923; 'the modern girl does not, and though given more consideration and liberty she often only abuses it.'[44] Servants became symbols of a new assertive modernity, fashioned by mass-produced clothes and cosmetics which suggested a girl could escape her place, if only fleetingly. After Emily Cleary – the aspirant confectioner – bobbed her hair in 1925, her disgusted mistress 'said "Now you look what you are, a common little slavey." Well I just turned round and walked out of the room.'[45] Employers' fruitless efforts to repress their maids' independence simply fuelled their workers' resentment – and their determination to leave service as soon as they could.

In the Georgian townhouses, Edwardian apartments and semi-detached villas of Britain, the bobbed hair, made-up faces and stockinged legs of the servants told of a subtle but significant social transformation. Even high unemployment, benefit cuts and long hours for low pay could not erode demands for financial and social independence that servitude could never offer. This was the 'upheaval' of which Woolf wrote. It had begun before the First World War, but had been exacerbated by two formative experiences. The first was war work. In the years between 1914 and 1918, the British workforce truly became industrialized. Many thousands of workers experienced similar conditions and found, in the new and urgent demand for their labour, unprecedented economic and political power. They used the strength of collective action to secure better wages – and won more leisure time in which to enjoy these.

The second experience was the return to peacetime 'normality'. The broken political promises of employment and homes, and the coercive measures that forced women back into domestic service, while their brothers and fathers languished in long dole queues, provoked resentment and anger against the government and employers. Just three years after Virginia Woolf had described this transformation, the class antagonism she hinted at would explode into one of the largest and most disruptive strikes that Britain has ever experienced.

3

Enemies Within

ON THE MORNING of 4 May 1926, twenty-two-year-old Harry Watson left his home in east London and walked to the docks where he worked as a labourer. But this was no ordinary working day. When Harry arrived, the crowds of men he joined weren't milling around hoping to be given a few hours' work – the usual sight that greeted visitors to the docklands – but holding a rally. Britain's General Strike had begun. That morning, as he listened to his workmates' speeches, Harry became convinced that 'we were going to win this one, because it was a national strike and [the older men] knew what kind of power and authority that exercised. There was no question that there would be capitulation by the government.'[1]

Between 1.5 and 3 million of a unionized workforce of 6 million walked out on 4 May – 4 per cent of the population – while millions more wives, sisters, friends and neighbours actively offered their support to the strikers.[2] On the previous evening, 3 May, Walter Citrine, the General Secretary of the Trades Union Congress (TUC) had announced that Britain's transport workers would strike in support of the country's miners, who were disputing savage pay cuts. But this was more than a protest about pay. 'The strike was really a desperate cry for manhood,' said Winifred Foley, then the twelve-year-old child of a striking miner. Her father and his workmates wanted 'to be able to do a full week's work in the pit, to be paid enough to fill the bellies of their families', without fear of unemployment.[3] The strike was a battle for economic citizenship: for the acknowledgement that those who laboured were contributing to the country's wealth and thus deserved to share in it. This was 'a staggering demonstration of working-class resolve'.[4]

★

The grievances that fuelled the call to strike had been brewing since the end of the war. From 1919, miners fought against successive wage cuts. In 1924 strikes had erupted in the coal and steel industries as a result of employers' attempts to cut jobs and wages, and in frustration at the very first Labour government, elected that year, which proved unresponsive to the miners' demands. Ramsay MacDonald, the Prime Minister of Labour's short-lived minority administration, admonished the strikers for 'disloyalty', and his Cabinet dismissed those responsible as proof of 'Communist influence' within the trade union movement. From then on, the trade union leadership would approach Labour leaders with a good deal more caution, realizing that a conflict existed between their members' interests and Labour politicians' desire to court a wider electorate.

The general election of November 1924 returned Stanley Baldwin's Conservative Party to government. In the following year the Chancellor of the Exchequer, Winston Churchill, placed the British pound back on the gold standard – a move that greatly exacerbated the tension between miners and their employers. Churchill wanted to raise the value of the pound against other national currencies; a morale boost for those who recalled Britain's imperial pre-eminence in the years before 1914 but – as the economist John Maynard Keynes predicted – disastrous for the British economy. In 1914 Britain's government and industrialists had been able to rely on the empire both to produce and consume British goods. But by 1925 British industrialists relied heavily on exporting goods, and manufacturers had to price their goods competitively in the free international market. Churchill's move made exports prohibitively expensive.

The coal industry was particularly badly affected. The colliery owners announced that they must reduce the prices they charged, and that these price cuts must be paid for by wage reductions. The miners reacted with anger. They had already suffered pay cuts since the end of the Great War, and argued that they couldn't cope with further reductions. They pointed out that the colliery owners could well afford to take a cut in the healthy profits they continued to enjoy. Baldwin's solution was to pay a subsidy to the colliery owners – a notably more charitable approach than his party adopted towards the country's unemployed.

In parliament, Baldwin claimed that the subsidy was necessary to avert a major confrontation between employers and workers in one of Britain's largest industries.[5] But in private, a more aggressive rationale emerged. Kingsley Martin, a Labour Party activist and lecturer at the London School of Economics, recalled that:

> Churchill and other militants in the cabinet were eager for a strike, knowing that they had built a national organisation in the six months' grace won by the subsidy to the mining industry. Churchill himself told me this on the first occasion I met him in person . . . When Winston said that the subsidy had been granted to enable the government to smash the unions, unless the miners had given way in the meantime, my picture of Winston was confirmed.[6]

Baldwin was more moderate – unlike Churchill, he refused to countenance allowing troops to fire on the strikers – but he was adamant that the trade unions must acquiesce to employers' demands. In August 1925 ministers discussed how to bring the emergency organization of supply and transport 'up to the highest possible point of efficiency' within 'the next few months', anticipating a general strike.[7] Baldwin warned the TUC against calling a strike: 'let me say that no minority in a free country has ever yet coerced the whole community . . . when the community has to protect itself, with the full strength of the government behind it, the community will do so, and the response of the community will astonish the forces of anarchy throughout the world.'[8]

At a time when the vast majority of British people were working class, Baldwin's presentation of trade unionists as a 'minority' committed to 'anarchy' was curious to say the least. Conservative ministers knew that, numerically, the trade unions were growing stronger. It was this that caused these politicians such concern. The trade unions' right to negotiate on behalf of their members had been established in skilled trades during the nineteenth century, and enshrined in law during the first two decades of the twentieth. The First World War had brought thousands of unskilled and semi-skilled workers into the movement and established new negotiating rights for them. There were many within the Conservative Party who were eager for an excuse to curtail the collective power of these workers.

In April 1926 the government stopped paying a subsidy to the colliery owners, and strike became a probability. Newspapers of liberal as well as conservative persuasion reflected Baldwin's horror and outrage that the working class might have the temerity to down tools. It was impossible, opined the liberal *Manchester Guardian*, 'to conceive that the country may be involved in anything of the nature of a general strike. Yet not only are these things on the cards, but there is little beyond instinctive belief in the latent sanity of most Englishmen to nurse the hope that they will not come to pass.'[9] The newspaper warned its readers that to surrender 'to the pressure of force' would be to admit that 'the days of majority rule in Britain would be numbered'.[10]

Like Baldwin, Britain's press represented the country's workers as a stubborn minority whose aims were beyond comprehension. Many liberal and left-leaning middle-class people simply took it for granted that they represented the mainstream of British society, and that their opinions were common sense, while those of trade unionists were either radical or irrational. These newspaper editorials were the first clue that, in a time of strife, many well-heeled supporters of Labour or the Liberals would jettison their party political affiliations in favour of defending their privileges against organized labour.

The TUC's leadership entered into the General Strike reluctantly. By acquiescing to a pay cut for the miners, the TUC believed that it would render the labour movement impotent. But these moderate men were not interested in 'holding the country to ransom' as Britain's newspapers suggested on the eve of the dispute.[11] On 2 May the TUC's General Council wrote to Baldwin's Cabinet offering 'in the event of a general strike . . . to enter into arrangements for the distribution of essential foodstuffs'. After 'some discussions between the government representatives and the General Council', agreement was reached that 'conversations of an informal character and of which no stenographic note would be taken' would continue to take place, in the event of a strike, to co-ordinate food and fuel distribution.[12] These discussions were kept secret from ordinary trade unionists. Many of them were dismayed when it became clear on 3 May that the TUC would only call for railwaymen, transport workers, printers, dockers, ironworkers and steelworkers to stay away from work.

On 4 May the strike began. The call to action brought an eerie quiet to the country's ports, railway stations, town and city centres. Newspaper stalls were bare; the drilling and banging of the shipyards ceased; the whistle of steam engines died away. As well as the railway workers, porters, omnibus drivers, shipyard labourers and welders who stopped work, other workers supportive of the miners downed tools without the TUC's say-so, many textile workers in Lancashire among them.

Over the next few days, these strikers became conscious that they had no leaders; the strike was a struggle between these or-dinary workers and the political establishment. The TUC leadership remained lukewarm, and leading Labour politicians offered the strikers little support. Some of those who came from aristocratic or upper-middle-class backgrounds were concerned that the strikers' interests might irreparably damage their own. Among them was Philip Snowden, Labour's first Chancellor of the Exchequer in the minority government of 1924. He was opposed to the strike, but was 'not sorry that this experiment had been tried. The trade unions needed a lesson of the futility and foolishness of such a trial of strength. A general strike could in no circumstances be successful . . . There is no country in the world which has pro-portionally such a large middle-class population as Great Britain.'[13] Snowden's logic was highly questionable: the Fourth Reform Act had massively expanded the electorate to include many outside the 'middle class'. His sentiments showed that he, together with the front benches of the Liberals and the Conservatives, took the concerns of these new voters far less seriously than those of the shopkeepers, schoolteachers and small businessmen who made up the middle class.

Baldwin's government labelled the strikers unlawful, unpatriotic and disloyal. 'The government's view is that there must be a govern-ment,' read one press release, 'and that it must govern, not as taking sides in the dispute, but as asserting itself as the supreme power of the community which must override all sectional interests.'[14] The strikers were represented as a 'sectional interest' while the colliery owners' interests were treated as synonymous with those of 'the community'.

Who composed Baldwin's 'community' became clear as the government's call for 'loyal labour' was answered in the early days of May. As the historian Rachelle Saltzman explains: 'University students and young businessmen costumed themselves in workers' uniforms, assumed roles as lorry drivers, bus conductors, and special constables . . . Society women offered rides to those without trans-portation, acted as telephone operators, served tea to the volunteers.'[15] Ellen Havelock had recently come down from Girton College, Cambridge. Within hours of the strike being announced, 'the call went out "our country needs you!"' on the wireless and in the press. 'And, of course, the best and the brightest responded including my fiancé who joined up at once and dashed off to London.' Many upper- and middle-class people shared Havelock's patriotism. 'Anybody who came from my type of home would have volunteered,' explained Phineas May, a middle-class Jewish Londoner who had recently left public school. He became a special constable because 'you felt it was the proper thing to do, in the same way, when there's a war, you join up.'[16] This war was waged on the organized working class.

Unsurprisingly, given high unemployment and the government's propaganda, many manual workers and unemployed men responded to the government's plea for volunteers. Eighteen-year-old George Richardson was among them. An apprentice engineer in Peterborough, his decision to volunteer was strongly influenced by his father, a skilled worker who had never been out of work. Peterborough was a town with a large number of transport workers but many of them were casual labourers; families like the Richardsons often had stronger links with agricultural workers in the villages from which they hailed than with other factory workers. During May 1926 George enjoyed his work at the local power plant because of the camaraderie and the feeling of heroism it inspired: 'we were keeping the power plant going! . . . We were so proud of what we were doing!'[17] For people used to being treated as socially inferior, being honoured as patriots was a heady experience.

Other working-class strikebreakers were hungry for work. In

Bristol, eighteen-year-old Alf Canning, a bus conductor, stayed at work when others struck. His father, a labourer, was 'non-union I suppose' and told Alf to keep his head down. Alf's seven brothers and sisters relied heavily on his wage, and in 1926 'if you had a job you was doing well'. With so many people desperate for work in Bristol, Alf and his colleagues 'had to be careful in all ways; you could be victimized if they didn't like the colour of your eyes.'[18] In several cities, unemployed young men were among those who volunteered, primarily in order to earn a few shillings, though some of them also expressed a conservative patriotic fervour. In Glasgow strikebreakers included members of the Billy Boys, a violent Protestant street gang who provided protection for local Conservative Party meetings throughout the 1920s and 1930s.[19]

But most of the volunteers came from far more privileged backgrounds. Some, like Mary Chitty, a wealthy student at Girton College, Cambridge, believed that the strikers were dangerous revolutionaries – 'after all, the Russian Revolution was quite young'[20] – while others had some sympathy with the strikers' plight. Some of these volunteers classed themselves as Labour or Liberal men. Ellen Havelock's fiancé was a Labour activist at Cambridge. Nevertheless, he volunteered because he viewed his country's interests as being at odds with those of the miners. Not everyone from his social background agreed: he later discovered that his grandmother, who recalled colliery lockouts of the late nineteenth century, had quietly sent money every week to the TUC support fund.[21]

The General Strike was a class struggle. It revealed the antagonism that so many of the upper and middle classes felt towards the labourers, servants, shop workers and factory workers who served them. The Hon. John Jones came from a county family in Suffolk and had recently graduated from Cambridge University. During the strike he drove buses in London.

> The whole thing was a joke. You got up on the bus and you had a 'Special' sitting beside you with a truncheon so if anyone tried to get up on the bus he'd knock him off . . . And people got on the bus . . . you'd say 'where do you want to go, love?' . . . As long as we got to the end eventually it didn't matter. And everyone was

roaring with laughter . . . we'd drop some of the dear old ladies that wanted a lift . . . And we had a lot of fun with this.

Those nine days in May saw 'upper-class women acting like servants . . . women dressing like men, upper-class people dressing and acting like members of the lower class . . . and a general atmosphere of festival license'.[22]

By 1926 provocative and violent 'larks' were part of life for London's fashionable clique, the Bright Young People – the crowd who took centre stage in Evelyn Waugh's 1930 novel *Vile Bodies*. 'Larks' and 'rags' were a means for the younger generation to assert their financial and social superiority. These 'larks' often involved dressing up as workers or the unemployed and mimicking their crudities. Jessica Mitford recalled that the General Strike provided enormous excitement in her isolated, rural, aristocratic household:

> There was a thrilling feeling of crisis in the air . . . Everyone was pressed into service for the emergency. Nancy and Pam [her older sisters], then in their early twenties, established a canteen in an old barn on the highway . . . in which they took alternate shifts serving tea, hot soup and sandwiches to the scabbing lorry-drivers. After lessons, Boud and I with our governess and Debo with Nanny would toil up the hill to help, Miranda [a pet lamb] strictly at heel in case a Bolshie should jump out of the hedge.[23]

Jessica's sister Pam was accosted in the canteen she ran for strikebreakers by

> a filthy tramp . . . 'Can I 'ave a cup o' tea, miss?' he leered at Pam, thrusting his dreadful face close to hers . . . 'Can I 'ave a kiss, miss?' and he put his arm round her waist. Pam, thoroughly terrified, let out a fearful shriek, and in her mad haste to get away from him fell and sprained her ankle. The tramp turned out to be Nancy [her sister] in disguise. All in all, we were rather sad when the General Strike came to an end and life returned to dull normalcy.[24]

Before the First World War, dressing up and imitating one's servants and labourers had been integral to annual celebrations like Christmas and the Harvest Home, when upper-class employers might wait on their staff.[25] Such rituals emphasized the bond of mutual obligation which 'service' was meant to define. They also implied that such role-reversal was a topsy-turvy, temporary transgression from the 'natural' order of things. But by 1926, this meaning was lost to the masquerades of the Bright Young Things. Many of their 'larks' were provoked by the political instability of the post-war years, and were a means of temporarily, provocatively and sometimes violently asserting their claim to social superiority.

Laughing at people was a serious business. '[T]hat was what broke the strike,' claimed John Jones; 'everyone who was my age, we simply treated the whole thing as a joke – which it was!'[26] Taking over the strikers' jobs suggested that the well-heeled volunteers, not the working class, were the backbone of Britain; the strikers were dispensable, their demands for equal treatment laughable. Diana Athill, who was a child in 1926, took her aristocratic family's sense of social superiority for granted. In her teens, however, she came to realize that this rested on a harsh truth: 'they despised almost all the rest of the world.'[27] We are the country, said the volunteers of 1926; we are necessary. You, the strikers, rely on our goodwill; not vice versa.

Important though voluntary labour was, the government knew that victory relied on its mobilization of the media, the police and, ultimately, the armed forces. In an effort to keep Winston Churchill's aggression in check, Baldwin permitted him to edit the *British Gazette*, the government's propaganda newspaper, and the only national daily published throughout the strike. Its sheets were filled with Baldwin's speeches and declarations that the strikers were aiming to 'starve . . . the country'.[28] The BBC followed the government's line; the corporation refused to broadcast an appeal by the Archbishop of Canterbury for the government and the TUC to return to the negotiating table, after the Cabinet expressed disapproval. Although the TUC produced its own news-sheet, the *British Worker*, this was often extremely hard to come by. This was part of a government strategy to prevent strikers communicating with each other as well as with the wider public. In Battersea, twenty-one-year-old railway labourer Harry Wicks, himself a striker, complained of being 'starved of news'.[29]

But as the strikers showed no sign of returning to work, the government decided to resort to force. On 7 May a notice placed in the *Birmingham Post* and a few other newspapers being produced by strikebreakers informed the public that 'Any member of the civil or military defences who prevent disorder are assured that His Majesty's government will support his actions, now and later.'[30] Troops were sent to work on the docks. Harry Watson and his comrades 'had word that there were troops in the docks unloading ships and the lorries were coming up the Victora Dock Road manned by the troops . . . sure enough when we got to the Barking Road outside Canning Town Station up came the lorries with barbed wire all round the lorries' canopy with troops with guns sitting behind the barbed wire.'

At this stage of the dispute, many workers – Harry Watson included – believed that the government was as committed to peaceful and democratic debate as its propaganda suggested. They were about to get a shock. At Canning Town

> The people were jeering and booing . . . but . . . [t]here was still a degree of good humour about it. [Then] the police started pushing from behind – instead of being in front of us they were behind – and they kept pushing and pushing and pushing and we were being pushed further into the road and . . . before we know it the police were laying about us with their truncheons and that caused more anger and a real explosion for about half an hour.

Shocked, Harry returned home to Battersea. But the strike became increasingly violent in the following days. The government's actions radicalized many workers. On 8 May the strikers of Canning Town plotted revenge:

> before they went up to the main road hundreds of the men slipped the iron railings out of the walls and took them along Barking Road. When I got there there were several lorries already that had been turned over . . . And then up from Victoria Dock Road came the lorries with the troops on it and again the police lined up . . . but before they could start anything the crowd turned on the police and started laying about with their iron bars.[31]

This was a short-lived victory for Harry Watson and his mates. Later that day, the army managed to break a picket line in order to transport food to a distribution centre set up in Hyde Park – a major victory that the *British Gazette* trumpeted as a demonstration that the government was in control of events. But the violence escalated elsewhere. On 10 May strikers derailed the *Flying Scotsman* as it sped through Northumberland. Miners in Glasgow were jailed for fighting with police as they sought to allow troops to enter the Kilmarnock tram depot.[32]

The government invoked the draconian powers of the 1920 Emergency Powers Act to repress protest. A miner in Penrith was jailed for three months with hard labour for distributing posters calling on workers not to break the strike.[33] One hundred and three strikers and their supporters were prosecuted for violence and disorder in Northumberland, 110 in the West Riding of Yorkshire and 183 in Durham county.[34] In County Durham, a striker was jailed for three months for allegedly warning that 'If Stanley Baldwin uses his forces – police force, Air Force, Army and Navy – we will meet them and they will go to the bottom . . . I am corresponding with a friend of mine in the Army and another in the Navy and they say that a good number will follow the Red Flag when the opportunity arises.'[35]

Men and women who had thought themselves law-abiding and respectable found themselves criminalized. Harry Musgrave was a miner's son in County Durham. His father was

> A very mild-mannered, law-abiding person . . . wouldn't say boo to a goose. That mild-mannered man broke the law during the 1926 strike – obviously in the beginning they went onto the spoil heaps picking out the coal until there was no coal left. So down in Bloemfontein woods . . . they started to work this seam . . . and of course it was against the law – someone was watching for a policeman. So that we had a fire.[36]

Men like Mr Musgrave came to realize that the laws of Britain were not primarily made for their protection. While government propaganda suggested that the strikers were a minority, or even 'communist agitators', many felt forced into criminal behaviour by the government's actions. For those who had prided themselves on being law-abiding folk, this was a shattering experience.

By 10 May the government's treatment of the strikers was provoking unease among many people who had initially been ambivalent about the dispute. Edith Holt of Bristol was among them. A factory worker with young children, she was 'sorry for the miners', but she was exasperated by the strike: 'of course the miners had put everybody else out of work [by going on strike].' But when the pitmen of South Wales marched to Bristol to hold a rally, she was shocked and intimidated by their reception. 'All the police was coming out on horseback and truncheons were going all over the place.' Edith found herself caught up in the mêlée as she returned home from the shops. 'The [police] were going anywhere at anybody. And I had my babies in the pushchair and I ran down over Newgate Hill to get out of the way.' While publicly presenting the strikers as a tiny minority, in reality Baldwin's government waged war on the working class as a whole, not stopping to distinguish between strikers and bystanders. In doing so, they provoked observers like Edith to reflect that they had much in common with the strikers themselves.[37]

On 12 May the TUC capitulated and declared the strike was over. The leadership had decided that it could never win against the government's propaganda machine and control of the armed forces. But ordinary trade unionists were devastated, rightly seeing this as a massive defeat for the working class. In Swansea, strikers were unable to believe it; when police and journalists told them of the decision they 'jeered at the news, singing "none of your leg-pulling"'.[38] When the news reached the crowd outside Battersea Town Hall, 'the workers just booed and shouted,' recalled Harry Wicks. 'We decided that we should march back to work. Most of the workers employed at Victoria Station were from Battersea so the branch decided to report for duty the following day and we marched from Battersea to Victoria Station.'[39] The same thing was happening all over Britain.

Only the miners held out, and by December 1926 they, too, had returned to work, defeated by the colliery owners who locked them out until the mining unions accepted the wage reductions that had provoked the General Strike in the first place. By Christmas, men like Mr Musgrave had either returned to work under harsher terms and conditions, or had been sacked by employers who condemned them as revolutionary militants. In 1927 Baldwin's government passed the Trade Disputes Act, which banned sympathetic or supporting strikes and placed strict limitations on picketing.

One of the most important legacies of the strike was that Britain's labour movement became firmly committed to constitutional change rather than militant or revolutionary action. There would always be dissenting voices, but the leaders of the TUC and the Labour Party were able to use the General Strike to their advantage. The leaders' support for the strike had always been ambivalent, and they were worried by the increasing militancy exhibited on both sides. 'As a last resort,' argues the historian Keith Middlemas, 'that strike was not unwelcome . . . from the point of view of government, NCEO [National Confederation of Employers' Organisations] and the TUC itself, if indeed the choice lay between class warfare and the collapse of capitalist society on the one hand and industrial harmony on the other.'[40] Successive governments of different political hues were content to discuss policy and co-operate with the trade unions and employers' organizations; the alternative – endless strikes and stoppages – was too costly, time-consuming and chaotic to contemplate.[41]

But for ordinary workers, the failure of the General Strike meant the loss of any hope that the labour movement would address their concerns about the shortcomings of British democracy. Labour leaders proved undecided about the use of workers' collective strength as a political weapon. Government policy contained working-class demands for new political and economic rights: negotiation on working hours, wages and conditions was now well established, but demands for anything approaching greater social and economic equality were outlawed as 'unconstitutional'.

Yet while it was a massive defeat, the General Strike testified to the existence of a vocal and angry working class. The experience of men like Harry Wicks explodes the myth that the British are essentially a moderate people, whose differences (including class) are less important than a shared interest in peaceable, law-abiding governance. The strike had rocked the British establishment, and those who lived through the nine days in May never forgot them. This was a class struggle, which showed the collective strength of the working class, but also the partisan interests of their country's rulers who used every weapon at their disposal to protect their property, profit and privilege. A generation of men and women would never lose that inspirational feeling that unity was strength, just as they would never forget the determination of a 'democratic' government to repress them. Little wonder that in many mining villages the strikebreakers of 1926 were still social pariahs decades later.[42]

One consequence was an increase in the working-class vote for Labour. Despite the lukewarm backing of the Labour front bench, local Labour Party branches had shown great solidarity with the strikers. Labour's support had not increased in municipal elections since 1920. But in 1926, for the first time, Labour won control of several important municipal councils, including Glasgow and Sheffield.[43] Alf Canning, the eighteen-year-old strikebreaker from Bristol, was among these new Labour supporters. Although he hadn't joined the General Strike, he was influenced by the solidarity shown by the strikers and their trade unions, and by his own poor working conditions – long hours, shift work and being at the beck and call of managers who warned Alf that the dole queues were full of willing replacements. Shortly after the strike ended, he joined the Labour Party's League of Youth. He signed up, he said, 'to create a fairer society'.[44]

The strikers' experiences, in turn, affected the outlook of their children. In 1928 fourteen-year-old Winifred Foley left home to enter domestic service. Her father, a miner, had been victimized by his employer after playing a leading role in the General Strike, and now found it hard to make ends meet on his reduced wage. 'I don't have to tell thee how much your mam and I wish we could kip thee at 'ome,' he told his daughter. 'Now mind what I do say: if they do work thee too 'ard, or not give thee enough vittles . . . we'll scrape the money up some'ow to get thee wum.' But Winifred Foley knew that her parents desperately needed their daughter to 'get her feet under someone else's table', although it broke her father's heart not to be able to keep his family together.[45]

Six years later, memories of the General Strike revisited Winifred Foley in different circumstances. She was about to leave domestic service, having secured a waitressing job that offered poor pay but the independence she craved. On her last day in service, 'I sang "The Red Flag" as loud as I dared among the clatter of pots and pans, and thought of my Dad and all the down-trodden workers of the world and nearly cried.'[46] The strikers of 1926 may have been defeated in their battle for full economic citizenship; but their dream survived.

4

Dole

IN 1934 THE writer Winifred Holtby – author of the acclaimed *South Riding* – declared that in Britain's industrial areas:

a new element has entered into the relationship between parents and children. As it is often easier for women than for men to find employment, so it is easier for adolescents than for adults. It therefore often happens that young girls are working in factories, private domestic service, shops and laundries, and using their small wage to support their parents . . . It is not always easy, even for generous and exploitable adolescence, to shoulder the adult burden of responsibility.[1]

Holtby was referring to the disastrous consequences of mass unemployment. She focused her ire on the government's new innovation to cut benefit spending: a household means test. Three years earlier, in 1931, the government had reduced unemployment benefit and had introduced a means test for those claimants not entitled to standard unemployment allowances. These included uninsured workers, such as domestic servants. They also included those insured workers who were unemployed for more than three months, and had exhausted their entitlement to the contributory unemployment benefit introduced by the National Insurance Act of 1911. Most of the long-term unemployed were adult men with families to keep and they all suffered the consequences. In 1934 the means test to which claimants were subjected was extended to include the incomes of all members of their household, and their possessions.

Unemployment dogged the inter-war working class – around 11 per cent were unemployed in the best years – but it rose dramatically in the years after the Wall Street Crash of 1929.[2] In 1931, 23 per cent of adult male workers were recorded as out of work, and 20 per cent of women. Thousands of uninsured, and therefore unrecorded, workers – juveniles and cleaners, for example – also experienced unemployment. As late as 1938, 14 per cent of men and 13 per cent of women were registered as unemployed, and a far higher proportion of people were on the dole in north-east England, the textile towns of the north-west, Scotland's Clydeside, and South Wales – Britain's industrial heartlands.[3] The unemployed included both men and women, in skilled as well as unskilled work. White-collar workers were affected by unemployment too, though manual workers were hardest hit.

The government's policies penalized the unemployed; the means test in particular suggested they were culpable for their own poverty. However, as the 1930s wore on, the unemployed themselves protested against their treatment in ways that demonstrated their desire to play a full and active part in a democratic society. Meanwhile, the hardship suffered by the wives and children of unemployed men provoked some important social surveys, which showed that poverty was a common experience of working-class life, and that it was caused by government policy rather than by personal fecklessness.

The government's establishment of a household means test testified to that persistent assumption made by the powerful and privileged that the wilful idleness of the poor caused poverty. Politicians and social investigators differed as to whether this was the primary cause of poverty, or simply the one that was most easily treated, but the principle that the poor could be held responsible for their hardship guided welfare policy throughout the inter-war years. In reality, however, government policy often prevented people from helping themselves or each other; in the case of the means test by penalizing those who had savings or any recourse to self-help networks within their family, neighbourhood or trade union.

Means testing wasn't new; neither was having to prove oneself deserving of benefit. The 1921 Unemployment Act had introduced a 'genuinely seeking work' test that all claimants of unemployment benefit had to pass. Until 1929, the Boards of Guardians who administrated the Poor Law were responsible for providing assistance to those who were desperate and without any entitlement to sickness or unemployment benefit. Carolyn Steedman, who grew up in the 1950s, recalled that her grandmother, 'means-tested in the late 1920s, had won the sympathy of the Relieving Officer, who ignored the presence of the saleable piano because she kept a clean house, with a cloth on the table'.[4]

Not all Guardians conformed to the letter of the law. In 1927 Stanley Baldwin's Conservative administration passed the Board of Guardians (Default) Act which enabled the government to reconstitute Boards of Guardians more easily. The Act was a vengeful response to the decision taken by some liberal Guardians to grant assistance to striking miners in 1926. More usually, however, the Boards regarded the poor with suspicion, and surplus chairs, for instance, could lead to a reduction in a claimant's unemployment benefit.[5]

In 1929 Baldwin's five years of government came to an end when the Conservatives lost that year's general election. Working-class women were partly responsible for this defeat. In 1928 their political power increased when the women's movement finally won the fight for the vote to be extended to women on the same terms as men. In 1918 the coalition government of Conservatives and Liberals had passed the Fourth Reform Act in the hope of avoiding a return to the industrial militancy and suffragette protests of the pre-war years. The Act gave the vote to all men over the age of twenty-one – but only to women over the age of thirty who were ratepayers. This excluded most working-class women, domestic servants among them.

If the government hoped that the 1918 Act would pacify the women's movement, they were wrong. Suffragists and members of other prominent women's organizations formed the National Union of Societies for Equal Citizenship (NUSEC), under the leadership of Eleanor Rathbone, the Liverpool social reformer who was an independent councillor for the city's Granby ward. Faced with pressure from women campaigners across the political spectrum, Stanley Baldwin had promised to equalize the franchise when he entered office in 1924, but over the next three years he continuously postponed a vote on the matter, recognizing that some of his own government might rebel. He was also influenced by Lord Rothermere, owner of the *Daily Mail* and a powerful Conservative supporter, who used the pages of his newspaper to warn against 'the flapper vote folly', arguing that young and working-class women voters would deliver a Labour government.[6] On the other hand, Labour was committed to equalizing the franchise, and Baldwin knew he could potentially gain the support of women by beating the opposition to it.[7] In 1927, with the end of the current parliament in sight, the women's movement and supportive MPs from all political parties intensified the pressure on Baldwin to fulfil his pledge. In these circumstances Baldwin's government passed the Equalization of the Franchise Act.

The general election of 1929 was therefore the first in which women aged between twenty-one and thirty had the vote, and in which working-class women over the age of thirty were enfranchised. For the first time, Britain was truly a mass democracy: over 32 million people had the vote compared with just 7.7 million in 1910.

The result of the 1929 general election appeared to bear out Rothermere's fears: voters elected Ramsay MacDonald's Labour Party. Initial signs were that this Labour government would enact the kind of social reform to which Conservatives like Rothermere were vociferously opposed. In 1929 Labour's Local Government Act abolished the Poor Law. In most places little changed, as the Boards of Guardians were replaced with Public Assistance Boards whose duties and personnel were almost identical to those of their predecessors. Still, the means test was abolished.

But the abolition of the means test, like the Labour government itself, was short-lived. Following the Wall Street Crash of 1929, and the global trade depression and mass unemployment that followed, MacDonald entered a National government 'of all parties'. The Conservatives dominated this new administration. The National government reintroduced the means test in 1931, and the household means test was instituted three years later, administered by the new Public Assistance Boards.

The Labour voters of 1929 were dismayed and angry. The household means test added to the problems of the unemployed rather than alleviating them. It affected those who had long been considered – and considered themselves to be – the respectable working class. Before the First World War, most of the unemployed were casual and unskilled workers, and often juveniles. But in the early 1930s, skilled, adult, male workers were highly vulnerable to long-term unemployment because the depression hit older manufacturing industries – like iron and steel production and coal mining – hardest.

Unemployment became an important, shared experience of working-class life, cutting across the divisions of skill, occupation, age and gender. Although men were primarily affected, many women also found themselves out of work, or forced to enter domestic service by government policy and their fathers' unemployment. The number of servants increased, reaching 1,554,235 in 1931.[8]

The government suggested that the unemployed had to help themselves, implying that those on the dole were responsible for their own hardship. In 1927 Baldwin's government had introduced a labour transference scheme, and the National government expanded this. The scheme, which took workers from the depressed north to jobs in southern England, testified to the stark regional division between the impoverished industrial areas and the richer south-east. Rather than seek to raise employment in the north, the scheme forced workers to leave their homes to take jobs hundreds of miles from their spouses or parents. The scheme failed. It relied on employers in the expanding light manufacturing industries that were beginning to spring up in the towns and cities of the Midlands and south-east England by the beginning of the 1930s. But these employers did not want to give work to older, more expensive adult men with a history of trade unionism, when they could use cheaper teenagers who lived on their doorstep. The majority of transferred workers were young women, many of whom had left school only months earlier. Some were sent to new factories, but 80 per cent of them were directed into domestic service; they were the replacements for the southern teenage girls who were now escaping from middle-class households into new factory jobs.[9]

The workers who participated in the transference scheme learned – if they hadn't already known – that Britain was composed of two nations, and they lived cheek by jowl. Social divisions were not simply regional. Although more men and women were unemployed in northern England, South Wales and Scotland's industrial heartland than in England's Midlands and south-east, this was not the full picture. In most major conurbations the inhabitants of the slums coexisted with prosperous, propertied car owners who could afford holidays and fashionable clothes. In 1933 J.B. Priestley walked up the old High Street in Southampton on an *English Journey* to assess the social and economic condition of the country. '[T]he mile of shops seemed to be doing a brisk trade,' he observed; 'it shared the taste of Fleet Street and the Strand for wine bars . . . I had lunch in one of these places, and it was full.' But down an adjacent side street Priestley quickly came upon 'narrow brick gullies . . . over-crowded rooms', and 'pitiful' small shops with 'fly-blown windows'.[10]

Priestley found more evidence of economic boom in Coventry, 'the famous old city of the three steeples, and the equally famous new city of bicycles and motor cars and wireless sets'.[11] But his guide, a young worker at the city's Daimler factory, sought to convince Priestley that this boom was based on an immense amount of hard work for relatively little reward. Coventry's inhabitants were often lonely, having moved miles away from family and friends to find work – like Priestley's guide himself who 'was not a Coventry man and did not like the place. Here he was in entire agreement with the head porter of my hotel, also not a Coventry man – perhaps there are no Coventry men.' The porter 'answered my questions about a possible evening's amusement with the most sardonic nega-tives'. The people, he said, were obsessed with work and focused on making money; presumably, in many cases, to send back to parents or children still at 'home'.[12]

These Coventry workers enjoyed a security unknown to their relatives up north, but life was far harsher for them than for the middle- and upper-middle-class sets Priestley found in the nearby Cotswolds. Yet as the dole queues grew, so too did middle-class anx-ieties about who would pay for the poor. Many salaried professionals and businessmen saw themselves – in the words of a *Daily Mirror* columnist – as 'sandwiched between the people who are unable to fend for themselves and the affluent who can well afford to do so'.[13] Their outrage was fuelled by the loss of privileges that had previously distinguished them from the working class. The right to vote was no longer a hallmark of middle-class status, but a right conferred on all adults. An expansion in local government, the civil service and shopwork meant that white-collar workers were no longer as distinct a social group as they had been before the war. And, despite the increase in the number of servants, demand exceeded supply, raising worries over whether the middle class could continue to depend on domestic help. Householders concerned about the survival of their social status and home comforts now constantly referred to their responsibilities – and potential exploitation – as taxpayers who shouldered the burden of poor relief.

But in fact many of the middle class were doing rather well. Far from shouldering a crippling financial burden, the man on £500 per year was subject to light taxation. From the mid-1920s, private house building increased, and middle-class home owners were the prime beneficiaries. Council house building remained slow and sporadic in the 1920s, and rents in new council houses were too high for most manual workers to afford. Salaried professional workers, on the other hand, were able to afford mortgages on modern villas in the spacious, green suburbs springing up on the edges of Britain's major cities.[14] Many could easily afford to employ domestic help, and a growing number of them wished to do so. 'The shortage of servants,' concluded officials at the Ministry of Education in 1937, 'must be due to a largely increased demand rather than to a decrease in the supply.'[15]

Middle-class ratepayers' resentment at paying for the unemployed was stoked by the National government's increasingly punitive treatment of the luckless thousands on the dole. In 1931 a *Times* editorial lauded the means test, claiming that the dole had become 'an alternative source of almost permanent maintenance'.[16] The unemployed, judged Francis Joseph in a letter published by *The Times* in August 1931, were 'drugged by the dole', content to live on handouts rather than energetically seeking work.[17] In December of that year the *Scotsman* – the newspaper read by businessmen, schoolteachers and suburban housewives north of the border – published an extraordinary letter from 'Lex', bemoaning that 'we have travelled far away' from 'the day when such was the independence of Scots that suicide seemed almost preferable to assistance from public sources'.[18] A correspondent signed 'An Inquirer' agreed: 'the income-tax payers are, unlike the unemployed, paying out and getting no return directly for their money,' the writer complained. 'Many of the workless marry and breed families while in receipt of the dole', adding to the taypayer's 'heavy burden'.[19]

Yet far from being able to rely on the dole for a comfortable lifestyle, the unemployed were the group most likely to live in poverty. This marked a change from earlier years. In 1924 A.L. Bowley, Professor of Statistics at London University, and his assistant, Margaret Hogg, had discovered that even in the depressed north-east mining town of Stanley, only 15 per cent of households living in poverty were in such straits because they were headed by an unemployed man. Most families were poor because their chief wage-earner was dead or too old to work, or because the wages earned by working members of the family 'were insufficient at full ordinary work' to keep their household.[20] But by 1929 the largest social survey ever conducted in Britain, the *New Survey of London Life and Labour* led by Hubert Llewellyn Smith, observed 'that the highest proportion [of families] in poverty is to be found where there is no adult male wage-earner', frequently as a result of unemployment.[21]

From 1932 the number of unemployed people began to fall as more jobs became available in light manufacturing industries, shops and offices. Nevertheless, unemployment remained a major cause of hardship in many areas, including relatively affluent ones. In 1936 about 4 per cent of York's residents lived in dire poverty, 30 per cent of them because of unemployment,[22] and the same was true of Bristol in 1938.[23] Jack Bell was born in 1922 and grew up in Hanham, on Bristol's outskirts. His mother was a factory machinist and his father hawked goods. Jack left school at fourteen to become a builder's labourer. He felt fortunate: 'it was a common thing to see men – little bunches of men on the corner of the street just talking and hoping that something would come along.'[24] Most unemployed men had to rely on the financial support of their relatives, primarily sons, daughters and wives, in that order.[25]

The architects of the benefits system, and those who policed it, insisted on behaving as though personal fecklessness caused poverty, and called on the unemployed to help themselves. But critics, like A.D. Lindsay, the Master of Balliol College, Oxford, warned that the means test was preventing people from helping themselves or their relatives; that it was in fact 'breaking up families'.[26] From 1934, the household means test reduced an unemployed person's benefit if they shared a house with wage-earners, and so some of those claiming dole left home – or pretended to have done so. Stanley Iveson grew up in Nelson, a Lancashire textile town that suffered high unemployment. As a teenage mill worker he witnessed the effect of the means test on the people in his street: 'there was a big building across [the road] . . . it was a model lodging house. And people used to – lads used to go and sleep there, during the week . . . It was a shilling a night . . . So they was able to draw the dole. But they went home for their meals . . . And it broke homes up in those days.'[27]

In other families, young wage-earners departed, so that their unemployed brother or father could retain their benefit rather than living on their meagre wage. In 1935 Jane Wright, a Labour councillor in Paddington, 'came across many cases in which a son or daughter, or both, who had been contributing towards the relief of their parents under the Means Test had left their homes in consequence. This naturally caused great anxiety to the parents.'[28] As late as 1937, a study by the Carnegie Trust noted that young men in the cities of Glasgow and Liverpool left the parental home at an early age in order to avoid the means test.[29]

The process of being means-tested was as humiliating as the principle of the test was degrading. Inspectors – or 'relieving officers' – had the right to inspect an unemployed person's home to see if they had goods they should sell before claiming benefit, or were spending money fecklessly. In 1934 twenty-two-year-old Ernie Benson of Hunslet, Leeds, was struggling to make ends meet. His labouring job had come to an end, and he was claiming dole. His wife Eileen worked in a mill 'on a three day week, the major portion of her wages was deducted from the amount we would normally have received in Public Assistance . . . I got a miserable 10s a week.' Altogether, the Bensons and their two young children were expected to live on 20s per week, at a time when the social investigator B.S. Rowntree calculated the average family required more than 43s to secure 'the necessaries of a healthy life'.[30] Ernie's money was reliant on the weekly visits of the Public Assistance Board's relieving officer, Frank Waters, 'a real mean sod':

I was sat in the house one day awaiting his visit. It was one of those dull, damp days and the fire was low in the grate. As I jabbed at it with the poker, the door opened without warning and Frank Waters stepped inside. Peremptorily he demanded 'Is there any change?' Was I angry . . . 'get out you unmannerly bastard. My wife could have been washing herself at the sink there, get, out, knock and don't come in until you're asked' . . . He went outside and knocked. I let him in and glared when he said, 'Is there any change in your circum-stances?' I snapped, 'Yes, there is – for the bloody worse.' 'Have you anything in your cupboard?' . . . After a hurried look [in the food cupboard] he said 'Alright, but I won't forget this.'

Shortly after Walters's fateful visit, the Public Assistance Board discovered that Ernie was secretly earning 10s per week repairing boots and shoes. 'My relief money was suspended for five weeks, which meant I had nothing for Christmas from Public Assistance.'[31]

People felt forced to commit fraud in order to maintain themselves and sustain their families. In 1931 twenty-one-year-old Frank Haynes of Abingdon found himself on the dole. He'd worked as an apprentice carpenter after leaving school: 'I stayed there till I was twenty-one when I got 10s a week. When I asked for a rise I got the sack.' The Public Assistance Board 'turned me down and told me my father could keep me', which Frank's father, a decorator with four younger children, disputed. A month later the Board granted Frank 10s, too little to live on, especially as he wanted to get married. So 'I done a little job unbeknown to them, decorating on a house.'[32]

In some cases, like Ernie Benson's, neighbours sought to settle old scores by dropping a hint that a man claiming benefit was working. In other cases, neighbours would help each other out. In 1934 sixteen-year-old Emily Swankie – one of twelve children, living in a Glasgow tenement flat – was a shop worker. Her older brother Charlie, in his mid-twenties, was unemployed. 'Two of my sisters and myself were working and so was my father. So Charlie's money was reduced . . . it was quite a serious thing for the family when first of all we lost Charlie's wages and then his dole money.' Charlie told the means test officials that he had moved out of his parents' tenement flat, in order to qualify for more money; in reality 'he just stayed out as much as possible.' Then 'neighbours would tell one another when they thought the inspectors were on their way', so that unemployed men like Charlie 'could hide'.[33] Such incursions into people's private lives fostered resentment, anger and suspicion.

Unemployment radicalized some. Emily Swankie joined the Communist Party and, in 1934, participated in one of the hunger marches organized by the National Unemployed Workers' Movement (NUWM) from Glasgow to London.[34] Ernie Benson became a stalwart of the NUWM and had fun disrupting the attempts of the Leeds Public Assistance Board to force unemployed men to undertake menial work in return for their benefits. Obliged to attend the local 'Occupation Centre', 'I did a fair amount of work there, but not for them. I borrowed a portable typewriter to type letters and cut stencils for leaflets for the [Communist] Party and the Unemployed Movement. When I first did this the workshop gaffers didn't know what the hell to say about it.' Eventually, the recalcitrance of Benson and his fellow participants forced the centre's staff to replace menial work with lectures, and eventually to shut down the centre.[35]

But it was the hopelessness of the long-term unemployed for which the thirties became known. In many families, unemployment touched two generations or more. Ewan MacColl was born in Salford in 1915. 'Of the four children my mother bore, three died in infancy. I was the survivor and, consequently, especially dear to her.' His mother, Betsy, was a charwoman and MacColl's father, William, was an ironmoulder at a local foundry. The older Mr MacColl's Communist beliefs and his trade union activism lost him several jobs in the 1920s. In 1929 Ewan MacColl left Grecian Street elementary school along with his other fourteen-year-old classmates, 'fearful of the future, infected by our parents' despair, waiting for tomorrow and wishing it would never come'.[36]

Like Emily Swankie and Ernie Benson, resistance to this fate catapulted Ewan MacColl into political activism – in his case via the Young Communist League and socialist theatre.

> The years between 1929 and 1934 were tumultuous ones . . . I leave school, I sign on at the unemployment exchange, I join the Clarion Players, I am employed at the wire-works, I am erect, I am unemployed again but still erect, I'm employed by the *Textile Trader* (with erection), unemployed again, form Red Megaphones

(less erect), become motor-mechanic's apprentice (and was quickly sacked). From then on, everything seems to happen at once. Two or three nights a week I am busy rehearsing and performing agitprop sketches and during the day I am up to the eyes in political work. At weekends I am off rambling in Derbyshire or North Lancashire or the Lake District and I am reading everything I can lay my hands on. I am also active in the Youth Council of the NUWM.[37]

But older men could find it difficult to summon up this energy and enthusiasm. In 1930 William MacColl was sacked for the last time; by 1931 'he had become just another reject among three million other rejects.'[38] He never found regular work again.

Many of the 'rejects' were taking to the roads by 1934. They were trying to follow the National government's advice to move to where the work was, and attempting to relieve the pressure on their wives and children – often without success. That summer, eighteen-year-old Laurie Lee left the crowded cottage in the Cotswold village of Slad that he shared with his mother and six siblings. He set out on the road for London, in search of work and adventure.

> I soon noticed there were many others, all trudging northwards in a sombre procession. Some of course, were professional tramps, but the majority belonged to that host of unemployed who wandered aimlessly about England at that time . . . They were like a broken army walking away from a war, cheeks sunken, eyes dead with fatigue. Some carried bags of tools, or shabby cardboard suitcases; some wore the ghosts of city suits; some, when they stopped to rest, carefully removed their shoes and polished them vaguely with handfuls of grass. Among them were carpenters, clerks, engineers from the Midlands; many had been on the road for months, walking up and down the country in a maze of jobless refusals, the treadmill of the mid-Thirties . . .[39]

There seemed, thought Lee, no escape for these men. He himself had his sights set on London and then hoped to go abroad as soon as he could afford a passage out of his depressed homeland. He reached London, and found work labouring on the capital's many building sites. One year later, he was on his way to Spain.

Laurie Lee was one of the lucky ones. Many families couldn't afford to allow their children to move far away. When young people left school, their employment opportunities were determined by who they knew. In 1923 the government had established juvenile employment bureaux, arguing that lack of information was a major cause of unemployment. But these bureaux couldn't invent jobs, and so they were unable to offer much to teenagers leaving school in the early 1930s. In larger towns and cities, school-leavers had more options than those in small villages or mining communities, but in a highly competitive labour market most relied on a relative or neighbour to 'speak for' them to a foreman or manager. A series of surveys into young people's working lives – provoked by concern over high unemployment – found that only a minority of sons entered the same trade as their fathers, but the vast majority were working in the same occupational grade. They had little chance of moving from unskilled into skilled manual work, and manual workers' sons had almost no opportunity to get higher grade clerical or professional work.[40] This was a labour market offering very little mobility; and when unemployment hit, disaster struck.

Among those who entered employment in the inter-war years, more slid down the social ladder than ascended it. Those who were lucky enough to get apprenticed to a trade found that there was not usually a job for them at the end of their training, the fate of engineering apprentice Harry Hardcastle in Walter Greenwood's 1933 novel, Love on the Dole.[41] In 1969 sociologist Richard Brown led an interview team into Wallsend's shipyards on Tyneside. Brown himself was concerned with the shipyard workers' experiences and attitudes in the late 1960s, but in the process of interviewing these men, his team amassed details of the employment history of 266 engineers, boilermakers and labourers. The majority of those men who had entered employment before 1935 (70 per cent of 187 men in total) experienced downward mobility during the 1930s. Many were forced out of their trade once they had completed an apprenticeship and qualified for adult wage rates. Most of them never got the opportunity to retrain or re-enter the trade for which they had trained. They ended up as labourers or semi-skilled workers.[42]

As this suggests, teenagers who were too young to qualify for adult wage rates were in greater demand than adult men: once they reached twenty-one they were dismissed. This was true in the older manufacturing industries like shipbuilding, and it was also true in those new factories making wirelesses and vacuum cleaners, and in the department stores and offices that sprang up in the 1930s. Young workers were cheap. Employers justified paying them low wages by claiming that they were 'pin money workers', who only worked for spending money. Yet the reality, as Winifred Holtby observed, was that young wage-earners bore heavy responsibilities. Norman Savage grew up in Manchester. His father's long-term unemployment led Norman to take casual jobs throughout his schooldays: he worked in a shop before and after school, and as a delivery boy in school holidays. When he left school in the early 1930s, he and his oldest sister became responsible for keeping their family of six: 'my sister worked in the mill . . . so there was only my wages, my few bob, and her few bob keeping the lot.'[43]

Fathers were often guilty and ashamed that they were unable to keep their children. Peggy Few, who grew up in Nottingham, felt fortunate to find work at the city's Players cigarette factory when she left school in the early 1930s. The factory paid good wages and conditions were reasonable; 'Players' Angels', as Peggy and her workmates at this factory were popularly known, worked in clean conditions, had shorter working days than many factory workers and enjoyed regular wage increases. In the mid-1930s, however, Peggy learned that this could be a mixed blessing. The day after she received a wage rise, her father's unemployment assistance was stopped: 'he cried like a baby and so did I, he fetched me out of work to tell me . . . and I said "It don't matter daddy, it don't matter, we'll get through somehow, we'll get through somehow".'[44]

Peggy's generation learned to blame the government or their employers for this state of affairs, not the fathers they sought to look after. Their experience would influence the course of history. They were the generation that gained the vote in 1945, and who, with one eye on the 1930s, gave Labour its first majority government.

Winifred Holtby was not alone in her anger. The means test galvanized the sympathies of many left-leaning writers, academics, social researchers and welfare workers. 'Both my parents were left-wing,' recalled journalist Katharine Whitehorn, the daughter of a public school housemaster, 'horrified by the conditions of the two million unemployed, the slums, the means test that meant you hid your last remaining treasures in the coal bin lest your dole be cut until you sold them. And like so many of their generation, the horrors of the First World War – during which my father had been a conscientious objector – had made them passionately pacifist.'[45] 'We now realize,' wrote A.D. Lindsay, the Master of Balliol College, Oxford, in a scathing attack on the means test printed by *The Times* in 1935, 'that most men . . . who are unemployed [are on the dole] through no fault of their own.'[46]

With Labour in disarray, and the dole queues still long, those concerned about the consequences of long-term unemployment turned away from formal politics and towards investigating the conditions of those affected. In 1934 two investigators, H.L. Beales and R.S. Lambert, published *Memoirs of the Unemployed*, a collection of testimonies from men and women. In the following year, the Labour-supporting Archbishop of York, William Temple, convened an Unemployment Committee of Enquiry under the auspices of the charitable Pilgrim Trust. Among its members was that self-described 'independent progressive' A.D. Lindsay of Balliol. Their wide-ranging study of the impact of unemployment on men and women in South Wales, north-east England, London and Liverpool was published as *Men without Work* in 1938.

These studies demonstrated that the poor were not to blame for their poverty. Beales and Lambert had shown that every unemployed person had a backstory – a personal history that usually involved hard work, when they got the chance, and being thwarted by sickness, old age or global recession. The Pilgrim Trust's researchers agreed with Beales and Lambert that unemployment was not confined to the feckless few. *Men without Work* concluded that 'in periods of depression thousands of men are thrown out of work by conditions outside their own control'.[47]

This was an important and controversial assertion. Conservative politicians and the conservative press had assiduously promoted the notion that those drawing unemployment benefit were those who had never prudently saved, or paid into the national insurance scheme.

In 1931 an editorial in *The Times* declared that the unemployed 'should have to prove the need of relief as a condition of receiving it', claiming that this offered 'moral advantages' in a system where the 'uninsured' composed such a large group of claimants.[48] What such proclamations conveniently ignored was the very large proportion of benefit claimants who had been unemployed for so long that they had exhausted their savings or the contributory benefit scheme funded by their national insurance payments.

By giving unemployed people voices, history and individuality, *Memoirs of the Unemployed* and *Men without Work* undermined the stereotypes of fecklessness and idleness that dogged press and political representations of those on the dole. An unemployed advertising agent spoke to Beales and Lambert of his 'despair' when he had to resort to selling 'my books and other oddments. Finally my wife had to sell what little jewellery she possessed. The worst wrench came when she had to pawn her wedding ring.'[49] He described his 'desperation' and 'horror' at finding himself in debt and unable to be the breadwinner his wife had married; of becoming 'embittered against all politicians of all parties'.[50]

Proponents of the means test assumed, as *The Times* suggested, that unemployment benefit would dissuade people from finding work. But the unemployed disputed this. 'I have always stood for independence,' said a forty-year-old miner from South Wales, 'but now I have been compelled to lose mine through no fault of my own, but simply because I am the victim of a vicious circle.' The stories such men told made clear that the problem with the dole was not its generosity, but its limitations, which cast so many families into poverty. This miner told Beales and Lambert that he found politicians 'hopeless'; being on the dole 'has made me very bitter', he said.[51]

The voices of the unemployed revealed that personal appearance, behaviour and spending patterns were not the causes of poverty, but its consequences. Some of those who spoke to Beales and Lambert recounted their journey from 'keeping up appearances' and aspiring to a particular sort of job to a realization of their common interests with those they had previously considered 'rough' or feckless. One 'Scottish hotel servant' wrote that his worst period was when he struggled to keep lodgings in 'a better-class district of Glasgow'. Finally:

I shed my pride . . . and took share of a room in a working-class locality where existence upon the dole is not an uncommon experience. I learned how to wash and iron my clothes . . . and mend my boots, and, more important still, learned how to secure the utmost value out of every penny spent . . . One can enter cheap clothing clubs . . . A lucky flutter on horses called a 'tanner double' brought me wealth to the tune of three pounds odd. This 'ill-gotten money' not only enabled me to buy boots, socks, shirts and underclothing . . . but also provided me with a trip to the seaside for a day. How I enjoyed that outing![52]

Stories like this man's stressed how thin the line between respectability and poverty was. They testified to the arbitrary nature of hardship, and challenged the notion that laziness or lack of savings plunged people into poverty. Living for today – enjoying the thrill of a horse race, a train-ride to the coast, a bag of chips on the beach – was a way of life forced on people by the circumstances in which they found themselves.

These were not new stories. That millions of people were vulnerable to living in poverty through no fault of their own, and that hardship had dire consequences for emotional and physical health as well as family income, had been documented by social investigators, journalists and novelists for more than a century – by men and women like Charles Dickens, Henry Mayhew and Maud Pember Reeves. Yet in every generation they needed retelling; for the myth that the poor caused their own poverty was a persistent one, precisely because it served powerful people's interests. That the unemployed were citizens too – that some of them had paid the rates once – was a truth that parliamentary politicians rarely acknowledged in the mid-1930s.

And yet some of the ratepayers and taxpayers were slowly changing their minds: the experience of mass unemployment led them to wonder whether it was really ethical to divide the 'undeserving' from the 'deserving' poor at all. A few came to this conclusion as a result of their own unemployment, for white-collar and professional workers were not exempt. Others, like Katharine Whitehorn's parents, were long-standing social progressives, whose views were confirmed by the hardship and distress the means test caused. But most had their minds changed by what they witnessed at work, on travels around their city or country, or by what they read. In 1938 the Pilgrim Trust's *Men without Work* found an enthusiastic publisher in Victor Gollancz, who had founded the Left Book Club in 1936. Gollancz hoped to provide a platform for working-class writers and for writings about working-class life; he also aimed to produce books affordable to a wide readership. It was Gollancz who published L.P. Coombes's account of life in a South Wales mining village, *These Poor Hands*, and George Orwell's *Road to Wigan Pier*. By April 1939 the club had 57,000 members, who eagerly awaited their copy of each 'Book of the Month'.[53]

Gollancz was not alone in his promotion of working-class writing. By the mid-1930s, many on the political left were captivated by the notion of a 'popular front', an idea that had originated with the Communist Party but was taken up and developed by a broader group of writers, artists, journalists and academics including Winifred Holtby, Lewis Grassic Gibbon and Cecil Day Lewis. In parts of mainland Europe the Popular Front exerted more direct political influence (France elected a popular front government in 1936) but it had a significant effect on British cultural life. The popular front comprised a loose collection of writers and artists; but the periodical *Left Review* was their platform. In close typeface, on the first page of its first issue in October 1934, *Left Review* provided readers with an introduction to the popular front:

> There is a crisis of ideas in the capitalist world today not less considerable than the crisis of economics . . . There are already a number of writers who realize this: they desire and are working for the ending of the capitalist order of society. They aim at a new order based not on property and profit, but on co-operative effort. They realize that the working class will be the builders of this new order, and see that the change must be revolutionary in effect.[54]

In this climate a handful of influential working-class writers such as Walter Greenwood, author of *Love on the Dole*, and Walter Brierley, who wrote *Means Test Man*, found publishers and an interested public.[55] It is difficult to know how large the readership for these books was, but Greenwood's *Love on the Dole* was a bestseller, reissued ten times between 1934 and 1937.[56] High sales, the large number of members that Gollancz's Left Book Club attracted and the multiple broadsheet newspaper reviews from which these books benefited suggest that many people were keen to learn more about working-class life than politicians' rhetoric or newspaper headlines told them.

Many of these readers were middle class – but not all of them. Working-class readers were sometimes critical of the social surveys and novels, which they thought represented them as ignorant or helpless victims rather than as thinking people with political opinions of their own. They included Ernie Benson, who helped establish a Communist bookshop in Leeds during the mid-1930s. He preferred working-class representations of urban life to that offered by George Orwell in his *Road to Wigan Pier*, an account of Orwell's visit to the depressed northern town and the people he met there. When Benson visited Wigan a year after Orwell's book had been published:

> [o]ne of the local party members, Jim Grady, told me that [Orwell] asked Jim's brother to take him round the slummiest areas of Wigan . . . He was interested in picking on the scruffy, ignorant workers, and . . . projected them as being typical of Wigan as a whole. How little people with such ideas know about us of the working class, of our aspirations and dreams, of our desire and ability to climb from the filth, poverty, wars and starvation which capitalism creates for us, and of our endeavours to create a more just and humane society.[57]

While only a minority of the unemployed were politically active, Benson was correct to point out that their experiences and actions were often neglected by social investigators, who chose to represent the 'typical' unemployed man as apathetic, resigned, or impotently frustrated. These writers were unwilling to acknowledge that working-class people might have the capacity to be agents of social change without the leadership of a liberal middle class.

By the late 1930s a wider range of middle-class voters were changing their view of the unemployed as innately apathetic or feckless. One reason was the rise of Fascism and authoritarianism on mainland Europe, personified in Hitler's appointment as Chancellor of Germany in January 1933. The Nazi Party, like Mussolini's Fascisti, made much of their populist appeal, organizing mass meetings and demonstrations. Suddenly the capacity of ordinary people to be agents of political change was inescapable. From 1932, Oswald Mosley's British Union of Fascists (BUF) tried to replicate Hitler's success. Mosley, a former Labour Party MP, attracted sufficient support to hold large rallies in several towns and cities, including the infamous and violent London Olympia rally of June 1934, which frightened several prominent Conservative MPs, and the conservative *Times* and *Daily Telegraph*, into denouncing Mosley's 'private army' for its 'violence'.[58]

Both the British right and the left claimed that the ordinary working class was on their side – but in reality, streets, neighbourhoods and towns were often divided. Mosley's message appealed to people who believed they were competing for limited jobs and housing with immigrants. Working-class docklands areas had always provided homes for recent immigrants: these were the places where new arrivals could find cheap shelter and casual work. In areas like London's East End, Tyneside's South Shields, or Liverpool's docklands, secure work was limited, housing overcrowded, and some were quick to support Mosley's claim that immigrants either caused these problems or made them worse. The BUF never fielded candidates in a general election, but in the 1937 elections to the London County Council Mosley's party received large numbers of votes in the East End constituencies of Bethnal Green and Shoreditch. On several occasions the BUF marched unopposed through East End streets.

Ultimately, however, the BUF could not galvanize the support that the Nazis had managed to foster among German working-class people. Partly, this was because unemployment in Britain was not as high as it was in Germany or Italy. Most of those on the dole were older men, many of whom were members of Britain's trade union movement, which was both stronger and more independent than the labour movement in Germany. The men who made up Britain's dole queues were very different in age and outlook to the young, disillusioned but energetic men who the Nazis were able to recruit.

Working-class support for fascism was weak; racial tolerance, if not acceptance, was a long-standing feature of life in the communities that Mosley targeted. In districts where different races, religions and cultures collided, tension was always a possibility, particularly in times of poverty and unemployment. But much of the time, most people simply got on with life, forging neighbourly relations and sometimes deeper friendships that crossed divisions of race and religion. Immigrants who wished to become British subjects had to list British-born referees in their applications, and people from all walks of life stepped forward to offer this support to workmates or neighbours. In 1919 John George Robinson, a long-time resident of South Shields – a port town accommodating Yemenis, Germans, Austrians, Russian Jews and Scandinavians – gave his support to George Edwin Anderson's application for naturalization. John had known George for years, 'having been postman on the walk for 17 years and knowing his father well'.[59] Even in London's East End the BUF failed to win any council seats: Labour remained the choice of most working-class voters. Despite Mosley's claims that the BUF numbered 50,000 members by 1935, he only attracted about 16,000.[60]

Many active fascists came from the wealthier echelons of society. In 1934 the Labour Party asked local branches to provide information about BUF membership in their area. The responses revealed that Mosley relied heavily on shopkeepers and businessmen, worried about financial crisis, and the upper middle class; in Harrogate, 'the younger members of the Tory Party' were attracted by the BUF's uniforms and sports; in Portsmouth the party relied on 'young men and women of independent means'; while in the Home Counties one of the most prominent BUF speakers was 'a Church of England vicar who is also a leader in the Boy Scout Movement'.[61] Arthur Rogers, a fifteen-year-old assistant in a small corner shop, recalled that in Oxford, university students were Mosley's most prominent supporters. 'On Saturday nights, the University had the Blackshirt movement, the Nazi throng – and they used to come over and stand around in the street and Sid [Arthur's friend] used to stand in the middle and argue with them. He knew more about it than they did.'[62]

But many supporters remained cautious and covert. The BUF's unpopularity grew as revelations about Hitler's brutality began to trickle into the British press. Nellie Driver, a BUF organizer in the Lancashire cotton town of Nelson, recalled that 'Some of our sympathizers were well known Tory businessmen and Nelson would have been astonished if they had known who they were.' She regretted that the more conspicuous BUF members 'were cranks – and worse'.[63] While the BUF's anti-Semitism and totalitarian convictions (and their uniforms and sports, if Harrogate and Portsmouth were typical) provided an outlet for discontented Tories, most were not so disenchanted that they considered departing from Baldwin's electorally successful Conservative Party.

Although Mosley loudly criticized those 'great interests' that controlled 'commerce . . . the press . . . the cinema [and] the City of London', he was receptive to support from aristocrats, industrialists and manufacturers.[64] Wealthy farmers assisted BUF campaigns in Suffolk.[65] In 1934 Lord Rothermere, until 1931 the owner of the *Daily Mirror*, secured two-thirds of a page in that newspaper for his article 'Give the Blackshirts a Helping Hand'. Rothermere condemned anti-Fascist 'panic mongers' and suggested that the Blackshirts' 'patriotism and discipline set a practical example to the young men and women of Britain, who are being defrauded by Old Gang politicians of the share to which they are entitled in the control and organisation of their country's affairs'. What kind of 'control' a one-party state would offer to Britain's youth Rothermere did not say.[66] The aristocratic Mitford family, who were never far from a crisis, also joined the fray. Unity and Diana visited Germany several times in the mid-1930s and became close friends with members of Hitler's inner circle.[67]

Militant opponents of fascism began to appear in the mid-1930s. Once Hitler was ensconced in power, anyone reading the newspapers became aware that violence, anti-Semitism and totalitarianism were intrinsic parts of his regime. This helped to galvanize opposition to the BUF in some working-class neighbourhoods – including east London. It was there, in 1936, that twenty-one-year-old Charlie Goodman, the son of Polish Jewish émigré parents, heard that Mosley's Blackshirts were planning to march through his neighbourhood. Like many of his friends, Charlie had been influenced by his family's left-wing politics and became involved in the Communist Party in his teens. Until the mid-1930s, however, the political activities of most of his friends and relatives were restricted to debates and meetings. Charlie's experience chimed with that of Willy Goldman, the son of Yiddish-speaking, Russian-Romanian parents who 'never allowed [us] to forget that we were foreigners. Our parents continually reminded us: "One bad Jew gets the whole race into trouble."'[68] Attitudes changed as unemployment increased and the BUF began to march. By 1936 both Willy Goldman and Charlie Goodman were part of 'the growth in opposition to fascism' alongside many friends and relatives. Charlie ascribed their increasing willingness to campaign actively against Mosley 'to what was happening in Germany'. In 1936 he was among hundreds of protesters who prevented the BUF from marching through Cable Street. For his part in this successful demonstration, Charlie was arrested for hitting a policeman and spent a year in jail at Wormwood Scrubs.[69]

In 1936 some of the unemployed departed the dole queues and hunger marches of Britain for a different battle. In July that year General Franco launched his attack on the new Spanish Republican government and the Spanish Civil War began. Certain that this marked the start of a sustained fascist attack on European democracy, more than 2,300 volunteers from Britain and Ireland joined International Brigades set up to assist the Republican forces.[70] The volunteers included a sprinkling of aristocratic fighters like Esmond Romilly (a cousin, and later the husband, of Jessica Mitford) and George Orwell, who tended to dominate breathless press reports about the war; but most were young men from ordinary homes in London, the north-east coalfields, the valleys of South Wales or the slums of Manchester. They included thirty-four-year-old Clement Broadbent, Dewsbury's youngest Labour councillor, who was killed in the Battle of Ebro in 1938;[71] and Nat Cohen, a Jewish pacifist living in London's East End, who 'studied military strategy and Spanish at night' before founding the Tom Mann Column of the International Brigades.[72] Many were unemployed, like twenty-five-year-old Phil Gillan, the first Glaswegian volunteer to reach Spain, who had had paid work for just a few months after leaving school and then had 'been unemployed for about ten years'.[73]

These volunteers viewed themselves as the guardians of democracy. Gary McCartney, a Scottish volunteer, was certain that his peers 'didn't go to Spain to usher in communism or anything like that. We went to Spain to continue the fight for the freedom of a people to put a cross on a ballot paper.'[74] Many hoped that success in Spain would destroy fascism in Europe. When Charlie Goodman was released from Wormwood Scrubs in 1937, he 'felt I would like to continue the fight physically against fascism with arms in hand' and quickly departed for Spain.[75]

The volunteers quickly came to be represented as defenders of democracy by newspapers and Labour politicians. Particularly influential was the *Mirror*, Britain's most popular newspaper, selling 4 million copies each day.[76] By 1938 the newspaper's editors had broken sufficiently free of Lord Rothermere's influence to champion the Spanish Civil War as a 'fight for the working classes'. Some of the newspaper's senior journalists were drawn from the first generations of working-class children to benefit from free state elementary education (established in 1874). Literate and adventurous, they brought to their work a commitment to reach and inform a working-class readership. They had also seen, first hand, the effects of unemployment on the families and communities where they grew up. 'We came from ordinary backgrounds,' said Hugh Cudlipp, the assistant features editor. 'I came from South Wales, which was a distressed area . . . If you've been through that, you don't forget it.'[77] The *Mirror*'s coverage reflected the view of many of the British volunteers in Spain: that full citizenship did not only mean the right to vote, but the right to play a full part in the economic life of the country too. Whether this meant the right to work, the right to negotiate economic policy at the highest level, or the right to complete political and economic equality was a matter of debate within the British left – but they all shared the sense that democracy offered working-class people a greater chance to realize their aspirations than Fascism ever could.

Those who fought in the Spanish Civil War, or against Mosley's BUF, were in a minority. However, their protests caught the attention of the press and the wider public because they suggested that working-class people might be Britain's true guardians of democracy, at a time when it appeared to be under grave threat. These campaigners, many of them unemployed, arraigned themselves against the much publicized friendships between British aristocrats and Nazis. Far from being feckless or helpless, they promoted the causes of anti-fascism and socialism. In doing so, they proposed a very different vision of the future from that being offered by Hitler's influential supporters.

Back home, in the valleys of South Wales, the slums of the East End, and the textile towns of Lancashire, unemployment continued to cause poverty. By the middle of the 1930s, the living conditions of working-class women were attracting the attention of feminist and labour campaigners. In the 1920s and early 1930s local and national government had focused on children's health when measuring the medical impact of poverty. Despite regional discrepancies, Ministry of Health officials were able to point to a gradual decline in infant mortality. But women's health presented a more worrying picture. Between 1923 and 1933 the maternal mortality rate actually rose by 22 per cent. Although the national rate of maternal mortality dropped during the mid-1930s, poorer areas continued to record as many as 10 maternal deaths per 1,000 live births.[78]

Concern over the plight of these women fuelled a campaign for better birth control advice and for state allowances for expectant mothers and young children. These were reforms for which women in the Labour Party and the co-operative movement – who came from a wide range of social backgrounds – had long been campaigning. After the First World War, they had succeeded in having a state maternity service, free medical care, home helps and free or low-cost school food and milk incorporated into Labour Party policy, although neither the 1924 nor the 1929 Labour governments implemented these reforms.[79]

Members of the wider women's movement shared some of these aims. Where some of them differed from Labour women was in their attitude to state intervention. Some, like Eleanor Rathbone, believed that the voluntary sector should provide those maternity and children's services that Labour women argued the state should manage. Among those who initially supported Rathbone's view was Margery Spring Rice, the daughter of a wealthy London solicitor, and a former student of Girton College, Cambridge. After leaving college in 1924, Spring Rice had joined some of her contemporaries in undertaking welfare work in London's slums. Her encounters with working-class women there convinced her that they were not to blame for the poverty in which they found themselves. During the following decade, Spring Rice helped to establish several maternity and child welfare clinics across London.

In 1933 Spring Rice joined the Women's Health Enquiry Committee, a non-partisan group that included representatives from major women's groups, including the Co-operative Women's Guild. The committee's work was inspired by the government's refusal to admit that poverty caused ill-health. By focusing on women and young children, the women's movement was able to challenge the assumption that the poor could be divided into the 'deserving' and the 'undeserving'. Sick and dying mothers were never vilified in the manner of unemployed men; and their children were clearly innocents. They were easily portrayed as defenceless victims of poverty.

Nevertheless, Spring Rice and her allies had to struggle against scepticism. Even many of those who accepted a connection between poverty and women's ill-health felt the solution lay with the women themselves. In 1934 a *Times* editorial on 'Maternal Mortality' – itself a sign of how pressing a political issue this now was – suggested that 'the state of nourishment of the mother determines to an important extent her safety in childbed'. However, this writer shared the view of many liberal thinkers that voluntary efforts, and education, offered better means of improving women's health than state intervention. The chief problem lay, he concluded, with 'the ignorance of many young mothers' about their needs.[80] In the same year, the Ministry of Health launched a series of regional investigations into maternal mortality, partly to quell the criticisms of campaigners. Yet even in its 1937 report on Wales, which grudgingly admitted that 'inadequate diet and wrong feeding may be factors' contributing to high maternal mortality in working-class districts, the ministry concluded that 'their influence cannot at the moment be accurately assessed'.[81]

The Conservatives strongly opposed Labour's demands that the unemployed be given more assistance and the public health services be better financed. In 1935 Stanley Baldwin took over as Prime Minister from the ill and frail Ramsay MacDonald, in a government ostensibly called 'National' but really dominated by the Conservatives. '[T]he spending of money alone will never save one mother's life,' declared the Conservative MP Mavis Tate in a parliamentary debate on maternal mortality in 1935.[82] Arguing against the expansion of state healthcare, she claimed that 'the magnificent work done by voluntary associations' was quite sufficient to meet the health needs of those people who could not afford a private doctor.[83]

Yet within three years Tate's view had been seriously undermined. The work of campaigners like Margery Spring Rice, and the (mostly Labour) local authorities who supported pleas for better welfare provision for the poor, was beginning to have results. At the same time, the Labour Party adopted a national commitment to state welfare and housing development, as it recovered from the crisis of 1931 and reunited under a new leader – Clement Attlee – in 1935. Labour scored several important municipal election victories, including winning control of the London County Council under the leadership of Herbert Morrison in 1934. These authorities prioritized improving health and housing in working-class areas.

Keen to ensure that Labour did not take the initiative on reform, Baldwin's government introduced the 1936 Housing Act. This charged local authorities with providing homes for 'the working classes', and led to a big expansion in council house building. Whereas the council houses of the early 1920s had been aimed at the most prosperous manual workers, this heavily subsidized scheme focused on the poorest. Cities such as Liverpool and Newcastle launched ambitious slum clearance programmes. Increasing numbers of people believed that the state should provide the basic essentials of life.

In 1938 the work of the Women's Health Committee culminated in the publication of *Working Class Wives*. Margery Spring Rice wrote up this study, which was based on interviews with 1,250 working-class women. They included the wives of wage-earners as well as women married to unemployed men, and country-dwellers as well as those living in the inner-city slums. The voices of this broad sample helped make Spring Rice's most powerful argument: that a rise in maternal mortality testified to widespread ill-health caused by poverty. 'The constant struggle with poverty this last four years has made me feel very nervy and irritable,' the wife of an unemployed man – herself a former typist – explained. 'Mrs L.C. of Cardiff', a former servant, complained of bad backache 'ever since her first confinement which was a difficult one'. Unable to afford the doctor's fee, she suffered 'unexplained palpitations and cardiac pains' and could find little respite with six children and no bathroom or hot water.[84]

Poverty explained these women's poor health. The behaviour of some husbands didn't help: 'I believe myself that one of the biggest difficulties our mothers have is our husbands do not realize we ever need any leisure time,' said one woman. 'My life for many years consisted of being penned in a kitchen 9 feet square, every fourteen months a baby . . . I used to feel I was just a machine.'[85] But over-crowding, low wages and unemployment, together with poor and expensive medical care, all played their part. 'Naturally there are some who seem to get more out of life than others,' Spring Rice admitted, 'but almost without exception it is those women who have very few children . . . and who for this or some other reason are in much better financial circumstances.'[86]

When *Working Class Wives* was published, debate still raged in parliament and the press over whether high levels of maternal mortality were due to poverty or to poor medical provision. The women and doctors to whom Margery Spring Rice spoke were in no doubt: poverty caused ill-health, while having to pay for medical care exacerbated the problem. In the same year that *Working Class Wives* was published, the ongoing debate about maternal mortality had forced the Conservatives to admit that government could do more to improve public health. The government increased expenditure on healthcare, made training for midwifery mandatory in 1936 and funded training for thousands of new midwives. The Ministry of Health published statistics showing that maternal mortality had fallen to 4.11 in 1935, the lowest rate recorded for ten years.

In 1937 Neville Chamberlain took over from Stanley Baldwin as Prime Minister. Chamberlain, who as Chancellor of the Exchequer had presided over the swingeing benefit cuts of 1934, heralded the fall in maternal mortality as a victory for Conservative health reforms. In future, he declared to an open-air meeting of supporters, 'every prospective mother, whatever her circumstances, will have made available to her the help of a qualified midwife.' More generally, he suggested, poor physique was due to lack of exercise, not to poverty. Chamberlain proposed a national programme of 'physical training' that would 'give our young people a new joy in life, a sense of their power to do what they want to do without undue fatigue' and would make them 'better citizens as well as better athletes'.[87]

Labour sounded a sceptical note, pointing out that the connection between poor health and hardship was increasingly apparent. Ellen Wilkinson, the young Labour MP for Jarrow, suggested that training midwives was only a piecemeal and partial treatment of a national problem caused by poverty. Labour MPs, she declared, 'have had much experience of what it means to have a child on the means test and to have to visit those homes'. They knew that 'nursing and midwifery, however excellent, are no substitute for good food and conditions.'[88] The government's critics pointed out that the fall in maternal mortality concealed massive regional differences. The Labour MP James Griffith noted that maternal mortality remained 'abnormally high' in his South Wales constituency, 'where we have had ten years of very bad poverty and unemployment . . . The mothers have paid the penalty for it.'[89]

In fact, the lowest rate of maternal mortality was found in working-class West Ham. In 1937 Kingsley Wood, the Conservative Minister for Health, suggested that as 'a poor borough with a population of over 280,000', West Ham proved that poverty did not have to lead to ill-health: proper medical attention, and instruction for working-class mothers on care for their children, were all that was required.[90] In reality, however, the good maternal health enjoyed by West Ham's women was the result of a Labour council's staunch commitment to generous, publicly funded health and welfare provision. West Ham council invested in midwives and hospital provision for those constituents too poor to pay medical fees. But crucially, West Ham also offered more financial assistance to the unemployed than any other local authority in Britain. As James Griffith pointed out, the lower maternal mortality rate there was 'due to the fact that they have been prepared to spend money in the interests of human life which other and far richer authorities have refused to spend'.[91]

By 1938, Margery Spring Rice could rely on finding a sympathetic readership for *Working Class Wives*. The welfare reforms introduced at West Ham, and more broadly at the Labour-controlled London County Council, had demonstrated that improvements in public welfare were not prohibitively expensive and that they could reap rich rewards.[92] Local initiatives like these gave form to the proposals of the economist John Maynard Keynes for greater state investment in, and organization of, employment, health care and housing; for a living wage and full employment.

The campaign against unemployment, orchestrated by the National Unemployed Workers' Movement and the trade unions (often in uneasy alliance, since the former was close to the Communist Party), had also played a part in changing opinion. In 1936 the Jarrow hunger march saw 200 unemployed men march from this devastated ship-building town in north-east England to deliver a petition to the Prime Minister, Stanley Baldwin, in London. The march attracted reams of press coverage and caught the public's imagination. For many middle-class inhabitants of the villages, towns and cities that the marchers passed through, the unemployed demonstrators provided their first encounter with the northern working class. Students from Girton College, Cambridge, served the men coffee and sandwiches as they marched through southern England. When they reached Bedford, 'each man was given cigarettes or tobacco by the Rotary Club' and 'offered free seats at local cinemas'.[93]

But when the marchers reached London, Stanley Baldwin refused to meet them. His action provoked widespread disapproval. On 5 November 1936 the editor of *The Times* noted approvingly that the marchers had used 'the constitutional method of petition' and deserved the government's consideration. 'The people of Jarrow,' stated the editor, 'are . . . the sufferers from decisions that they could not influence and that have been to the benefit of other places. They have done what they could for themselves.' He urged ministers to recognize that 'it is much too late in the day to suggest that the condition of industry and the location of industry are not direct concerns of the government' and declared that 'new industries are required to save the distressed areas from a lingering death; and, if private enterprise stands aside, it becomes the more necessary that the government should act.'[94] This was the first time that *The Times* had shown such overt sympathy for the unemployed.

By the time *Working Class Wives* was published, Spring Rice had changed her earlier view that voluntary effort alone could provide for people's health and wellbeing. Her committee's enquiry power-fully argued that the government should adopt the example of authorities like West Ham by reducing unemployment as well as making healthcare more accessible. While Spring Rice still saw a secondary role for voluntary agencies, she now believed that only state welfare provision and a proper economic plan could address the urgent needs of these women and their families, by offering comprehensive, uniform and continuous care. 'There does not appear to the Committee to be anything revolutionary, visionary, extravagant or socially unsound about [these recommendations],' Spring Rice declared. She pointed out that a national health service, better unemployment benefit and state intervention to create work would result in 'an incalculable saving of expenditure in the cure of disease and the tinkering with destitution'. While voluntary and charitable organizations had done a great deal of good, they necessarily focused on those in most dire need of help; what was required was a new emphasis on prevention. These were goals for which many labour organizations – including the Co-operative Women's Guild – had been campaigning for decades. In the 1930s they found new allies, whose change of heart was provoked by the immense distress suffered by the unemployed.

Spring Rice also argued that the welfare reforms she proposed could protect the country against the threat of dictatorship, now rearing its head across Europe. The 'principle of democratic develop-ment of individual happiness and welfare through communal services offered to every citizen,' she argued, 'will always be an integral part of wise government.'[95] This was an argument for universal entitle-ment to the basic means of life; an entitlement derived not from household income or the lack of it, nor from one's moral character, but simply from being born.

Yet this form of democracy was one intended to offer top-down help to the working class, rather than to encourage political and economic equality. Spring Rice's proposals foresaw no central role for those organizations that working-class people had established in order to promote collective self-help – the trade unions and the Co-operative Women's Guild among them. The notion that working-class people could be important agents of change was still one that many middle-class observers – including those sympathetic to the unemployed – found disturbing. When Guild members themselves published a collection of members' first-hand accounts of poverty, the publisher – the Hogarth Press, owned by Leonard and Virginia Woolf – prefaced this with a letter from Virginia Woolf herself, in which she described the contributors' writing as important, but as lacking 'detachment and imaginative breadth, even as the women themselves lacked variety and play of feature'. The result, she claimed, was 'half articulate speech'.

Woolf was very open about her own fears that working-class women were not yet capable of fully participating in democratic debate.[96] Spring Rice's study was different; it was, after all, based on an enquiry that included representatives from the Co-operative Women's Guild and from the Standing Joint Committee of Industrial Women's Organisations, which was composed of trade unionists. Nevertheless, her proposals stressed the need for state intervention, rather than for working-class organization. This vision of the future was certainly an improvement on the dire reality of the dole queue, but it was at odds with the aspirations of many of the Jarrow marchers, the NUWM sympathizers and the strikers of 1926, who had hoped for more active participation in the political system.

For millions of people the 1930s meant unemployment – and unemployment meant destitution and humiliation. The experience of being on the dole cut across the divisions of the skilled and unskilled, the 'respectable' and the 'rough'. Government policies focused on dissuading the unemployed from becoming reliant on the state, and on providing incentives to seek work. Yet as successive social surveys proved, this focus was misdirected; it partially placated middle-class

ratepayers, but did not address the underlying causes of unemployment, nor did it prevent the hardship of those who endured it.
Ironically, the government's household means test ensured that unemployment directly and poignantly affected thousands more people
than those who formed the dole queues: the wives and children
who became responsible for keeping their families, on wages that
were usually grossly inadequate for the task.

These days did, however, leave a positive legacy. The sight of dole
queues filled with miners, craftsmen and clerks – the so-called
'respectable' working class and even the lower middle class – made
many middle-class opinion-formers realize that hardship was arbitrary.
Means-testing added to people's indignities at a time of great stress,
and for little gain: punitive welfare did nothing to reduce the number
of those who were unemployed, and could severely damage the
health of women and children, as well as that of unemployed men.
The means test was designed to limit welfare provision but its implementation assisted a campaign to make social welfare a universal
entitlement.

The hunger marchers, social investigators, feminist campaigners
and Labour politicians who declared that poverty was caused by
social inequity, not personal behaviour, still had little political
influence in the late 1930s. That would change in the 1940s, in ways
that would bring benefits to a new generation of working-class
voters. The strong memory of the 'hungry thirties', and particularly
of the invidious means test, would prompt those children who had
shouldered family responsibilities in the inter-war years to vote, in
1945, for a Labour government committed to a welfare state and full
employment.

But the 'never again' rhetoric of the 1940s was unknown in
1934, to the men on the dole queue and their families. The Jarrow
marchers of 1936 would eventually be commemorated for having
helped to shape a national debate about unemployment and the
causes of poverty. But that unknown future could not compensate
them for returning home workless and hungry, in the knowledge
that their Prime Minister refused to see them. It could not eradicate the humiliating experience of applying for public assistance,
or assuage the anger provoked by the fact that, after decades of

fighting for the vote, the political power of working-class people remained so limited; the only legitimate role offered them by either politicians or liberal social investigators was that of helpless victim. For too many people, these were years of cruel privation and despair.

Interlude I

A Star is Born

I was born in 1936 in Castleford, Yorkshire. You'll find it on the map – I'm the bugger that put it there.

Vivian Nicholson, Play for Today, 1977

O N 3 APRIL 1936 Vivian Asprey was born in a 'two-up, two-down' council house in Wallington Street in the West Yorkshire town of Castleford. 'Where we lived, all the fellers were coal-miners,' she explained years later. 'Except my dad – he was a full-time, fully-paid-up, fully-fledged bastard.' On the census return, though, he too was listed as a 'miner'. Miners were the men whose labour made Britain great, 'blackened to the eyes, with their throats full of coal dust, driving their shovels forward with arms and belly muscles full of steel', as George Orwell admiringly, half enviously, described them in his *Road to Wigan Pier* of 1937.[1]

The reality was somewhat different. 'Miners are storytellers,' their wives would sardonically warn social scientists twenty years later, as they conducted a study of life in a Yorkshire mining town. Their jobs were hard and dangerous, but responses to that could include taking the odd day off to get drunk, as well as the heroics Orwell revelled in.[2] Their work was also unhealthy. Viv's father spent most of his time 'on the sick', due to epilepsy, asthma and his love of a drink. His five children – Viv was the eldest – depended on the pittance that their asthmatic mother could earn from potato picking on the local farms.

By the time Viv was born, most of Castleford's young women were able to turn their noses up at the agricultural labour and domestic service that their grandmothers and mothers had had to undertake. Factory work had arrived. Employers manufacturing textiles, liquorice, sweets and chemicals wanted young women to work for them; they were cheaper than adult men, and, unlike married women with families to look after, teenage girls wanted full-time work. A girl could earn more in a factory than in the fields, but such work wasn't without its dangers. Six years before Viv's birth, Castleford had come to national prominence when an explosion at Hickson and Partners, a dye manufacturers, killed thirteen workers and injured thirty-two more. Three hundred houses were rendered uninhabitable. British Pathé News reported the accident at cinemas across Britain: 'Castleford: Like an Earthquake', the newsreel proclaimed.

Away from work, young people enjoyed nights out watching Hollywood's latest hit at the town's Queen's cinema or the New Star picture house, while dances at the Co-operative Ballroom attracted large crowds. The music hall and the theatre were popular, too. Visiting Bradford in 1933, J.B. Priestley had commented that 'in communities that have suffered the most from industrial depression, among younger people who frequently cannot see what is to become of their jobs and their lives, these theatres have . . . acted as outposts for the army of the citizens of tomorrow, demanding to live . . . a life at once more ardent and imaginative and more thoughtful than their fathers and mothers ever knew.'[3] Priestley was less enthusiastic about the cinema, but by the time Viv was a child it certainly served a similar purpose.

Viv recalled her family home: 'They were drab buildings and looked as if they were falling down.' The family was overcrowded; with just two bedrooms for the household of seven 'there was no space to play about.' From the time she could toddle around, Viv played outside with the neighbours' children. They played on the street; no house had a garden and 'the front doors opened straight in to the pavement.'

Life could have been worse. 'Your lavvy and your coal house were at the bottom of the yard,' and there was 'no bath, no hot water' and no prospect of that changing that anyone could see. On the other hand, at least they had a yard. If the Aspreys had lived in one of the big industrial cities, like Leeds, they might well have found themselves living in one of the one-up, one-down back-to-back houses that composed so many slums; these only had windows and ventilation at the front of the house and residents shared an outside lavatory at the end of their street.

And there were advantages to being a miner's daughter. Viv's home was a council house and these were generally kept in better condition than those owned by private landlords. Those built since 1918 tended to be more expensive than privately rented houses, but Viv's home had been built in the 1900s, after the passing of the 1900 Housing of the Working Classes Act gave municipal councils the power to build, redevelop and maintain accommodation for their neediest residents. The West Riding of Yorkshire had taken up the challenge, under pressure from miners' unions who wanted decent and affordable housing for their members. Thousands of other workers had to wait for the 1936 Housing Act before they had a chance of a council house.

There were other compensations. The houses in Wallington Street may have looked drab, but 'inside they were comfortable'. In *The Uses of Literacy* Richard Hoggart wrote about his 1930s childhood in nearby Hunslet: 'the cluttered and congested setting' of his childhood home which forged strong family ties and fostered neighbourliness in 'small worlds, each as homogeneous and well-defined as a village'; a life of 'peculiarly gripping wholeness'.[4] Viv would have agreed; growing up in Castleford was, she thought, 'a really good happening'; it was 'a tough area but a nice one in many ways'. Looking back from adulthood, she found it hard not to be nostalgic and to see the past through a romantic haze: 'you know, you even seemed to have longer summers.' But although she may have dwelled on the good times, nostalgia is usually based on some reality; at times adults really did sit out in the street 'and chat and laugh, and giggle and smoke and drink a beer with each other' while the kids played into the evening.

As a child, Viv had plenty of benchmarks against which to judge her surroundings and find them wanting. Long days, months and years of hard industrial work and ill-health provoked a desire for the good times – the chat and the giggle and smoke and drink on the street on a summer's evening – to last longer. The furthest Viv ventured was the fish and chip shop at the end of the street, but her experience and that of her family was sufficient for them to know there should be more to life than sickness and poverty. The Hollywood films offered a different reality, but finding a means of escape that didn't end when the lights went up wasn't easy. Richard Hoggart celebrated his childhood home as 'a burrow deeply away from the outside world',[5] but for Viv and her family the outside world was tempting, yet tantalizingly remote, its opportunities confined to the silver screen.

5

Politics at the Palais

IN 1938 A new dance craze swept the country. 'You . . . can find them doing the Lambeth Walk in Mayfair ball-rooms, suburban dance-halls, cockney parties and village hops,' reported a new book, *Britain by Mass Observation*. The authors were Tom Harrisson and Charles Madge, two of the founders of Mass Observation, a new and progressive social research organization that was dedicated to examining how ordinary people lived.[1]

Lambeth Walkers testified to a new age of prosperity that even humble costermongers could enjoy. By 1938, unemployment was falling and wages were rising. The hungry thirties were apparently over. At Lambeth Baths, the annual dance of the Lambeth-walk Traders' Association was well attended that year, and the nation's journalists were there to see the partygoers. Those attending all joined in the 'Walk', reported the *Daily Express*, with 'the fervour of a Waltz in Vienna, a Charleston in New York, a Tango in Spain, and no one ever danced the Lambeth Walk half as well as Harry, the Toffee Apple Prince, after his fourth brown ale and a baby's head (meat pudding)'.[2] Here was a new, modern working class, no longer fractured by unemployment but united by a commercialized leisure culture that spoke of reasonable wages and time in which to enjoy them.

By the mid-1930s, there was prosperity as well as poverty. Working-class families in south-east England and in pockets of the Midlands and the north – in bustling cities with plenty of employment like Manchester – began to enjoy more holidays, greater leisure time, and luxuries in the home. Particularly prominent among these new consumers were young men and especially young women. By day, in the factories of Britain, they produced the wirelesses, bicycles and fashionable clothes that sustained a new leisure boom. By night they consumed the fruits of their labours. They were suggestive of a new, more equal Britain, in which everyone had access to the good things in life. In 1926 strikers had been represented as anti-democratic. But by the mid-1930s, as the threat of Fascism and totalitarianism rose across Europe, the energies and aspirations of ordinary workers and consumers increasingly looked like Britain's best defence against dictatorship.

The Lambeth Walk was only a dance – but dancing mattered in the 1930s. The popularity of dance halls testified to a working-class leisure boom, the effects of which were anxiously debated by writers and politicians. In 1933 J.B. Priestley visited the textile town of Leicester. At the Wolsey Hosiery works he found 'hundreds of girls' at work on assembly lines which had 'the dumb secrecy and uncontrolled orderliness of a bee-hive or an ant-hill'. These workers, he noted grimly, 'are simply cogs and levers'. He admitted that they 'are not bullied or even nagged at; their very weaknesses are elaborately taken into account; their comfort is considered; but between the time when they "clock in" and "clock out" their central human dignity, which entitles them under our democratic system to a vote as good as anybody else's, has no real existence.' And once they left work the 'danger is, of course, that this robot employment will alternate with robot leisure'.

Here lay Priestley's central concern: that this silk-stockinged working class, who he left 'gaping behind me' when he departed, might give up on democracy. Content to be automatons at work, finding fulfilment in Hollywood films and fashions, swayed by the new, American-style billboards advertising soft drinks and holidays on every roadside hoarding, this new generation might let Fascism or Communism in by the back door – or, more worryingly, the ballot box.[3] For Priestley was writing just five years after women had finally been enfranchised on the same terms as men, and as Hitler seized power in Germany.

Many middle-class observers shared his concern. Men of the political left and right – including George Orwell, the journalist Ivor Brown and the poet Louis MacNeice – worried that the assembly line would destroy democracy and civilization.[4] In 1930 MacNeice graduated from Oxford and took up a lectureship at Birmingham University, where he stayed for six years. Sympathetic to the left but sceptical of Marxism, his overriding political sentiment was antipathy to the totalitarianism of Italy and Germany. In 1941 MacNeice wrote of his years in Birmingham that

> When the wind blew from the south the air would thicken with chocolate; we were only a mile from the Cadbury Works . . . I thought myself that, if I had had to be employed in mass-production, I would rather not mass-produce chocolate. The girls in their white aprons each with her own little monotony, flicking a pink bauble accurately on to a bonbon, for ever and ever and ever – a million baubles on a million bonbons, and another girl puts them in a million frilly paper cradles and then they are marshalled in boxes with perpetual June on the cover and are shot around the world to people's best girls and mothers and the frilly paper is trampled underfoot in cinemas and railway trains and stadiums and every day is somebody's birthday.[5]

Here MacNeice captured an element of mass production that worried many of its critics: the transformation of humans into machines who could no longer think or feel independently.

MacNeice, like many other middle-class liberals and socialists, believed that assembly-line production embodied all the evils of modern work and its increasingly unskilled, repetitive and mechanized nature. 'So effectively had he transformed himself into a machine,' wrote Winifred Holtby of a bank worker in her 1927 novel, *The Land of Green Ginger*, 'that he found it increasingly impossible to effect the transformation from machine into man.'[6] In 1934 the *Manchester Evening News*, in a series about modern working girls, referred to a shop cashier as 'The Adding Machine'.[7] MacNeice captured associated worries about the mass consumption of the fruits of mass production: the reduction of culture to a drab uniformity, the taste of cheap chocolate in anonymous cinemas or stadia and the homogeneity of mass-produced birthdays.

Observers like MacNeice remind us that mass production, conducted on assembly lines in factories employing hundreds of people, was a startlingly new development in the 1930s and not one that was universally welcomed. The American entrepreneur Henry Ford had popularized mass production in his American motor factories and the method was marketed most assiduously by his fellow American, Frederick Taylor, who dedicated his working life to calculating the most efficient means of producing goods. Taylor broke down every production process into minute tasks, and then used a stop-watch to time how fast a worker could complete a single operation, whether installing a bumper to a car, drilling a hole, or machine-sewing a seam. He advocated paying workers by the piece – the task – in order to give them an incentive to work speedily and consistently. Taylor argued that there was no need for workers to understand anything about their workplace and its function other than their own task; his method ensured that they would not be 'distracted' as their whole attention would have to be given to completing the required number of tasks in the required time.[8]

By the 1930s, disciples of Taylor included Charles Bedaux, a French millionaire who amassed a fortune in the United States. By 1931 Bedaux was making friends in high places: they included Prince Edward, the Prince of Wales, and several leading members of Germany's National Socialist Party.[9] Bedaux was responsible for introducing Taylor's methods to British manufacturers with whom he had close links. The 'Bedaux system', as it became known, was attractive to those entrepreneurs producing clothing, vehicles, cosmetics, domestic appliances, furniture and processed foodstuffs. The expansion of these industries has led historians to reassess the 1930s as a decade of plenty rather than poverty. But behind this development lay a dramatic change in people's working conditions, whose nature and effects cannot simply be summed up as 'progress'.

Factory workers were not as naïve or impressionable as commentators like Priestley feared. The new liberties to which MacNeice pointed – the money and time to spend on films and chocolates – were hard-won by the workers themselves. Among them were the young textile workers at Leicester's Wolsey plant, the factory that Priestley visited. In 1931, two years before his visit, they had walked out en masse. The reason they gave was their firm's proposed introduction of 'scientific management' – the Bedaux system.

In 1931 the Wolsey workers were engaged in one of those industries that economic recovery relied upon – the production of hosiery.

Most of those who deserted their benches were young women, many of them paid by the piece. They walked out, so they told the local press, because they feared that the introduction of the Bedaux system would reduce their earnings. The Bedaux system invariably led to workers being set highly demanding targets for hourly and daily production. The women at Wolsey were highly sceptical that the introduction of machinery or assembly lines would benefit them. On 7 December 1931 those 'gaping' women, who Priestley had found so frighteningly apathetic, downed tools and walked out of the factory.

The Wolsey strikers earned themselves the disapproving title of 'Boisterous Workers' in the local press. The epithet suggested that their spontaneous action – there was no single leader – was provoked by the young women's frivolous attitude to work; much was made of their 'singing and dancing' as they formed a picket line outside the factory. Initially, the Leicester Hosiery Union (LHU), which enjoyed a good relationship with Wolsey's management, appeared to agree. It was not until 10 December, three days after the young women had walked out, that the LHU formally agreed to support their dispute. The union leaders had previously avoided the contentious issue of the Bedaux scheme. Their sympathies lay with those skilled, male workers who were not required to undertake automated tasks and so were unlikely to be directly affected by the reforms.

After the women had endured three days on a wintry picket line, they could no longer be accused of frivolity or 'boisterousness'. '[A]s a result of the dispute over the introduction of the Bedaux system,' admitted Horace Moulden, the LHU's Secretary, 'the Union has been compelled to face up to the issue of whether or not it is prepared to accept the principle of Bedaux as a wage-payment scheme.'[10] By 15 December most of Wolsey's 3,000-strong workforce had joined the strike and the LHU's support encouraged many women to join the union. But two months after the strike began, on 11 February 1932, the LHU announced to the workers that they must return to work. Negotiations between the LHU's officials and management had ended with an agreement that Bedaux would be introduced – albeit in a modified form that would allow the trade union to negotiate with the firm on pay rates for piecework.[11]

Although the Wolsey dispute ended in disappointment for the strikers, it was not a complete failure. The workers' modification of mass production was slight, but nevertheless important. The strikers secured significant bargaining rights for unskilled and semi-skilled workers, which would enable these workers to have a small but vital stake in industrial relations in the decade to come. In fighting for a living wage, they and others like them also ensured that a generation of working-class people had the money to buy the new wirelesses, cosmetics, clothes and foodstuffs that they made each day on the production lines.

Most importantly, in an age when political 'common sense' presented the ballot box as the agent of change, strikers as dangerous militants or fecklessly frivolous, and an ever faster assembly line as the only route out of economic depression, these workers offered a different worldview. The Bedaux system symbolized a new form of factory production, a new approach to work that these workers opposed. They suggested that there were some things more important than speed, productivity and profit. Asked by the *Leicester Evening Mail* to justify her opposition to the Bedaux system, one young Wolsey worker said simply, 'It is inhuman.'[12]

As the 1930s wore on, similar disputes erupted in other industries. Unemployment and the 1926 General Strike had precipitated a fall in trade union membership. By 1933, 3,661,000 men and 731,000 women were members of trade unions, a decline of over 50 per cent for both sexes since 1920. But from the mid-1930s trade union membership began to increase, as more workers were recruited to light manufacturing plants, and they in turn joined trade unions. In 1939, 1,010,000 women were trade unionists, 16 per cent of the female workforce; 5,288,000 men were trade union members, 39 per cent of the male workforce.[13]

These new trade unionists were often engaged on unskilled and semi-skilled factory work. In 1929 Llewellyn Smith's *New Survey of London* noted that 'a great proportion of the additional labour which has recently entered the metal-working trades, and the larger part especially of female labour, is engaged on what are virtually new industries, rendered possible on a large scale by the invention of mass-production processes.'[14] While many men were facing unemployment, new manufacturing industries were employing growing numbers of younger men and women. They were in demand, and as a result had greater bargaining rights.

Many of these factory workers had formerly been domestic servants. It was as servants that they honed their bargaining skills, for by the 1930s service was a very different occupation to a decade before. In the cities, the rise of factory employment added to the servant shortage. High demand for servants in middle-class households meant that young maids could leave for a better post in a different household if they were so inclined. Many of them were. By the early 1930s their masters' and mistresses' chief grievance was that their maids were increasingly likely to desert their post. Servants could afford to be more assertive, as Eileen Balderson recalled. 'Domestic servants are said to have been exploited. I do not agree,' she stated in her autobiography. 'Exploitation applied much more to other workers . . . Girls sought advancement through domestic agencies, always asking for a bigger wage than they expected to get. There was no need for a girl to stay where conditions were poor.'[15] But increasingly servants simply deserted the occupation. Winifred Foley got her chance in 1934, when she finally got a job as a 'nippy' – a waitress in one of the growing number of Lyons Corner Houses, which served tea and lunches to the new army of young office and shop workers in Britain's city centres. 'The money was awful, the hours were long,' she recalled of her job in central London; 'but I had my independence.'[16]

More servants left for the factories. They took with them an eagerness to protect those elements of factory work that they had long admired: shorter working hours and a living wage. But their unions did not always support these new members. Many labour leaders saw women and juveniles as a threat to men's jobs, rather than as constituencies they should seek to represent. In 1932 the London Trades Council expressed anxiety that 'The progress of science is evolving machines which can be handled by female labour in their teens . . . this raises a problem of tremendous import to male workers.'[17]

When the 'female labour' began striking or sabotaging their workplaces, these trade unionists were nonplussed. In 1935 most workers were still not entitled to any paid holiday. Mary Abbott, a young Lancashire textile worker desperate to enjoy the seaside delights of Blackpool, met hostility from her local union branch when she and her young workmates requested that delegates raise the question of holidays with pay at the union's national conference. When she subsequently defied the local officials by sending a telegram to the national executive detailing their request, the secretary of the local committee summoned her: "'That's not right," he says, "they'll think we've got a lot of militants in this area now." "Well," I said, "we could probably do with some."' Her determination was fuelled by the support of her father, an active trade unionist.[18]

One union adopted a different approach. Under the astute leadership of Ernest Bevin – who had worked his way up from dock labourer to General Secretary of the Transport and General Workers' Union (TGWU) – the TGWU became Britain's largest labour organization. By the mid-1930s, TGWU officials were engaged on a determined recruitment drive targeted at those women and young workers employed on Britain's assembly lines. A women's page appeared in the union's magazine. Union officials suggested that young workers' 'enthusiasm for dancing, cycling, rambling, football, gymnastics, and other organised sports and pastimes can usefully be diverted into trade union channels'.[19]

The TGWU's hope of harnessing workers' leisure aspirations was not quite as patronizing as it sounds. In 1935 Hubert Llewellyn Smith, author of *The New Survey of London Life and Labour*, optimistically concluded that a 'new civilisation' had sprung up, in which Londoners' rising rates of pay, access to new housing and ability to patronize dance halls and department stores shifted 'the main centre of interest of a worker's life more and more from his daily work to his daily leisure'.[20] Holidays and time off were becoming increasingly important to ordinary workers and their representatives. In 1930 the Youth Hostels Association was established; by 1935 cycling and rambling had become fashionable. Car ownership – on the increase, but still confined to the middle class – and cheap motor bus tours encouraged entrepreneurs like Billy Butlin to open holiday camps, and fuelled a passion for picnicking, caravanning and camping.[21]

Among those who benefited was Frank Gogerty. Born in 1916,

Frank had been illegitimate and his mother had been too poor and too ashamed to keep him. He was brought up by his aunt and uncle in rural Warwickshire. He had attended school in Rugby, before leaving to find work at the age of fifteen. Frank had hoped to enter clerical work or a trade, but his aunt and uncle lacked the money, or the will, to see him through an apprenticeship, and there was no office work available for a boy with such a limited education. Following a row with his relations over money, he found himself homeless in 1934, and walked to Coventry in search of work in one of the city's factories 'with nothing, literally nothing in my pockets. I was hungry for days.' Two years later, twenty-year-old Frank was working in one of Coventry's car factories, which paid good wages and generous overtime. He spent his wages on a bicycle: 'cars were just coming into their own, and motorbikes. You couldn't afford a motorbike, you couldn't afford a car, so the next thing was a bike.' He cycled 'every day' and toured Warwickshire with a local cycling club each weekend. Later that year he got engaged to Rita, a waitress he met in one of the cafés he could occasionally afford to patronize for tea and a bun. Rita 'couldn't ride, so what did I do? I went out and bought a tandem, secondhand . . . lasted us years.'[22]

Workers like Frank responded with enthusiasm to the TGWU's call. Many of them hadn't ever been approached by a union before. They included the Bristolian tram driver Alf Canning. In 1935 'the TGWU decided they would try and organize the workers.' This was a slow process. At first twenty-seven-year-old Alf was among the majority of tram drivers reluctant to join, fearing that his boss would victimize him – a worry that had prevented him from joining the 1926 General Strike. But 'three or four joined . . . and then the union leaders said that anyone being victimized, they wouldn't allow it, they'd step in for you.' This made an impact on Alf, who disliked the existing system whereby a worker with a grievance had to approach the manager directly, and had no one to speak for him if a foreman complained about his work. 'The fear was that if you had to speak to the manager, you might be dismissed,' he said. 'With the trade union, you would have someone who would put your case and that could make a very big difference.' All the same, it took two years to unionize the workers at Alf's Kingswood tram depot – just one of many, many battles being fought by union organizers across the country.[23]

Among the union's pioneers were the workers of Ingrams Rubber Factory in Hackney Wick. Ingrams was one of the area's largest employers and one of its oldest. In 1933 the firm had made more than £300,000, but paid low wages: just 9d per hour to men, and less than 25s per week to women. The workers had no overtime pay and no paid holidays. In April 1936 workers at a nearby wood factory helped establish a branch of the TGWU – union branch 1/149. By August, 170 Ingrams workers had joined this, ranging from adult men to teenage girls. When the Ingrams family contemptuously announced that they were unable to meet the workers' representatives to discuss union recognition wage rates because they were 'on holiday', the 'Organized workers in your factory' wrote to announce that they had 'withdrawn our labour until such time as an agreement has been reached'.[24]

At lunchtime on 8 September the strikers – determined to ensure their protest was as conspicuous as possible, in an area where poverty-stricken workers often felt powerless to act – marched to the factory gates, carrying hastily erected banners. 'When we arrived,' recalled Harry Fortt, 'it was to see a great crowd of men, women and children gathered.' Inspired by their own daring, and encouraged by the audience, some of the young women began to dance. Their marches and dances became a daily spectacle in Hackney Wick, until on 20 September the Ingrams family capitulated to most of their demands. Some of the strikers were victimized when they returned to work, leading at least ten young women to leave the factory.[25] Similar disputes were happening all over the country, and the efforts of those involved paid off: by 1939 the TGWU was Britain's largest union.[26]

By 1938, Britain appeared less riven by class than in 1918 or even 1930. Increasing numbers of families were making new homes in the light, modern houses built in Britain's expanding suburbs. Newlyweds Frank and Rita Gogerty were among them. They couldn't afford to buy their own home – 'we'd got no money saved up, everything we had we'd been putting aside for the furniture' – but they could rent a three-year-old suburban house in Coventry. 'We'd got two bedrooms, a bathroom inside, a damn good cooking range and everything else – and it was perfect.'

By the end of the 1930s, inter-war suburban housing estates accommodated a wide range of workers, from civil servants to factory workers. The Moulsecoomb estate in Brighton had been home to clerks and teachers since its establishment in the 1920s, but by 1939 it was also home to labourers moved out of the town's slums.[27] 'People read about the houses being built here . . . and came to see for themselves,' recalled one Liverpool tenant. She was proud that 'there were always people walking up and down our road.'[28] Norman Lewis was born in Lancaster in 1931, the oldest child of a bargeman. He was just six when his family of four was moved into a council house on the city's new Marsh estate, but this significant event passed into family lore, such was the luxury of hot water and an indoor bathroom: 'we had a list of the relatives that were coming down to us to have a bath.'[29] A small but significant minority of other workers were becoming owner-occupiers for the first time. In 1938 almost 20 per cent of British manual workers owned their home or had a mortgage on it.[30]

Unemployment was falling. Bristolian Clare Stevens was ten when, in 1938, her father finally got a job – his first in fifteen years. He was taken on by a local removals firm, whose business was increasing as more families took advantage of private housing, and had the money to pay for professional removal of their goods, and for the deliveries of new chairs and tables from Bristol's growing number of department stores. At the end of her father's first week at work, 'he came in and put all his money on the table, so proud at last to be working and earning money.' His wife paid off their debts and then began buying a washing machine 'on H.P. [Hire Purchase]'.[31]

Rearmament meant work for thousands more. When Percy Wiblin left school in Abingdon in 1923, he had gone to work at Thatcher's builders 'as a handyman, that's all the shit jobs' – but there was nothing else to be had. By 1935, however, life was changing. As Britain began to rearm, Percy – by now a married man – was able to get work building the nearby Harwell Aerodrome for better conditions and more pay. Munitions and housing work gave Percy new negotiating opportunities. He moved on to another aerodrome. 'Then one day it was blowing a gale, wind, and I thought, "I can't have much of this, I'm not cycling in this," so I went down to see the foreman of the firm building the [council houses] on Saxon Road . . . he said, "Can you start tomorrow?"'[32]

The children of these families were ambitious. They were determined to use new employment opportunities – in factories, shops and offices – to carve out a more independent and affluent life for themselves and their families. By the late 1930s, white-collar work was the most rapidly expanding occupational sector in Britain. In 1935 fourteen-year-old Elsie Smith left her Manchester elementary school to start work. The daughter of a factory worker and a char, Elsie was determined to become a clerk: 'I'd rather have had a pen in my hand than a bloody machine on my knee. And this "walking tall" . . . I thought, "I'm going to hold my head up like anyone else, and nobody's better than me." . . . If I'm dressed and I feel good, that's what I feel and I can hold my head up . . . I did feel I wanted to be better.'[33]

Marriage was no longer a young woman's only means of climbing the social ladder. Fashion and leisure were important in constructing a better sort of life, and office work provided a means of attaining them.

The rising generation of modern women exhibited an assertiveness that startled observers – and attracted young men. Modesty and deference got you nowhere in this new world: initiative, ingenuity and independence were the watchwords of those who wanted to get on in life, as Frank Gogerty discovered:

> when we started tandem riding, the gear for cycling clubs was corduroy shorts, corduroy jacket and that was that and the all-weather gear if it was raining. And not many girls in that particular period would be seen in shorts, not many. But Rita accepted it, she went in shorts. Some of the neighbours used to say 'brazen hussy', but she wasn't. She was up there and that was the sort of person she was. You wouldn't muck around with Rita.

Young women looked for similar virtues in young men. In an era when unemployment was still high, finding a reliable breadwinner wasn't easy. Instead, inventiveness, taking the initiative and asserting your rights were all proof of a man's potential to make something of himself if circumstances ever permitted.[34] Mrs Hughson was a servant in Manchester when she got engaged in the 1930s to a man who could only find casual factory work. 'I persuaded him to buy an insurance book – because there was money in those days in building up an insurance book.' But when her fiancé failed to take the initiative in organizing their wedding or saving money for a deposit on a flat, Mrs Hughson began going out occasionally with another man. 'When I saw my young man I told him, "Now I've been friendly with this chap . . . so it's up to you to fix the date – otherwise I'm going back in service." He said, "Alright – we'll have the fifteenth of August,"' and his decisiveness reconciled her.[35] Couples like the Hughsons and the Gogertys were taking their place in a new, modern, assertive working class impatient for the good times to begin.

In 1938 these workers achieved an important victory. The Holidays with Pay Act marked the culmination of a twenty-year campaign for paid leisure time in which the TUC – and particularly the TGWU – had played a pivotal role. The Act entitled most factory, shop and office workers (though not casual workers, or domestic servants) to a week's paid holiday each year. The energetic work of social researchers and women's groups, like the enquiry into women's health headed by Margery Spring Rice, played an important part in persuading the Conservative government to support one week's annual paid holiday (although this fell short of the fortnight for which the labour movement had lobbied). 'An annual holiday adds greatly to the health of the worker and his family,' declared Ernest Brown, the Minister of Labour, when he introduced the Bill to the House of Commons. But he quickly made clear that workers' welfare alone was not a sufficient argument for state intervention; more important was that an 'increase in the wellbeing of the general worker means an increase in the efficiency of the industry, and this in its turn means an increase in our general wellbeing'.[36] The Conservatives still saw the world in terms of 'us' and 'them': 'our general wellbeing' referred to those who did not work in industry.

Nevertheless, as Sandra Dawson, the historian of the Holidays with Pay Act, points out, the new law 'legitimated the leisure . . . of the working class' and in doing so, 'redefined who was considered a legitimate consumer of pleasure'.[37] Perhaps consumption of leisure and luxuries could overcome, or at least compensate for, inequalities in work and income. 'The acid test of any social reform,' argued the Labour MP Gordon MacDonald in a parliamentary debate on working hours in 1937, 'is that it ultimately enables the worker to enjoy longer leisure, and to enjoy it in a better way.'[38] For similar reasons, the Lambeth Walkers were greeted with pleasure by both press and politicians: they appeared to herald a new age of comfort, an end to poverty, and a society in which everyone could partake of the good things in life.

Yet there was much still to do. Although young workers were able to consume new kinds of leisure, their other opportunities remained limited. For some, a white blouse and money for the cinema were consolations for the education they had wanted but never received. Most working-class children left school at the earliest possible age – fourteen – after receiving the very basic academic training offered by the state's elementary schools. The 1936 Education Act raised the school leaving age to fifteen, but postponed the introduction of this measure for three years; war then intervened and it was not implemented until 1948.

Those children who wanted any further education had to attend a secondary school, but these charged fees. Only those lucky enough to win one of the small number of local education authority (LEA) scholarships were able to benefit from a free secondary education. In 1938 the Spens Report on Secondary Education noted that although the number of LEA scholarships had risen during the 1930s, it was still very low. Scholarship pupils comprised less than a quarter of all secondary school students. Even the few working-class children who won a scholarship often could not take it up because their parents needed their earnings. In 1934 Margaret Sharp, a millworker's daughter in Clitheroe, Lancashire, 'won a scholarship, but I never went'; her family needed her to earn money as quickly as possible so she followed her mother into the local mill.[39] Less than 15 per cent of those children who left school in 1938 had received any secondary education; the rest were fourteen-year-olds who had only attended elementary school.[40]

These young wage-earners had the consolation of new kinds of leisure, but many older people continued to struggle in poverty. Those living in the depressed industrial regions of north-east England, southern Scotland and South Wales remained badly affected by unemployment and insecure work. Fourteen per cent of the workforce was still on the dole in 1938: over 1 million people.[41] Thousands of people were still subject to the household means test. In 1937 a government investigation revealed that a man on unemployment benefit received just two-fifths of the average wage.[42] Those who were in work could enjoy nights at the dance hall, but their leisure was often a means of forgetting the heavy financial burdens they faced, as sons and daughters keeping unemployed parents.

Even among those in work, the late 1930s were hardly affluent. Those who lived outside the cities were virtually untouched by the new developments in leisure and shopping. Jack Bell grew up in the village of Hanham, near Bristol. In about 1930, eight-year-old Jack watched 'a crowd of women come up through Hanham giving out samples of Kellogg cornflakes', but that was the beginning and the end of Hanham's encounter with processed and convenience foods until the late 1940s: 'diet was a pretty standard thing', because no one could afford the new goods. The late 1930s were good to his family in one way: a building entrepreneur who built an ambitious private housing development in Hanham found that, in fact, few of the locals could afford the £400 he demanded for a house, and so 'we moved into the new development – the builder couldn't sell them so they just rented them out.' The new fashions, with rising and falling hemlines, passed the girls and boys of Hanham by. 'It was no good to change fashion,' said Jack, 'because people couldn't afford to buy new.'[43]

Even in the large cities, where job opportunities were growing, people's prosperity proved insecure. Many families relied heavily on the contributions of wage-earning sons and daughters to afford the new consumer goods, holidays and cinema trips that the late 1930s offered. Dolly, who began work in a Manchester factory in 1938, explained: 'I know what I felt when I started work, I'd been kept until I was 14, and it was my turn to put something back into the house. I'd got younger brothers and sisters, and my wage – it was

10 shillings a week – I'd got to put back into the house. You'd got the feeling you wanted to help . . . My ambition was to have a nice home, more than ever when I started work' – an aspiration she shared with her mother and with countless others of her generation.[44] Dolly's family achieved this goal while she was still a teenager because 'several of us were out at work by then'.[45] But when children moved out of their parents' house maintaining this lifestyle could prove precarious. Relying on paid work was in any case a gamble in an era of scant welfare benefits and limited employment. Those in work often suffered poor health due to poor nutrition, accidents in the workplace, and doctors' fees. Political and Economic Planning, an influential independent research agency, calculated that working days lost through illness cost the economy £120 million each year.[46] Those who fell ill had little recourse to sick pay; before long they, too, became subject to the means test.

Some on the left wondered whether the attention that politicians and the press were paying to working-class leisure skilfully glossed over the problems still afflicting millions of people's lives. In 1938 Mass Observation invited people to send in diaries and reports on those social phenomena that the founders considered of interest. Most of the Mass Observers who volunteered were middle-class, a majority were young, and many were left-wing. One young man wrote that 'I have seen [the Lambeth Walk] danced on rambles and at the WEA [Workers' Educational Association] social and I hate it . . . It leads to the viewing of slum-life with all its poverty, dirt and misery through the rosy spectacles of the wise-cracking Cockney and the glamorous Pearly King.'[47] Whether better leisure could overcome the indignities and suffering caused by social and economic inequality was a question that few politicians posed during the 1930s. In the following decade, the need to address working people's lack of power in workplaces and formal politics, to which this young man referred, would become more urgent.

The British working class of 1939 looked very different to the working class of 1918 – or even of 1930. More workers were employed in factories and offices than in domestic service. Wage-earners were no longer servants; they increasingly worked with large numbers of other people in shops, offices and factories, reinforcing their sense of collective interest and their bargaining power. They had fought for and achieved greater recognition for trade unions, whose leaders now played a role in regulating the working hours and wages of millions of workers. In the evenings young workers enjoyed their financial independence at cinemas and dance halls, where Hollywood glamour and raucous dance routines allowed them to explore their dreams of a better life than that of their mothers and fathers.

Yet in the summer of 1939 what hadn't changed was just as evident as what had. Unemployment had not gone away. In the factories, young men and women were working long hours for low pay; thousands of their fathers remained unemployed and their families still endured the hated means test. As the threat of war grew, employers and the government disappointed thousands of workers by revoking their new right to paid holidays. Employers, politicians, trade union leaders and journalists told the workers that their compensation for boring work, job insecurity and continued political and economic subordination came from a new consumer culture: nights at the dance hall, cinema matinees on their half day, suburban homes at high rent, chocolates, gramophones and – perhaps at war's end – holidays in Blackpool. In August 1939, however, it remained debatable whether people would go to war to defend this version of democracy.

PART II

The People, 1939–68

6

The People's War

O N 5 JUNE 1940 the Dorset town of Bridport was 'crammed to suffocation' with exhausted soldiers evacuated from Dunkirk; military police; day-trippers fruitlessly seeking respite from the war news; trucks, guns, uniforms – and a team from ENSA (the Entertainments National Service Association) recently arrived from London. Basil Dean, ENSA's director, had his orders: non-stop film showings for the troops while the bigwigs decided what to do with them. That evening, he met with colleagues to discuss the project:

> In a small pub . . . we exchanged impressions and made further plans, listening to the seething soldiery (yes, that is the only adjective to use) expressing blasphemous resentment at what had happened to them. There was a typical 'Sergeant Troy' in the bar whose loud-mouthed criticism of the junior officers of his Ack Ack unit in seizing the only available transport and making for the French coast, leaving their NCOs and men to fend for themselves, was gaining angry corroboration among his listeners. These dismayed men, savagely wounded in their pride, were seeking relief in bitter criticism of those set over them.[1]

A defeated army in mutiny against their officers did not bode well for Britain's chances against an enemy marching swiftly across France. Dean worried that the conversation he had heard was being repeated all over the country, and that it suggested a country too socially divided to find the unity and strength to win the war.

But between June 1940 and the general election of July 1945 Britain experienced a social transformation. Basil Dean could not have dreamed that, by the time he felt able to speak of that evening in Bridport, Dunkirk would have been immortalized as a victory for the British; and its army as representatives of 'the people' – the workers who, victorious in war, deserved to win the peace. He could not have envisioned Labour's landslide election victory in 1945, on a pledge to maintain full employment and a welfare state as thanks to the workers on whom victory had depended.

The Second World War was the people's war. It marked one of two major turning points in the twentieth century, heralding a period of full employment and comprehensive welfare provision that was only brought to an end by the second turning point: the election of Margaret Thatcher to government in 1979. During the war the government struck a contract with the people: work hard in return for a guaranteed job, a living wage and care in times of need. This bargain evolved because the demand for munitions and men created full employment in Britain for the first time, and the workers themselves used this to strengthen their collective bargaining power.

But to call the Second World War 'the people's war' does not mean that Britain became classless. The government sought to win the war by demanding ever greater sacrifice and effort from the workers in the factories and from ordinary troops. Only when the crisis absolutely demanded it did they oblige middle- and upper-class people to share in some of these sacrifices. Most politicians had little interest in making Britain a more equal society. In fact, their notion of how to win the war was predicated on the assumption that economic inequality was a natural and helpful part of British life. The country had many millions of people who needed to work for a living, therefore they could be the war workers.

The workers were able to use the unprecedented demand for their labour to secure greater political and economic rights, but these gains were hard-won. The Conservatives, who dominated the wartime coalition government, believed that ordinary people required only the most basic welfare provision, and that voluntary initiatives could organize this. During the war the popularity of welfare assistance and full employment grew, faith in state intervention as a means of delivering a better society increased, and people asserted their rights to better remuneration and welfare provision, at work and at home. But the working class remained just that: a class of workers who depended on earning a living, and were in that way distinguished from the rich who lived on the labour of others. In the 1940s the

Servants were a ubiquitous presence in Britain's towns and cities until the 1930s. This maid is cleaning the steps of a large private house in London, *c*.1910

After the Great War many veterans and their wives found themselves without homes or jobs, like this family photographed in London's Fleet Street in November 1919

Workers at the Burton's clothing factory in Leeds show off their silk stockings and patent sandals, 1932

Jean Donnelly, the author's grandmother, pictured in 1935, shortly after she arrived to work at Woolworths in Leeds from her home in Hawick, a textile town in the Scottish Borders badly hit by industrial depression

Frank and Rita Gogerty enjoying a holiday at Skegness, c.1937

Young women at Cadbury's chocolate factory in Bournville, Birmingham, 1932

Join this march to
PROSPERITY
AND
PEACE

under
NATIONAL
GOVERNMENT

The Conservative-dominated National governments of the 1930s took credit for a rise in factory work and earnings in southern England and the Midlands

Jarrow hunger marchers, headed by Labour MP Ellen Wilkinson, receive support and sandwiches from villagers near Luton as they walk to London in 1936

Go through your wardrobe

Make-do and Mend

During the Second World War working-class skills like thriftiness became increasingly valued

In 1945 voters elected Britain's first majority Labour government

VICTORY DAWN

ZEC

Women and children on Clydeside wait on a street with the few possessions left to them after a night-time air raid in the winter of 1941

Betty and Michael Ennis (right) outside the migrants' hostel in Coventry where they lived until being rehoused in the early 1950s

A new council housing estate at Croydon in 1948, featuring spacious semi-detached properties. Tenants often moved in while neighbouring houses were still being built and before the muddy fields around them had been landscaped

Bill Rainford and his sister outside their new, prefabricated house on Liverpool's Belle Vale estate, *c.*1950

"Look what we made with our new Electric cooker!"

Electric cookers have thermostat control on the oven, quick-heating boiling plates, and new, variable switches which give perfect heat-control from fast boiling to slow simmering — *and lower*, if you want it!

Go round and see one at your Electricity Service Centre. They are friendly, knowledgeable people there, and will be glad to help you. They can also let you have details about easy payments, and the new, free book, full of clever ideas for saving work, ELECTRICITY IN YOUR KITCHEN; or you are welcome to write for a copy to EDA, 2 Savoy Hill, London, W.C.2.

ELECTRICITY
a Power of Good in the kitchen

Advertisers and politicians encouraged people to spend their wages on new domestic appliances in the 1950s, using recently relaxed credit arrangements. This advertisement promises 'easy payments'

Many families continued to live in the inner cities in the 1940s and 1950s like the Hirst family in Hunslet, Leeds. Pictured are Fred (left) and Jack Hirst outside their home, 1948

Cars were beyond the budget of most families in the 1950s, but holidays were not. This group, enjoying a women's weekend in Blackpool in 1951 — and the chance to pose in a photographer's car — includes the author's grandmother and mother, Jean Hirst, née Donnelly (centre front), and her seven-year-old daughter Ruth (centre back)

A career for tomorrow for young lads of today

You're paid to learn a trade in the Country's COALMINES

In the post-war years near-full employment promised men a job for life in nationalized industries

Many men wanted to become more involved with family life as working hours shortened and family size dropped. Terry Rimmer is pictured here with his first child, Michelle, in 1959

Ann Lanchbury, née Kiddey, and her father outside their Coventry council house in the 1950s

By the end of the 1950s many families enjoyed socializing in their increasingly comfortable and well-equipped homes. Pictured are Hazel Wood, née Watson, and her boyfriend John at Hazel's parents' council house, 1959

Work provided many young people with a wage to spend on their social life, and friends to enjoy it with. Pictured are Judy Walker (third from left) and colleagues from Coventry's British Home Stores, c.1958

Harry, Ruth, Ralph and Neil Hirst of Hunslet sport their new clothes, bought for Whitsuntide, in the late 1950s

people's new role in the nation's economic and political life was still a subordinate one: as other people's employees, as the recipients of wages rather than an equal share of the profits, and as the beneficiaries, but not the architects, of social welfare.

Nevertheless, working people came to see themselves as a collective force – a class – in new and profound ways. They shared even more experiences than they had done before the war as factory work eclipsed domestic service as the country's largest employer, and the unemployed entered the workforce. In these circumstances, workers clearly had a great deal to gain by joining together and fighting collectively for shared needs. They did so from a new position of strength: no longer were they caricatured as enemies of the state – as in the General Strike of 1926 – or viewed as helpless victims, like the dole claimants of the 1930s. They were now recognized by politicians and the press as being the backbone of the nation, on whose labour Britain depended. Their interests became synonymous with those of the country.

In the summer of 1940 these gains were unimaginable. Most working-class civilians shared the frustrations of the soldiers whom Basil Dean observed in Bridport. Regular soldiers had borne the brunt of the country's lack of preparations for war. There was anger, but little surprise, that the wealthy and privileged seemed to be having a very different war to the ordinary troops and workers. Press reports – censored by Chamberlain's Conservative government – suggested that the soldiers returning from Dunkirk were greeted with bunting and cheering crowds, who remained plucky despite fears of a German invasion. But Mass Observation – commissioned by the government to prepare confidential reports on public morale for the duration of the war – emphasized just how far from the truth this representation was.[2] Mass Observers warned that antagonism towards 'the old gang' and 'vested interests' was growing daily. This was particularly so on the south coast, where 'anyone with any money' had already departed 'en masse'.[3]

More worrying than anger and frustration, however, was apathy. Faced with the threat of invasion, Mass Observation found that 'middle-class people were concerned for personal, economic, luxury and independence reasons.' But many 'working class people said it wouldn't make much difference to them, anyway'.[4] The harsh truth was that many British workers weren't sure that Nazi tyranny would be any worse than the poverty they had already endured in the name of 'democracy'.

The government's attitude did nothing to assuage such scepticism. By June 1940, Mass Observation was complaining that government propaganda and information was 'impersonal', 'indecisive' and 'out of sympathy with . . . mass reaction'. With the threat of invasion growing daily, the government issued a leaflet, 'If the Invader Comes', to every household. Recipients were unenthusiastic, one young woman calling it 'defeatist'. The leaflet, judged Mass Observation, sounded like 'the upper class talking to the stupid mass'. The assumptions that this leaflet made – that people would 'flee', and needed to be told to 'put your country before yourself' – indicated that the government thought the people couldn't be relied upon in a time of crisis.

The government and the military top brass shared what Tom Harrisson, one of Mass Observation's founders, called a 'deeply ingrained contempt for the civilian masses'. Ministers' plans for invasion and aerial bombardment aimed at containing hysteria, by evacuating children from the cities, ordering adults to stay put, and assuming that 'the proletariat were bound to crack, run, panic, even go mad, lacking the courage and self-discipline of their masters or those regimented in the forces.'[5] The people themselves were given no positive reason to act against a potential invader. 'Herbert Morrison's GO TO IT,' concluded Mass Observation of the government catchphrase designed to provoke factory workers to higher productivity, 'has a condescending ring vaguely reminiscent of YOUR COURAGE . . . WILL BRING US VICTORY.'[6]

Few men went gladly off to war. Quite apart from the fear of never returning, the troops endured poor pay and conditions. In September 1939 men aged between eighteen and forty-one had become liable for conscription under the National Service (Armed Forces) Act. Those who were not awarded an officer's commission received a low rate of pay – less than most manual workers' earnings. This was a boon for those who had been unemployed, but less satisfactory for those white–collar and manual workers who had been the chief or sole breadwinner in their families. Frank Gogerty was a motor mechanic in Coventry when he was called up. He rued the fact that he hadn't had the presence of mind to get ensconced in a 'reserved occupation' like engineering. The war, he said, 'mucked around' with his life, depriving his wife Rita and their two young sons of Frank's earnings for the foreseeable future (in his case five long years). Men like Frank were wary of doing the dirty work of a government that had offered them nothing worth fighting for.

Staying put at a factory, as Frank Gogerty had wanted to do, made good sense. War workers benefited from increased wages and job security. The war factories were the centres of economic and political change – the agents of change their workers. By the autumn of 1940, unemployment was virtually unknown in Britain. By 1943, over 90 per cent of single people of working age had a job; more than a third of married women were out at work too. Most of these workers were in factories, producing munitions, tanks and guns, and earning better wages than factory workers could have dreamed of before the war.

Despite the fear and uncertainty that 1940 brought, the war offered a new security to these workers. In February 1940 a Mass Observer visited a London Labour Exchange, where he found a large selection of domestic servants, delivery boys and office workers waiting for appointments. Gone was the despair of the 1930s. A twenty-year-old woman who had left domestic service to work at one of the Royal Ordnance Factories summed up the prevailing mood: 'If I don't like it I'll walk out,' she told her questioner. 'I don't put up with no nonsense!'[7]

The unnamed former domestic servant who spoke to Mass Observation exemplified a widespread suspicion of government. After an initial burst of enthusiasm in the autumn of 1939, productivity in the factories had fallen: workers were fatigued by the long hours imposed by employers. By May 1940, the government itself was beginning to recognize that this distrust must be overcome if they were to have any chance of winning the war. Following Chamberlain's resignation, Churchill became Prime Minister that month, and he brought several Labour members into his Cabinet. Among them were Clement Attlee, leader of the Labour Party and now Lord Privy Seal, and Ernest Bevin – former General Secretary of the Transport and General Workers' Union (TGWU) – who became Minister of Labour and National Service. In May 1940 this new government passed the Emergency Powers Act, which granted them unprecedented control over people and private property. Attlee stressed that the Act would ensure that everyone – 'rich or poor' – was required to 'perform service and give up their property' if required.[8]

But increasingly, those on the political right as well as on the left realized that winning the war would take more than increasingly centralized control of people and property. On 1 July 1940 an editorial in *The Times* made a plea for clear war aims that explicitly benefited ordinary workers and soldiers. Post-war Britain must uphold liberty and democracy, and 'beware of defining these values in purely nineteenth-century terms. If we speak of democracy we do not mean a democracy which maintains the right to vote but forgets the right to work and the right to live.'[9]

Ernest Bevin did more than any other politician to transform this rhetoric into concrete war aims. In 1940 he successfully argued that the government, rather than the employers, should control manpower, wages and working conditions. The Emergency Powers (Defence) Act conferred on Bevin 'a role comparable in civil life to Churchill's in the direction of the war'.[10] Bevin put productivity before civil liberty; he swiftly introduced Order 1305, which made strikes illegal and introduced harsh penalties for unofficial strikers. Factory workers were required to be at their benches for ten or twelve hours each day. Paid holidays were suspended 'for the duration'. But Bevin argued that conscription into the factories, the illegality of strike action, long hours and no holidays with pay would only increase productivity if trade unions were granted a central role in Britain's industrial life, and workers' welfare was prioritized. He began in May 1940 by cutting working hours in Royal Ordnance Factories, increasing the number of workplace canteens, building workers' hostels and improving the medical services available to factory workers. Bevin professed himself determined to ensure that 'no industry . . . lack trade agreement' by the end of the war; by which he meant that every industry must institute collective bargaining between employers and trade unions, thereby granting the latter a new and permanent form of power.[11] Workers needed to feel they had a vested interest in what they were doing, otherwise they wouldn't be motivated to work at the rate the war effort required of them.

Bevin won his case because, as the historian Keith Middlemas points out, 'labour rather than machinery or capital had become the scarcest and most prized industrial commodity.'[12] In other words, the war effort depended on workers – lots of them, working as hard as they possibly could. That had been true in the First World War, but in 1940 it was already clear that Germany's military power, and the importance of aerial warfare, meant that each combatant in this war would require three times as much economic support – in the form of munitions, transport and equipment – as one of his predecessors.[13] And Bevin's certainty that greater worker satisfaction would increase productivity was quickly proved right. Within just three months of his appointment, Britain's factory workers were working harder and faster.[14]

Bevin saw the new demand for factory workers as an opportunity to turn the working class into 'the people', whose political as well as industrial interests had to be considered at the highest level. His strategy had a dramatic, lasting impact on Britain's workers. He argued that the leaders of the trade union movement were the democratic representatives of Britain's workforce. It was trade unionists, not MPs or the electorate at large, to whom Bevin turned for consent to his new powers. On 25 May 1940 he invited 2,000 TUC delegates to come to Westminster, where he asked them 'virtually to place yourselves at the disposal of the state. We are Socialists and this is the test of our Socialism . . . If our Movement and our class rise with all their energy now and save the people of this country from disaster, the country will always turn with confidence to the people who saved them.'[15]

Although Bevin claimed this was a 'socialist' strategy, his approach also set the unions outside party politics, by suggesting that a negotiation structure for wages, working hours and the control of industry were not party-political issues, but in the national interest. That clearly offered a new platform to the trade union leaders. It also offered a new logic for nationalizing industries, on the basis that the interests of the workforce were synonymous with those of the nation. But this new arrangement also relied on trade unionists accepting the economic system of which they found themselves a part. They might bargain for more wages; they couldn't bargain for a different way of organizing work and wealth. The days of 1926, when many grassroots trade unionists had argued that the capitalist system of industry was inequitable, seemed very long ago.

Yet if the militancy of 1926 no longer seemed possible, the workers of 1940 were at least as assertive, and certainly more organized, than those who had supported the General Strike. Unions that had jealously guarded the privileges of skilled men began to open their doors to the unskilled and semi-skilled workers who swelled the ranks of the wartime workforce. The Amalgamated Engineering Union (AEU) finally admitted women in 1942. These new factory workers were just as conscious as the craftsmen that the high demand for workers strengthened their bargaining rights. They expanded the trade unions, which had represented 39 per cent of men and 15 per cent of women in the workforce in 1939, but by 1943 were representing 46 per cent and 30 per cent respectively.[16]

But this workforce remained one stratified by class. In 1941 the government introduced conscription for women, beginning with the young and single, but reaching married women by 1942. In practice, though, conscripts were almost exclusively working class. Few middle- or upper-class women entered the factories. If a woman could show that she was assisting the war effort through voluntary activity – such as part-time work in a soldiers' canteen, or for the new Women's Voluntary Service – she could be exempted from conscription. Only middle- and upper-class women could afford to do this.

Among them was Eleanor Humphries, a forty-year-old housewife who lived in London's Blackheath with her husband Horace. She believed that Bevin should be 'absolutely ruthless' in dealing with the TUC's opposition to the conscription of working-class women (Walter Citrine, the TUC's General Sectetary, believed that married women should be encouraged, but not obliged, to take up part-time work). Nevertheless, she admitted to her diary in 1942 that 'I'm frankly angling to have just enough [voluntary] work to keep me from being directed to a part-time job.'[17] Her weekly voluntary efforts comprised two afternoons of secretarial work for the Citizens' Advice Bureau and the Invalid Children's Aid Association. Margot Harper, a middle-class housewife living in Bristol, was eventually conscripted in 1943, but was allowed to take a part-time office job rather than enter a factory. After a few months, her eighteen-year-old daughter, Joyce, became ill and Margot took time off to nurse her. But when Joyce was better, Margot decided that she preferred being at home and didn't notify the Labour Exchange that her nursing duties were at an end; in 1944 she reported triumphantly to her diary that she had 'been "lying low" for some time'.[18]

While these women actively sought to evade official scrutiny, the government was clearly in sympathy with their plight. The Ministry of Labour made huge allowances for those women like Humphries who were 'servantless'. Even at the height of the war, the ministry allowed servants' employers to request their maids' exemption from conscription, although by 1942 officials noted, with some consternation, that many servants 'left of their own accord to take up war work'.[19] Many Labour Exchange officials conscripted working-class mothers into the factories, but readily accepted that servantless middle-class women were fully occupied with running their homes.[20] Home Intelligence Officers reported 'considerable resentment among women who are already working that the middle and upper classes are still being allowed to "get away" with voluntary war-jobs'.[21] Wartime Britain was a society in which the government expected the working class to fulfil its traditional role – providing labour – for greater rewards, in the form of better pay, job security and more regulated hours than people had hitherto enjoyed. It was certainly not an equal society, nor one in which either government or employers wanted to introduce social equality.

Many policymakers and civil servants were clearly content to uphold the social privileges of the middle class. Bevin himself was unwilling to instigate any confrontation over the controversial issue of married women's work; he described their conscription to the House of Commons as 'an unhappy thing'.[22] In practice, the government was able to find the requisite number of women workers among working-class wives and mothers. In 1942 the Ministry of

Labour issued a pamphlet to employers that urged them to consider introducing part-time work in order to recruit more married women. Assuaging fears that this might lead to full-time workers demanding part-time hours, the ministry assured employers that 'many women who are working full-time need the extra money'.[23] As Richard Titmuss, the historian of wartime social policy, pointed out, many working-class women needed to work because the allowances paid to servicemen's families were very low.[24] The government's organization of labour actively sustained an economic system in which a large swathe of the population desperately required a wage, and then used this group as a pool from which to recruit war workers.

Bevin's reforms achieved a great deal, but they did not entirely satisfy many workers. As the discontent detected by Home Intelligence officers suggested, some workers resented the extensive control exercised by employers and government. Despite the illegality of strikes, many workers began to protest, demanding equal pay and greater popular participation in the control of production, particularly over the value assigned to different tasks. Before the war, the trade unions had jealously guarded the rights of those workers whose jobs were designated 'skilled'. During the war, the importance of craftsmanship declined. Employers sought to introduce mass-production techniques, like the Bedaux system, and then to define workers who staffed them as 'unskilled' or 'semi-skilled' – which justified paying them lower wages.

One of the earliest strikes occurred at the Smethwick works of Guest, Keen and Nettlefold in 1941. The firm's attempts to pay women – designated 'semi-skilled workers' – less than male workers led hundreds of workers to walk out. Most of the strikers were women, but some male, skilled workers joined them. The strikers pointed out that the firm had used the conscription of some of its male workers to reorganize production around the Bedaux system. The women conscripted to work in the factory were then designated 'semi-skilled' by their employer – with the collusion of trade union officials. This enabled the firm to pay the women less than skilled workers were entitled to. At Guest, Keen and Nettlefold, as in other disputes, the strikers argued that assembly-line production should only be introduced after proper consultation with the workforce.

They also argued strongly that assembly-line work should not automatically be defined as 'semi-skilled', pointing out that this did not take into account the exhausting and valuable contribution that such workers were making to production.[25]

Another significant dispute took place at the Bath Co-operative Society in December 1941, when young clerks initiated an illegal 'sit-down strike' over their employer's decision to reduce wages and their union's reluctance to do anything about it. The instigators were young women in their late teens and early twenties. Their work was not considered essential war work, and so in 1941 they were facing conscription. Many of them had accepted this with equanimity, until the Co-op's managers declared their intention of reducing the wages for women in their age group, and simultaneously introducing new bonuses for young school-leavers, who were cheaper to employ. The women worried that if this was allowed they would be replaced by younger workers and would not have jobs to come back to. Behind this, they detected their employer's intention to 'de-skill' office work by breaking down their jobs into menial tasks that recent school-leavers could undertake. These young workers struck on 23 December – perfectly timed to disrupt Christmas trade. Faced with crowds of angry customers, the Co-op's management capitulated to their demands, and restored the old rate of pay.[26]

These strikers were alert to their employers' attempts to use the war for their own advantage. '[W]e were not on strike for a rise in wages,' one of the Bath strikers wrote to her local newspaper. 'We, junior staff, wanted the cancellation of the new wage scale, which tended to be a flattering attraction to new juniors coming into the Society's employment, but an insult to those who had served three or four years . . . [we] just wanted them [sic] readjusted to their former rate.'[27] The Bath strikers reflected a widespread fear that employers would use the war effort as an excuse to renege on pre-war agreements over wages and status.

Often, strikers expressed their anger with trade union leaders who acquiesced to the employers' demands as long as they didn't interfere too much with those workers who many trade unionists still considered to be their most important constituency: skilled men. In many factories like Guest, Keen and Nettlefolds, disputes over equal pay broke out in part because the AEU was unresponsive to women's grievances, while at Bath the National Union of Distributive and Allied Workers (NUDAW) was primarily concerned with securing a wage rise for the male branch managers, and failed to keep abreast of the young women workers' grievances. The workers themselves were furious at this, and walked out without consulting their trade union leaders.[28]

On the whole, strikers received a sympathetic hearing from Bevin's Ministry of Labour. Illegal strikes provoked government enquiries, and in January 1943 the Ministry of Labour instigated one into the dispute at Bath. The team who conducted this enquiry criticized the Bath union officials and managers rather than the strikers. They judged that 'the worst feature of the whole affair . . . is that the workers would not have secured the advantageous result obtained had they not acted as they did and held up the Management Committee to ransom.'[29] Employers and trade unions were now expected to work together to agree equitable wage rates and regulated working hours.

The strikers were often confident that they would not be prosecuted; as early as 1941 they were claiming their right to democracy at work as well as at the ballot box, evoking the war aims of Churchill, Bevin and the press. As one of the young strikers wrote to the unsympathetic *Bath and Wiltshire Chronicle and Herald*: 'Surely we, as human beings living in a free country, are at least entitled to a hearing by the people who employ us?' She signed herself 'the daughter of a serving soldier'.[30] In a period in which labour was badly needed, workers were aware that they had more negotiation rights. This did not only apply to skilled men but to those workers who had lacked trade union representation before the war, like young and unskilled wage-earners.

These workers shared a strong sense of entitlement to better treatment, at a time when they and their families were supporting the war effort, whether as soldiers, skilled craftsmen, white-collar clerks or assembly-line operatives building tanks. At times, they sought to advance this further than government expected or wanted. It was a tribute to the workers' unity that few strikers were in fact prosecuted. The government enquiry that followed the Bath strike was typical in concluding that no further action should be taken against the strikers because their prosecution could lead to further protests and 'the effect upon the future of industrial relations and the war effort generally might prove disastrous'.[31]

The strikers had some qualified successes. As a result of their protests, and Bevin's shrewd handling of them, manual workers' earnings more than trebled during the war, with unskilled and semi-skilled workers enjoying the biggest gains of all.[32] But the workers failed to gain any greater power over the organization of production, or popular participation in negotiations over working conditions. At Bath, the government enquiry concluded that the workers were 'unrestrained by their Union' – implying that the union's job was to curb direct, popular participation in workplace relations.[33] Bevin's bargain of 1940 with government and the trade union leaders had been based on a presumption that workers would not seek to control or disrupt production in return for greater government regulation of their working hours, wages and welfare – in consultation with trade union leaders as well as employers. Workers were expected to be the passive beneficiaries of change, rather than the drivers of it. This was the people's war – but the people were certainly not going to achieve equality.

'Fair shares' and 'equal sacrifice' were the watchwords of civilian life, but some were more equal than others. If that was evident at work, it was even more conspicuous in those areas of home front life over which Bevin and the trade unions had less control: rationing, evacuation and air-raid protection. The government remained firmly committed to a laissez-faire approach to welfare. In 1939 intelligence reports suggested that war with Germany would quickly cause dire food shortages. Several ministers advocated rationing food and fuel, in order to avoid scarcity, panic-buying and price rises that might make essential goods too expensive for ordinary consumers. However, Chamberlain resisted rationing in the autumn of that year because of a campaign orchestrated by the right-wing press – led by the *Daily Express* – which argued that rationing was 'government control gone mad'.[34] The government finally introduced food rationing in January 1940, initially restricted to a few basic foodstuffs. However, the dwindling supply of imported goods meant that most basic foods, clothing and fuel were rationed within two years.

Churchill's coalition government promoted rationing as offering 'fair shares'. Each person received a ration book, which contained coupons that shopkeepers cut out or signed when people bought rationed goods. All adults received the same rations, in the same buff-coloured ration book – but not everyone's needs were the same. True, when Churchill took over the government swiftly issued special green ration books to nursing mothers and children under five, which granted them a free daily pint of milk and a double supply of eggs. Feminist campaigners had been fighting for free milk for pregnant women and infants since Pember Reeves's time; it took total war for government to acquiesce. In the late 1930s the families of factory workers and agricultural labourers had consumed far fewer calories than those of managers and company directors. By 1943, these groups were consuming a very similar number of calories, and working-class families were eating more meat and dairy than they had been able to afford in the 1930s. The supply of free milk to nursing mothers and young children clearly improved their health.[35]

Nevertheless, rationing certainly did not deliver 'fair shares'. Those who could afford to pay could still find plenty to spend their money on, especially in the early years of the war. Until 1941, rationing was confined to a few essential foods, and those with the money could still buy many delicacies, as well as clothing and fuel. Rationing was never extended to restaurants. 'We have yet to hear of the wholesale dismissal of chefs employed by the upper classes,' declared the Women's Co-operative Guild in 1943; 'people with money and influence go short of nothing.'[36] Meanwhile, Ernest Bevin lost his fight to have the rations of manual workers increased to reflect the physical effort required of them. The Conservative-dominated government proved highly reluctant to erode the privileges of the wealthy. It did just as much as was required to keep the nation healthy, and no more.

Government responses to bombing were similarly characterized by a desire to do the bare minimum. They also indicated that the Conservatives were still reluctant to commit to state intervention in welfare, preferring to rely on voluntary efforts. In the early hours of 1 September 1939 the first major, state-orchestrated evacuation scheme ever seen in Britain began. Neville Chamberlain's government had decided to implement this scheme in the belief that war would lead to disastrous air bombardment: in 1937 an official government estimate calculated that 1,800,000 people would be killed or seriously wounded in the first two months of a war.[37] Despite this, the government was adamant that the evacuation scheme should be voluntary. Participation was not obligatory, and voluntary organizations were given responsibility for managing the scheme, with only minimal assistance from local authorities and none from national government. In practice, many of the rich simply used their wealth to opt out. They could afford to send their children abroad, or to rural boarding schools, or to move to a country cottage *en famille*; the writer Vera Brittain did all three.[38] Most of the 1 million evacuees who left Britain's cities on the official scheme were working-class children. So were most of their hosts, who received a paltry allowance on which to keep their new charges.[39]

Evacuation highlighted that voluntary organizations couldn't cope with caring for very large numbers of people. The government took responsibility for zoning the country into evacuation and reception areas, but the rest was up to local authorities. In the summer of 1939, twenty-seven-year-old Hilda Dunn was one of the thousands of 'infuriated and exhausted' teachers whose 'ordinary work was constantly interrupted for the purpose of making lists'. Hilda and her fellow teachers at Newcastle's Washington Road School were in an evacuation zone. They were responsible for delivering to the local authority the names of the children to be evacuated from their school. Then, in August 1939, Local Education Authorities (LEAs) made arrangements for the evacuation of their children, liaising with the billeting officers in reception areas. These billeting officers had the tricky task of arranging for the arrival of the children, finding host families, and matching evacuees to billets. The government made very little additional money available for areas hosting evacuees, either for paying officials or host families. Consequently, many billeting officers juggled their new workload with their day job, like G.M. Bland, Lancaster's billeting officer who was also the City Librarian.[40] Some heeded the government's encouragement to delegate their responsibilities to voluntary organizations like the Women's Voluntary Service; others, like Bland, did the best they could in difficult circumstances. In most cases their efforts proved insufficient to cope with the mammoth task with which they were charged.

The experience of evacuation was frequently chaotic. On 1 September Hilda Dunn arrived at Newcastle's Central Railway Station to take her thirty charges to their unknown destination. After several hours on a train they arrived, 'their cotton frocks crumpled, their faces grimy and their hair awry. They had come from "the slums" and they looked the part.' Hilda Dunn's party was lucky: a reception committee awaited them with 'kind smiles, hand shakes, steam from the tea-urn' and details of the children's new homes. Hilda herself appreciated how much effort this must have taken. Sadly, John McGuirk's experience was more typical. He was evacuated from Bootle to Southport in 1940, at the age of seven. 'That was a culture shock for me,' he said, 'because I came from a really basement type of family, rough and ready, we had next to nothing.' Still, he came from a loving home in a neighbourhood where 'everyone was on a level – poor', and this made his arrival in Southport an unpleasant revelation. 'We were put in this churchyard as a group,' he said. 'People came around and picked you like they were picking dogs out of pet shops.'[41] Experiences like his were reproduced across the country.[42] They showed up the woeful inadequacies of a scheme left almost entirely in the hands of volunteers, with little training and few resources.

Relations between evacuees and their hosts reflected the social chasm that fractured Britain. Middle- and upper-class people often refused to help. In some reception areas, noted a Home Intelligence officer, villagers asked to give up rooms to the evacuees 'frequently suggested that the owners of large country houses are shirking their responsibilities' – a complaint that he and his colleagues found to be justified.[43] A Liverpool University survey of evacuation concluded that the upper and upper middle classes were most likely to refuse to take evacuees. Middle-class and upper-class hosts were most likely to complain about their evacuees and to show their resentment openly through cold or callous treatment of the children in their care. As one Scottish billeting officer observed: 'working-class hosts either got down to it and cleaned their guests up, or, being of the same temper, felt quite at home with them. The more comfortable hosts, in spite of having more facilities, raised Cain, in most instances, until the children were removed.'[44] John McGuirk and his brother were billeted on a businessman and his wife, who owned a large house in suburban Southport but fed their charges meagre meals, housed them in the coldest and smallest room in the house, and let the boys know in no uncertain terms that their hosts 'thought we were scum'.

Evacuation sharpened many children's sense of class. Those children who stayed in middle-class homes, like John McGuirk, frequently found that their presence was resented. The playwrights Jack Rosenthal and Arnold Wesker recalled similar experiences. In Rosenthal's case his mother eventually took him back to Salford; Wesker, however, spent six years with various foster parents and 'never stopped longing to get back to London' and his 'poor but happy' family.[45] Twenty years later, both men would make their name by writing about the rich emotional life of the working-class families and communities they had been forced to leave behind.

The experience of evacuation convinced some teachers and welfare workers that working-class parents and homes had hitherto-overlooked virtues. A few days after arriving in the village of Arnistone, Hilda Dunn visited the 'sandy faced, sharp nosed' Smithson sisters, who had been billeted at a remote, poor hill farm:

> a stout woman, perhaps forty . . . led the way into a stone-flagged kitchen that might once have been a midden by the smell . . . A black cauldron was bubbling over the peat fire and emaciated hens ran in and out of the open door . . . the two girls came running to the door. They looked like something out of a pantomime, each in two pairs of thick dark socks and enormous clogs. But their faces were rosy and alive.

The Smithson sisters settled well at their billet. 'In the course of many visits to that farm,' recalled their teacher, 'I never saw cleanliness or efficiency.' Hilda Dunn wondered if she should move them; 'there were better-off village homes . . . but could a compulsorily billeted child have had even a dog's life?' Hilda came to realize that 'there were other things' that mattered even more than cleanliness – and that love and affection might be found in a poor home just as readily as in a prosperous one.[46]

Joan Cooper also began her career as a teacher – in her native Manchester during the 1930s depression. The experience led her to seek posts in child welfare during the Second World War, and she became head of the evacuation programme in Derbyshire. The ad hoc arrangements made for billeting children on sometimes callous hosts led her to advocate that the state, rather than charities, should care for vulnerable children. Her experience of the love and affection she witnessed in the working-class families whose children came to Derbyshire, and among the working-class host families, strengthened her conviction that, whenever possible, children should be kept with their parents rather than being consigned to institutional care. Such wartime experiences were to have a major impact on the post-war welfare state, when women like Cooper would become instrumental in delivering educational and social policy reforms. Prior to the war, charities had taken a lead in caring for vulnerable children, and institutionalizing them was the norm. Joan Cooper helped to implement the 1948 Children's Act, which gave the state greater control of children's care, introduced smaller children's homes, and kept children with their birth parents whenever possible. She rose to become Head of the Children's Department in the Home Office.[47]

Back in the cities, the hysteria that Chamberlain's government had predicted air raids would provoke never materialized. In the autumn of 1940 the Blitz began, but most people continued to go to work and to look after their families. The neighbourhoods hardest hit by bombing were those by the docks. These were districts like Stepney in London, where dockers, factory hands, labourers and shop assistants were crammed into rented rooms and damp, dilapidated one- or two-bedroom houses accommodating an average of twelve people.[48] Anyone who visited the blitzed East End couldn't fail to be impressed by the residents' courage – but the journalists who visited the people there also observed anger. The Blitz brought home how ill-equipped Britain was to deal with disaster, and how wilful was government neglect of ordinary people. A government committed to voluntarism had encouraged people to build Anderson shelters in their gardens, but those who couldn't afford the time or materials, or lacked the space, endured terrible privations. After visiting the cramped, stinking air-raid shelters of London's East End one American journalist warned that 'these people were beginning to lose faith – faith in all degrees of people higher up.'[49] Coventry was badly bombed on 14 November 1940. The following evening, Mass Observation's Tom Harrisson found survivors who had not fled their homes making their way to the city's woefully inadequate air-raid shelters: 'always very damp' and ankle-deep in 'foetid floor water'. Harrisson noted that 'a good deal of the housing in the centre was too crowded for garden Andersons'. He also observed that many of the public shelters were unsafe; brick-built and above ground, several had been bombed, their occupants killed.[50] Thousands of people took the initiative in the face of the authorities' neglect. Londoners flocked to the capital's underground Tube stations, commandeering them in lieu of the shelters their government had failed to provide.[51]

Twenty-two-year-old Bristolian Bert Sheard was on active service abroad when the Blitz began. A former factory worker, 'it annoyed me when I used to see the papers and they had headlines like "We can take it, let them send it". I didn't hear anyone say that when I came home. They were all saying "We can't stand much more of this".' To Bert, the press reports 'were just propaganda' which suggested that victory depended on the people affected to keep smiling through, rather than on government investment in medical support, shelters and troops.[52] Bert considered such reports patronizing – a view shared by many of those questioned by Mass Observation – in their assumption that ordinary people were too stupid not to know or intuit what morale would really be liked in the bombed areas. Such blatant propaganda only fed rumours about how bad conditions must be in cities like Coventry.

Those left homeless by the Blitz received limited, grudging assistance. The government charged the Public Assistance officials who had administered pre-war poor relief with helping the people bombed out of their homes. As Mass Observation noted, many of them were the same men and women who had run Britain's workhouses before 1929, and administered the means test of the 1930s.[53] Their belief that applicants for assistance needed only the bare minimum died hard. In London, they opened rest centres designed to shelter 10,000 people on any one night. This was a woeful underestimate of what was required: on several nights in November 1940, 25,000 people crammed into these centres, one of which a horrified journalist described as a 'frowsty underground den'. Long-term inhabitants were offered typical workhouse fare – weak tea, bread, corned beef and scrapings of jam.[54] Clearly, pre-war poor relief was not an efficient means of dealing with a national emergency. Faced with widespread hardship, those in charge of public assistance had long fallen back on the fallacy that only a minority of the poor 'deserved' assistance. The war demonstrated that this dangerous myth glossed over the harsh truth that a lack of resources and will prevented Britain's neediest citizens from receiving the help they required. In March 1941, at Bevin's behest, the government quietly abolished the household means test.[55] The Blitz had brought home an important lesson: that the victims of disaster were rarely its perpetrators.

The hysteria that the government had feared did not materialize. Mass Observers and journalists spoke of ordinary working-class people as the quiet heroes of the home front, while more prosperous residents appeared selfish and unpatriotic. In badly bombed areas like Coventry and Portsmouth, Mass Observation found, people were 'seriously shaken' but 'not defeatist'. It was the rich who were most likely to flee. In November 1940, on the day after Leicester's first air raid, Mass Observers discovered that 'rich people are already considering buying houses outside Leicester, and many with cars are taking their cars out into the country . . . and spending the night there.' Following several night raids on Portsmouth, 'there was adverse comment among the working classes about the better-off, who largely drove out in cars during the first few days and often had space in their cars.'[56] The Blitz, like evacuation and rationing, brought home to many social investigators and journalists that social and economic inequality had pervasive and dangerous political consequences. The desire of the wealthy to hang on to their privileges was actively unhelpful in a time of national crisis.

By contrast, ordinary people appeared to be the heroes of the hour. Those in rural districts often took evacuees into already over-crowded homes. People in the cities continued to go out to work while enduring nightly air raids. And by 1942, many families knew that their boy in the Mediterranean or the Far East was never coming home. That sacrifice wasn't confined to one social group, of course;

but working-class families lost brothers, sons and husbands who before the war had been stigmatized as feckless or idle. In 1941 Emily Swankie's brother Charlie, who had been made unemployed in 1928, had had his dole money cut by the means test in 1932, and had had to spend years pretending to live away from his parents' flat, 'was lost at sea when his ship was torpedoed in the Bay of Biscay'.[57] Far from being feckless or hysterical, Charlie and millions more like him kept the war effort going.

By 1942, the media and government routinely presented the workers as the people – the mass of the populace, whose interests and desires should shape British culture. By 1941 it would have been folly to suggest that middle-class tastes exclusively set the standard in the British media. In 1940 Bevin had won the battle to introduce 'Music While You Work' – light music programmes broadcast by the BBC for factory workers – in order to raise morale. He appeared on *Workers' Playtime*, the BBC variety show established in 1941 that was broadcast from a factory canteen 'somewhere in Britain'. Variety shows like this made use of the talents they found in the factories they visited, with workers being invited to sing a song or tell jokes to a live national audience. As the historian Geoffrey Field points out, the result was that 'radio sounded more like the mass of the nation talking to itself' than the upper-middle-class dinner party it had often resembled before the war.[58]

By 1942 supplies of food and clothing were scant. The war at sea was drastically depleting Britain's supply of imported foodstuffs. In this time of hardship and uncertainty, working-class strategies for existing on very little – honed in the inter-war depression – were publicly acclaimed. In government propaganda and in the media, the supercilious tone that had caused Mass Observation such despair in the first year of the war gave way to a new voice – one that was more likely to hector the upper middle class than the workers. 'Don't come over all superior at the mention of fish and chips,' Charles Hill, the BBC's Radio Doctor, advised millions of listeners. 'It's not only very tasty and very sweet – it's first-class grub. That's true whether it's dished up with dignity to the duke in his dining room, or scoffed by the nipper from a newspaper spread out on his knees.'[59]

In 1943 the Board of Trade urged Britons to 'Make Do and Mend'. The leaflets and posters reminded housewives that 'a neatly patched garment is something to be proud of nowadays', rather than a shameful sign of poverty.[60] Making do was no novelty for working-class women, but being praised for their initiative was a new experience.

The stress on equal sacrifice and 'making do' in the media and government propaganda created a climate in which those who 'got away with it' were openly criticized for letting down the nation. Government posters and leaflets emphasized the importance of establishing 'fair shares' through rationing. Civilians were urged to 'stay put' in aerial bombardment and to 'do their bit' in the factories. Many middle- and upper-class people were able to avoid doing so, often with the assistance of a government that saw no good reason to destroy social inequality. Nevertheless, the legitimacy of social inequality was constantly, if subtly, challenged by the war effort. Less subtle, but no less significant, was the increasingly heroic position that working-class soldiers, munitions workers and thrifty housewives assumed in both press and propaganda.

By the middle of the war, Allied victories were turning people's minds to what the post-war world might look like. First and foremost they hoped work wouldn't dry up. 'The fear of post-war unemployment,' warned one 'Private' in the army in the Labour newspaper *Tribune*, 'is not likely to evaporate in promises and prophecies.'[61] Full employment had delivered economic security, and a new bargaining power. 'It was a planned economy that worked,' was how twenty-one-year-old Peggy Charles felt about it, having worked at an aircraft factory for three years. She and thousands of others wanted the wartime gains to be secured in peacetime.[62] At the end of 1942 a receptacle for post-war aspiration appeared in the form of the Beveridge Report, which promised 'cradle to grave' welfare provision. Even war-weary Frank Gogerty, kicking his heels at an army camp outside Bournemouth, perked up when he heard about this: 'The expression used was "from the cradle to the grave" and we had high hopes on what it would be. We all thought that a new revolution was about to begin, or happen. We realised or we thought we realised that it would take years to do, a few odd years to do it. From the cradle to the grave, we will look after you. It was a wonderful expression.'

To understand the strength of such feelings, we should briefly recall the pre-war situation. The needy had to rely on contributory insurance, if they had sufficient money to pay for this. If they did not, they were reliant on the locally organized Poor Law or, from 1929, the locally administered Public Assistance Boards; or on private charities. Assistance was means-tested. Unemployment benefit remained inadequate for those who had families to support. Those who were sick, but too poor to pay for a doctor, had been able to use local voluntary hospitals, or Poor Law hospitals where these existed; but provision varied from town to town.

The deficiencies of this system had prompted many valuable voluntary initiatives, including those welfare clinics established by inter-war campaigners like Margery Spring Rice. However, such voluntary provision could not overcome the problem of poverty, as the increase in maternal mortality among unemployed families during the 1930s had shown. By 1939, many liberals and left-wing politicians and thinkers – among them William Beveridge, John Maynard Keynes and Margery Spring Rice – argued that the state needed to intervene more directly in order to improve health, education and economic security. They differed on the role they wished the state to fulfil. While Beveridge believed that voluntary organizations could continue to take a primary role, others, like Herbert Morrison, argued that central planning was the way forward and that the state should take chief responsibility for its citizens' welfare. That view gained support during the first two years of the war. The image of evacuees as lousy, dirty and frail was a caricature, but as the social scientist Richard Titmuss was to point out, it possessed sufficient truth to highlight the inadequacies of existing welfare provision.[63] Meanwhile, Bevin won his fight for better sanitary and medical facilities in Royal Ordnance Factories, success-fully arguing in Cabinet that a healthy workforce was a productive workforce. But what no one had yet suggested, in 1942, was how these gains might be consolidated and expanded in peacetime.

Into this breach stepped William Beveridge. A leading Liberal,

Beveridge had been commissioned to review all existing social insurance schemes by Arthur Greenwood, Labour Minister for Health in the coalition government. It was a sign of the trade unions' newfound power that Greenwood's action was prompted by a TUC request to introduce a comprehensive social insurance scheme. Beveridge's committee published its report – *Social Insurance and Allied Services* – on 1 December 1942.

In the weeks leading up to publication, word leaked out that the report's dry title belied exciting proposals. Beveridge had long viewed the contributory national insurance scheme as a foundation for social welfare. He firmly believed that the contributory principle prevented people from being idle or becoming too dependent on the state. He was also convinced that any growth in social welfare provision should only be granted in return for people's commitment to work, wherever they were able and willing to do so. But until the war, Beveridge had been firmly committed to the notion that voluntary provision was the best way of expanding welfare assistance. The first two years of Blitz, evacuation and conscription led him to conceive of a more central and ambitious role for the state than he had hitherto believed either possible or desirable.[64]

Thousands eagerly queued in the bitter cold for a copy of the report (the 635,000 that had been published quickly sold out). 'It's extraordinary the interest people are taking in it,' one middle-class man told Mass Observation on 2 December. 'When I went down to the Stationery Office to get it, there were queues of people buying it; and I was looking at it on the bus, and the conductor said "I suppose you haven't got a spare copy of that?"'[65]

Beveridge's report was published at an auspicious moment. That year, 1942, had seen the United States enter the war, and Hitler's disastrous decision to declare war on the USSR. The war was, finally, going Britain's way. Many in the Labour Party were already considering the future. In April Ernest Bevin had welcomed the International Labour Organisation's emergency committee to London with the words: 'This is a people's war: it must lead to a people's peace.'[66] Less than a month later, delegates at the Labour Party conference passed a motion to defend the wartime political truce that existed between Labour, the Conservatives and the Liberals – but only by the slimmest of margins. The continuing political truce meant that no one had given form to the aspirations that underpinned Bevin's speech and inspired the dissident conference delegates. Beveridge's report offered them important ammunition. Mass Observers noted that the readers included many manual workers and their families, most of whom welcomed the report's main conclusions. On 2 December the *Daily Mirror*'s front page summed these up: 'Beveridge tells how to banish want; Cradle to Grave plan; all pay – all benefit'. It was a simple, straightforward message that was immensely popular.

Beveridge's proposals aimed to free all Britons from want, disease, ignorance, squalor and idleness. The state should be responsible for ensuring that its citizens had the basic means to live (a 'national minimum'), though workers would contribute to this through insurance payments. This element of the scheme was necessary, he said, so that workers would experience 'the duty and pleasure of thrift'. Underpinning his scheme, he stressed, must be a government commitment to full employment.

Beveridge's stress on self-help and his assumption that 'free donations' would lead to 'idleness' indicated that older suspicions about the moral fibre of the working class hadn't disappeared. Nevertheless, by arguing for universal welfare provision that wasn't policed by a means test, Beveridge destroyed the distinction between the 'deserving' and the 'undeserving' that had penalized so many needy people before the war. His stress on the crucial role of central government was also new.

Political responses to the Beveridge Report highlighted a growing division between Conservative and Labour members of the government. The Conservatives refused to endorse Beveridge's central assumption of universal provision. Churchill argued that inflated wartime promises might lead to post-war unrest if they were not met in peacetime – and made clear that he considered them to be unaffordable luxuries. 'The broad masses of the people face the hardships of life undaunted, but they are liable to get very angry if they feel they have been . . . cheated,' he cautioned in a confidential note sent to the War Cabinet in January 1943. 'It is because I do not wish to deceive the people by false hopes . . . that I have refrained so far from making promises about the future.'[67] But the language of economic realism and 'common sense' that had served the inter-war Conservative Party well was no longer popular in wartime. Home Intelligence reported that Churchill's stance provoked widespread 'anger' and 'despondency, especially among working-class people'.[68] That their wartime sacrifice entitled 'the people' to peacetime reward was now firmly established with many sections of the population and the press – but not among senior Tories.

Outside parliament, Beveridge's proposals met with massive support especially from the working class. Factory workers, clerks and shop assistants were particularly enthusiastic. One twenty-eight-year-old skilled working man summed up the prevailing mood: 'It would be all right to be able to stop worrying about tomorrow, or your old age, or what was going to happen to the kids,' he told Mass Observation.[69] 'It should be passed as quickly as possible,' declared another working-class man. 'I don't see how anybody can oppose it, except perhaps the insurance companies, but they . . . have feathered their nest long enough.'[70] Middle-class people expressed greater caution. One middle-class housewife, married to a businessman, thought that 'we pamper the workers . . . with their canteens and music. They ought to work harder.' However, she admitted that her opposition was outdated and 'selfish . . . I've been one of the lucky few and I want to remain so.'[71] This was very different to the easy sense of entitlement expressed by so many servants' employers less than twenty years earlier. And Mass Observation found that 'opponents of the scheme were in a minority' even among the middle class; in February 1943, for example, only one person opposed Beveridge's recommendations for every seven people who approved of them.[72]

Labour embraced Beveridge's recommendations – and reaped the benefits. From 1942, by-election results indicated disenchantment with the Conservatives. For the duration of the war, the major political parties had agreed not to contest elections against each other. But by-elections were fought where sitting MPs died or retired, and from 1942 the voters made clear they were eager for change along the lines that Beveridge, Bevin and Labour were suggesting. Turnout was high, and candidates who advocated radical social change along broadly left-wing lines were popular – among them many Communists.

Away from the ballot box, other signs of popular commitment to social change were appearing. In the cinemas, audience surveys and Mass Observers found that, understandably, the most popular films were those that offered a complete escape from the war – slapstick comedies or historical romances. But among the war films on offer, the most popular were not those that espoused national unity above class division, but those that acknowledged that 'The world's made up of two kinds of people.'[73] Those were the words of Charlie, the foreman in the 1943 film *Millions Like Us*, the story of women from diverse social backgrounds sent to work at a Royal Ordnance Factory in the countryside. They are shown to have very different outlooks on life as a result of their different class backgrounds; and Jennifer, the most privileged of them all, is the laziest and least patriotic at first. 'Oh, we're together now there's a war on – we need to be,' Charlie tells Jennifer, who becomes his girlfriend (the working-class girl had not yet attained glamour status; Jennifer remained the film's heart-throb). 'What's going to happen when it's over? Shall we go on like this or are we going to slide back?' It was no coincidence that Charlie's speech was made on a hill overlooking England's green and pleasant land; inequality, he suggested, was not a part of the 'British tradition' that 'the people' were fighting this war to defend.[74]

Labour's appeal was not simply based on claiming solidarity between the working and the middle class; this solidarity was also invoked against the powerful and wealthy, who were now popular scapegoats. Home Intelligence found that supporters of the Beveridge Report were concerned that 'vested interests' who 'want to go back to 1939' would ensure that its recommendations were never adopted, despite its popularity.[75] 'The [Labour] party's publicity campaign in December 1942,' argues the historian Laura Beers, 'is notable for its emphasis on the practical benefits of social welfare and state direction of the economy, not only to the working classes, but to the nation as a whole.'[76] 'The Tories are concerned about the future for private profits,' declared one of Labour's election pamphlets in 1945. 'Labour is concerned about the future for the people.'[77]

This was a popular sentiment in 1945. Fear that the poverty of the past decade would return was rife. People remembered the broken promises that had been made in the last war, and the long dole queues of 1919. One woman munitions worker told Mass Observation that, while she'd like to leave work at war's end, 'you don't know how things will turn out . . . we might be selling matches in the streets.'[78] Another woman said pessimistically, 'I think it's going to be just as bad as the last time, or even worse.'[79]

The war in Europe ended in May 1945. Two months later came the general election. Before the war, profit-making had been widely accepted as the basis of any civilized society. This was no longer the case. Churchill's ill-advised warning that Labour's commitment to collective provision could be compared to the Gestapo showed the party leader to be startlingly out of touch with the public mood.[80] But Labour did not simply win because of Conservative failure. *Let Us Face the Future* – the Labour manifesto published that year – offered a powerful message that resonated with many middle-class voters as well as with the working-class electorate. Herbert Morrison, the man in charge of Labour's election campaign, claimed that collective and comprehensive state welfare provision would benefit all of Britain's 'useful people'. 'There is no cleavage of interest between hand workers and brain workers,' he declared, a sentiment regularly echoed by the party's leader, Clement Attlee.[81] Such was Morrison's faith in this vision that he left his parliamentary seat of South Hackney – a predominantly working-class constituency – to contest the more middle-class East Lewisham in the 1945 election. His faith was borne out: a seat that the party had previously considered unwinnable fell to Morrison with a 15,000 majority.

Across the country, the picture was repeated: Labour made huge gains in formerly Conservative constituencies. The common sense of the 1930s – that the middle class would never pay for welfare provision; that private enterprise was the only means of organizing society – was shown to be false. Labour's success testified to the party's ability to unite clerks, miners and schoolteachers as 'productive citizens' – Morrison's phrase – against the 'vested interests' of the rich. Successive opinion polls conducted between April and August 1945 indicated that this was not an election simply won on anti-Conservatism; it was a positive vote for Labour's policies. Throughout the spring and summer of that year, opinion polls found that more than 60 per cent of those questioned (from a range of social backgrounds and political sympathies) supported nationalization of industry.[82]

But the Labour victory rested above all on the votes of working-class people. In August, more than 50 per cent of Labour supporters who responded to a Gallup poll said they had voted Labour because the party was 'best for the working class'. Kitty Murphy was among those first-time voters who put Labour into power. She had grown up in the East End of London, and had witnessed the effects of unemployment on her father and uncles. By 1940 she was a young married woman, working at the Woolwich Arsenal with her mother, father and younger brother while her husband fought abroad. In 1945 she was demobbed, and cast her vote while awaiting her husband's return. The Labour slogans of 1945 – 'Never Again' and 'Ask Your Dad' – made sense to her. 'We didn't intend going back to how it was,' she explained. 'The Labour party promised us that they'd do this and they'd do that and they did, they done it . . . whereas I don't think that would've happened had Churchill got back in.'[83]

The Blitz spirit, the sense that 'we're all in it together', was certainly mythologized, both during and after the war, but it was a myth based on a reality of collective effort for collective gain. Labour promised that this could continue in peacetime, a claim that proved highly attractive to many people who had lived through the years of inter-war poverty and wartime uncertainty. Attlee's Labour Party entered government with a majority of 146 and 48 per cent of the popular vote.[84]

Labour's victory was a tangible result of the people's war – a vote for the maintenance of full employment and for better social welfare as a reward for the exhaustion, effort and loss that the people had endured as they battled to win the war. The conflict had shown just how valuable ordinary workers were to the country's economic, military and political prowess, and what impressive results planning, unity and decent pay could bring. As an economic and political force the strength of working-class people grew, thanks to the new demand for their labour and the negotiating rights they fought hard to establish. Britain at the end of the war was certainly not an equal country, but the gaping social chasm of 1939 had narrowed slightly in favour of wage-earners, thanks to rationing and rising wages. In 1945 millions of voters showed that they wanted certain aspects of wartime life to continue. First and foremost was full employment, but a close second was a welfare state in which the state looked after the people's needs. The voters' aspirations testified to a transformation in the relationship between the state and the people. Those responsible for this change were the workers on the home front and the troops now returning from abroad – those whom Ernie Bevin called 'our people', and who had now become *the* people.

Interlude II

On the Lloyd George

VIV BEGAN SCHOOL in 1941. The war made little difference to her life; mining was a reserved occupation and her father was, in any case, too sick with epilepsy to be called up. Her brothers and sisters were all younger than she was, so her mother wasn't required to take up war work.

By the time the war ended in 1945, Viv and her four brothers and sisters had been joined by her two cousins, Michael and Margaret. Her aunt had died and 'my mother took them in because there was nobody to have them.' There were now nine people living in four rooms, but the family had no chance of being rehoused; there were no bigger houses nearby. 'Me, Jess, Maureen and Margaret would sleep in one bed and my mother in a single bed, in one room,' while the boys and Viv's father shared the second bedroom. Viv enjoyed escaping from her cramped home whenever she could, but with so many young children in the house, as the oldest daughter, she was expected to help her mother. 'I had to get up at six o'clock in the morning, get the washing out and boil all the water up,' before rousing her younger brothers and sisters and getting them ready for school.

With Viv's father not working, and so many children to feed, the family felt none of the benefit of rising wages during the early 1940s. They remained reliant on what Viv's mother could earn in the fields to supplement the help they received from the local Public Assistance Committee (the body that had administered the means test).

Viv took to truanting from school because 'we had our clothes given to us [by the Committee] . . . and it used to worry me whether they'd belonged before to one of the kids at school who would notice me and say "Hey, them's my shoes!"' Although the Unemployment

Insurance Act of 1934 meant that unemployment benefit rates were set nationally, not locally, the committees still had a great deal of discretion about how they helped those who were out of work through sickness, or were earning wages too low to support their families (as judged by the stringent means test). Many committees, including Castleford's, preferred to make donations 'in kind', like clothes, believing that this would prevent families from spending their money in the 'wrong' way.

In 1948 – the year that the Labour government introduced the 'cradle to grave' welfare provision recommended by the Beveridge Report – Viv turned twelve. Large families like hers didn't always experience 1948 as a transformation. This was the year when Viv's mother began putting her 'to work in the fields in school bloody time'. Viv protested – she hated the back-breaking work of picking potatoes and peas. Her mother told her they had no choice because her father 'only got the "Lloyd George", as we called the National Assistance'. The name showed how little any of them felt had changed since pre-war days; the much heralded welfare state seemed to Viv only to lead to her having to 'queue up to take this cod-liver oil every Monday morning'. She hated it and 'always ducked my turn. Eventually I'd end up bloody last and the teacher – Mr Smith – would see me. He would grab hold of my cheek, force my mouth open.' She got her own back: 'I was sick on him once.'

Nonetheless the new approach to welfare made a difference to Viv, for the late 1940s gave her a sense, not only of what she was missing, but of what she should be entitled to. Cod liver oil and education suggested she mattered – and they sparked anger and a desire for a different sort of life. What that life might consist of was hinted at in 1949 when 'my teacher, Miss Wilson, suggested I should change schools'. In 1948 Labour's Education Minister, Ellen Wilkinson, had overseen the passing of the 1944 Education Act. This meant, explained Viv's headmistress, that Castleford's art school was now free, open to all who could pass an examination proving they had the requisite ability. She 'asked me if my parents would be interested in me going.' Viv was 'dead chuffed about it' but her father said no, 'we can't afford it.' – Viv's wage was needed to support his four younger children, not to mention his drinking. Even after Viv's headmistress wrote another letter 'saying it wouldn't cost me father a penny . . . as it would all be provided by the government or something' her father wouldn't hear of it: 'Tha's leaving,' he said when Viv turned fifteen in 1951, 'and tha's going to make a wage.'

7

New Jerusalems

ETWEEN 1945 AND 1951 the lives of working-class people greatly improved. Labour took power committed to maintaining full employment and collective bargaining, and to introducing cradle-to-grave welfare provision. Hazel Wood was born in 1941, the youngest of three children. In 1940 her family had come to Coventry from Sunderland, hoping to find work for Hazel's unemployed father. Hazel's mother had been the oldest girl in a large family, who she had had to keep on her shop assistant's wage because her father, a blacksmith, was unemployed. She had left that life behind when she married in 1939. By 1945, her husband had a skilled job in a car factory and Hazel's mother stayed at home to look after her three children. 'She laughed a lot,' said Hazel. 'She'd known tough times and she was so happy to have come through them.'[1]

Her experience was shared by thousands of other people. Labour's maintenance of rationing (not fully abolished until 1954) and the introduction of comprehensive social security helped ensure that the income gap between the richest and the poorest, which had narrowed in the early 1940s, remained static. Wages rose, with manual workers and lower grade clerical staff enjoying the biggest gains. Most importantly, full employment eradicated the major cause of pre-war poverty. Clement Attlee's post-war government established the political framework for the next thirty years. Less than 2 per cent of the working population was unemployed between 1948 and the beginning of the 1970s.[2]

However, government policies simultaneously constrained working-class people's power in ways that provoked popular frustration. Labour's front bench was not committed to establishing economic or political equality. They promoted equality of opportunity. Workers were not granted any control over industry, but were instead expected to submit to the authority of managers. Welfare was paid for not by income redistribution but by insurance. This placed a heavy responsibility on husbands and fathers, and made women and children heavily dependent on them. The Labour government maintained private housing, education and healthcare, and differential wage rates that rewarded salaried professionals and managers more than manual workers. These measures were intended to help create a meritocracy, in which anyone could get on with hard work and talent. But in reality, these policies reinforced existing social divisions, by encouraging middle-class voters to see themselves as a separate interest group from the working class. The 1945 rhetoric of 'the people' against 'vested interests' rang increasingly hollow.

Hazel Wood's vision of the late 1940s is very different from the usual portrayal of dreary austerity. That dismal representation is summed up by Doris Lessing, writing of her arrival in London from South Africa in 1948, the manuscript of her autobiography *The Grass is Singing* in her suitcase:

> No cafes. No good restaurants. Clothes were still 'austerity' from the war, dismal and ugly. Everyone was indoors by ten, and the streets were empty. The Dining Rooms [British Restaurants], subsidized during the war, were often the only places to eat . . . The sole civilized amenity was the pubs, but they closed at eleven . . . Rationing was still on. The war still lingered, not only in the bombed places but in people's minds and behaviour. Any conversation tended to drift towards the war, like an animal licking a sore place. There was a wariness, a weariness.[3]

Lessing's memory contains a good deal of truth. But we need to ask whose truth this was. For those who were used to a comfortable way of life, the late 1940s was an uncomfortable period of privation. But for those who had grown up in the depression and had survived the Blitz, the immediate post-war years heralded the start of a new life. Between 1945 and 1951 ordinary working-class people's lives dramatically improved.

The welfare state, and particularly full employment, made the transition from war to peace easier than many people had feared. In June 1948 thirty-two-year-old Frank Gogerty, an army conscript since 1943, was finally told he could go home to his wife Rita and their two small sons. It was the day he had dreamed of for five years; yet when it arrived he felt apprehensive:

> I came out of the demob office with a suit, a pair of shoes, a hat and a tie and a shirt, I thought, well, this is a new life. And I really began to wonder because for five years I had been in the army where everything was done for you. You hadn't got any responsibilities owing to the army and when I came back on that train I was thinking, 'Crikey, I've got a house in Coventry, I've got a wife, I've got two kids. I've got to look after them.'

Frank had 'a little bit of doubt' about whether he could really do this. Fortunately, he quickly settled into life back home: 'I think the self-doubt vanished as soon as I saw Rita,' he said. What also helped was that Ernest Bevin had ensured that Frank's old job as a skilled metal worker would be open for him. 'If I go back,' he said to himself, 'they have got to employ me for a year, so I've got a year to rehabilitate myself.'

Economic security couldn't cure the trauma that returning soldiers and particularly prisoners of war had to deal with, but it helped. Labour's policies aimed to give 'the people' decent living standards, but also political and economic citizenship. 'Full employment,' declared the Labour MP Charles Pannell in 1948, 'means a regular wage at the end of the week . . . But it can mean something more . . . It means that the great bulk of the self respecting working classes . . . can stand on their feet in the full stature of manhood and be men on their feet rather than toadies on their knees.'⁴

This form of citizenship was extended to disabled veterans as well as to able-bodied men – to men like twenty-five-year-old Robert Rigby, who in 1945 married Nellie, a nurse he had met while recovering from horrific injuries sustained as a soldier. When Robert was demobbed the couple moved to his home town, Liverpool. By 1948, the Rigbys were settled in a new council house at Belle Vale, an estate of prefabricated houses hastily constructed on Liverpool's southern outskirts. Robert's injuries left him in constant pain and permanently lame. Nevertheless, the Rigbys were reassured both by their council house and by the knowledge that, in Nellie's words, 'there was a scheme where disabled veterans would be found jobs.'[5] The Labour government had guaranteed this. Robert was not in fact found work until 1952 – at a local factory – but his war pension, their new home, and the fact that Nellie could find work locally helped them get through. Full employment, as Charles Pannell had said, was not simply about giving people work – it also granted them a modicum of control over their lives.

For many people the end of the war did not feel like a return to peacetime normality, but the start of a better life. Many workers had a little extra spending money in their pockets. Skilled manual workers continued to be paid more than their unskilled workmates, and the gap between salaried professionals and manual workers remained substantial, but these divisions narrowed, with manual workers enjoying far higher and more regular wage rises than professionals.[6] In the late 1940s most people spent about one-third of their income on rationed goods; quite a change from the 1930s, when many families had had to spend at least two-thirds of their income on food and clothing. 'Rationing was a great leveller,' said Norman Lewis, who was a teenager in the late 1940s and living with his widowed mother in Lancaster. Although their circumstances were hard, 'We were all a bit better off, because of the earning power.'[7] In 1949 Mass Observation interviewed 2,040 people across England about their income and spending patterns. The investigators discovered widespread satisfaction, especially among manual workers and their families: 'a third say that they have no particular wants beyond those that they can afford.'[8] This marked a dramatic improvement since the hungry thirties.

People spent more on leisure than ever before. 'The six or seven years of austerity and restriction, and often self-denial and sacrifice,' explained the social investigator Ferdynand Zweig in 1949, 'have produced a relapse and reversion of the trend in a hunger for pleasure.'[9] Far from wishing to retreat from the communal habits of wartime into their homes, many people took advantage of the end of the blackout to get out and about. Wage-earners and their families flocked to British Restaurants, the state-owned canteens that had opened during the war to offer affordable meals, and which survived for more than a decade. Almost half of all factory and shop workers went to the cinema at least once a week.[10] Carol Blackburn grew up in Swinton near Salford. Her parents were both millworkers, who had endured years on the dole before the war. Their new-found security meant that, for the first time, the family was able to take regular advantage of the town's cinemas and cafés. 'We used to go to the pictures on a Friday night,' Carol recalled. 'My father used to take us. It was a family thing. We'd go to the pictures and then we'd go to the chip shop.'[11] Pubs boomed as well as fish and chip shops: beer consumption rose from 2 million barrels in 1938 to 3 million barrels in 1945.[12]

Rationing remained – and remained popular. In 1935 the average factory worker had consumed only 87 per cent of the calorific intake of the top 20 per cent of wage-earners (mainly salaried professionals). By 1947 that gap had disappeared.[13] Working women complained about having to use their precious free time to queue for groceries, and most people weren't averse to accepting a little butter or sugar from 'under the counter' of a trusted shopkeeper.[14] Those who circumvented the law were often represented by their relatives or friends as Robin Hood characters, seeking to redistribute goods that profiteers or the army sought to keep to themselves. When Brian Thresh's demobbed uncles returned home to Manchester bearing 'blankets, clothing, old torches' they were hailed as heroes. Unfortunately, the police weren't far behind: 'they got picked up, actually, because they were stolen property,' but taken from the army which was considered fair game; it was 'all ex-army stuff that people really needed in the days after the war'.[15] There was a sense that people were entitled to take what they needed – but no more.[16]

Most people were prepared to accept that the government was *their* government and committed to their interests. In 1947 heavy snow stopped coal being transported to power stations. The government imposed power cuts and urged people to preserve fuel. Some workers barely noticed the difference. Among them were an Essex railwayman and his colleague who told Mass Observation that they 'were willing to work over the weekend clearing coal wagons, but we were not required'. Their families, like many working-class households, did not suffer in the crisis because the amount of fuel they used each day was so slight. 'We have been warm enough indoors as we have plenty of logs,' said the railwayman.[17]

Labour provoked more anger by lifting controls on food and fuel than by extending them. In 1948 the cash-strapped government accepted America's Marshall Aid in order to pay off war debts owing to the United States government. The terms of the Marshall Plan, which was designed to promote capitalism and thwart the Soviet Union's expansionist ambitions, committed the government to promoting a free market, which meant a gradual end to rationing. By 1951, most people were spending less than 10 per cent of their income on rationed goods, so price rises hit ordinary consumers hard. The newspapers were full of accounts of working-class women's concern about how far and how fast prices rose after goods stopped being rationed. In February 1951, for example, Elaine Burton, Labour MP for Coventry South, demanded that local shopkeepers 'Stop Week-End Veg Ramp'. She told the *Daily Mirror* that 'Housewives in Coventry had given her examples of price rises on Fridays and Saturdays compared with Mondays to Thursdays . . . Cabbage up 1d or 2d . . . oranges as much as 1½d each.'[18] Many of these women demanded greater government control over prices, not less. They had excellent grounds for their fears. After 1951, the difference in the calorific consumption of the poorest and the richest began to grow once more (though it remained far less significant in the thirty years following the war than it had been in the 1930s).[19]

The year 1948 was seminal. On the one hand, the government accepted the poisoned chalice of Marshall Aid. On the other, Labour abolished the Poor Law and instituted a new system of social security, free healthcare and free secondary education. Opinion polls showed overwhelming support for these reforms. 'The biggest factor liked about the new scheme is its cheapness to the individual,' Mass Observation reported in 1949. 'This is followed by the creation of equality among all people.'[20] Free healthcare was particularly valued. Years later, asked to comment on what had made most improvement to her life, Beryl Gottfried, born in 1929, commented, 'You don't have to pay for the doctor anymore.' Her father, a railway signalman in Oxfordshire 'used to take people's teeth out for them' because they couldn't afford the dentist.[21] Moira Gordon, a former domestic servant, was particularly well placed to observe the change, having had two children before 1948 and one just after the National Health Service was introduced. She was married to an agricultural worker, living in a village near Stirling: 'You'd to pay for a doctor and for a midwife and then when the weans were a wee bit older you'd to pay for an inoculation and it was actually compulsory and you'd to pay for that you know. But then all that stopped in 1948. So I had two before that, 1940 and 1947 but by 1948 it was all into the National Health so [when I had my younger children] it was a lot better.'[22] Infant mortality fell rapidly between 1941, when 50 deaths were recorded per 1,000 births, and 1955, when this figure had fallen to 27 deaths.[23]

Crucially, this welfare provision was part of what Labour called a 'social contract' with the people. The government would guarantee the workers' welfare in return for their labour. To ensure that workers' needs were met at work as well as at home, the trade unions were assured a seat at the national negotiation table. 'The individual citizen will still feel that society is on top of him,' declared Aneurin Bevan, Labour's Minister of Health and Housing, 'until he is enfranchised in the workshop as well as at the ballot box.'[24] Everyone had the individual right to vote, and to sell their labour to whoever they chose. But workers also required a collective freedom, to organize and to negotiate with their employers.

However this collective independence was severely limited. There was no suggestion that workers would be given any control over industry. Behind this lay Labour's commitment to establishing a meritocracy. The government agreed with William Beveridge that welfare reform should be paid for through social insurance rather than a redistributive tax system. Many Labour politicians believed that social insurance and higher rates of pay for professionals and managers were important in a society determined to reward hard work and talent. In 1946 William Jowitt, Labour's Lord Chancellor, explained their thinking to the House of Lords. Sixty-one-year-old Jowitt had served in the wartime coalition government, latterly as Minister of National Insurance, a post he used to implement several of Beveridge's proposals. Among these was the introduction of family allowances.

In August 1946 Jowitt announced that the state would pay five shillings a week to the mother for every one of her children except the first – a great help to many families, including those headed by women. These allowances were essential, he declared, because 'the remuneration which the worker gets must depend upon the services which he renders. It cannot depend upon the size of his family.' Family allowances would thus ensure 'that children of all sections of the community may have that equal opportunity which we all desire'.[25] In Labour's meritocracy, the government put time and effort into offering children equal chances at birth, but differential wage rates were promoted as an incentive to work hard and a reward for doing so.

The 'top-down' nature of these reforms explains a growing disillusion with the government. Striking remained illegal under Attlee's government, but despite the possibility of imprisonment, hundreds of workers did strike over pay and conditions. In striking, they asserted their right to have more say over their working life than Labour's reforms allowed them. Workers found that their union officials were granted a seat at the negotiating table, where they frequently became management's spokesmen, especially in the nationalized industries that were supposedly run in the interests of 'the country'. Miners and steelworkers who had cheered nationalization were dismayed to find that the rigid managerial hierarchy of pre-war days was retained – often with the same faces in charge. Most worrying for the government was the spate of strikes in Britain's docks between 1947 and 1950. Before the war, dock labourers had been casually employed; most were hired by the day or week by different employers. In times of high unemployment, this granted employers enormous power, and robbed the labourers of any security. Ernest Bevin delivered on his promise to regularize dock labour by establishing the Dock Labour Board in 1947. But many dock workers were disgruntled at the loss of their hard-won localized negotiation rights, and their employers' continued right to hire workers by the day (only abolished in the 1960s).[26] Four major unofficial strikes erupted in the London docks between 1947 and 1950 and smaller disputes occurred in the provinces. Few of the strikers were in a trade union, which Mass Observation ascribed to 'a sense of impotence and isolation' among workers who felt disenchanted with their trade union leaders and the government.[27]

Those working-class people who fell outside the remit of the trade unions were more dissatisfied. Hundreds of thousands of people continued to live in poverty. In 1948, 495,000 old-age pensioners and 143,000 others below pensionable age received the National Assistance supplement that provided a basic income for those who had no other means to make ends meet. National Assistance was means-tested. Labour failed to introduce a subsistence-level pension as Beveridge recommended.[28] Many older people continued to suffer the indignity of having their income assessed in their own homes.

Also suffering were those women bringing up families alone – including many war widows. As well as family allowances, the introduction of National Assistance in 1948 offered a boon to lone mothers. If they had school-age children at home, they were no longer required to register for work in order to claim benefit. But their benefit was means-tested and could be stopped if they were suspected of living with a man.[29]

Widows and women who had separated from their husband found making ends meet a great strain. In the late 1940s, nineteen-year-old Norman Lewis was living on Lancaster's Marsh estate with his younger sister, a schoolgirl, and his mother. Norman's father, a bargeman, had died in 1943: 'He fell in the canal and drowned. What a romantic death. Company gave us nothing.' A few years later Norman's mother fell ill 'and the doctor kept calling to the house . . . I grabbed him one day and asked him what on earth was wrong with Mum. He said in no uncertain terms, "She's starving herself to feed you two."' Norman left his joinery apprenticeship: 'I had to earn more money . . . without saying anything to Mum, I took a job as [a] labourer, so my wage leapt.'[30] Women with younger children were often very poor. In 1948 Mrs Annie Pye of Birkdale, Merseyside, was fined £10 for selling her ration books. 'Living apart from her husband and with four children to keep on less than £2 a week,' reported the *Liverpool Echo*, she was 'unable to send two of the children to school because they had no boots'.[31] The welfare state did not eradicate poverty.

Labour ministers too easily assumed that full employment would sweep away hardship. The government failed to act on Beveridge's recommendation that other forms of support be established for those groups – like single mothers – who could not easily fit into a social insurance scheme, and who were not always able to work outside the home.[32] Instead, as the 1940s drew to a close, Labour prioritized the repayment of American loans and, as the Cold War escalated, increased defence spending. In vain did left-winger Aneurin Bevan suggest that creating a great welfare state, with an NHS 'the envy of the world', might be a more civilized (and practicable) route to international prestige than aggressive diplomacy.[33]

Closer to home, the government was preoccupied with reviving the economy by increasing domestic demand for consumer goods. This meant promoting manufacturing, which in turn required unskilled and semi-skilled workers to staff the assembly lines. In 1945 thousands of married women had left the war factories. Most did so voluntarily and thankfully. '[I]n the services, and overwhelmingly so in the factories, marriage and domestic life remains the almost universal post-war hope,' a Mass Observation study of working women had noted in 1944.[34] Within two years of war's end, however, the government was encouraging married women to return to the factories to meet a labour shortage. On 1 June 1947 George Isaacs, the Minister of Labour, launched the government's 'Back to Work' appeal over the wireless. He explained that the country urgently needed to produce more exports in order to increase the national income, and that 'there are just not enough people to do the job'.[35]

But the government proved reluctant to acknowledge the needs of working women. Wartime nurseries were closed down. In 1951 nursery school provision was available for only 3 per cent of children – the same proportion who had benefited from it in 1936.[36] Isaacs disingenuously suggested that 'people prefer to make their own [childcare] arrangements – a working arrangement with neighbours or someone else in the family.'[37] But this was not possible everywhere, as Nellie Rigby found when she went out to work in the late 1940s. Few residents on her out-of-town housing estate had relatives living close by, so 'working women were desperate for help'. Robert Rigby was able to look after their young daughter before he returned to work in 1952, but when he did so Nellie herself became a child-minder 'because people really needed this and there weren't any nurseries where we were'.

The government refused to address the needs of women workers both because of potential expense and because of their short-sighted belief that most working women would eventually be replaced by men. Isaacs stressed that women's return to the factories was 'a temporary business – we will catch up in time'.[38] Yet a wide-ranging economic survey commissioned by the government suggested that women's labour would be essential for many years to come. Britain's economic recovery depended on the mass production and domestic consumption of cars, domestic appliances, electrical goods and clothing. As this survey pointed out, employers in these industries preferred to employ cheap, unskilled and semi-skilled workers – primarily juveniles and women – rather than more expensive adult men.[39] But Attlee's Cabinet clung to the notion, long enshrined in the labour movement's campaigns, that the ideal family was one that could be kept by a single male breadwinner. Women's pay and conditions were treated as matters of secondary importance. In 1946 the government pleaded financial pressure as a reason to ignore the recommendations of a Royal Commission on Equal Pay, which advocated equal pay for men and women in teaching and the higher grades of the civil service. In 1948 female factory workers earned, on average, 74s 6d per week – about half the average male wage.[40]

The biggest disappointment to Labour's voters was, however, housing – or the lack of it. In 1945, 100,000 families lived in houses that had been officially condemned as unfit before the outbreak of war. A further 200,000 people were living in homes that would have been condemned had war not broken out. Two and half million more occupied houses that were unsafe as a result of wartime bombing. Countless more were living in overcrowded conditions with relatives or friends. About 10 per cent of the population was enduring substandard housing.[41] Minister for Health and Housing Aneurin Bevan – or Nye as he was known – promised to build 240,000 new homes each year. His 1948 Housing Act stipulated a generous minimum standard for council houses: they were to be solidly built, well-insulated, well-ventilated, light and airy and equipped with that luxury – an indoor bathroom.

Bevan was determined to make council housing available for all who needed it. The 1936 Housing Act had charged local authorities with housing 'the working classes'; Nye Bevan's 1948 Act boldly proclaimed that local authorities would house all those in need. Bevan recognized that war damage had affected a variety of people; but his Act was also shaped by his conviction – provoked by the overcrowded slums of pre-war Britain – that local authorities would provide better, and better-planned housing, than private landlords or builders would.

The majority of new homes were to be situated on the outskirts of towns and cities, or in the eighteen new towns that Labour planned to build. Land was cheaper outside the city centres, but Bevan had another reason for wanting to build communities from scratch: he wanted to ensure social diversity. '[W]e should try to introduce . . . what was always the lovely feature of English and Welsh villages,' he declared in 1949, 'where the doctor, the grocer, the butcher and farm labourer all lived in the same street.'⁴² Bevan himself had grown up in a mining village, in the valleys of South Wales; he wanted to encourage the collective support he had known there, while eradicating the poor housing that his family and their neighbours had endured. Districts in new towns like Crawley were built around their own 'village green' lined with shops and amenities.⁴³ Bevan was determined to eradicate the distinction between home owners and council tenants and the geographic divisions that had existed between inter-war council estates and more salubrious suburbs.

The lucky ones relished their new homes. 'It is like heaven,' was how the wife of a demobbed sailor described their flat to the *Manchester Evening News*, which proudly reported that these, the city's 'first post-war flats . . . might have been transplanted from London's West End'.⁴⁴ In 1948 Bill Rainford's family moved out of the small, dilapidated house they shared with relatives in Everton in Liverpool and into a newly built council house at Belle Vale. Bill himself was just a baby at the time, but he grew up knowing how much his parents welcomed the move, and how proud they were of their new home. The Rainfords' new neighbours shared their conviction that this move meant more than a new house: it meant consigning poverty and destruction to the past. 'They were putting the war behind them,' Bill explained, 'and just trying to rebuild their lives.'[45]

But families like the Rainfords were the lucky few. Bevan's ministry consistently failed to meet its annual target of 240,000 new homes, although an impressive 900,000 new houses had been built by 1950. One survey estimated that at the current rate, hundreds of applicants for council housing in Birmingham alone would wait more than twenty years.[46] By 1951, housing was voters' biggest grievance.

Significant though these difficulties were, the late 1940s positively transformed many people's lives. The fear and uncertainty of war were over, but the country did not simply return to pre-war normality. The six years that followed Labour's 1945 election victory witnessed the rapid development of a more comprehensive welfare state than Britain had ever known. This gave everyone free access to healthcare and secondary education, and offered an important safety net to those who could not benefit from full employment. Economic security enabled people to plan for the future while also enjoying life in the present. People could afford to hope – they could even afford to go out and enjoy themselves. They valued what they experienced as real improvements.

At the same time, many people – whether 'workers by hand' or 'workers by brain' – remained supportive of the new egalitarian, compassionate society that Labour seemed to offer. Philip Gilbert was born in Stepney in east London in 1920 to a working-class Jewish family. By 1950, thirty-year-old Philip was working in a factory in Hackney. Looking back over his life from the 1990s, by which time he was living in a prosperous area of Oxford, where he ran a bookshop, he identified the 1940s as the only time for which he felt nostalgia. 'I think there was more caring and feeling in our country during the war years and just after that.'[47]

Alan Watkins thought this feeling lasted 'for about ten years after the war'. He was a schoolboy in Coventry during the late 1940s, growing up in a ramshackle house in a cramped medieval court close to the centre of the blitzed city. After the war, he said, people tolerated the poor: 'I think it was, "there but for the Grace of God". Because, you know, lots of people were down on their luck. A bomb could have got a businessman's house same as a working man's.'[48] Alan was happy to describe his family as 'a bit rough', seeing no value judgement attached to this; in post-war Britain people understood that families found themselves in circumstances they wouldn't necessarily have chosen: in the Watkinses' case, this meant existing on his father's unskilled wage, in a blitzed city with a dire shortage of housing. Norman Lewis agreed. If some families on his estate didn't keep their home as neat as others did, this was no reason for condemnation, but due to circumstances beyond their control, like 'the women whose husbands were killed', including his own mother. Norman consciously eschewed the idea that some families were more 'deserving' or 'respectable' than others. 'My values then were not whether we were any better or worse than others. We liked to think that we were all equal.'[49]

One result was that Labour won the general election of 1950, albeit with a reduced majority. The Conservatives' confidential post-mortem on this election illuminates the reasons why. Local activists, voting figures and opinion polls revealed that Labour had continued to poll strongly in working-class constituencies, though the party had lost ground in some middle-class areas. The Conservatives concluded that Labour's attractions were, in order of importance: 'full employment, the National Health Service and social services, Fair Shares, bigger wage-packets [and] "Tory Misrule"': voters vividly recalled the hungry thirties. While some middle-class voters were greatly attracted by the Conservatives' commitment to cut income tax, working-class voters in particular were put off by the 'vagueness of [Conservative] policy for full employment', 'cuts in food subsidies' – including the promise to end rationing – and by 'Churchill – seen as a warmonger'.[50]

Yet just one year later, on 26 October 1951, the Labour Party lost the general election. Winston Churchill's Conservative Party returned to power. Their victory was not a surprise – opinion polls had been predicting a comfortable majority for the Tories, the press speculating that this was due to voters' fatigue with austerity. Rearmament was taking a financial toll on the economy, in a country still reliant on importing 60 per cent of its foods at high prices. Writing in the *Guardian* five weeks before the election, the journalist Alastair Cooke prophesied that a Conservative victory would be brought about by voters' fears of a 'winter of discontent' characterized by fuel shortages, continued rationing and inflation.[51] In fact, polls showed that the shortage of housing was the most important reason why some working-class voters had switched to the Conservatives; the Tories promised to build far more houses in a far quicker time than Bevan had managed. Many voters considered rationing and price controls reasonable prices to pay for full employment and welfare, and in the event Winston Churchill was returned to Downing Street with a slim majority of just seventeen seats, which the BBC judged a 'disappointment' for his party.[52]

But the Conservatives' victory was not the result of widespread popular disillusion with austerity. Although frustration at Labour's broken housing promises helped them, the Conservatives lost the popular vote in 1951, with more voters casting their ballot in favour of Labour than ever before – even in 1945. Churchill was carried back to Downing Street on a fresh wave of middle-class antipathy to Labour. The Conservatives' slim majority was mainly drawn from voters in affluent constituencies, and from a large middle-class turnout in more socially mixed areas.[53] These middle-class voters, most of whom were employed in senior roles in the private sector, saw themselves as the losers of Labour's regime. They were more likely to have experienced the late 1940s as a period of privation than were working-class people. 'Shortages may be more galling and scarcities less easily acceptable,' concluded Mass Observation, 'if both variety and abundance have commonly been achieved on a balanced budget.'[54] During the fuel crisis of 1947 Mass Observation found that a minority of middle-class people consciously engaged in 'fuel wasting (part political, part spiteful)'. One Mass Observer reported on an elderly woman in south-west London, who 'insists upon using her hall light every night because she hates Mr Shinwell [the same Emanuel Shinwell who had been convicted following the Glasgow riots of 1919, now a Labour minister], and would do anything to get him and the government out of office'.[55] 'If the interwar decades conjured up images of poverty and dole queues for workers,' writes the historian Geoffrey Field, 'for the middle classes they became a lost Arcadia of low taxes and cheap servants.'[56]

Not all middle-class voters fell out of love with Labour. The government remained very popular among public sector workers, including teachers, civil servants, technicians and administrators. Many of those to whom Mass Observation spoke clearly benefited from, and appreciated, Labour's welfare reforms. Some of them shared Norman Lewis's and Philip Gilbert's strong support for egalitarianism. Others were attracted by Labour's promotion of an elite of planners and technical experts, which offered a new and distinct role for the middle class.[57] In 1948 Mass Observation asked people why they considered themselves to be middle class, and how they saw the future. One middle-aged man offered a typical response when he confidently predicted that 'the managerial and intelligentsia part of our class will be much in demand' in the new welfare state.[58] Workers like him saw the welfare state as offering them new opportunities, and not only in career terms. Many clerks, schoolteachers and junior civil servants had struggled to afford school fees or medical bills before the war, and they welcomed Labour's reforms. Middle-class take-up of universal benefits and services was very high, and Mass Observation reported strong support for free secondary education and healthcare.[59]

Those who disliked Labour's programme were those who had managed comfortably with privatized services before the war, and now regretted the loss of their privileged status. 'We've got a Health Scheme,' wrote Nella Last, a housewife married to a small businessman in Barrow-in-Furness, 'and less time for doctors to find out what's wrong with you.' By 1950, she was even more indignant about the 'worry' that free secondary education caused her friends with children.[60] Middle-class families who had previously paid the relatively low fees charged by grammar schools, or captured the few scholarships available, were now faced with increased competition for places at these academically selective secondary schools. '[I]t is heartbreaking to hear of children of good intelligence from good homes who have ambitions say "I wanted to be a doctor etc, but I can't be now because I never passed to the Grammar school,"' wrote a twenty-seven-year-old grammar school teacher in 1949. '[W]hen I see (and teach) some of the children who do (somehow and heaven knows how) pass into our Grammar schools, it certainly makes me think.'[61]

Meanwhile, Labour had lost the confident vision of 1945, when the party had promoted the interests of 'the people' against those of 'vested interests'. The government had encouraged 'workers by hand' and 'workers by brain' to believe that they shared some important interests, by virtue of their common need to work for a living. Labour had been able to build on the experience of total war that these voters had shared. But by 1951 the situation had changed. The collective spirit of war was a fading memory. And many Labour politicians – themselves the products of middle-class homes – believed that there was an important distinction between manual workers and educated non-manual salaried employees. 'I think we are a pretty important class,' declared Labour's Attorney General, Sir Hartley Shawcross, during a widely publicized election address in 1950. 'We have supplied many of the best brains in the professions often because parents have been prepared to make great sacrifices in order to give their children the best possible education.'[62] The top-down nature of Labour's reforms, with its emphasis on managers and planners, emphasized a distinct role for the educated middle class.

Although many middle-class people (Nella Last among them) worried that Labour would abolish private education and healthcare, the government did not do so. Yet they failed to win votes from the middle-class private sector workers and managers who they hoped would be appeased by this caution. Some Labour ministers, Herbert Morrison among them, argued that building up better state provision would lead private provision to decline. But this overlooked the fact that many middle-class people chose private education or healthcare precisely because, as Nella Last or Mass Observation's anonymous schoolteacher suggested, such provision was restricted to only a few. Those who used these private services saw them as an important means of asserting, and maintaining, their 'distinction' from other wage-earners.[63]

Labour's reluctance to erode these privileges reinforced the notion that the middle class was a distinct social group entitled to special treatment. Even the left-winger Nye Bevan agreed that ordinary workers should have cheaper and smaller houses than managers and professionals, advising that managers of the nationalized coal mines be given 'villa-style' houses.[64] Professional and senior white-collar workers were encouraged to believe that they deserved better provision than manual workers, which only aggravated their sense of deprivation when Labour failed to deliver lower taxes, and made them inclined to support the Conservatives, a party unashamedly committed to private enterprise. The wartime alliance between workers by hand and by brain against 'vested interests' was broken.

The 1940s was, in many ways, the heyday of 'the people'. They gained much from collective bargaining in the workplace, and universal provision of social security, education and healthcare. As well as improving their living conditions, full employment granted workers a significant degree of economic power which they could and did use to boost their political strength.

But these gains came at a price. They were conditional on 'the people' accepting an older power relationship that left control of workplaces, and the lion's share of the country's wealth, in the hands of the few. Attlee and his ministers claimed that Britain's social structure was now based on merit rather than birth. Yet as long as economic and political power was concentrated in the hands of a minority – through differential wage rates and selective entry to the universities and the professions – then most people's opportunities would be limited, however hard they worked. Just as the 'people's war' had not been classless, so the 'people's peace' was riven by class.

Interlude III

Setting the People Free

IN 1951 VIV left school to begin work in the local liquorice factory. The newly elected Conservative government had promised in its election manifesto to 'set the people free' from such restrictions as rationing, to deliver 'liberty' (as opposed to the state socialism associated with the Soviet bloc), to reward 'individual effort' and to replace 'class war' and 'envy' with 'abundance' and 'the unity of the English-speaking peoples'. Churchill aimed his appeal squarely at the middle-class housewife, calling for 'thrift and good housekeeping' and berating Labour for creating 'Queuetopia'. The prosperous Britain he promised was alluring – but in reality ordinary wage-earners found affluence elusive throughout the 1950s.

Magazines and Hollywood films promoted new fashions as offering luxury rather than austerity, like Christian Dior's full-skirted 'New Look' dresses. In 1951 *Picture Post*, the popular weekly magazine, proclaimed a 'revolution' in tennis: 'A Sportswoman's New Look has been launched.' The writer applauded the rejection of 'Severe Styles for Serious Sportswomen' – or serious women anywhere; the emphasis was on 'frivolous innovation' rather than functionality, on 'going feminine' rather than being 'mannish', on 'freedom of action' rather than seriousness of purpose.[1] The message was that prosperity was just around the corner. In this unprecedented period of economic growth, all women could apparently aspire to a hitherto upper-middle-class ideal of leisure and pleasure.

For those who, like Viv, felt themselves to be on the margins of this dream, life was only made worse by the suspicion that someone (probably wearing a New Look dress), somewhere (perhaps Paris, possibly Leeds), was having a far better time of it. Clothes rationing had ended in 1949 and by the time Viv left school the browns and

greys of wartime wear were replaced on the fashion pages of magazines by taffeta in Princess Elizabeth's 'favourite shade of blue . . .
exactly matching her eyes'.[2] But these fruits of 'liberty' remained
beyond the reach of thousands of women like Viv, even if they spent
all day producing them on an assembly line.

In 1952 Viv packed in her factory job to become a cinema usherette.
The cinemas were still packing in large audiences, and usherettes got
to watch all the films. 'I loved it!' recalled one woman who, in her
twenties, worked as an usherette in Portsmouth: 'fancy being paid
to do something you enjoyed so much!'[3] The smart uniform added
a touch of glamour, and Viv began to backcomb and bleach her hair
in the style of 'Monroe, Bardot and Mansfield'.[4] There were opportunities to make a bit of extra money, too: 'We had lots of films
about people being lost in the desert,' recalled an usherette who
worked in the 1950s. 'On those nights the manager would tell the
projectionist to turn the heating up because this would mean an
increase in the sale of ice cream. I know it's laughable, but it worked
. . . We usually took it in turns to sell ice cream and in that way
earned a few extra shillings.'[5]

Viv used that trick, too, but her father got wise to the fact she
was pocketing the additional cash from ice-cream sales and turned
up each night to escort her home. After he'd taken most of her 15s
wage, she had just a shilling or two to spend at the local dance hall
– the Kiosk – but 'for two nights' pleasure a week, it wasn't bloody
worth it'. The cinema and the dance hall were still entertaining
thousands of young wage-earners each week, but, as Viv found, they
were often only a partial consolation for hard work.

A different kind of escape came a year later, with the coronation
of Elizabeth II. 'When it came to the coronation of a new young
queen,' recalled Katharine Whitehorn, a recent graduate of Cambridge
University and an aspiring journalist, 'people started talking about a
New Elizabethan Age.'[6] This was the first coronation to be televised:
the royal family – the queen who sported New Look dresses, her
young children and her dashing Greek prince – was a quintessentially
British answer to Hollywood celebrity. Thousands crammed round
television sets to enjoy the pomp and splendour.

For many people, the coronation captured a different memory of the war to the military victories with which Churchill assiduously associated himself. The sociologist Maurice Broady concluded that the coronation was, for lots of Britons, a chance to relive wartime comradeship – or, even more pertinently, to enjoy the chance of an unexpected holiday. His study of working-class districts on Merseyside concluded that many of the organizers were not prompted by strong royalist sentiments, but by a desire to mark how much their lives had changed. Their enjoyment of sweets, cakes, lemonade, beer and dancing harked back to VE Day and was 'fostered by the experience of difficulties and privations which the local people have shared in common. Their recollections of the economic depression during the 1930s are particularly vivid.'[7]

If street parties were a survival of an older form of working-class community, many people – Viv included – hankered after a taste of the new luxuries: the domestic appliances, the cars and the fashionable clothes advertised in every newspaper and on every street hoarding; and a home of their own. Making do was all very well in wartime, but the message of the early 1950s was that affluence and ease were the signifiers of success.

When Viv turned sixteen, she began courting Matt, a local miner. 'Just falling pregnant was a way of escape,' and she and Matt 'had' to get married in 1952. Viv claimed she 'didn't love Matt, not ever'; and her parents were more understanding than she'd expected. Her father advised her not to get married, showing a care for her she'd rarely seen before. 'We'll all just have to muck in one way or another so tha stays at home,' he told her – belying the myth that the 1950s was a repressively conservative decade, in which illegitimate children and their mothers were banished from family life.

But Viv couldn't see a future for herself in her parents' house: 'I wanted independence,' she said, and there was little chance of having that as a single mother, even in the era of the welfare state. The average age of marriage fell dramatically after the Second World War. Many couples didn't see the need to wait, given plentiful work; they didn't have to save for years to begin their life together as their parents had often done. And yet early marriage also testified to the limited pleasures of leisure and work: getting married remained a working-class girl's most likely route out of her parents' home. It was a desire that might just have a happy ending like the fairy tales and the films, with her prince turning her rags into riches, and making her into the queen of her own palace.[8] In the brave new post-war world, such things were meant to be possible.

A home of their own was the dream shared by thousands of young couples in the late 1940s and the 1950s. In their 1951 election campaign, Churchill's Conservatives boasted that they would build 300,000 houses each year.[9] This promise proved highly attractive to thousands of people languishing in Britain's condemned slums. In the early 1950s many voters – regardless of how they had cast their ballot in 1951 – fervently hoped that this was one promise that the government would keep.

8

Communities

IN 1954 TWENTY-SIX-YEAR-OLD Betty Ennis lived in a one-bedroom council flat on the outskirts of Coventry. The daughter of an Iranian mother and a British father, she had ended up in Coventry's Baginton Fields hostel for migrant workers and refugees in 1946, when her father brought his family 'home' from the Middle East. By the beginning of 1954 she was married to Michael Ennis – an Irish labourer who had lived in a neighbouring hostel – and the couple were expecting their third child. Betty eagerly awaited the completion of the nearby Willenhall housing estate, where, the council informed her, the Ennis family would be rehoused. 'I used to come and watch it every day getting built,' said Betty. Eventually, Betty and Michael were told they could choose a three-bedroom house near the centre of the estate. 'When the builder asked me which house do I want, this one or that one? . . . I picked that one.'[1] Here was a rare opportunity to exert some control over their lives – council housing was to help them shape a new and brighter future.

For Betty Ennis and the other two and a half million people who moved into council housing over the next twenty years, their new home was not just a house, but an important step towards independence.[2] Council housing offered freedom from the rules of relatives with whom so many young couples had lodged, from the slum landlords who had taken tenants' rent but never repaired their homes, and from the fear of finding themselves homeless should they complain about their conditions or find themselves in rent arrears. Most welcomed the security and space this afforded them. But during the 1950s, just as tenants were settling into their new homes, successive Conservative governments were distancing themselves from Bevan's commitment to constructing socially mixed communities.

They sought to revive the pre-war understanding of council housing as accommodation for the poorest, and assiduously promoted home ownership. The new estates and neighbourhoods became communities because of the efforts their inhabitants made, often in the face of government indifference or hostility.

Britain was on the move in the 1950s. In 1951, three years before the Ennises moved into their new house, 18 per cent of households rented their home from a council or from one of the corporations that managed the twenty-two post-war new towns. Ten years later, Betty Ennis's family was one of the 25 per cent of households to do so, a figure that rose to almost one-third of British households by the 1970s. Thousands of others bought their own homes. In 1951, 31 per cent of householders were owner-occupiers, but 44 per cent owned their own homes ten years later. The proportion of households renting from a private landlord fell dramatically from 51 per cent in 1951 to 31 per cent in 1961, and had sunk to 19 per cent by the 1970s.[3]

During the 1950s, planners and social scientists continued to harbour Nye Bevan's faith that new neighbourhoods could become vibrant, socially mixed, self-reliant communities. Although this faith was not new to the post-war years, it heralded a new and widespread confidence that working-class people could teach the rest of the country a thing or two about community. The Blitz had cemented the idea that an unquenchable collective spirit defined working-class life. In 1952 Lewis Womersley, Sheffield's City Architect, waxed lyrical to a conference of town planners about 'the friendliness of the slums', and warned that new neighbourhoods must protect this vibrant community life.[4]

Social scientists set out to investigate working-class life and how best to plan new communities in areas as diverse as inner-city Liverpool and suburban Oxford. They found much to support Womersley's claim. In 1957 social researchers Michael Young and Peter Willmott published *Family and Kinship in East London*, a groundbreaking study based on their interviews with, and observations of, Bethnal Green's residents. Young and Willmott highlighted that residents enjoyed close ties of friendship and kinship with their neighbours. They warned that these residents deserved consultation about where they would like to live, revealing that 'few people want to leave the East End'. They criticized the policy of slum clearance for failing to consider people's strong 'sense of belonging' to the areas in which they lived. Surveys conducted in areas as diverse as Banbury and Sheffield discovered that many people did not want to move away from the inner cities, though they wanted better quality housing.[5]

These researchers' findings have been influential – perhaps too influential – in creating an image of what 'traditional' working-class life was like. Young and Willmott's study became a bestselling paperback and has never been out of print since its publication. But these researchers overlooked one vital aspect of working-class 'community': work. Ann Lanchbury, the daughter of a car worker and a former servant, grew up in a council house on a Coventry street named Pinley Fields. What she loved about it 'was that it had life': women chatting on doorsteps, children playing in the street, and a stream of pedestrians and cyclists on their way to or from the local factories that gave work to Ann's brother and their neighbours.[6] The playwright Shelagh Delaney was to say something similar about her home town, Salford: 'the streets were full of life,' she told Ken Russell in a television documentary shot in the early 1960s, precisely because people had work and shops locally available.[7] By focusing on single neighbourhoods, and the relations between people on a single street, the researchers of the 1950s implied that working-class life took place in hermetically sealed neighbourhoods that were entirely shaped by the virtues or otherwise of those who lived in them. The researchers were well intentioned, and highlighted many important aspects of working-class life, not least the need to consult working-class residents about the shape that new neighbourhoods should take. But they paid scant attention to the ways in which employers, landlords and policymakers shaped the quality of life in all neighbourhoods, new or old. They neglected the reality that the reciprocal childcare, loans and companionship that impressed Lewis Womersley were provoked by poverty. They missed what really made people working class: the fact that they lacked power.

Terry Rimmer could have told them about this. In the late 1950s

Terry was living with his mother in a small terraced house in a working-class district of south Liverpool that they rented from a private landlord. Terry was in his early twenties. He'd recently returned from National Service, having stayed on in the army for an additional third year 'because we needed the money at home'. His mother, a war widow, was a factory worker with three younger children to keep. Shortly after moving into their new home, Terry and his mother discovered that their neighbours had no electricity so Terry, a burly railway labourer, 'punched a hole in the wall so they could [use our supply to] watch television'.[8] People helped themselves and each other because these were important ways of getting by and enjoying some of the new temptations of post-war life – of which television was an important one.

While social investigators enthused over neighbours' willingness to lend a hand, those who had to survive on such strategies took a less romantic view. Some would have preferred more privacy – or at least less dependence on the neighbours' goodwill. Terry's own experiences led him to treat neighbours with cautious respect. As a child, Terry had heard neighbours gossip about his mother 'because she was a single parent . . . and she had a boyfriend'. Those who did enjoy good relationships with neighbours or relatives still valued having some independence from them. In 1954 seventy-year-old Sheila Adams was keen to move from Liverpool's inner city to a council flat in the suburb of West Derby, where one of her daughters lived. 'What I want,' she told a visiting social scientist, 'is comfort and peace and knowing there's relations nearby.'[9] Most pensioners wanted to live independently, near but not with their children if possible, or with easy access to domestic help or nursing should they require it.[10]

People wanted different things from their home depending on their stage of life. Older people were often reluctant to leave behind friends and relatives in the inner cities, fearing isolation on new estates. But many younger people were delighted to escape the streets where their parents lived. In 1957 the social scientist D.V. Donnison found that most manual workers, clerks and shop workers moved because they 'wanted more room'. In 1955 social scientists asked almost 600 families in inner-city Liverpool about where they'd like to live. Older people wanted a flat (easier to manage than a house) near the city centre. Those with young children wanted to move to the suburbs. They wanted their children to grow up in a 'healthy' environment, 'with clean air, and a park to play in', as one mother wistfully explained.[11]

Those who were most desperate to move wanted to escape the claustrophobic community in which they lived. Some were unhappily living with a tyrannical father or mother; others had attracted disapproval by marrying someone of a different religion or race.[12] Overcrowding and poverty led some residents of the slums to define community narrowly, identifying and excluding 'outsiders' from the limited support on offer. In casting such judgements, they could make a meagre claim to authority. Bill Rainford's parents were on the receiving end of this. They were typical of those who wanted to move: a young couple who were sharing a home with their parents, siblings and their own young children. Mr and Mrs Rainford were also a 'mixed marriage': she was Protestant, he was Catholic, in a city still riven with sectarian prejudice; they shared Mrs Rainford's family home but her parents could barely bring themselves to speak to their son-in-law. 'They wanted,' said Bill, 'to get us out of that environment.' When Mr and Mrs Rainford moved into a prefabricated house on the city's southern outskirts, their new neighbours included both Protestants and Catholics, united by a desire to 'start a new life', in Bill's words. There were bigots in working-class communities, but there were also many who seized the opportunities presented by post-war reconstruction to get out and start again.

The Rainfords and the Ennises were fortunate. In 1954, when Betty Ennis was rehoused, millions of people still hankered after council accommodation. This was particularly so in Britain's largest industrial cities, like Glasgow, Liverpool and Newcastle, where housing conditions were especially poor. Here, as in Birmingham, Leeds and Manchester, thousands of residents languished on the long housing waiting lists that local authorities introduced in the face of heavy demand. Most of those who wanted a new house or flat were tenants of private landlords, living in desperately overcrowded and insanitary conditions.[13] In 1955 Mr and Mrs Mahoney of Liverpool lived in a small terraced house on Mount Vernon Street, a major thoroughfare between the university and the city centre. When social scientists visited them there they found the couple and their three children living in near darkness. Their window frames were rotten and the landlord had 'nailed up' the windows rather than repair them. In the single bedroom, the floorboards were weak; the 'legs of the bed come through the ceiling'. The Mahoneys were suffering no worse than the majority of their neighbours.[14]

To those living in such conditions, council housing offered almost unbelievable luxury. Council houses built before the mid-1950s tended to be of far higher quality than privately rented housing – or indeed many owner-occupied houses. Bevan's Housing Act of 1948 stipulated generous provision for council houses, with spacious rooms and an indoor bathroom. In 1957 Donnison's national survey found that most would-be home-movers 'are likely to prefer the larger newer, and better-equipped dwellings available to the Council tenant', rather than taking their chances in the private sector.[15] By 1964, 80 per cent of households renting from a local authority enjoyed sole use of a sink, a fixed bath, a washbasin, a hot water supply and a toilet. Only 61 per cent of owner-occupiers had these amenities and only 57 per cent of private tenants.[16] Commercial builders and landlords, who were primarily concerned to make a profit, lacked any incentive to modernize their accommodation at a time when many people were desperate for any kind of home.

Churchill's Conservative government kept its election promise to build 300,000 houses each year, but did so by returning to a pre-war conception of council housing as inferior to private building. It relaxed Bevan's stringent regulations, encouraging local authorities to scrimp on space and to use cheaper materials in order to meet housing targets. It also lifted controls on private building. 'Local authorities and local authorities alone can clear and rehouse the slums,' acknowledged the Housing Minister, Harold Macmillan, in 1954, 'while the general housing need can be met, as it was to a great extent before the war, by private enterprise.' Home ownership, he declared, encouraged 'independence'.[17]

The millions of people who needed a home disagreed with Macmillan. Many of them considered council houses better than private accommodation, both in quality and in the security they offered. Christine and Jack Elliott were among them. In 1951 they were renting a tiny, dilapidated cottage in Willenhall village, on the outskirts of Coventry. Jack, an unskilled factory worker, was employed at one of the city's car plants, while Christine worked as a cleaner at a local hotel. Home should have provided respite from their exhausting jobs, but it did not. By 1951, there were six occupants of the cottage: Christine and Jack, Christine's invalid mother and her increasingly frail father, and Christine and Jack's daughters, nine-year-old Carol and seven-year-old Pauline. There was no indoor lavatory or electricity. 'I had my dad, my mother in bed, my husband and two children to look after,' said Christine. 'I often wonder how I got through.'[18]

With no chance of a council tenancy (the Willenhall estate, where Betty Ennis would find a home, was still at the planning stage) the Elliotts jumped at the chance to buy a new house from a local builder. Their three-bedroom house cost them £1,500. They were lucky that Jack's father, a postmaster, gave them a deposit of £500, but paying back the mortgage relied on both Jack and Christine remaining in regular work for the next twenty-five years – something that didn't prove possible when, in the late 1950s, Jack began to get sick with increasing regularity, meaning Christine had to take on more paid work. Christine would have preferred a proper bathroom; this house had only 'a toilet outside' – an inconvenience outlawed in post-war council houses. But in 1951 'we were desperate – there was no houses to be had.'[19] In 1960 one-fifth of home owners nationwide would have preferred to rent.[20]

For those who did get a council house, the event was a memorable and happy one. Particularly noticeable is the effect that the move had on children. Their delight and their vivid recollections of it reveal the extent to which worry over housing permeated family life in the 1950s. Vera Goldsmith grew up in Liverpool, where her parents shared a 'one-up, one-down' terraced house in the inner city with their young daughter and her maternal grandmother. Vera's mother found the situation particularly difficult; her daughter was acutely aware that 'it really got her down'. When Vera was ten a letter arrived from the council:

my mum was working at Smithdown Road Hospital [as a waitress] but my Nin [grandmother] saw the crest on the letterhead and she knew it was from the Council and she said, 'this must be for the house', so she ran with me all the way down to Smithdown Road Hospital with this letter and got my mum. She showed her the letter and she had been allocated this house in Lee Park estate, so my Nin got the bus with me up to Lee Park to see this house . . . we were all excited over it.[21]

Dorcas Kelly was a teenager when her family moved into one of the 5,000 prefabs in south Liverpool's Belle Vale. 'The family all under one roof – our roof! A lovely new home of a higher standard than most working people could enjoy! A fitted kitchen with a fridge!'[22] Council housing offered thousands of people the chance of their own home – and a good home at that. But once they moved in, the hard work of making their new neighbourhoods into communities began.

Those who moved on to new estates in the 1950s found themselves in strange and inhospitable landscapes. Vera Goldsmith's first impression of Lee Park was that 'everywhere was all muddy', making it difficult to keep houses clean, or to get about easily. The planners hadn't anticipated the needs of pedestrians, optimistically envisioning neighbourhoods of car owners – but few council tenants could afford a car in the 1950s. On Coventry's new Willenhall estate, which bordered the Elliotts' village, roads became busy with traffic cutting through to local car factories; but no paved paths joined the estate to the existing village, where the school and the bus stop were. This meant that Betty Ennis had to take her children to school across a muddy field 'which was difficult with a big pram', and walk back home across this same, unlit field when she returned from working the evening shift at a local factory.

The estates were often situated away from the city centres and inner-city neighbourhoods that the inhabitants knew well. In 1954 social investigators visited a large council estate in Sheffield. Although the estate was by that time twenty years old, and the residents lived less than a mile from the city, 'they were . . . almost completely isolated from other residential districts.' The estate was surrounded by 'waste ground' and the railway line divided its inhabitants from the rest of Sheffield. Local authorities only had limited funds with which to construct the estates and its location meant that the land was cheap; this was to dictate the situation of many other post-war estates, too.[23]

Residents felt both fenced in and isolated. In 1955 ten-year-old Lorna Sage and her parents moved from her grandparents' vicarage in the Shropshire village of Hanmer into a small new council estate on the edge of the village. 'The council put up concrete posts and a chain-link fence,' she recalled, but 'it wasn't a boundary you could believe in.'[24] Just beyond estates like hers was the countryside; a sign of unplanned existence, out of the reach of politicians, but also a reminder that the residents were on the edge of society, and could easily be forgotten.

The new estates were built on a shaky foundation: politicians' faith in private enterprise to deliver jobs, shops and recreation. In 1945 the New Towns Commission planned eighteen new towns, all to be situated in areas where land was plentiful and cheap, so as to attract employers. In 1946 Attlee's government introduced subsidies to encourage manufacturing firms to locate plants on new industrial estates in those areas that had been hardest hit by the 1930s depression: Clydeside, Tyneside, Merseyside and South Wales. In the Midlands and the south-east, the government hoped to lure businesses away from London by offering employers cheap land close to new towns with good road links to major ports and cities. 'Their special purpose,' declared the Ministry of Housing in a report on the new towns, 'is to provide homes with work near at hand.'[25] The same could be said of the new estates.

The reality proved different. Labour's subsidies did not attract as many firms as the government had hoped. Those that did appear were often light manufacturing firms that preferred to employ cheap young and women workers rather than adult men.[26] In Liverpool, the industrial estate at Speke, several miles south of the city centre, provided very little work until the early 1960s when Ford arrived. In 1955 Peggy Brooke was living with her husband and their two teenage children in a dilapidated, privately rented house in Liverpool's inner city. She would have loved to move to a new council house at Speke but concluded that it 'is too far from [my] family's work'.[27] Meanwhile, London County Council was busy resettling the residents of Bethnal Green on a new council development at 'Greenleigh' (Young and Willmott's pseudonym) in Essex. But at the end of the 1950s, almost half the men who had moved there continued to work in the East End.[28]

Then, in 1957, the Conservative government cut the industrial subsidies that Attlee's administration had introduced. This was part of a raft of cost-cutting measures intended to reduce public spending and to stimulate the private rental market. But the cut consigned thousands of existing and planned estates to a future as dormitories, whose residents would remain reliant on distant town and city centres for work. In 1959 tenants of Manchester City Council who had been housed on the Langley estate – over five miles north of the city centre – endured daily commutes of up to two hours, 'industrial expansion not occurring locally as had been hoped'.[29] People felt tied to the inner cities not only by family and friends, but the need to work.[30] While successive governments promoted council estates as offering new, planned communities, they did little to provide the jobs that residents badly needed in order to pay their rent and enjoy whatever amenities the local area had to offer.

The lack of local work affected women as well as men. With wage-earners having to travel long distances each day, women found themselves spending hours alone at home. Few had relatives or friends close by to call upon, and there were hardly any local shops, so making ends meet could be a burden. In 1960 Margaret Jones and her family moved from inner-city Liverpool to the new Lee Park estate on the city's southern outskirts. 'I find shopping very frustrating in this area,' she complained in 1963. 'Food is definitely dearer. Only mobile shops.'[31] The cost of food was important, for living expenses on the estates were often higher than residents had anticipated. In 1946 a council tenant was expected to pay an average of 9s rent per week, but the rents paid by private tenants were often lower, reflecting the parlous state of most privately rented accommodation.[32] Bus fares were an unexpected and unwelcome cost as those who moved had been told that the work would come to them.

The residents themselves gradually created the amenities they needed. The neighbourhoods became communities, but only because of the residents' hard work. Tenants were forced to act by the short-sighted vision of the planners, and the reluctance of politicians to invest properly in the new neighbourhoods they had built. Belle Vale's tenants 'built the Labour Club themselves', recalled Bill Rainford. 'There was nothing there. There was one bloke who was a builder, and he organised the others.' In Willenhall, Betty Ennis and her neighbours volunteered as lollipop ladies for the local primary school until the council installed proper traffic lights. Residents' associations sprang up: Michael and Betty Ennis were among the founders of Willenhall's association.

As neighbours got to know each other, some turned into friends. Their spacious houses took the place of streets in social life.[33] Betty and Michael Ennis lived too far from Coventry's dance halls and pubs to go out as often as they would have liked. During the week, they stayed in and watched television with their children. But each Saturday night, 'we went to a different house. And we'd have sand-wiches or curry and rice or spaghetti or something like that. And drink and put the records on and we'd have a dance in the house.'

The planners should not shoulder all the blame, since they were not responsible for the changing political climate.[34] In the late 1940s it was perfectly understandable that planners should assume that government investment would sustain the estates and help them to grow. Bevan and his supporters enthusiastically advocated the benefits of parks, libraries and leisure centres. But after 1951, when the Conservatives returned to government, this changed. The government increased house building, but at the expense of constructing public amenities. From 1954 the line hardened: Harold Macmillan announced that local authorities would only be concerned with slum clearance; general housing needs, he argued, could best be met by private enterprise.[35] The Conservative manifesto for the 1955 general election announced the party's intention to establish 'a property-owning democracy', and the subsequent 1956 Housing Act was designed to encourage this.[36] The Act obliged local authorities to focus new housing on the residents in greatest need. Those voters who could afford to buy their own home were to be encouraged to do so. Municipal councils were given the power to sell off their housing stock, although very few did so. Council housing became a less attractive option: local authorities used cheaper materials, and focused on building housing as quickly as possible. The Conservatives jettisoned Bevan's vision of socially mixed communities through investment in high-quality homes and public spaces, in favour of the quick construction of high-rise flats.

Social divisions began to fracture the new communities. Municipal councils sometimes exacerbated these. Two tiers of council housing became apparent – that built before the mid-1950s, and that built after – and councils chose who to house where. Many municipal authorities, including London County Council, assumed that the families who came from the inner-city slums were likely to misbehave and concentrated them in the poorest housing available.[37] Elaine Leather moved into a council house on Coventry's Willenhall estate in 1958. By this time, four years after Betty Ennis had chosen her house there, certain streets had gained a reputation for being 'rough'. When Elaine Leather was told where she would be housed, she breathed a sigh of relief that it wasn't one of the roads which 'had a bad name' for being 'dirty . . . [and] full of rubbish, litter'. At first, Elaine was among those who tut-tutted at the behaviour of families who lived on these streets – 'there were lots of children, they were all dirty' – but after living on the estate for a few months she came to believe that 'the council sometimes caused this' by accommodating large families in houses that were too small for them, and placing them together on a single street.[38] Many councillors continued to believe that those in need could be divided between the 'deserving' and the feckless.

Among those who faced the worst housing problems were Commonwealth immigrants. The number of people entering Britain from the Caribbean and Asia increased after 1948, as a result of the Attlee government's recruitment drive for the new manufacturing industries. Many of these immigrants had been brought up to believe that Britain was their 'mother country'; some had fought for the Allies during the Second World War. 'We were born British,' said Leo Jones, a black Barbadian. Born in 1933, he came to Britain in 1951 'to improve my cricket' and get work. With few job opportunities in the Caribbean islands, and historic links to both Britain and the United States, many islanders grew up assuming they would spend a few years working abroad. Leo, who had worked as a labourer on a plantation after leaving school, was among them; he came to work at a factory in Reading. 'In Barbados you grew up calling white people master this and master that,' he said; he wanted a different sort of life. 'I came over thinking it was for five years'; fifty years later he was still there.

At first life was very hard: getting work was easy but 'people used to put up signs [that] said "room for rent" and as soon as they see your black face they would say "Sorry – it's already gone."' So Leo and his immigrant workmates felt 'you have to look for your own place'. Leo bought his first house – one in a small Victorian terrace – just two years after moving to Britain, from 'a chap that owned all these houses. He gave me the house at £2 a week, paying £600 with no interest', because he liked Leo's cricketing ability (and was making a handsome profit). Leo set up the Reading West Indies Cricket team, and white factory teams began to play against them. 'We became so friendly that people were begging you to come and live at their place.' All the same, Leo knew there were certain boundaries not to be crossed: 'if any white girl or woman was to come into a pub where the black people were they'd be called prostitutes.' He married a Barbadian nurse in 1958. 'She was the most beautiful Black woman I ever seen in my life.'[39]

Most immigrants found themselves living in working-class areas – even if they considered themselves to be middle class in origin. Esme Lancaster had a more difficult time finding work than Leo Jones did, for she had higher aspirations. She was a young Jamaican schoolteacher who came to Britain in 1954 because 'you needed English qualifications to become a senior teacher back home'. Esme was black, but her training had been partially paid for by a paternalistic white plantation family for whom she had worked as a nanny.

In the Caribbean, hierarchies of race intertwined with class relations. In Jamaica Esme was treated as socially inferior to white people, but at the same time she commanded respect as an educated woman. In Britain she discovered that her education counted for little or nothing. Esme considered herself 'lucky' to find accommodation with a family friend in Birmingham: one room in shared lodgings in a working-class area of the city. Work was harder to come by. Although there was a shortage of teachers in Britain, many head-teachers and local councils considered that black immigrants would not be up to the task. 'I was sent to one school and the headmaster just stared,' she said. 'I wasn't given a class, I just sat in the staffroom all day. He wouldn't put me in front of a class.' The following Monday 'I received a phone call from the local authority. The school governors had complained about me being in the school. So the placement was over.' The racism shown towards Esme Jones by the headteachers of Birmingham schools meant she was unable to get the teaching experience that her training required.

Esme was reluctant to return to settle in Jamaica without the qualifications she needed. On the island, the legacy of slavery remained strong, the existence of plantations, still headed by wealthy white families, a constant reminder of why racial hierarchies were so perva-sive there. While Britain was racist, Esme felt she hadn't explored the full potential of a country that had near-full employment, and nothing like the strict racial hierarchy she had encountered back home. Like Leo Jones, she believed her stay in Britain would be temporary, but hoped that, as the years passed, it might be possible for her to gain the training she wanted to pursue her ambitions back in Jamaica. In the interim, she trained as a social worker in Leicester, and eventually became a foster mother in the late 1950s, looking after the children of black parents whose own accommodation was overcrowded, damp, infested with insects or insanitary. 'In those days, many West Indians were sending for their children, but they had nowhere to put them,' she said. 'If social workers or schools found out then the children would go into care. So I began looking after the children of people I knew, and then later social services would send children to me.' This job paid just enough for her to afford the rent on a home of her own. By 1960 'I realized that maybe I wouldn't go back. It became harder once I had the [foster] children: where could I leave them? Suddenly I had responsibilities here.'[40]

Racism and sectarian prejudice shaped many people's housing preferences. In 1955 many inner-city Liverpudlians wanted to move house because they disliked 'the coloureds' living nearby. Protestant residents remained bitter about the influx of 'new' Catholic tenants who had been moved there from the dockland slums twenty years earlier.[41] It was from this area that Ellen Halliburton, a white twenty-five-year-old, fled with her black boyfriend Alf when her father discovered they were courting and threw his daughter out. After fruitlessly confronting several hostile landlords, they were offered a handful of suburban council flats, but turned them down in favour of 'a slummy flat' near the city centre because of the hostility that prospective neighbours showed them.[42] Their experience was far from unusual: a study of London showed that mixed-race couples encountered hostility from their neighbours and their landlords.[43]

But policymakers – particularly the Conservatives – were often responsible for causing or exacerbating racism. In the summer of 1958 race riots erupted in the inner-city district of St Ann's, Nottingham, and in London's Notting Hill. One catalyst was the lack of housing. In 1957 the government had passed a Rent Act that removed all rent controls from unfurnished properties with a rateable value in excess of £40. Landlords could also have rent controls removed from empty properties worth less than £40. Ministers argued that this would give more impetus to the private housing market and encourage landlords to reinvigorate those inner-city areas where people still wanted to live. In reality, profiteering landlords flourished, among them, London's infamous Peter Rachman, who bought up dilapidated houses, evicted white tenants, kept the accommodation empty in order to have rent controls removed, and then took on recent immigrants as new tenants. At a time when black migrants found it hard to get housing, Rachman was able to charge them exorbitant rents for overcrowded and insanitary conditions.[44] In the summer of 1958 the shortage of affordable housing was one reason behind the frustration of those white youths who launched violent attacks on local black residents.[45] Both St Ann's and Notting Hill housed a large number of young white men who were either un-employed or employed in low-paid casual work; not only were they missing out on housing, but on any sign of post-war affluence.

Some politicians deliberately stoked their constituents' fears about immigration. If poor housing and youth unemployment played their part in sparking the violence, so too did some white residents' virulent dislike of black men courting white women. In both St Ann's and in Notting Hill, young white men's violent attacks initially focused on mixed-race couples.[46] But local politicians were often guilty of inflaming these tensions by suggesting both that there were only a limited number of jobs or houses to go round, and that immigrants deserved neither. In 1964 residents of London County Council's Loughborough estate signed a petition protesting against the allocation of a flat to a black railway worker. The petition was organized and presented by local Conservative parliamentary candidate Kenneth Payne, who argued that people 'who were born and bred in this country should have first choice'.[47] The following year, a dispute erupted between London County Council and Conservative-controlled Mildenhall Council in Cambridgeshire over racial discrimination against black Londoners. London County Council gave financial support to several firms wishing to move to Mildenhall, in a bid to relieve demand on the capital's housing supply. When it became clear that black Londoners were among the workers hoping to move, some of Mildenhall's councillors attempted to institute a colour bar.[48] Trevor Hagger, the Conservative vice-chairman of Mildenhall Council, told journalists that 'They do not have the same standards we have . . . They buy all the property and sleep ten to a room.'[49] However, when London County Council threatened to withdraw financial support if Hagger's 'obnoxious opinions' became policy, local people wrote to the newspapers to disown his opinion that they 'would not be happy' with black neighbours. In this case, immigrants were bringing new homes and jobs to the area, and the council's racist sentiments found little sympathy with residents. Mildenhall Council reluctantly withdrew its colour bar – but quietly established a quota to limit the number of black residents.[50]

As Ellen Halliburton – herself a white, working-class woman – showed, not everyone who grew up in the inner cities was racist. Far from it: many working-class districts were the reception areas for immigrants; tolerance and adaptability were demanded of both old and new residents to a level that was rarely required of the suburban middle class. And the status of immigrants themselves was never entirely homogeneous: class played a part in how they were perceived and treated, as Clare Stevens discovered. As a young woman, she worked in a shop in a middle-class suburb close to Bristol

University. One of Clare's regular customers let a room to an Indian lodger 'and I got to know him and he introduced me to the tennis club I belonged to.' Belonging to a tennis club was a step up for this working-class girl. She enjoyed socializing with the students and young professionals she met there, and quickly became attracted to an Indian student. The feeling was mutual, and the couple courted for two years in Clare's early twenties. Clare 'was quite proud to be going out with him because he was very intelligent and he went to Bristol University'. His status as a middle-class student may also have helped keep her parents quiet: 'I think my father was a bit put out but he never said anything.'[51] Courting a university student with a professional career ahead of him was a different proposition to going out with a sailor with no fixed abode, as Ellen Halliburton had done. The colour of his skin still mattered, but class was important too.

There was no single 'white working-class' attitude to race. In 1960 Robert Colls was a teenager in the small Tyneside town of South Shields, a white, working-class boy who made it to grammar school, living in a street of Tyneside flats (in which a small terraced house is divided into a ground floor and an upstairs flat). But 'this was a working class that wasn't all white', for many Yemeni seamen had settled in the area, living in lodging houses and so slightly separate from family life. 'Not everyone was friends with them,' Colls recalled, 'but there again, not everyone was friends with everybody else.'[52]

The riots of 1958 sparked government and university-led enquiries into immigration and its consequences. Some of these reached surprising conclusions. A study of a Bristol estate found that white residents who lived close to black tenants were less likely to feel hostile towards immigrants, and that the shared experience of parenting young children forged some friendships between black and white mothers.[53] That was Betty Ennis's experience in Coventry. Her Iranian ancestry made her feel conspicuous in the city centre, particularly in the 1950s, when the number of immigrants resident there was very low. On one of her shopping trips, 'a boy followed me calling "nigger, nigger" . . . I felt like a stranger.' She felt more comfortable back on her estate where 'I knew everyone and they knew me', and where her friends included white Coventrians as well as recent migrants from other parts of Britain and from overseas.

Betty Ennis's experience of estate life was made easier by Coventry Council's sensitive planning strategy. Coventry was a Labour authority that received a large amount of government investment during Attlee's term in office, to help its people recover from the terrible Blitz of 1940. The council poured this money into the city centre – where a large theatre and shopping precinct were opened – but also into those neighbourhoods where ordinary workers lived. Coventry Council added mobile classrooms to Willenhall's two primary schools to cater for the influx of children from the Baginton hostels where Betty and Michael Ennis had first lived. Consequently, the large number of migrants in the area did not lead to overcrowded class-rooms or resentful parents. By the time the hostels' inhabitants began to move on to the Willenhall estate, many of them – including Betty Ennis – already knew some of the established residents of the village. The council began building Willenhall's shopping precinct shortly after the first houses were constructed on the new estate, and made clear that these shops were meant for all Willenhall's residents, not just the estate's tenants. As a result, many of Willenhall's established working-class residents welcomed the new estate. Christine Elliott hoped that 'the estate was going to give our children homes when they got married'. Christine's daughter Carol was a teenager by this stage, and was 'just really excited because we'd never had shops or many young people around before'.[54] In this way, tension between established residents and newer migrants was avoided.

Relations between working-class council tenants and their middle-class neighbours were frequently more fraught. While owner-occupiers in Willenhall were sanguine about the new estate in their midst, middle-class owner-occupiers often worried that council housing would reduce the value of their homes. In the 1930s some of Oxford's middle-class residents had constructed two walls to divide their prop-erties from the small Cutteslowe council estate built nearby, with the support of Conservative councillors. Tenants faced a lengthy walk to nearby shops and the main thoroughfare into the city. Oxford's Labour council finally demolished the Cutteslowe Walls in 1958, in the face of vociferous opposition from the home owners.[55]

Yet just as the Cutteslowe Walls were being destroyed, middle-class opposition to new housing developments was growing elsewhere. In reserving council housing for the poorest, the Conservatives' 1956 Housing Act exacerbated home owners' suspicions that council tenants would be undesirable neighbours.[56] In 1963 sociologists asked Luton's factory workers: 'What is the boundary between the working class and the middle class?' Andrew Brown spoke for many when he cited housing as important: 'Well here's a case in Luton. There was a private estate and a council estate and the private built a brick wall to separate them. That's typical of how people look at themselves.'[57]

The Act also kindled resentment among those taxpayers who felt they were paying for welfare benefits from which they would never personally benefit. Across the country, middle-class owner-occupiers and tenants complained to provincial newspapers about the feckless-ness of working-class council tenants. 'Working class people, with their subsidized houses . . . look down on us professional classes, who have to live in top floor or basement flats for which we pay exorbitant rents in order to keep them in the luxuries they demand,' wrote Gertrude Jordan of Hove to the Brighton *Argus*.[58] Such senti-ments were reminiscent of the grievances expressed by ratepayers in the early 1930s over the cost of unemployment benefit, or by those middle-class voters who in 1951 had argued that post-war welfare reforms cost them dear. In the late 1950s, as in these earlier years, their complaints had no economic justification. Rather, their griev-ances were based on a strong sense that their hard work and social position entitled them to enjoy better living standards than their working-class neighbours. The Conservatives' selective use of benefits exacerbated their anger. There was an echo of the early 1930s, when the National government's very selective use of benefits had encour-aged taxpayers to scrutinize whether anyone really 'deserved' help more than them.

Both Conservative and Labour politicians encouraged middle-class residents to 'look at themselves' as having a distinct and important role to play. Those post-war housing pioneers who called for council housing to create 'mixed' communities often had a hierarchical vision of community in mind – one in which the middle class took a leading role. We have seen that Attlee's Labour government assumed that managers and professionals would require better housing than their workers. In the 1950s municipal councils, middle-class residents and Conservative politicians often went further, by blaming many of the problems of the early estates on a lack of middle-class leadership. In 1953 the rector of Crawley New Town wrote to *The Times* to complain that 'higher income groups are not being attracted . . . in a sufficient proportion'. This, he claimed, was leading to a 'deficiency of local leadership'.[59] Liverpool's City Architect and the city's Director of Housing attributed a lack of local employment on the Speke estate to 'the lack of suitable housing accommodation for key men to act as instructors of new operatives'.[60]

When Harold Macmillan became Minister for Housing in 1951 he put pressure on local authorities and new town corporations to sell off some of their housing stock in order to attract the middle class.[61] But many middle-class residents showed little interest in providing community leadership and, regardless of the quality of accommodation they were offered, rapidly exchanged their new neighbourhood's replica of a village for the real thing. In Worcester, social scientist Janet Madge discovered that large houses and gardens were not the only reason why many of the town's salaried professionals chose to live outside the city's boundaries; some did so because 'they feel that it raises their status'.[62] Far from recognizing that this desire for social distance posed a more pervasive threat to 'community' than working-class residents' behaviour, policymakers simply pandered to it in their building plans.

In 1962 journalist Bill Rogers visited Kirkby, a new 'urban district' on Merseyside. He found 'housewives' blues' and 'bored and frustrated teenagers'. However determined and enthusiastic the new inhabitants might be, they could never entirely overcome the problems of the estates and new towns. Their out-of-town location meant that family and neighbourhood networks were broken up, with particularly severe consequences for women, who, as Bill Rogers suggested, could experience great isolation. After 1956 these districts increasingly became stigmatized as sink estates for the poor, rather than as new communities for the people.

Yet after conducting extensive interviews, Rogers concluded: 'Problems? Kirkby has them in abundance. But they are mostly growing pains.'[63] Despite the neglect of the Conservative governments of the 1950s, many estates were flourishing. 'A generation has now grown up at Dagenham,' researcher Peter Willmott was able to report by 1963. The large London County Council estate he visited had been built in the 1920s. In its early years, the estate had shared 'all the initial inadequacies – the lack of local industry, schools, transport and the rest, the "one age-group" population' that investigators found on post-war estates. But by the early 1960s, 'extended families . . . have grown up . . . on the estate, and so have local networks of neighbours.'[64]

The residents of Dagenham and elsewhere had worked hard to turn muddy fields with houses but few amenities into vibrant communities. Their commitment demonstrated just how enthusiastic millions of people were at escaping the dilapidated housing of the inner cities and the power of private landlords. Also important was the availability of local work. Communities could not be created out of residents' determination alone. If people had long and expensive journeys to work, they could not invest time, energy or money in their new neighbourhoods. By 1960, two-thirds of Dagenham's workers were employed in local factories, shops and offices. Their ability to earn a living close to home enabled them to afford the rent on their comfortable council house and to have a bit extra – enough to visit ageing parents left behind in the East End, buy home furnishings and enjoy the local cinema and dance hall.[65] For those of the post-war generation who could live close to work, council housing offered unprecedented security and comfort; but if the work ever dried up, their situation would radically alter.

Despite their frustrations and annoyances, Betty and Michael Ennis knew themselves to be lucky. Those who moved into council housing experienced a new level of comfort, but also a degree of control over their lives; ultimately, their landlords were accountable to the voters, whereas private landlords had been accountable to no one. But ordinary workers' housing was never any post-war government's most important priority. Labour was busy trying to provide jobs and welfare services; the Conservatives focused on reviving private sector housing. And all the governments between 1945 and 1960 invested time and money in accommodating managers and employers, whose presence in the new communities was believed to be crucial, and to rely on superior housing. Consequently, as the 1950s drew to a close, millions of people remained in overcrowded slums. On the eve of the 1964 general election, the *Daily Mirror* published a picture on its front page of a woman hanging out her washing in a decrepit inner-city backyard. The headline summed up the dashed hopes of the last nineteen years: 'Is This the Promised Land?'[66]

Interlude IV

Love and Marriage

B Y 1956, VIV was a mother. She knew she had a lot to be thankful for: Matt didn't earn much as a miner but he was in regular work and was 'thoughtful and helpful'. He 'was going to work steadily and bringing in money so we weren't poor'. Matt was a good provider. He was in secure work, and benefiting from the gradual increase in wages that manual workers had experienced since the late 1930s. He was also considerate of his family: he gave most of his wages to Viv for housekeeping. The couple were able to 'make do with what we had and we could go out when we wanted', which Viv knew made her life better than her mother's had been in the bleak 1930s. Viv's mother wanted her daughter to have an easier time of it; the house that Matt and Viv rented was one that 'my mother got me' by speaking to the council's rent man about the need for this young couple with a baby on the way to have a home close to Matt's work.

Viv's married life was different from her mother's in another way: she and Matt were able to limit their family to just one child. By 1940 the average family had two children, but this average hid some important class distinctions: middle-class families were generally smaller than working-class ones. Middle-class couples had long enjoyed greater access to information about birth control – in publications like Marie Stopes's *Married Love* – and they could pay for private healthcare, at a time when state-funded clinics were forbidden from prescribing contraceptives (something that wouldn't change until 1968). Viv herself had little idea about contraception; it remained illegal for NHS doctors to give advice on this, and she simply told Matt that he must find out about it, or do without sex. But what did change in the 1950s was working-class women's determination that they would not be tied down by childcare in the way that their mothers had been; nor would their children endure the poverty they had known. Many of their husbands wholeheartedly agreed, and these couples used the limited range of contraception available to them – condoms and the with-drawal method – to achieve their aspirations. As the historian Kate Fisher says: 'To "plan" one's family . . . reflected a forward-looking and optimistic approach to life.'[1] Full employment and welfare encour-aged Viv and Matt, as well as thousands of other working people, to adopt such an approach.

Yet once Viv's son Stephen was born, she began to find life a strain. She and Matt had a home of their own, a council house, but it was one of those built before 1918, and was small and dilapidated, dark and difficult to keep clean. Motherhood was more demanding than Viv had expected. Stephen had serious health problems that entailed regular trips to the hospital several miles away. Healthcare was free now, but buses were not. Secure work, a good wage and a home of your own were meant to provide a better life for members of Viv's generation; but life was still hard when you had young children to look after, and a decrepit home as well.

When Stephen was two, Viv did what so many married women were beginning to do across the country: she found a part-time job. In larger towns and cities, women benefited from an expansion in factory work; employers badly needed assembly-line workers, and the pre-war marriage bar never returned. In Castleford, job oppor-tunities were more limited. Viv returned to the cinema where she had worked as an usherette, and then got work as a barmaid at a local pub.

Many women took work because they needed the money. But 'Matt would work a double shift sometimes to really bring the money in if we desperately needed it,' Viv admitted. However, 'poverty was the excuse I used to get me mother to look after Steve for me.' Providing for your kids could justify a woman working outside her home. The reality was that Viv did need money, but not for what were considered 'essentials' in a 1950s pit village. She wanted a tele-vision, new clothes and an occasional night at the dance hall: 'I just wanted to be out amongst the girls and have that enjoyment, the bright lights, again.' She told her parents 'that Matt wasn't working and he wouldn't give me any money . . . All they said was, "Oh, bring [Stephen] down here and we'll have him and then you can go to work."'

Viv felt a fleeting shame – Matt was a thoughtful and considerate husband, after all – but this soon passed, because she knew her parents wouldn't think badly of him. Many men withheld their wages for their own leisure, only allowing their wives a few shillings for 'house-keeping'. In mining villages that offered little work to women, men's retention of a large portion of their earnings for themselves was widely regarded as their 'right' (at least by them) – compensation for their dangerous job and being the sole breadwinner. That wasn't true in Viv's case, but at times the old traditions and stereotypes could work in your favour and this was one of them. People could accept that a man might withhold his money, desperate for some independence and a reward for his hard work. That a woman wanted more than marriage and children – especially if she was wedded to a reliable worker – was less comprehensible. 'I lied, but I was desperate': desperate for distraction from domestic drudgery, her sick baby and an early marriage she was beginning to regret.

9

Never Having It So Good

IN 1951 THE renowned social researcher, philanthropist and chocolate manufacturer Seebohm Rowntree announced that post-war
welfare reform and full employment had 'all but ... eradicated'
poverty.[1] This was the conclusion of *Poverty and the Welfare State*, a
major social survey conducted by Rowntree and his collaborator
George Lavers. It appeared just weeks before that year's general
election; Labour hailed it as a ringing endorsement of the welfare
state, while the victorious Conservatives claimed it provided a
mandate for fostering prosperity rather than focusing on helping the
poor. Both parties agreed that poverty was all but destroyed, an
orthodoxy that persisted through the fifties. In 1956 the Labour MP
Anthony Crosland cited Rowntree in his influential book, *The Future
of Socialism*, which argued strongly that 'the worst economic abuses
and inefficiencies of modern society have been corrected.'[2] The
following year, Conservative Prime Minister Harold Macmillan
announced that 'most of our people have never had it so good.'[3]
During the 1950s, Britain had apparently become an affluent society.

But the voices of working-class Britons offer a different view. Far
from being a period of unprecedented prosperity, the 1950s were a
decade of insecurity and fear for many people. The Conservatives
retained their pre-war reluctance to intervene in welfare or industry.
The income gap between the rich and the poor, which had dramatically narrowed during the 1940s, widened in the 1950s.[4] Poverty –
practically a taboo in political circles – continued to be endured by
the elderly, the sick, and large families, and remained a very real fear
for thousands of ordinary workers. The generation having families
in the 1950s could still remember the hard times of the inter-war
depression, and were acutely aware that the new comforts of the

post-war years might be temporary. For a generation who craved security, the Conservative path to prosperity – reliance on credit and the free market – was one that was bound to generate anxiety.

In the 1950s working-class 'prosperity' was manifested in a hitherto unknown array of consumer goods: televisions and three-piece suites, fridges, cookers and convenience foods. But working-class consumers got these alleged signs of affluence 'on tick', through hire purchase (HP), or by long hours of overtime. In the early 1950s the social investigator Ferdynand Zweig interviewed hundreds of male workers at several factories in a range of towns and cities, including Birmingham and Luton, where many men had well-paid, skilled manual jobs. Zweig discovered that many of these workers 'achieved a relatively high standard of living but not without hard work, with a great deal of overtime and shiftwork'.[5] Families could only attain 'affluence' by working harder than ever. It took a lot of hard work, debt and a bit of luck to have it so good in fifties Britain.

Working-class people's living standards were certainly better than in the 1930s. Cars and houses were beyond the pockets of most, but many people could afford the rent on a new council house, hire-purchase payments for the television, the odd holiday and treats for the children. Jobs were abundant – less than 2 per cent of the workforce was unemployed in the early 1950s – and manual workers' wages rose.[6] Men's largest employer was the metal industry, which employed 15 per cent of the male workforce in 1951 and the majority of men in cities where the car trade was based, like Coventry. Alan Watkins left school in Coventry in 1956 and walked into an engineering apprenticeship in a local firm. As a school-leaver, he knew that 'you went from apprentice to engineer, and then you'd work your way up from there.' The unemployment that his father had experienced in inter-war South Wales was a distant memory.

Nevertheless, the regional differences that had driven the elder Mr Watkins to Coventry remained important. For men in unskilled work, secure jobs were harder to find. Transport was men's second-largest employer, and, together with construction, provided work for thousands of unskilled men. Men living in port cities like Liverpool, in London's docklands, and in Newcastle and Glasgow still found it hard to find any work other than unskilled labouring on the docks, railways, or in the manufacturing firms that were opening. People here didn't enjoy the rise in skilled work from which those like Alan Watkins, who lived in the centres of light manufacturing and engineering, benefited. Those firms that opened branches in the former industrial heartlands sought to exploit these regions' history of low pay and continued casualization. The Ford Motor Company opened a plant in South Wales in the late 1950s and then one at Halewood on Merseyside in 1962. Ford's managers chose their locations carefully, believing that 'unemployment means low wages and a vulnerable workforce.' The workers at these plants were paid lower wages than employees at Ford's first British plant, at Dagenham in Essex.[7]

Nevertheless, the reduction in unemployment was an important gain. In 1952 fifteen-year-old Liverpudlian Terry Rimmer left school. He would have preferred to get more education, or to take up an apprenticeship, but his widowed mother needed him to get the most lucrative job available, and that meant labouring. His first job was as a warehouseman at Liverpool's Lybro clothing firm in 1952. After a few months of getting bored and 'larking about', 'I was due to be sacked, he [the boss] rescinded it and I said, "No it's alright, I've already got another job". Because in those days, there was lots of labouring jobs.' 'Now the Boys Interview the Bosses!' declared the *Daily Mirror* in 1955.[8] The teenagers who entered employment in the 1950s were the first generation to find that 'you could walk out of one job on a Friday and into another on a Monday'.[9]

People had more money – and more goods to spend it on. In 1954 the Conservative government ended food rationing. By 1956, 12 per cent of British holidaymakers were taking holidays abroad. A survey of inner-city Liverpool households conducted in 1955 found that even one-quarter of this relatively poor group had had a holiday away from home in the previous year.[10] In more affluent Coventry, Frank and Rita Gogerty were among those who relished a range of new comforts. By 1950, Frank was a skilled chargehand in one of Coventry's car plants, and, with their two sons at secondary school, Rita had taken a factory job. 'When we got the money,' said Frank, 'we didn't spend it wastefully – but I think we enjoyed it to the full.' This included buying a car – Frank was the first man on his street to do so, at a time when less than 5 per cent of Britons owned one – and 'furnishing our house, which not many people could afford to do then'. In the mid-1950s, with their sons in work, Frank and Rita began to take holidays abroad. On their first trip, to San Sebastian in Spain, 'we felt like pioneers'. By 1955 the package holiday had arrived, as entrepreneurs sought to lure this new British market to the stretch of coastline around Benidorm that they renamed the 'Costa Blanca'.[11]

The Conservatives' promotion of these new consumer goods – by ending rationing, and by making it easier for working people to get credit – helps to explain why they won the 1955 general election and then increased their majority in Parliament when the country went to the polls once more in 1959. Yet people's delight at the new consumer goods was tempered by the insecure nature of their prosperity. While the pawnshop – once a pillar of every working-class neighbourhood – was in decline, hire-purchase agreements (which, because they demanded regular payments, depended on having a reliable income) increased. In 1953 the *Daily Mirror* reported that over 70 per cent of Hartlepool's residents relied on credit: 'They Even Get Married on Tick!'[12] In 1955 most families in inner-city Liverpool relied on credit for such essentials as clothes and home furnishings.[13]

In the late 1950s the number of people with consumer goods like televisions increased, but their insecurity remained, especially in those areas of northern England and Scotland's industrial belt that had been hardest hit by inter-war depression. In the early 1960s sociologists studied 500 households in inner-city Liverpool and a more prosperous southern suburb, Woolton. They found that more than 80 per cent of these families relied on some form of credit. Among them was Joan Hicks, a forty-one-year-old housewife who lived in Woolton with her husband Bill, an engineer, and their two teenage children. The Hicks family owned their small terraced house, and Bill was in skilled work. Nevertheless, when Joan was asked if she had trouble making ends meet she replied 'yes' without hesitation. 'Have to go without in order to keep up mortage payments and pay for groceries and TV,' she said. She would have liked 'more money to save, and to spend on clothes for Bill and the children'.[14]

Life had improved since the mid-1950s, they could afford luxuries that she hadn't previously hoped for – but the precariousness of their position worried Mrs Hicks. Many families shared her dissatisfaction; opinion polls demonstrated their strong aversion to debt.[15] The growing array of domestic goods in ordinary workers' homes revealed only part of fifties reality. Many people's purchases had a backstory of sacrifice and worry.

Why, then, did people get into mounting levels of debt? A major reason was political pressure. The Conservatives actively encouraged people to rely on credit. Like Labour before them, the Tories believed that post-war economic growth relied on stimulating consumer demand for the goods being produced by British manu-facturers. However, reliance on manufacturing was risky. As demand for goods rose, manufacturers increased prices, either to limit demand or to increase their profits; at a certain point, these price hikes deterred consumers, who would stop buying the goods, causing unemployment.

Labour's price controls, including rationing, had regulated both production and consumption, but the Conservatives were firmly committed to a free market. They had to find other ways to stimulate consumption and support profit-making, and credit was one of them. In 1954 the Conservatives relaxed restrictions on mortgages and hire purchase, making it possible for thousands more families to acquire both.[16] In 1955 Rab Butler, the Chancellor of the Exchequer, introduced purchase tax on basic household goods such as washboards, while exempt-ing from taxation most of the more expensive domestic appliances, including automatic washing machines. 'Tories Hit the Housewife', screamed the Labour-supporting *Daily Mirror*'s front page.[17] All these measures made mass-produced consumer goods increasingly attractive to working-class wage-earners and, apparently, affordable.

Those who looked longingly in the shop windows had good reasons to buy what they saw there. Vacuum cleaners, fridges, cookers, televisions, holidays, wirelesses, three-piece suites, cars and motorbikes all promised to make life easier and more luxurious. This was a time when millions of people were still waiting for a new council house, but wanted to relish life after the privations of war, and give their children the best possible start in the new post-war meritocracy.

Advertisements offered guidance on how to do so, proliferating in magazines and newspapers and, from 1955, finding a new outlet on Independent Television, Britain's second television channel and its first to be privately owned. Crown Paint promised to 'make your house a home'; Crosley's cookers would create 'a care free kitchen'. Campbell's soups offered wives and mothers the chance to 'begin with the best' when cooking for their families; Butlins told husbands they could provide 'the perfect holiday for mother'. All guaranteed a better life at 'an unbelievably affordable price'. Consumer goods were becoming a means of combining the multiple roles that people were meant to fulfil in post-war Britain: responsible breadwinner and loving husband; glamorous wife and selfless mother; or healthy, happy children.

Meanwhile, Labour's appeal to the people was almost entirely negative. The party's 1955 manifesto began with the warning that 'the Hydrogen Bomb looms over all mankind', and suggested that the pressing question for voters should be: 'What can we do to meet that menace?' Labour pointed out that many pensioners continued to live in poverty, and that shareholders' dividends were rising faster than wages. But Labour politicians seemed unable to offer a positive alternative, at a time when the major parties agreed that the most serious threat to peace was Soviet Communism. The Conservatives' message – that in an era of instability, ordinary people could at least enjoy peace and prosperity in their own homes – was one that many people found more attractive.

Yet although the Conservatives' policies encouraged people to consume more goods, they also limited the economic power of working-class consumers. Their priority was to maintain the wealth of their core voters – employers, managers and businessmen – by keeping regulation of trade to a minimum and taxes low.[18] In 1956 the Conservatives lifted the last of Labour's significant price controls, when they removed the subsidy that had reduced the price of bread. The government declared that this would offer consumers greater 'freedom' of choice, by stimulating competition among food production firms which was declared to be a sure way of keeping prices low. But the price of bread went up. Conservatives' policies hit ordinary workers hard, by removing any certainty about the prices of basic goods, and by adding taxes to the appliances they bought. Conversely, the middle and upper classes enjoyed lower taxes than at any time since the early 1930s. At the same time, the gap between manual workers' earnings and those of professionals widened; both experienced pay rises, but professionals enjoyed a much bigger increase.[19] The supposedly affluent society was in fact one that was incredibly socially divided.

Many workers worried about the future. Although manual workers' earnings rose by 50 per cent during the 1950s, price rises meant that in real terms their earnings only increased by 30 per cent.[20] While this was still a significant rise, it happened in fits and starts across the decade, and people could never be certain that each new gain would last. The government worked hard to reduce prices directly before general elections in 1955 and 1959. This helps explain the Conservatives' victory in both (though in fact most manual workers voted Labour throughout the 1950s), but post-election price rises were keenly felt by voters. Sir Michael Fraser, the Conservative Party's most senior adviser, reflected in 1959 that the party's habit of providing generous pre-election budgets could lead to economic recovery 'spectacular both in extent and speed, but this very fact made some people suspicious of the stability of the resulting situation'.[21] This state of affairs robbed people of the power to plan ahead and to enjoy themselves that many had relished for the first time in the late 1940s.

'The people' were not as united as they had been in the immediate post-war years. The gap between the earnings and working conditions of skilled and unskilled workers grew in the early 1950s, when skilled workers enjoyed bigger wage rises than the unskilled and semi-skilled.[22] As more firms moved towards mass production, trade unions representing skilled workers jealously protected their members' rights to higher wages and security. Prominent among them was the Amalgamated Engineering Union (AEU), which was active in Britain's car plants. These employed many semi-skilled and unskilled workers whom the AEU resolutely excluded from membership.[23]

Even within the most prosperous towns and cities, workers could see enormous differences in their living standards. Trade union agreements, and the needs of employers, meant that unskilled and semi-skilled workers bore the brunt of the boom and bust – or, as the Conservatives' critics called it, the 'stop-go' economy of the 1950s. They didn't have the job security that more skilled workers enjoyed. Carol Hinde's father, Jack Elliott, was a factory hand who worked at several of Coventry's car plants in the 1950s; 'he was never in work all that long,' she recalled, 'because he was unskilled, so he was always first out,' when demand for cars dropped and workers were laid off.

Many unskilled and semi-skilled workers resented their skilled workmates. Not only were skilled workers' earnings better than theirs, but the rewards available to them – in the shape of food, furniture, houses and holidays – grew in the early 1950s as the Conservatives ended rationing and supported private house building, and credit became easy to come by for those who had a secure income. Aggrieved unskilled workers often harked back to the war, invoking the 1940s rhetoric of equal sacrifice and 'fair shares' to justify their anger. Demobbed servicemen expressed resentment at the skilled men who had remained in their reserved occupations. Howard Blake was born in a working-class suburb of Coventry in 1941. Howard's father had served with the RAF during the war, but after being demobbed in 1948 he returned to his job as a bus driver. Mr Blake resentfully pointed out to his young son that 'the first car on the street would go to a guy who worked in a factory, the first telephone in the street would go to one . . .'[24]

But those unskilled workers who had stayed in the factories returned this frustration with interest. Many of them envied demobbed soldiers like Frank Gogerty who were able to return home to their former jobs. Ann Lanchbury's father, Mr Kiddey, 'resented the soldiers, he saw them as coming in, taking jobs'. By the 1950s, there was no hard and fast division between the living standards of those who had served in the forces and those who had stayed at home; Mr Blake and Mr Kiddey pointed to the re-emergence of a pre-war fracture between the living conditions of skilled workers and those of the rest of the working class.

These disgruntled men believed that the promises they were made in the 1940s had been broken. Many of them experienced the 1950s not as a time of rising living standards, but as a period when their hopes of attaining – or returning to – skilled work were dashed. As a result of inter-war unemployment and wartime disruption, many thousands of men had slid down the occupational ladder. Ann Lanchbury's father was among them. A trained carpenter, he had been laid off in the hard times of the 1930s. During the war he had become a semi-skilled worker at Coventry's Jaguar plant, where he took pride in making 'all the wooden insides of Jaguar cars'. He continued to love his trade, making toys for the children who lived on his street each Christmas. In the 1940s Mr Kiddey's hopes that life would get better were high; Ann recalled him as 'the life and soul' at family parties. But by the mid-1950s this had changed; he 'had to work a lot of overtime' to make ends meet, had given up on the idea he might ever become a carpenter again, and was 'a very disappointed man'.

Life in the 1950s did not only differ between families on the same street, but within families like Mr Kiddey's. The 1950s has long been recalled as a 'golden age' of family life, when divorce rates were low and marriages long.[25] But behind many doors in 'family Britain'[26] lurked tension and disappointment. By the mid-1950s, social investigators were pointing out that many men in unskilled or semi-skilled work appeared unwilling to keep their families. In a survey of family budgets, Michael Young suggested that a pre-war trend, which saw many wage-earning men withhold a very large portion of their wages from the housekeeping budget, had survived the Second World War.[27] Other investigators claimed that this was a primary cause of hardship. In the early 1950s a series of reports compiled by the Family Service Units, a voluntary social work agency that worked closely with local authorities, criticized working men who failed to 'provide adequately for their families', suggesting that their reluctance to work, or to give their wages to their wives, caused poverty.[28]

Some men certainly were reluctant to put their family's needs before their own. Mr Kiddey, for example, became 'a very sensitive man [who] could be very volatile, especially after drink', which he indulged in with increasing regularity in the 1950s. Ann Lanchbury recalled tense Friday and Saturday evenings at home with her mother, who 'knew jolly well he was spending her money' in the pub. When her father returned, he could be violent. 'He didn't look angry, he looked sort of – "Look at me, I'm a peacock . . . I rule this place".'

Mr Kiddey was grappling with a tension that stretched back into the nineteenth century. Generations of working-class men had sought to fulfil two distinct roles. The first was that of the family bread-winner, the figure championed by Attlee's government. The second was the independent, hardy, working man; tough and self-reliant. These roles could be mutually reinforcing, but they could conflict, especially in times when men found it hard to be competent bread-winners. In the 1950s many men found it hard to keep their families in the style that prosperity seemed to demand.[29] Fortunately, not all of them reacted with the impotent rage of Mr Kiddey, but exerting control over money and family could be important for men who keenly felt they had lost any hope of control at work. Her mother taught Ann Lanchbury to attribute her father's behaviour to his 'disappointment', both with his work and his inadequacy as a breadwinner.

Unskilled workers, then, were losers in the affluent society. So too were older people and large families. Even the optimistic Rowntree and Lavers had pointed out that pensioners and families with three or more children were still likely to live in poverty, because state benefit levels were too low to support them.[30] During the 1950s their circumstances worsened. In 1955 the Conservative Cabinet charged a Social Services Committee with outlining a strategy for cutting expenditure. However, opinion polls indicated that adopting the committee's central recommendations – which involved reintro-ducing the means test – would be electorally disastrous.[31] Instead, the government cut or froze many benefits, including the family allowances on which large families relied.[32] At any one time in the 1950s, 7 per cent of British households were living below Rowntree's stringently defined poverty line.[33]

By the end of the 1950s, however, life was changing for the better for many ordinary people. Mr Kiddey was finally able to become the kind of breadwinner he'd aspired to be. 'Dad was happy, nobody felt threatened, nobody was going to be drunk,' Ann remembered. 'My whole world improved.' When Ann married in 1960, 'my father wanted, as he'd not been able to pay for his other daughters' weddings, he wanted to pay for mine,' and this touched her. Shortly after her wedding, Ann's father bought his first car and her parents began to enjoy holidays away from home for the first time in their lives.

Two changes in the late 1950s had had a profound impact on the Kiddeys and on thousands of other families like them. One was the increase in slum clearance, which meant that the Kiddeys had finally been allocated a new council house, after years on the waiting list. At the same time, the wages of unskilled and semi-skilled workers finally began to rise, as unions like the AEU at last woke up to the importance of this expanding group of workers and agreed to represent them.[34] As well as being able to enjoy council housing, workers could now afford a few luxuries for their new homes. In 1955 a third of British households had a television. By 1960, 90 per cent owned or rented a TV.[35]

But these families' growing financial security was also due to a second dramatic transformation: married women's work. Working-class wives had always gone out to work in many areas of the country, but the proportion doing so rose during and after the war. A third of them had a paid job in 1951, and almost 40 per cent ten years later. Not only did more of them go out to work, but they stayed in the workforce for a longer period of time. Rather than leaving work when they became mothers, the women of the fifties were the first generation likely to remain in paid employment throughout their adult lives, with only a temporary break to have children.[36] They were also able to earn more than earlier generations. A minority of women benefited from the gradual implementation of equal pay in the public sector; following the government's 1955 commitment to equal pay in the civil service (a move that primarily affected salaried professionals), trade unions began to negotiate successfully for parity between men and women in local government and at the Post Office. More women were affected by the post-war manufacturing boom, which required plenty of workers willing to staff assembly lines; employers across the country introduced housewives' shifts to recruit mothers for work in school hours or in the evening.

Working-class women pioneered this change. In 1965 a study of 10,000 households showed that the wives of manual and junior clerical workers were far more likely to go out to work than those married to professionals or men with private income.[37] Some social investigators argued that women's work testified to families' fecklessness. '[I]ts main economic effects,' said Seebohm Rowntree, 'are to counteract the lack of skill of some housewives in spending their resources and to enable working-class families to enjoy luxuries that would otherwise be beyond their means.'[38] But in the late 1950s a study based on interviews with 1,200 working mothers concluded that most went to work due to 'financial pressures, usually very real [and] often directly related to housing shortage or to the desire to give children higher material and educational standards'.[39] In other words, they went to work because they needed to. As the social researcher Pearl Jephcott discovered from working women in Bermondsey, 'the aim was a higher standard of living for their families'.[40]

Politicians' views of working wives and mothers were never straightforward. A study by the Council for Children's Welfare pointed out that 'the government is either ambivalent or without policy. One minister may denounce working mothers as contributors to juvenile delinquency at a time when another department is seeking to attract them into teaching or into hospitals.'[41] Married women's work was vital to both employers and working-class families. But in the affluent society, women's work, like credit, was often represented as an 'extra', a 'luxury'; doing so prevented the government having to acknowledge, let alone address, the limits to affluence.

Working mothers themselves were unmoved by scare stories of delinquency. The factory workers of Bermondsey 'argued that the neglectful mother was the one too indifferent and too indolent to seize today's golden, and perhaps fleeting, opportunity to benefit the children by raising the physical standards of the home'. Many of their husbands agreed, and helped with housework and cooking so that their wives could get a job.[42] 'That's why I went out to work,' Mrs Edwards of Liverpool told a social investigator in 1955; 'to see the children get on.'[43] Her husband was a labourer; she was a part-time char and waitress; they lived in a shabby home and had three children. Such ambitions weren't new, and neither was women's determination to offer their children financial assistance – but by the end of the 1950s new jobs gave mothers new opportunities to fulfil their ambitions.

The enduring image of the 1950s as a decade of lipsticked and aproned housewives was only true in the advertisements. By the early 1960s, the children of the 1940s were growing up to believe that 'good' mothers went out to work. Jean McLoughlin resented her mother who 'never had a job, well, she couldn't, because she always had a baby'.[44] Hazel Wood, who grew up in Coventry in the 1950s, understood that 'many women had gone out to work during the war' and when her own mother became a waitress in the mid-1950s 'this was just normal'. Her father, a factory worker, 'didn't like it at first, but he soon got used to it', and her three children relished the new clothes and books for school that their mother's work bought them. Hazel knew, too, that her mother's earnings were important for her own self-worth and pleasure. She was 'handy with a needle' and used some of her earnings to buy cheap material from the market, but she didn't scrimp on design. In the early 1950s she spent hours making herself a New Look dress that required acres of material – she wasn't going to let dingy Coventry and domestic chores stop her enjoying the fruits of her labours. 'I can see her now, bent over that machine, this determined look on her face,' Hazel recalled fifty years later. The dress was a reward for her own hard work; the message her daughter took from this was that women deserved some of the pleasures in life – but that they'd have to work for them.

For many people, the 1950s was a paradoxical decade. They were better off than their parents had been but they weren't as well off as the advertisements and government rhetoric seemed to suggest – and they weren't sure that the gains they had made were here to stay. In 1957 Harold Macmillan fed their fears in his 'never had it so good' speech. In this widely publicized address, he called for a debate about whether full employment and a welfare state were really sustainable. A freer market would bring greater prosperity to those who worked hard, he argued. It was an alluring message, but one that condemned a very large number of people to a lifestyle maintained only through credit, uncertainty and fear.

In 1957 many ordinary people felt they were yet to experience the affluence that Macmillan described. For those families in work, 'prosperity' did not mean a life of ease and plenty, but long hours on a never-ending assembly line, a lino-floored council house, a rented television, a three-piece suite paid for by hire purchase, regular spending money for the kids, the odd splurge on a Saturday night or a long-saved-for week at the seaside. All these gains were important and cherished by families for whom the 1930s was still a vivid memory – but they relied on two parents working, long hours of overtime, debt, saving and sacrifice. The affluent society relied upon their labour, but working-class people received a very small share of its fruits.

Interlude V

The Affluent Society

IN 1956 TWENTY-YEAR-OLD Viv was desperate for a bit of the excitement and glamour she saw on the Hollywood films she glimpsed as an usherette. She dyed her hair blonde and went dancing whenever she could persuade her mother to babysit her son, Stephen. She spent ages decorating and painting her new home with odd bits of paint her parents could spare, and wallpaper for which she and Matt saved up. Viv reminded herself that 'at least Matt and I had a home of our own' – what she said she'd always wanted, what was meant to be the key to contentment for working-class people in the 1950s. But the role of wife and mother wasn't easy on a limited income. Viv visited her parents' house to get a taste of the good things in the affluent society; with more of their children at work her father and mother could now afford teas of tinned salmon or corned beef, before 'watching the goggle box'. It was hardly the consumer society of Conservative rhetoric, but Viv returned to her own home increasingly dissatisfied: 'I'd stare at four walls, we didn't even have a radio.'

Then in 1957 a new cartoon character appeared in the *Daily Mirror*: Andy Capp. This pint-sized, cloth-capped northerner was too idle to work or help his long-suffering wife Flo around the house, but always had the energy to hoodwink her out of enough money for a trip to the pub or the bookies. Reg Smythe, Capp's creator, claimed to have based his cartoon on his own father in Hartlepool where, he said, not much had changed since the 1930s. Within weeks, Capp was receiving sackloads of fan mail from the *Mirror*'s readers, women and men alike. 'Andy Capp is secretly every man's dream of what he would like to be,' wrote Mr D.L. of Watford to the *Mirror* in 1957. 'Fifty years ago if a man wanted to go out of an evening he just told the wife – and went. Now he has to ask for permission! Let's get back to the good old days.' Women also liked the cartoon. 'I was engaged to be married to an "Andy Capp",' wrote 'Name Supplied' of Gosport. 'His dry humour always amused me and *his* word was final. But alas! I married a southerner, and although he is immaculate in appearance and manners, I do miss the masterful, rough and ready "Andy".'

Viv hankered after the same sort of man – someone who was independent, and wouldn't be cowed by the demands of work and family, and the fear of debt or unemployment. Then she met Keith Nicholson, a sixteen-year-old miner. Compared to her dreary life of drudgery, their illicit courtship was akin to 'a sexy and romantic film'. But eventually reality caught up: she found she was pregnant with Keith's child and told Matt she wanted a divorce. Her unwanted pregnancy made Viv feel anew that she had no control over her life – doctors were only supposed to prescribe contraception on medical grounds (and the contraceptive pill would only become available in 1961) – but at least she could now get a divorce, which Attlee's government had made cheaper and more accessible for working-class people. Matt moved back in with his mother, and Keith moved into Viv's house.

Keith earned less than Matt. His trainee miner's wage was £7 per week, but he often couldn't be bothered to get up and go to work. He told Viv the pit was stiflingly hot and dusty, the work exhausting and boring. In winter he never saw daylight, leaving home when it was still dark to work in a poorly lit pit shaft. Viv couldn't bring herself to blame him: 'the little bit he did get wasn't blinding worth it, it didn't go far.'

That was the problem with the 1950s: the good things in life were tantalizingly close, and holidays, cars and domestic appliances all promised a life of ease; yet getting and holding on to them required constant hard work and a sprinkling of good fortune. That he saw through this was part of the appeal of Andy Capp. His wily ruses to remain outside the control of the boss, the state and his wife were tinged with humour, but also with regret and anger that affluence – or, more accurately, a modicum of extra security – came at such a high price. Andy Capp appealed to those who wondered if the welfare state and life on the assembly line had robbed men of their rightful responsibilities – and their power. 'Name Supplied' of Edgware told the *Daily Mirror* that he liked 'Andy Capp because he represents the inner man that rebels against the humdrum and regimentation of our daily lives'.[1] Viv, too, condoned Keith's rebellion against the routine work that brought so little reward; but romance couldn't put food on the table.

10

The Golden Age of the Grammar School

BY THE TIME Macmillan announced people 'had never had it so good', two cohorts of children had enjoyed a radical post-war innovation: free secondary education. The 1944 Education Act, introduced by Labour's Education Minister Ellen Wilkinson in 1948, made secondary education free and compulsory for all children aged between eleven and fifteen. Wilkinson shared the aim of the Act's architect, the Conservative Rab Butler, to provide 'equality of educational opportunity': merit, rather than wealth or family background, would determine the education of future generations. But educational expansion after 1948 did not create equality of opportunity. Instead, government policy created a highly selective schooling system that reserved the best places for a few. Ultimately, both Labour and Conservative governments put the demands of employers before the aspirations of working-class parents and children, and created an education system that channelled most young people into the factories on which peacetime 'prosperity' relied.

Equality of opportunity had certainly not been available before 1948. Secondary schools had charged fees, which prevented all but a small minority of working-class children from attending them. In 1938 just 14 per cent of elementary school pupils in England and Wales progressed to secondary schools, most on one of the limited number of council scholarships available.[1] While a higher proportion of Scottish children had a secondary education, few working-class children entered the senior secondary schools (those offering a full secondary curriculum and external examinations).[2] Wilkinson believed that achieving equal opportunity relied on education being tailored to each child's talents. She accepted the recommendation of the cross-party Norwood Committee, which in 1943 had proposed that secondary education be introduced on tripartite lines. Most children in England and Wales would attend a secondary modern school, 15 per cent a technical school – designed to educate planners, architects and technicians – and another 15 per cent the academically selective grammar schools from which the nation's doctors, lawyers and academics would emerge. This system was similar to the one that had already been introduced in Scotland, where secondary education was made freely available in 1936. Here, a binary form of secondary education existed, with most children attending a three-year course at a junior secondary school, while IQ tests determined the minority admitted to study for the academic five-year course offered by senior secondary schools.

Working-class parents strongly supported the introduction of free secondary education. In 1945 Mass Observation interviewed hundreds of people about the new Education Act and revealed a widespread desire for 'everybody to have an equal chance'. Significantly, the popular enthusiasm for free education was particularly strong 'amongst those with elementary education only'.[3] They included people like Ian White's father. Ian, a miner's son from Lancashire, was 'what they call a Blitz baby', having been conceived during an air raid in 1941. In the late 1940s, 'my dad took me to the top of the pit, and he said, "you've two things now, you get educated, or else you go down this place", and we stood at the top of the colliery, and the updraught was coming up from it, you could smell sulphur, it was like being in hell, so I thought, it's education for me!'[4] Schooling was grasped as a passport to a better life.

Wilkinson, herself the winner of a scholarship to grammar school, had two 'guiding aims' which, she told Labour's 1946 conference, 'come largely out of my own experience'. Born into a working-class home in Manchester, Wilkinson had 'had to fight my own way through to the University'. She was determined to ensure that 'no boy or girl is debarred by lack of means'.[5] Entry to selective secondary schools would be determined by a ten-year-old child's performance in an intelligence test – the 'eleven-plus' examination. Education was to be the foundation of Labour's new meritocracy, in which effort and talent would matter more than hereditary privilege.

Wilkinson and her government had a third aim, however: to meet the needs of employers. The three types of secondary school endorsed by Wilkinson were not based on what teachers, parents or children had requested. Instead, they were shaped by the kinds of workers that the government thought the post-war economy would need. The architects of the Education Act hoped that grammar schools would direct 'the nation's abler children' into university study, while pupils of the technical schools would contribute to 'the design and craftsmanship sides of industry' as well as to post-war planning.[6] But most children would face a different future. At Labour's 1946 conference, Wilkinson defended herself against the party's numerous and vocal supporters of comprehensive (non-selective) secondary education, many of whom were teachers themselves, by declaring that 'not everyone wants an academic education. After all, coal has to be mined and fields ploughed.'[7] Her claim betrayed a naïve assumption that people's talents and desires would fit easily with what employers wanted. And what many employers wanted by the late 1940s was assembly-line workers.

By the late 1950s, Wilkinson's reforms had achieved a good deal. Working-class children were receiving more formal education than ever before. In 1951 less than a quarter of sixteen-year-old boys and girls had been at school across Britain; just ten years later, almost one-third were. Children born in the 1940s were almost twice as likely to obtain formal qualifications as those born in the inter-war years.[8]

But if working-class children were receiving more education than their parents, they were at a disadvantage to their middle-class peers. Eighty per cent of children were educated in Britain's non-selective secondary modern schools during the 1950s.[9] The vast majority of them were the children of manual workers. These schools were the poor relations of the grammar schools. Many were, in fact, simply the old elementary schools renamed. In 1951, 628 schools in England and Wales were still housed in buildings that had been condemned as 'unfit for use' in 1920.[10] Among them was Liverpool's Granby Street School, where Her Majesty's School Inspectors were horrified to discover children from five to fifteen crammed into overcrowded classrooms 'seriously affected by dampness'.[11] In 1958 Geoffrey Lloyd, the Conservative Minister for Education, acknowledged that most of Britain's secondary moderns lacked 'the facilities needed for proper secondary education, above all in scientific and technical subjects'.[12] But government investment in the secondary modern schools remained low.

Working-class children had very little chance of entering the academically selective grammar schools. 'We are creating a new middle class,' declared the headmaster of Manchester Grammar School in 1958. '[T]he grammar schools are really the spearhead of the movement of social mobility.'[13] But less than 20 per cent of manual workers' children won a grammar school place, while more than 50 per cent of the children of professionals and business owners did.[14] In Liverpool, reported the city's *Daily Post*, 'to take the [inner-city] Paddington area as an example – only 10 per cent of the children from that district go to grammar schools after eleven. This percentage rises to 70 and 80 per cent in [middle-class] areas such as Childwall and Mossley Hill.'[15]

A large number of journalists and politicians – from the left as well as the right – suggested working-class parents were to blame for the low educational attainments of their children. In 1951 *The Economist* judged that the large number of grammar school pupils who left at sixteen indicated that 'not all of those who clamour for entry make their choice with a full sense of responsibility, nor are many of their parents aware how rigorous a grammar school course can be for the borderline child.'[16] The researchers J.W.B. Douglas, J.M. Ross and H.R. Simpson suggested that the low number of working-class grammar school entrants 'perhaps stems from low ambitions on the part of the manual working class pupils and their parents' – though their study of 5,000 schoolchildren offered no definitive proof.[17]

It was certainly true that some parents were reluctant to see their children endure the stress of the eleven-plus examination, and the overwhelming possibility of failure. In the late 1950s J.G. Ballard – former public schoolboy and later an acclaimed science fiction writer – came across some of these parents while selling encyclopedias door-to-door. These were a valued addition to many working-class families' bookshelves[18] but not, Ballard found, in Coventry. 'Here, people were more interested in taking me inside to show me their TV, or three-piece suite . . . education meant very little.'[19]

Ballard, who would choose to educate his own children privately, didn't understand the aspirations of the parents he met, most of whom had experienced the desperation of seeking work and striving to make ends meet. For them, one of the most important benefits of post-war full employment was that it gave their children the chance of a more carefree existence. Among them were Jack and Christine Elliott of Willenhall in Coventry, whose daughters, Carol and Pauline, failed the eleven-plus in the 1950s and left secondary school with no formal qualifications. Twenty years earlier, Christine had wanted a secondary education for herself, but her years at elementary school had been clouded by her father's unemployment and the family's poverty, so much so that she had had a nervous breakdown at the age of nine. In 1934 'I got back [to school] and I'd missed so much so I was a dunce. They didn't bother, and I didn't bother.' By the 1950s, her daughters were able to find well-paid factory work at fifteen, and were apparently assured of a job for life. In Coventry the proportion of children sitting A-levels was slightly lower than in England as a whole, reflecting the availability of factory and office work.[20] 'I just wanted them to be happy,' said Christine, and that meant avoiding the stress and strain she had experienced, and which the hurdles of examinations necessary to enter, and then to succeed at, grammar school implied.

Some parents were also wary about their children climbing the social ladder. Paul Baker was born in Coventry in 1948, in a 'cardboard prefab' in the city's suburbs. He was the son of a milkman who had seen active service during the war. Paul recalled that his father 'was more interested in the job, life and friends I suppose [than education] – what he got by with in six years during the war, survival'.[21] Solidarity with one's friends, keeping a steady job, surviving: these were important virtues, and it was sometimes hard for fathers to acknowledge that sons would have to reject them in order to get on in life. But many parents were also suspicious and sceptical of an education system that equated 'success' with middle-class status. Christine Elliott, for example, worried that further education would lead her daughters to 'think they're better than everybody else . . . if you went to university . . . you thought you was better than the other people, but you weren't no different. Just your imagination.'

Some parents – generally fathers – thought that education wasn't necessary for their daughters. 'He didn't believe in education for girls,' recalled Ann Lanchbury of her father; he had insisted that Ann's older sister, Pam, leave grammar school as soon as she could to begin work in 1947. The Education Act helped to change this practice, if not the underlying attitudes. When Ann herself began life at the same grammar school in 1952, she was aware that 'my father took absolutely no interest at all', but 'the fact it was free meant he couldn't do anything about it'. Surveys of workers in Luton and Tyneside in the 1960s suggested that men saw education as less important for their daughters, with many fathers believing that home economics was more valuable than English or maths. This was particularly the case in families that hailed from areas with a strict sexual division of labour, like agricultural districts and the north-east coalfield, where jobs for women were scarce; though it was evident in other house-holds, too.[22] Norman Lewis of Lancaster married when he was twenty-one, in 1951. By the early 1960s, his three children – Yvonne, Carol and David – had all sat, and failed, the eleven-plus. 'There was never any talk about the girls going to grammar school,' he recalled; but Norman would have liked it for David, and went to the primary school to find out what he could do to help. 'I wanted David to do well . . . I assumed that the girls would get married and their life would reflect on the type of partner they chose.' David was different, in his father's eyes – he had a living to make.[23]

A changing labour market helped to shift these attitudes. In fact, across the country as a whole, slightly more boys than girls left school at fifteen during the 1950s. Many of the expanding clerical and technical jobs open to girls demanded formal qualifications that could only be taken at the age of sixteen. Ann Lanchbury herself benefited from this; her chosen profession of nursing was expanding when she reached her teens, whereas her sister Pam's occupational choices had been more limited.[24]

Some working-class parents were ambivalent about their sons entering white-collar or professional work. Some, perhaps, were jealous of their sons' greater opportunities, but mixed with this was a suspicion of the petty authority wielded by middle managers and bureaucrats. Many men saw entering such occupations as nothing to be proud of, however the Registrar General might classify the status of such jobs in the decennial census. In the mid-fifties, Peter Willmott and Michael Young found that 'a sizeable minority of men' in Bethnal Green believed that clerical workers and managers were 'not doing anything' worthwhile. These fathers encouraged their sons to get an apprenticeship, which could offer a job for life and a set of skills that could be important bargaining tools.[25] These men were not seeking to hold their children back; rather their values were at odds with the hierarchy of manual worker–clerk–manager that successive post-war governments promoted. As the employment prospects of white-collar workers grew, so men's ambitions changed. In 1963 sociologists discovered that Luton's car workers overwhelmingly hoped their sons would enter office work, which was considered cleaner, safer and more interesting than a factory job. Bernard Harris wanted his son James to get 'a nice technical job, nice office, nice white shirt, really classy draughtsman . . . it's more interesting than my job and . . . it's a job you can take with you wherever you go.'[26]

But working-class mothers often had a much stronger desire for education for its own sake. 'It's the mother that educates them,' one Huddersfield man told the social scientists Brian Jackson and Dennis Marsden when they studied the experience of the town's working-class grammar school entrants.[27] Some of these women had lost out on education in the 1930s, when families faced with tough choices about who to educate were more likely to choose sons than daughters. They rarely had the chance to experience the skill, pride and camaraderie that many men believed was embodied in skilled manual work, and consequently they had different hopes for their children. Paul Baker's mother was among them. She was a cashier for Coventry Council, who had been denied secondary schooling and was determined that both her son and her daughter would do well. Paul was the elder of her two children. She named him Paul Vincent Baker because, he recalled, 'at a very early stage she got this vision of me going to Oxford or Cambridge and becoming a barrister, and she thought that a double barrel name – Vincent-Baker – would sound quite nice.' While Paul's father didn't say much about school, 'Mum knew that education was going to be a very, very important part of life after the war.' She used her earnings to pay for the children to have piano lessons, and 'she'd always try to help with the homework, or with reading books.'[28]

Most parents wanted the very best education for their children, regardless of what job they might end up in. In 1954 the *Daily Mirror*'s 'Spotlight on Education' published parents' grievances over the narrow curriculum that secondary modern schools offered. 'My fourteen-year-old daughter is bright. Yet she can't spell very well. Why?' asked 'Worried Mother' of Weston-super-Mare. 'Because she spends too much time at school learning how to cook, how to sew, how to wash up and how to shop. She can do all that at home.'[29] In 1959 Her Majesty's Inspectors of Schools observed that parents and children at a large secondary modern in Coventry were unhappy with the lack of opportunity to stay on at school and sit examinations. They could not do so because 'there is not sufficient provision of post-compulsory education to meet demand.'[30]

By 1959, their thirst for learning was becoming hard to ignore. The government commissioned a committee headed by Geoffrey Crowther to advise on the education of children between the ages of fifteen and eighteen. The Crowther Report concluded that the biggest grievance among parents 'in every kind of neighbourhood and occupation' was 'that their children, through failure to secure admission to a grammar school, have been condemned to an abbreviated schooling'. What was more, 'the demand for a longer education is even greater among the boys and girls than among their parents.' Sixteen per cent of boys and 23 per cent of girls attending secondary moderns 'said they would have liked at least a year longer at school'.[31]

As this eagerness for education suggests, a child's chances in life were determined neither by their aspirations, nor by their parents' expectations. The majority of children had a non-academic secondary education because government policy restricted academic success to only a few. This caused thousands of children and their parents disappointment and shame. In 1949, despite the encouragement his father offered, Ian White, the miner's son from Lancashire, failed the eleven-plus exam. He attended a local secondary modern, where the only qualification he gained was a certificate in gardening. 'I educated myself later on,' he recalled fifty years later; the memory of his 'failure' still pained him.

'[P]reference for the grammar school,' concluded the social scientists Jean Floud and A.H. Halsey after conducting an exhaustive study in the mid-1950s, 'bears no relation to the realities of the outcome of the process of selection.'[32] Bill Rainford knew this. He sat the eleven-plus in 1958. Like Paul Baker, Bill had a mother who was 'very ambitious for her kids', and used her earnings as a shop assistant 'to buy us books and toys'. Her husband worked at the local Dunlop factory, and was, said Bill, 'not less interested in us, but I don't think he saw education as offering so much as she did'. After all her help and encouragement, Bill was confident that he would pass the exam and fulfil his mother's high hopes:

> I was desperate to join the Scouts and my mother made it a condi-
> tion that if I passed the eleven plus you can join the Scouts and I'll
> never forget that day . . . When I got home . . . my dad was sitting
> there having his tea and I said, 'Has it come?' and my dad went 'Yeah',
> and he looked at me and he went [shakes his head], so I got a bit
> upset and I went upstairs and I think my mum was a bit disappointed
> as well but as she said to me later, 'After you've had your tea,' she
> said, 'get washed and go to the Scouts.' So I said, 'But you said I had
> to pass the eleven plus.' She said, 'Never mind.'

Mrs Rainford was not alone in having her aspirations dashed. 'Parents in the manual occupational groups,' observed J. Bynner, in one of the largest surveys of parental attitudes to education – his team interviewed thousands of mothers and fathers – 'seem to suffer a series of dis-appointments with their children's educational achievements.'[33]

Those most likely to fail were working-class children. A difference in material living standards was one reason. Middle-class children were more likely to have plenty of books, a warm and quiet room in which to do their homework, a comfortable house and no financial concerns. In 1954 a government enquiry into early school leaving concluded that 'bad housing' was crucial in explaining why more manual workers' children left school at an early age than those from any other occupational group. Children from large families or whose parents were out of work were likely to perform poorly at school and to leave education at the earliest opportunity in order to find paid work.[34]

If hardship helped explain working-class failure, class bias in the eleven-plus examination assisted middle-class success. By the end of the 1950s, social scientists like A.H. Halsey were highlighting that the exam consistently used middle-class cultural reference points. Private tuition for the examination – affordable for middle-class parents but rarely available to working-class children – boosted a child's chance of success.[35] All this undermined proponents' claims that this was an objective test of 'aptitude' rather than of teaching.

By the end of the 1950s, some social investigators were suggesting that the eleven-plus was an insidious means of keeping most children at the bottom of the pile, rather than helping the talented to rise to the top. In 1955 a report by Robin Pedley, a researcher in the Education Department of University College, London, caught the attention of the *Daily Mirror*: 'he points out that in 1953 ONE IN THREE of the children who originally entered the Castle Rushen comprehensive school . . . gained Certificates of Education – but in England and Wales as a whole, only ONE IN FIVE children is even admitted to grammar schools.'[36] Pedley's suggestion that the eleven-plus actually underrated the academic potential of the nation's children was increasingly echoed in Labour Party debates. In 1956 the party conference voted to adopt a different education policy, which favoured non-selective comprehensive schools over the tripartite system. The Conservative government, however, remained implacably opposed to ending educational selection.

That other large provider of education, the churches, also proved reluctant to provide proper schooling for their working-class pupils. In Liverpool, the Catholic Church was responsible for the secondary education of one-third of the city's schoolchildren, but was unwilling to offer any more than the most basic schooling to its working-class parishioners. In the late 1940s Liverpool Corporation's plan for post-war secondary education was criticized by the Ministry of Education for its 'inadequate Grammar provision'. As the Corporation explained, this was because the Catholic Church was 'not prepared . . . to contemplate full Grammar School provision'.[37] Nor was the Church willing to invest any new money in those dilapidated inner-city 'all age' schools that continued to accommodate most working-class schoolchildren.

One of those to feel the effects of this was Jean McLoughlin. Born in 1947, she was one of fifteen children who grew up in a two-bedroom council flat in inner-city Liverpool. The McLoughlins lived on Myrtle Parade, just a minute's walk from the University of Liverpool campus and ten minutes' walk from the city's famous Lewis's department store and Lime Street Railway Station. The city centre and the university seemed a world away from Jean's early life. 'My dad wasn't really a provider,' said Jean. His children weren't sure what he did for a living, but they knew every father had to have a job, so, 'we asked our mother and she said "he's a whoremaster." So at school, when they asked what your father's occupation was, my brother put "a whoremaster".' This was at St Anne's, a Catholic former elementary school still catering for five- to fifteen-year-olds in the 1950s. 'The nuns thought my mother was wonderful,' Jean recalled; 'they'd say, "Fifteen children, thirteen of them raised!"'

Bearing children and keeping them alive and clean was an achievement to be admired at this school, but it wasn't sufficient for Jean herself. When, at the age of ten, she 'failed' the eleven-plus, 'I was disappointed but I loved the nuns and if you failed you stayed at St Anne's.' But by the age of twelve, Jean's attitude to school had changed. She became the oldest girl in her family not yet out earning a wage. Consequently, 'my mother started to keep me off every Friday to look after the little ones while she did the washing [at the neighbourhood's wash house] – and I hated it.' Jean realized how much she loved learning new things, but her schoolteachers didn't say anything about her absences, let alone try to intervene or suggest that Jean's own life could be any different from or better than her mother's. It was assumed that Jean would leave school at the earliest opportunity and find work – as she did, at the age of fifteen, when she began working in the local clothing factory.

In 1960 Joan Brothers, a Liverpool University postgraduate, found that the Catholic Church's resistance to social and educational change remained strong. Her investigation of the relationship between Church and school discovered that most priests would have preferred their working-class parishioners to remain in Catholic elementary schools. Their major grievance, however, was that grammar school pupils had the confidence and capacity to question the priest's religious and social status. 'They think they have learned a lot,' said one priest disapprovingly. 'They seem to think they're in a position to answer you back.'[38] Many parents preferred their children to attend the newer and better equipped secular state schools, like Bill Rainford's mother, who, after he failed the eleven-plus in 1958, 'fought tooth and nail' to get him into the new Gateacre Comprehensive School near their modern council estate. Council officials told her that this modern, well-equipped school wasn't open to Catholic children, even those who had been educated in local secular primary schools, as Billy had been; they were meant to be bussed to a crumbling Catholic secondary modern in the inner city. Billy's mother won her fight, but other parents and children were condemned to a third-rate education simply because of their religion.

For the few who did leap the hurdle of the eleven-plus, grammar school often initially appeared to be the promised land. Many were aware at having delighted their parents; Howard Blake recalled it as 'one of my Mother's happiest moments'. The grand buildings, ambitious aims of the staff, and the honours boards that adorned the walls of their new schools helped to inculcate a sense of pride in their achievement. In 1959 Paul Baker passed the eleven-plus (to his mother's delight) and was 'very proud' to become a pupil at Coventry's Bablake School. 'The message was "you will all succeed."' Children with a love of learning revelled in the new and exciting subjects on offer; their studies were far in advance of anything their parents had experienced at school. Lorna Sage, the daughter of a car mechanic, grew up in Hanmer, a small village on the Welsh borders. In 1955 she became one of just two or three in her class to pass the eleven-plus examination, a feat she ascribed to her headteacher who invigilated the exam and, through judicious cheating, 'let one or two of us off the fate of being muck-shovellers . . . I owed my privileged position to the Vicarage connection [she was the vicar's granddaughter].' Lorna recalled her first term at Whitchurch High School for Girls as the beginning of a new and exciting life: 'the bus picked me up every day . . . at 8.15 and dropped me off again at 4.30; in between it was just me and all sorts of Latin.'[39]

But far from being a classless environment, the social distinctions between themselves and their middle-class peers soon made many grammar school entrants acutely aware of their social background. 'I suppose that was when I realized I was working class,' said Howard Blake, who found himself among the sons of businessmen and solicitors. In 1952 Ann Lanchbury also passed the eleven-plus in Coventry, and attended a girls' grammar school. 'I wonder if the fact that you were on a council estate did influence your passing [the eleven-plus],' she reflected, 'because I can't remember, truly can't remember any girls that lived on council estates.' Despite relishing her studies at Whitchurch High School, Lorna Sage felt 'like an evacuee or a displaced person'.[40]

These working-class children's sense of difference and inferiority was exacerbated by their classmates. Most grammars were situated some distance from working-class neighbourhoods, in city centres or — most frequently — unfamiliar middle-class suburbs. Wealthier schoolfriends often knew the area and many of their classmates before starting school. Some of the middle-class pupils ostracized their few working-class peers precisely because of their background. '[M]iddle-class children were almost obsessively sure they were clean and others were not,' revealed Brian Jackson and Dennis Marsden.

> Several . . . referred to working-class children at school as being very 'scruffy' or dressed like 'tramps'. There may have been unusual cases of poorly dressed children at the school, but on the whole this was very difficult to accept as a general fact. We were included to feel that we were here recording on the borderline where the exceptional instance supported a social stereotype . . . 'I don't think it's fair,' said Christopher Farrell, 'these snotty-nosed children should be given a chance — but not at a place like [his grammar school] Marburton College.'[41]

Far from overcoming social divisions, selective schooling exacerbated them, by implying that only a few 'deserved' to get on in life.

The schools themselves perpetuated subtle but significant forms of discrimination. After their joy at passing the eleven-plus, children from primary schools in working-class districts were likely to find themselves in the bottom streams of the least popular grammar schools; something that social investigators found had little to do with exam results.[42] Grammars could and did charge for 'extras': stationery, school trips, uniform and sports kit were often prohibitively expensive but lacking them could lead a child to be stigmatized. Ann Lanchbury's older sister 'bought me a satchel, because she'd been to grammar school and she knew these things mattered'. Paul Baker's parents 'fixed it so that I went to my grandmother for lunch every day, which was a long journey, but I realized later that they didn't want me to be the only one in the playground having sandwiches'. His parents couldn't afford school dinners. Jackson and Marsden reported that working-class parents complained that they were never invited into the schools to discuss their children's progress, though certain other parents were made welcome.[43]

Children had to choose whether or not to conform to the schools' resolutely middle-class ethos. Many grammars dissuaded pupils from involving themselves in neighbourhood youth clubs or sports teams.[44] 'Boys who seek their leisure amusements in the clubs and societies organised by the school,' reported Bablake School's hand-book for parents, 'prosper academically more than those who join external clubs and societies which may conflict with school loyal-ties.'[45] But this meant that working-class pupils had to give up their neighbourhood friends in order to fit in school homework and sports. The lack of rugby league or soccer irked working-class boys; grammars played rugby union, just one way in which they imitated Britain's public schools.[46] These elements of school culture had nothing to do with fostering academic success; they simply promoted and perpetuated social elitism.

Children were torn between two worlds: they wanted to make their parents proud, but were being taught that success depended on them rejecting their parents' experiences. Margaret Forster passed the eleven-plus in 1949. She was the daughter of a factory worker; her mother had been a local government clerk until she married, and was clearly not entirely fulfilled by domesticity. She encouraged Margaret to do well but, as her daughter progressed through Carlisle County High School, '[a]ll she could see were problems looming, a gulf emerging.'[47]

'I didn't see much of my parents around that time,' said Paul Baker of his first four years at Bablake School. His entry to grammar school coincided with his father, previously a milkman, getting a better paid factory job; the family bought their own house in Coundon, a slightly more prosperous suburb, and Paul, 'as the boy, got the bigger bedroom'; his younger sister, Vicky, got the boxroom. Paul would retire to his room with the excuse of doing his homework; it was true that he had plenty, but he also felt ambivalent about his parents' lifestyle. They'd given up so much, and continued to help in many ways – in Paul's bedroom stood a large bookcase that his father had made in his spare time for his son's schoolbooks. At the same time, they didn't understand how his own horizons were being broadened. They worried that he might find home wanting when he saw the posher houses of his classmates, but this wasn't the problem for Paul. More of an issue for him was that school opened up a world beyond Coventry that felt new and exciting, but could seem threatening to his parents. 'When there were school trips and so on to France, or ski-ing, I couldn't go; they'd say it was passports and money, and it was – but it was also that they didn't know why anyone would want to do that. It wasn't part of their world.' His mother couldn't see the sense in throwing good money away on foreign trips: what did that have to do with getting on and getting a good job? Like Margaret Forster's mother, she may well have worried about the social distance that her son's education seemed to be creating between them.

Many pupils eventually rebelled. Paul Baker was among them. By the age of fifteen, he had changed from a proud eleven-year-old desperate 'to succeed' into 'an outsider . . . I felt like a liability that they [the school] legally had to bring these . . . poor people . . . I felt a little bit ostracized.' While his schooling gave him an insight into worlds beyond Coventry, the school itself failed to support his ambitions, insisting on a narrow curriculum that was geared primarily towards excellent examination results. A group of children emerged whose path seemed to be leading towards university, but Paul was not among them. 'They never included my parents in discussions or anything like that,' he said; 'but there were others who were always at events, whose children went on the trips.' Others shared his experience. 'We were all scruffy kids – it was the ones who had better clothes and houses who got on best at school,' one eighteen-year-old former grammar school boy from London's East End told an interviewer in 1956. 'I always hated them.'[48] The vast majority of grammar school pupils left at sixteen – but working-class pupils were far more likely to leave than their middle-class contemporaries.

Far from being active agents of social mobility, grammar school teachers dissuaded many working-class entrants from staying on into the sixth form. An exceptional and determined few were encouraged, and some were lucky to meet inspirational teachers. 'I had a brilliant English teacher, Miss Wynne, who was helping me to be A Reader,' recalled Margaret Forster. 'She gave me a list of all the authors a well-read person should have read. It was exactly what I needed and wanted but it irritated my mother, she saw it as creating that very gulf she dreaded.'[49] Later, in sixth form, teachers produced booklets about the Oxbridge women's colleges which inspired Margaret to apply successfully for university. But most of that small minority who made it to sixth form were channelled into technical or industrial work rather than encouraged to apply to university. The Crowther Report highlighted that the few working-class children who did stay on after fifteen often took the wrong A-levels or O-levels for university entrance, or were unaware that government grants and scholarships were available for university students.[50] Schools with large middle-class intakes didn't bother to inform pupils about the process of applying to university, assuming their parents would do so; and often presuming that their working-class pupils weren't fitted for advanced study. Paul Baker's dream of becoming a barrister was dismissed by his headmaster, who belatedly pointed out that Paul needed Latin O-level to study arts at university. Many working-class girls were pushed into teacher training despite achieving the grades required for university entrance.[51] Far from opening up new horizons, grammar school was, for many children, a series of examination hurdles to be jumped as one trudged along an ever narrower and more circumscribed path to 'success'.

A fortunate and determined few made it through, but they were a tiny minority. Just 4 per cent of eighteen- and nineteen-year-olds attended university during the 1950s, although a quarter of their age group achieved the entry requirements.[52] There simply weren't university places available for them – a state of affairs that eventually led Macmillan's government to appoint the Robbins Committee in 1961 with a brief to 'review the pattern of full-time higher education'.[53] But Robbins's recommendation that universities expand was not implemented until Labour took power once more in 1964, too late for the first generation who had received their secondary education under the 1944 Education Act. The grammar schools were not solely responsible for this situation, but they helped to ensure that those selected for university were from privileged social backgrounds.

Nevertheless, those working-class children who did attend grammar schools were likely to enter different occupations to their parents. Paul Baker left school shortly after his seventeenth birthday. He had been talked into science A-levels by teachers who convinced him that they would make him more employable; but the hard grind seemed stultifying and he didn't complete his exams. Instead, he became an accountant. He remained disappointed that 'all my interest in the arts – in French, in literature, the cinema' remained unused in his daily work, but he donned a shirt and tie for work and had more power over his working life than his father had ever enjoyed.

Young women's occupational choices were also broadening. In 1956 sixteen-year-old Hazel Wood, the daughter of a Coventry car worker and a former shop assistant, became a nurse. She was inspired by visiting the local hospital with a friend 'and I knew it was what I wanted to do . . . no one in the family had been a nurse so they didn't really know anything about it', but Hazel's schoolfriend Ann Lanchbury had discovered that they could begin training as soon as they were sixteen and a half. 'A lot of our neighbours and friends, they automatically left school and went into the factory,' said Hazel, 'but that wasn't even thought about . . . because I'd gone to a grammar school.' Former grammar school pupils were more likely than secondary modern school-leavers to enter clerical jobs and they filled the increasing number of middle-management posts and technical professions, becoming laboratory technicians, chemists and draughtsmen.

These new opportunities were not the result of a changing education system, but a consequence of a revolution in the workplace. In the 1950s and 1960s demand for technicians, nurses and middle managers grew, thanks to the expansion in local government and the National Health Service, and the growth of the electrical and technical industries. In 1951, 6 per cent of workers were employed in the professions and 3 per cent were in managerial positions. By 1971, 10 per cent were in the professions, and 6 per cent were managers.[54] As the sociologist J.H. Goldthorpe pointed out, the grammar schools themselves did not expand access to the professions; what mattered was increased demand for teachers, technicians and nurses.[55] The education system simply determined who got the chance to compete for these posts.

Most of the fortunate few only travelled a short distance up the social ladder. Working-class grammar school pupils were as unlikely to find work in the most prestigious and remunerative professions like law or the civil service as they had been before the Second World War.[56] The grammar schools remained resolutely middle class, and the private education sector survived the post-war reforms. Clement Attlee, himself an alumnus of Haileybury public school, resisted calls by Labour's left wing to end the charitable status of these expensive and elitist institutions. Throughout the 1950s private schools educated 5 per cent of the population but provided more than half the undergraduates at Oxford and Cambridge.[57] Barristers, professors and senior civil servants continued to be drawn almost exclusively from the small pool of public school and Oxbridge graduates.[58]

Those working-class children who had made it to grammar school often perceived their limited success as failure. Unlike many of their primary school classmates, they worked in offices, owned their own houses, and lived in suburbs remote from their families' homes. But nurses and technicians earned no more than most skilled manual workers in the 1960s and had few promotion prospects. As Jackson and Marsden found among their sample, they could become frustrated at how little their hard work had achieved.[59] Few of them attained the dreams their parents had harboured for them. Paul Baker spoke of his lifelong 'guilt' at 'letting my mother down'. Hazel Wood was conscious that her parents saw nursing as 'poorly paid and they just wanted their family to do well and get good jobs and have plenty of money . . . they thought because I'd gone to a grammar school I was going to be a doctor or [an academic] . . . they suddenly had ambitions and I let them down.'

Hazel's generation found that attaining the ambitions their parents had harboured did not always deliver happiness. Luckily, Hazel herself enjoyed nursing and her parents quickly became 'quite proud of me'. Tom Courtenay, a dock worker's son from Hull, felt less fortunate. His mother strongly supported him through grammar school and university. An avid reader, she had once written to her son that she 'could have cried because I wasn't educated'. But her son found academic success boring. 'It is hardly surprising that when at UCL I found that getting a good education had become an almost intolerable burden, I felt very, very guilty.'[60] He failed his degree. Tom Courtenay's story had a happy ending: he managed to get a scholarship to RADA, and his parents proved more understanding than he'd dared to hope. But many of Jackson and Marsden's interviewees felt 'unsettled' and 'disillusioned' several years after beginning work as technicians or schoolteachers.[61] Meanwhile, the most privileged jobs in Britain remained in the hands of a tiny minority, who were unwilling to let anyone else break into the circle.

Fifty years on, politicians and journalists from across the political spectrum created a consensus that the 1950s was the 'golden age of social mobility'.[62] But in reality, selective secondary education ensured that there were very few golden tickets to go round, and most of them went to the children of privileged parents. Many manual workers had high hopes that their children's opportunities would be greater, and did all they could to make this possible. But the post-war economy required thousands of assembly-line workers and thousands more to undertake routine clerical work; and successive governments ensured that the education system was tailored to provide them.[63] The 'lucky' few discovered that 'success' meant treading a narrow path of unquestioning conformity, which offered some material rewards, but rarely the educational fulfilment or professional advancement they had hoped for. Their 'success' relied on the failure of the many. Their schooling made many children acutely aware of just how unequal Britain remained.

By the late 1950s, some were beginning to question whether mobility into the middle class should really be an aim of education. In 1958 the television journalist Jack Ashley produced the ground-breaking BBC television series *Does Class Matter?*. Ashley wanted to examine 'the problem of social class in its modern setting', including the extent of prosperity, the impact of slum clearance, and the effects of education and social mobility. He chose to interview a young working-class Oxford undergraduate about them: his name was Dennis Potter. He told Ashley that while he hoped to escape from the poverty and parochialism of his parents' mining village, 'I certainly want to keep a sense of identity, as it were, with that background.'[64] By the end of the 1950s, an increasing number of people were echoing Potter's assertion that their everyday experience gave working-class people a unique and valuable identity, one that didn't simply disappear if they earned more money or gained a degree. Being working class was about to become fashionable.

II

Working-Class Heroes

IN OCTOBER 1957 Margaret Forster began a history degree at Somerville College, Oxford. She came from a council estate in Carlisle: her father was a factory worker; her mother a former clerk; her older brother, Gordon, had failed the eleven-plus exam and now worked in a chemist's shop and her younger sister, Pauline, was still at school. To her surprise, she found at Oxford that 'being working class at the end of the Fifties . . . was *the* thing . . . instead of being embarrassed by our class, or concealing it, we flaunted it, to great effect, realizing how special it made us.'[1]

During the late 1950s and early 1960s, a cultural revolution took place in Britain. Being working class became fashionable. Teenagers could take some of the credit. Although 'affluence' remained limited, young wage-earners were increasingly significant consumers. The few who managed to climb the social ladder, like Forster herself, also played a pivotal role. They did not look like their parents and they led very different sorts of lives – to many journalists and politicians they symbolized a prosperous, meritocratic society in which working-class people could play significant roles.

If a generation of teenagers played an important part in this transformation, so too did a small number of upwardly mobile writers, actors, journalists and television entrepreneurs. They brought working-class heroes of the post-war generation to an audience of thousands, and at times millions, of ordinary people. They created 'angry young men' like Joe Lampton in *Room at the Top* and Billy Fisher in *Billy Liar*, and *Coronation Street*'s duffel-coated Ken Barlow, whose Oxford degree and frequent fits of pique distinguished him from the other characters on Britain's most successful soap opera. These young men personified a very modern dilemma: whether to use new post-war opportunities to pursue wealth and social status, or to reject these in favour of the community and solidarity that working-class life could offer. None of the new novels, films or television shows resolved this question – but all of them suggested that working-class life was of intrinsic interest and value.

This cultural revolution changed the lives of some working-class people for ever, as they found celebrity as writers, actors or pop stars. But it also touched millions more people, who saw their lives and experiences portrayed as being both normal and note-worthy. Those who came of age in the late 1950s and early 1960s were particularly affected, as they came to believe that they deserved a better life than their parents had experienced, in which they would find not only a steady job, but more excitement and independence.

Just a year before Margaret Forster arrived at Oxford, no one could have predicted this transformation. Although the vast majority of people in 1950s Britain were working class, middle- and upper-class life dominated stage, screen and literature. BBC Radio offered *The Archers*, an 'everyday story of country folk' which focused on a rural squirearchy. The first television soap opera – the BBC's *Grove Family* – followed the quiet, comfortable, suburban life of an English middle-class family headed by Jack Grove, a self-employed builder. Hollywood romances and costume dramas dominated the cinema, at a time when audiences relished escaping wartime memories and the over-crowded reality of home. In January 1956 theatregoers had a final chance to see Terence Rattigan's middle-class drawing-room drama, *Separate Tables* at London's St James's Theatre, before its two-year run ended – the greatest success a play had ever achieved on that stage. New middlebrow literature included Kingsley Amis's *Lucky Jim*, a light-hearted look at academic life. 'Normal' life was apparently lived in drawing rooms and universities, and centred on witty small talk, not anxiety about whether affluence would last, anger about the survival of privilege, or aspirations for life's luxuries.

Kenneth Tynan, the *Observer's* influential theatre critic, was among the crowds who flocked to see John Osborne's *Look Back in Anger* in 1956. The play focused on Jimmy, an 'angry young man' from a lower-middle-class or working-class background, and his upper-middle-class girlfriend, Alison. Radically, the play was told from Jimmy's point of view rather than from that of his social superiors. Tynan declared *Look Back in Anger* to be the most innovative play to appear since the war. In his opinion, 1956 would be remembered as the year when 'there issued the distinct sound of barricades being erected'.[2]

Then in April 1957 came John Braine's novel *Room at the Top*. This told the story of Joe Lampton, a young working-class man on the make in post-war Britain. *Room at the Top* sold 34,000 copies in hardback within a year of publication and was rapidly serialized in the *Daily Express*. The working-class hero was born. A new wave of writing explored the challenges faced by a generation of young, northern, working-class men and women (but usually men) who wanted to get on in life without losing their roots. In 1958 Alan Sillitoe's novel *Saturday Night and Sunday Morning* followed Arthur Seaton, a Nottingham factory worker (as Sillitoe had been himself). In the same year, eighteen-year-old Shelagh Delaney from Salford scored a hit in London's West End with her play *A Taste of Honey*, the tale of Jo, a working-class teenage girl who leaves home, has a brief affair with a black sailor, and finds herself pregnant. Keith Waterhouse's novel *Billy Liar* followed in 1959; the protagonist, a frustrated bohemian, hailed from Waterhouse's native West Yorkshire. The next year saw the publication of Stan Barstow's *A Kind of Loving* and David Storey's *This Sporting Life*.

By 1960, working-class life was also appearing on screen. Nine of the so-called 'kitchen sink' novels, plays and short stories were swiftly adapted into successful films that defined British cinema's new wave. In 1961 *Saturday Night and Sunday Morning* was the third-biggest box office hit in Britain, outstripping every other British-made film released that year. Most significant of all was the broadcast of *Coronation Street* on Granada Television from December 1960. Twenty-three-year-old Tony Warren described his new soap opera as 'full of characters all stamped with a strongly-flavoured, doughty and impudent scepticism of the Lancastrian North'.[3] Granada had initially planned to restrict broadcasts to the north-west, but such was the appeal that *Coronation Street* quickly became Britain's most popular television programme.

Many of these writers were provoked by frustration that post-war literature and film resolutely ignored their experiences and those of their families and neighbours. Shelagh Delaney was a Salford factory clerk, who was inspired to write *A Taste of Honey* after seeing Terence Rattigan's *Variations on a Theme* at Manchester's Library Theatre. Delaney derisively dismissed his depiction of 'safe, sheltered, cultured lives in charming surroundings – not life as the majority of ordinary people know it'. She was tired, she said 'of plays where working-class people simply appear as imbeciles, to be laughed at'.[4] The team behind *Coronation Street* was highly critical of what Derek Granger, one of the programme's first producers, called 'the stock figures in a stock formula – Mr and Mrs Everyman from a sweetly antiseptic, dehydrated no-class land'.[5]

By the late 1950s, many writers also believed that working-class people were challenging the social hierarchy in ways that should not be ignored. 'The bright young men from the provinces were no longer content to sit back and accept what was given to them,' said Stan Barstow, the Yorkshire draughtsman who wrote *A Kind of Loving*. 'The air crackled with a new energy. Anything seemed possible.'[6] But these young men demurred from the political celebration of the 'meritocracy', eschewing the idea that people could, or necessarily should wish to, escape from working-class life. They questioned whether the middle class was socially or culturally superior, and asserted that working-class people possessed values – a strong sense of community, loyalty, creativity and sincerity – that social mobility or slum clearance might threaten. 'I wanted,' said Alan Sillitoe of his creation Arthur Seaton, 'to write a novel about a working man who, though not necessarily typical of the zone of life he lived in, belonged to it with so much flesh and blood that nothing could cause him to leave it.'[7]

Barstow was not alone in believing that working-class people were assuming a new control over their lives. By the late 1950s a generation had grown up knowing full employment and the welfare state. They symbolized what Keith Waterhouse – in a feature for the *Daily Mirror* published in 1958 – called the 'Beanstalk Generation'. The epithet captured the health and affluence of those babies born after the war, who were now becoming teenagers and whose prospects were, said Waterhouse, better than those of 'any previous generation'.[8] They had no family responsibilities and so enjoyed a large disposable income. In 1958 Marc Abrams, a researcher at the London School of Economics, excitedly announced the emergence of a new 'teenage market' that was 'almost entirely working class'; unlike most of their middle-class peers, these young people were earning a wage by their mid-teens. They were the producers and the chief consumers of cosmetics and cigarettes, records and scooters; they patronized dance halls and coffee bars.[9] For these young people, the 'hungry thirties' were an unknown past.

The newspapers that entered working-class homes encouraged teenagers to see themselves as pioneers of a newly prosperous kind of ordinary life. Accounts of Teddy Boy violence or fights between Mods and Rockers studded the press during the 1950s and early 1960s and fed into political panics about whether working mothers and the desire for new consumer goods produced juvenile delinquency. But journalists also offered more optimistic observations of teenagers, particularly in the latter half of the 1950s when they could be viewed as heralding affluence. 'Beanstalkers are Big Business!' declared the *Mirror*.[10] In 1958 the *Manchester Guardian* reported on a conference of youth workers that concluded that 'the Teddy Boy movement was a hopeful thing'; Leslie Paul, the founder of the socially progressive youth movement the Woodcraft Folk, pointed out that the 'modern display of £25 suits is the protest of young men with money, who live still in the dismal back streets, against a past they disown'.[11] Here was a generation experiencing unprecedented prosperity and opportunity. In an era of rising wages and full employment, teenagers were encouraged to aspire not just to a steady job and the economic security that would bring, but to creativity and emotional fulfilment.

Politicians also shone the spotlight on working-class teenagers. In 1960 Leslie Paul accepted an invitation to join the government-commissioned Albemarle Committee, charged with discovering what teenagers needed and wanted. Other members included Richard Hoggart, who had 'passed the scholarship' to secondary school in the 1930s and had then graduated from Leeds University, before becoming an adult education tutor after the war and writing *The*

Uses of Literacy, published in 1957. The committee's report sanctioned shopping, fashion, lounging in coffee bars and jiving the night away as significant cultural activities, 'charged with an emotional content', that offered young people an outlet for 'creativity' that might be otherwise stultified in monotonous factory and office jobs.[12] All this suggested that working-class teenagers had much to offer the country, and deserved to have their aspirations taken seriously.

For a fortunate few, these years brought stardom. Young men like Albert Finney, who played Arthur Seaton in *Saturday Night and Sunday Morning*, and Tom Courtenay, who starred in *Billy Liar* and *The Loneliness of the Long Distance Runner*, were the first in their working-class families to enter higher education. Courtenay found himself a couple of years behind Finney at RADA, at a time when 'it was the thing to be working class, and ambitious young men in London would compete to demonstrate their credentials.'[13] The same was true for a tiny minority of women. When twenty-two-year-old Shirley Ann Field, an actress from Bolton, was cast as Doreen in the film of *Saturday Night and Sunday Morning*, 'Tony Richardson [the director] said they'd been looking for a working-class heroine and I felt a bit affronted' – she'd been trying to lose her accent for years. 'I don't think the north was so much ignored as patronized,' she said.[14] In 1961 Tony Richardson brought *A Taste of Honey* to the big screen, and sided with Shelagh Delaney against the powerful production company who wanted to use Audrey Hepburn as the lead. Richardson and Delaney successfully argued that an 'unknown' would do a better job and a nineteen-year-old Liverpudlian, Rita Tushingham, got the part.[15]

A small but smart coterie of upwardly mobile journalists and writers assiduously promoted these working-class heroes. In *The Uses of Literacy* Richard Hoggart suggested that working-class communities championed values that Britain was in danger of losing: neighbourliness, mutual help, sincerity and integrity.[16] Hunter Davies was a generation younger than Hoggart, and preferred to promote working-class pioneers of change. In 1964 Davies, who hailed from a working-class home in Carlisle, was a journalist on the *Sunday Times*. When he took over the newspaper's 'Atticus' column, he 'dumped all interviews and stuff about bishops and establishment figures', focusing instead 'on the new confident cockney photographers, cocky Northern actors, young fashion designers, new TV playwrights, working-class novelists and young football stars'.[17]

Journalists and politicians were quick to use these rising stars as proof of a new meritocracy. Far from eschewing their working-class past, these new celebrities were encouraged to embrace it – and to invent one if necessary. 'I wasn't really working class,' recalled Rita Tushingham three decades later. 'As I kept telling journalists, I came from a middle-class home, but they kept saying I was working class.'[18] Politicians' talk of a meritocracy and journalists' celebrations of working-class teenagers' affluence suggested that being working class meant being innovative and hard-working: hailing from a working-class background meant a star had 'got on' through merit and popular appeal. In the late 1950s, John Lennon, a grammar school boy who had grown up in lower-middle-class suburbia, met Paul McCartney, then at the city's most prestigious grammar school, the Liverpool Institute. They never made any attempt to hide their background but were quickly hailed by the press as working-class heroes.[19] Press features on Jane Asher's relationship with Paul McCartney focused on 'the doctor's daughter with a Beatle boyfriend', and quoted her as saying 'class doesn't matter anymore'.[20] All this suggested that class inequalities were dying, if not dead – being replaced by a new, swinging, meritocratic generation.

In 1964 Brian Epstein, already well-known as the Beatles' manager, boasted to the *Daily Express* about his latest signing, Cilla Black. 'Cilla comes from the roughest, toughest area of Liverpool, and is full of the most fabulous, burning natural vitality,' he said.[21] Like the 'angry young men', Epstein suggested that working-class people possessed an authenticity derived from their daily experience of struggle. They were unfettered by the stuffy conventions of middle- or upper-class life, and no longer hampered by the poverty that their parents had endured. The pop stars of the early 1960s sang about ordinary life and wore high street fashions; like contemporary actors Albert Finney and Tom Courtenay they proudly retained their regional accents. By the early 1960s, they were deliberately challenging the narrow definition of 'success' that post-war policymakers and grammar schools offered.

The millions of people who didn't become famous were nonetheless affected by this new understanding of working-class teenagers as both ordinary and special. As Alan Watkins of Coventry put it:

[W]e never looked . . . at our parents as role models and actually I don't think they wanted us to. I think we wanted to get on, do something different and I think that they wanted us to do better as well. I think the encouragement was from them . . . You know, 'You can do that . . . I never had a chance to do it, I couldn't do it, but you do it' and my dad was very much like that. He would always push, you know, 'have a go'.[22]

One way of 'having a go' was succeeding at school, but that path was only open to a few. Many parents and teenagers preferred (or had no choice but) to remain rooted in their neighbourhood, among family and friends. Rather than trying to escape their background, they proudly asserted their working-class credentials. Judy Walker was born in Coventry in 1940. After leaving school in 1955 she became a shop assistant at the city centre's new branch of British Home Stores, and later worked in a smart new boutique 'aimed at young girls'. By eighteen, Judy was 'rocking and rolling six nights a week' in Coventry's dance halls. She preferred jiving to the twist, she said, because 'there was more room for self-expression'.[23] Dancing and fashion had long provided working-class teenagers with outlets for a creativity denied them at work, but in the late 1950s and early 1960s their affluence and their large numbers (due to the rise in births during the mid- and late 1940s) made them more conspicuous, while the interest of journalists, politicians and parents imbued their activities with a new significance.

Other teenagers, particularly young men, formed pop groups. Ian White of Lancashire, who had failed the eleven-plus in the late 1940s, became part of a skiffle band in the late 1950s. Terry Rimmer of Liverpool, who had had to give up his dreams of art school due to his mother's poverty, was in 'loads and loads' of bands during the Merseybeat era of the early 1960s. Few of these men were in serious pursuit of celebrity. The social scientist Peter Willmott discovered that only 10 per cent of teenage boys in Bethnal Green aspired to become 'the entertainers, the pop stars and the professional footballers who achieve success and, in some sense at least, retain contact with their origins'.[24] But, as Ian White found, making music out of a washboard gave him a creative outlet that factory work could never offer. In the early 1960s Alan Watkins formed a band with a group of workmates, all engineering apprentices like himself. They called it 'The Sentors', 'after a piece of the Rolls Royce engine' on which they worked: a statement of pride in what they did and who they were.

These teenagers, and many of their parents, consumed the growing array of books, films and television shows about working-class life. As wages rose, more people could afford books, which were in any case becoming cheaper as the cost of producing paperbacks fell. 'Richard Hoggart's *The Uses of Literacy* had made a great impression on me,' recalled Tom Courtenay, who read the book in the year he left his Hull grammar school for London University. 'He spoke unselfconsciously about the working class that I knew. I loved seeing the people I had grown up among taken seriously.'[25] One Saturday afternoon in 1960, sixteen-year-old Robert Colls read *The Uses of Literacy* in his family's small terraced house in South Shields. He was surprised to read about the people whom he could see from his bedroom window, and was astonished to find a writer 'saying that the lives they lived were cultured, and worthy of attention'. When Colls put down the book, 'I saw that what I was looking at from the window was indeed a "community" . . . it was fairly big news for a grammar school boy who, at the time, was being trained to purge himself of who he was and where he came from.'[26]

Other working-class teenagers came across the British 'new wave' at school. While grammar schools tended to focus on examinations, teachers in secondary modern schools and further education colleges could be more adventurous. In 1963 Janet Hill, a Lambeth librarian, undertook a survey of teenagers' reading. She received a letter from 'three girls in an intermediate approved school [who] enthusiastically reported that "our teacher has read us *The Loneliness of the Long Distance Runner*."' Eva Fulleylove, who tutored day-release students at a Manchester college, wrote that '*A Taste of Honey* proved very popular' with them, partly because of its content and partly because it 'was in their idiom'.[27] These books, films and plays told this generation that their background and experiences were important – that they themselves deserved consideration.

The small screen had an even bigger impact. By 1960, more than 90 per cent of British households had a television set. On the evening of 9 December that year, nineteen-year-old Carol Hinde, the oldest daughter of Christine and Jack Elliott, and now a factory worker, was 'down in John's [her fiancé's] mum's and we were all looking forward to this new thing on television. *Coronation Street*. And I remember Ena Sharples . . . it was new and it was wonderful, and it was so funny to see just people sat round the kitchen table just talking . . . People like us.'

In 1961 the *Manchester Evening News* celebrated the soap's first birthday with a reader's feature: 'What *Coronation Street* Means to Me'. Readers young and old wrote in with fulsome praise. 'This programme recaptures, for many of us, the spirit of old Lancashire,' wrote M.V.H. of Sale, a sentiment shared by others who felt the soap showcased the neighbourliness that slum clearance, out-of-town housing estates and affluence might threaten. And *Coronation Street*'s contemporary elements attracted younger viewers too. Thirteen-year-old Linda Haig thought that it was 'typical of Lancashire life' in the present. The variety of comments, and heated debate over who was the favourite character (no votes for Ken Barlow, but plenty for matriarch Ena Sharples, no-nonsense pub landlady Annie Walker and Sharples's risqué *bête noire*, Elsie Tanner) reflected the programme's clever combination of the culture people associated with the old inner cities with the economic security of the 1960s. Regardless of whether they thought the programme nostalgic or up-to-date, many working-class viewers agreed with J. Taylor of Flixton that *Coronation Street* offered an enjoyable 'slice of reality'.[28] At a time when very few other programmes depicted working-class life at all, this was an innovation.

By the early 1960s, working-class people could see their lives reflected in bookshops, on library shelves, in cinemas and on television. This cultural revolution was to contribute to a new political assertiveness among the generation who had come of age on the cusp of the 1960s.

According to many journalists and politicians, Britain was entering an age of prosperity, in which class would become a personal, cultural identity, divorced from economics or political allegiance. Young pop stars and actors were applauded for their working-class authenticity (through their rejection of dinner jackets and upper-class accents), suggesting that a new generation of teenagers would retain the best of working-class values while enjoying unprecedented affluence.

But this focus on the fortunate few neglected the thousands of working-class people who didn't choose the circumstances in which they lived. Looking back from the late 1960s, the Australian journalist John Pilger sounded a note of caution: 'Behind a façade of new-found egalitarianism, such as the lionizing of working-class pop stars, fashion designers, and actors, "modernizing" society meant bringing poverty up to date, as in moving people from old slums to modern wastelands. The message was that these were swinging times and progress was progress.'[29]

Pilger was correct. Class was not simply a cultural identity, to be chosen or discarded on a whim. Away from the television and the cinema screen, people continued to experience profound inequalities, in education, at work and in their neighbourhoods. As the 1964 general election grew closer, the gap between political hyperbole about classless celebrities and the reality of people's daily lives gave rise to a new wave of anger and discontent.

Interlude VI

Spend, Spend, Spend

B Y 1961, VIV was happier than she'd ever been. She was married to the man she loved and 'we had a three-piece [suite], nice red carpet, nice little table lamp, [and] a rented TV'. She made sure that Keith and her children sat down to a hot dinner every night and was proud that 'those kids really had their fill'. She wasn't the only one to feel that life was finally looking up. In 1960 the average weekly wage was £14 10s. It had tripled since 1950.[1]

Yet by September 1961, the Nicholsons were only weeks away from losing everything. The reason was credit: their furniture, television and even their clothes were 'all got on tick, of course, with some help from me mum'. Viv regretted that she and Keith hadn't saved up before getting married. 'We were wondering if we had really made a mistake in being together,' said Viv, 'because we used to hear others saying, "I'm getting married when I've saved up enough to put down on a house or to have so much towards the furniture."'

Secure work and rising wages meant long engagements made good sense by the early 1960s – though they weren't always much fun. Full employment and, in the 1950s, the availability of housing meant that people were marrying at ever younger ages – a trend that would only end in the 1970s – but they needed to save up first to afford the homes and comforts they wanted. Yet in the households of dockers, labourers, miners and steelworkers – jobs where insecurity or danger were ever present – long years of saving made less sense. Viv had no certainty that Keith would complete his training and, meanwhile, credit was a temptingly easy way of getting hold of the good things in life. The Labour MP Nye Bevan condemned the alleged affluent society as a 'brash materialism shot through with fear'.[2] He could have been talking about Viv's daily life. She didn't tell Keith that they were drowning in debt. She feared he would leave if he couldn't enjoy the odd night at the pub with his mates and 'I'd have been left on me own with the bloody kids' – for, by 1961, she was a mother of three. The authors of *Coal is Our Life* had observed that in many mining communities, '[i]t is for him to earn the money and for her to administer it wisely' – but even if a husband didn't bring home the cash, his wife had to put food on the table for her family.[3]

Making ends meet remained a struggle; the new home comforts concealed an enduring poverty of which women bore the brunt. In 1960, when Viv gave birth to her third and last child, Howard, she weighed barely eight stone. She 'hardly once sat down to a square meal'. In the year of Howard's birth, researchers in London carried out a study of 734 families in the capital and found that women were more likely to suffer ill-health than men, with those in the poorest homes being most vulnerable to digestive disorders, back pain and joint problems – all medical conditions caused or exacerbated by a poor diet and exhaustion.[4] The problems documented by Margery Spring Rice in the 1930s had diminished, but they had not disappeared.

Viv knew that her family's home comforts – and, indeed, their home – depended far more on her job as a barmaid than Keith cared to admit. However, her ability to go out to work relied on her mother's willingness to care for her grandchildren. By 1961, her mother's chronic asthma was getting worse and she announced, 'I can't look after them kids no more.'

On Tuesday, 19 September Viv had 'six pounds between me and starvation'. On the following Friday, the TV rental man called at the Nicholsons' home, demanding that Viv pay her arrears. Worried by the threat of bailiffs, Viv paid up. 'That Friday evening I said to Keith, "Does tha know what I think we'll do, lad? We've two pounds left. Shall we blow it?" "Those are the best words I've heard for bleeding months," he said. "We'll get drunk."'

Working-class women weren't supposed to manage their finances in this manner. The post-war welfare state rewarded hard work; fecklessness was frowned upon. But on Saturday, 23 September, while

Viv was getting ready to go to the pub, Keith sat in front of their rented television and, together with 14 million other people, checked his Littlewoods football pools coupon. As the announcer read out the results, Keith could hardly believe his ears. He ran down to his father-in-law's house, taking his ticket with him. 'Tha's got eight draws, lad,' Viv's father confirmed, and the Nicholsons' lives changed for ever.

The *Daily Mirror* knew that its headline of 28 September 1961 – 'Girl Who Dreamed of Being Rich' – would grab readers' attention. 'Blonde Vivian Nicholson always dreamed of having money. LOTS of money,' began the article telling readers of Keith's historic win. Glossing over Viv's collapse when Bruce Forsyth handed Keith the cheque, the tabloids concentrated on what happened once she recovered: 'She grabbed a bowler hat and umbrella which someone had left lying about, gave a high kick, and yelled: "Yippee – we're in the money! From now on I'm going to SPEND and SPEND and SPEND!"'

Viv's aspirations resonated with the desires of those millions of people who filled in pools coupons each week. She wanted 'to throw big parties and not have to bother about the cooking'; to buy a 'big American car' – America was the land of the free and affluent – and most of all, to give her children a better life than her own. 'I bought them so much I don't remember what,' she said of that trip to London to collect the cheque; among these purchases, the *Mirror* reported, were 'bigger dolls and better dolls than the one Vivian coveted as a child, and finally bought for herself with cash earned by running errands'. This was post-war affluence writ large, with the constant echo of pre-war hardship to remind people what good times they were living in.

Viv hadn't won the money – Keith had; but the press was fascinated by her. (Keith barely got a mention, except as a means of telling readers that Viv's 'first marriage was dissolved'.) Journalists speculated on how she would spend the money; underpinning their articles was anxiety about whether working-class women could handle affluence wisely. In 1958 the *Mirror* had reported on 'blonde Barbara Carter' who 'Just Loved Signing Men's Cheques'. Miss Carter had paid for her fashionable clothes by forging her (numerous) boyfriends' signatures. The newspaper's account of her trial for forgery concluded with a combination of admiration and moralizing that was common to tales of women's profligacy: 'In the dock she was smartly dressed in a slate-grey suit, pale blue hat and elbow-length gloves. But, after sentence, her smart clothes were exchanged for the drab garments she will wear in Holloway Prison . . .'[5]

Men got on in life by hard work; women got by with luck, deception and sex; or so such stories implied. Behind these tales lurked a fear that the economic independence that affluence offered – through paid work or easy credit – might unleash working-class women's rapacious sexual and materialistic appetites.

After the initial euphoria faded, the press tried hard to present Viv and Keith as a model modern couple committed to hard work and judicious saving. Journalists instilled a moral in their tale by suggesting that Keith deserved his win after years as a hard-working miner. Five days after their win, a *Mirror* feature on the Nicholsons' homecoming painted a picture of Keith ('an ex-miner – "Stress the ex"') and Viv as 'ordinary folk with simple tastes, who have known hard times and hard work for much of their young lives'. Vivian – now given her longer, more sober-sounding name – had apparently revised many of her expectations: 'The big American car?' Vivian said. 'They're a bit showy for Castleford, aren't they? And not very good for our roads.' Keith chipped in: "We'll settle for a British family car, luv.'

'Vivian's Dad up the road' allegedly told the *Mirror*: 'If they buy me a nice set of false teeth I'll be content.' 'Vivian' and Keith planned to stay 'on at their council house living as simply as they were last week', and Keith apparently regretted his decision to leave work and become a man of leisure.[6]

Viv's recollections of those first few weeks of wealth were very different. 'For the first time in my life I had been to a big hotel where you had your breakfast brought to you and everyone was always fussing round you,' she remembered in her autobiography. 'So Keith and me stayed at me mum's' – living it up while searching for the car of Viv's dreams. They eventually settled on a large, American Chevrolet Impala. It was so vast that when they came to search for their next long-desired dream – a house – Viv insisted they confine their search to new estates where the roads would be broad enough to allow her to drive easily. They settled on a large show home on a private estate several miles from their old home. Keith noted, thankfully, that it was well away from the pit; he never thought of returning to work, whatever the *Mirror* might say.

The media found that their story of the tragic pools winner who misses the simple life did not appeal to most readers. 'What a joy to read about people who are going to spend, spend, spend!' wrote Mrs B. Henton from Slough in a letter published by the *Mirror*. 'Usually we are treated to such dreary sentiments as "We are going to carry on working, money will make no difference" from pools winners.' Mrs Woor of Ipswich agreed. 'At last a young couple have won the pools. And how sensible they are in wanting to spend the money,' she wrote. Only 'Retired Schoolmaster' of Cardiff declared himself 'disgusted' at a woman 'whose idea seems to be spending on herself. Alas, this philosophy is widespread in Britain today.'[7] Most people didn't agree. They didn't believe that people must show themselves to be 'respectable' and 'deserving' before enjoying good fortune. Spending on oneself was, in any case, a legitimate pleasure in the affluent society, one constantly promoted by advertisements on newspapers, on billboards, and on the new television channel, ITV.

Viv's story seemed to herald a new era. The old constraints appeared to be lifting in the early 1960s; maybe it would be possible for a young, working-class couple to make a better life for their family – and have a good time in the process.

12

A New Middle Class?

O N I JANUARY 1960 Alastair Hetherington, editor of the *Guardian*, spoke of the coming decade as 'the Political Sixties'. He believed that the late 1950s had seen the emergence of 'the new middle classes': car workers, technicians, nurses and clerks, who had 'made . . . astonishing material gains in the fifties'. But the 1960s would, he believed, see even more profound changes. '[T]his new class has not been numerous enough to count politically, nor self-confident enough to know what it wants,' he declared. 'In the coming decade it is likely to grow more numerous, and more confident.'[1] He was right – but his assumption that this group would see themselves as a 'new middle class' was wrong.

In the early 1960s sociologists descended on the manual workers and clerks of Britain's towns and cities, determined to discover how far affluence and white-collar work had changed working-class people's political affiliations and identity. They found that most people who began work in the late 1950s and early 1960s were substantially better off than their parents. Nevertheless, most of them identified themselves as working class – much to the astonishment of many politicians. Their explanations of why they did so illuminated a growing frustration with Conservative policies that reinforced social and economic inequality and were, by the early 1960s, threatening to end full employment and weaken the welfare state. What the sociologists heard told them a great deal about the limits to the social progress they were meant to be assessing, and indicated that Britain was very far from becoming a middle-class country.

It was in the 1960s that most working-class people experienced affluence for the first time. The 1950s was the decade when television entered most British homes and a council house became an aspiration for many people. During the 1960s that aspiration became reality; by the end of the decade overcrowding had fallen, families could expect to begin life in their own home rather than their parents' household, and the TV was joined by a cooker, a fridge and a twin-tub washing machine. Workers' earnings were rising: between 1960 and 1970 most white-collar and manual workers saw their pay packet double in size.[2] Unemployment was a dim and distant memory for most people, and unknown to the youngest workers. Memories of the war were also fading: in 1960 no one under twenty could properly remember it and by 1970 an entire generation had grown up and started families in peacetime.

This social transformation astounded those who could remember life before 1939. Among them was Tom Harrisson, an anthropologist and one of the founders of the social research organization Mass Observation. In 1960 Harrisson and a team of researchers decided to return to Bolton in Lancashire, where they had undertaken many documentary surveys of everyday life in the 1930s and 1940s (using the pseudonym 'Worktown'). Strolling round Bolton's streets, Harrisson saw that children still played outdoors, but now they played with toys and they wore shoes. But the biggest change of all was the people's expectation of economic security. 'In 1936–7 it is fair to say that the whole *atmosphere* breathed insecurity and dread of unemployment,' Harrisson wrote in 1961. 'In 1960 we seldom felt such winds of fear, either among old-timers or younger folk.'[3]

The people Harrisson met felt able to enjoy their security and plan ahead. So did workers elsewhere. In 1963 Alan Watkins completed his engineering apprenticeship in Coventry and stepped straight into a skilled job in one of the city's car plants. Alan and his fiancée Veronica knew what they wanted from life – a car, a house and regular holidays – and they were sure they would be able to achieve their goals. As a child, Alan had identified a neighbour as 'posh' because 'he had a car, unbelievable! – he had a car'. Yet just ten years later, 'we saw a car as something we were going to have . . . you knew we were going to have a car, we were going to get married, we were going to have a house.'

The children of the 1920s had seen their hard work as an investment in their children's future, but by the mid-1960s Alan Watkins's generation was able to enjoy some of the fruits of their labours themselves. Brian Thresh was born in Manchester in 1941. His parents had done all sorts of jobs to make ends meet in the 1930s, his father as a factory labourer and his mother as a cleaner and shop assistant. In the late 1940s, he had seen demobbed uncles greeted with gratitude when they returned with the spoils of war: blankets, clothing and cigarettes that were hard to come by. By 1959, though, Brian's own life was very different. After leaving school he got a secure factory job in Trafford Park, the local industrial estate. He married a woman who also worked in a factory, and with these two wages coming in they were confident about setting up home together. 'Even when the kids were coming along, we had us weekends away,' he said.[4]

In Liverpool, Ron and Edna Jones also enjoyed the spontaneity that having a little extra spending money allowed them in the early 1960s. Ron had left school at the age of fourteen in 1947. He had wanted to stay on at school, but wartime evacuation meant 'I missed the scholarship exam' – this was before the 1944 Education Act came into force – and in any case Ron's family needed him out at work: his father was a poorly paid van driver, and 'unfortunately, in those days, only one parent worked'. Ron was fortunate: after he completed National Service in 1953 he got a well-paid job as a bus conductor for Liverpool Corporation. He met Edna, a city clerk, at the corporation's social club in 1959. In 1963 they got married and moved into a council flat: 'We did mad things Edna and I. Many is the time we got up of a weekend, Friday night finish work, Saturday morning "what will we do today? Oh bugger it, we'll go out" and we would go up to Morecambe, book in bed and breakfast overnight. People used to say "you're mad" but we saw life, we didn't sit around.'

Ron's lack of a secondary education, and Edna's own love of her work, meant that there was never any question that she would give up her job when they married; she in fact continued working until their third and final child was born in the late 1960s.[5]

Left-wing politicians and social scientists feared affluence was eroding working-class identity. In 1959 Labour suffered a third consecutive general election defeat, one that senior party members blamed on the party's limited appeal to the acquisitive desires of the electorate. In 1960 Michael Young – one of the architects of Labour's 1945 manifesto – argued that 'class based on production is slowly giving way to status based on consumption'.[6] While the kitchen sink novels and films had given working-class identity a new cultural cachet, Michael Young suggested that class was no longer a political force. People did not see themselves as part of a collective group of workers, who shared political interests defined by their need to sell their labour. They were now individualists, only interested in how much they could earn, in order to buy more goods for themselves and their families.

In the midst of this debate, J.H. Goldthorpe, a sociologist at Cambridge University, set out to test whether the 'new middle classes' had really arrived. He discovered that election results in 1959 'suggested that this decline in support for Labour was most marked in those areas of the country that were most prosperous . . . in the New Towns and in constituencies in which extensive rehousing programmes had been carried through'.[7] Consequently, he and a team of social scientists set out to discover how affluence was changing working-class life and, most especially, people's political behaviour.

It was difficult to design a study that could rigorously answer the questions: how do people identify their class, and what effect does this have on their political affiliations? But Goldthorpe found a way. His research team set out to interview 'affluent workers' in Luton, a town that had been won briefly by Labour in 1945 but had had a Conservative and National Liberal MP since 1950, whose majority had increased at the 1959 general election. It was exactly the sort of place that Labour would have to win if the party was to have any chance of forming the next government.

Goldthorpe's team chose their respondents from some of the town's factories that paid higher-than-average wages. Most of their 229 respondents were employed at the Vauxhall car plant. They interviewed the workers once at the factory and once at home, in order to get a rounded picture of their lives. When they visited the workers at home, the sociologists tried to include the workers' wives in the interview. Goldthorpe set his team the task of discovering from this group whether a transformation was under way 'among certain sections of the British working class towards middle-class lifestyles and social attitudes'.[8]

Inevitably there were weaknesses in this pioneering study. Those questioned were not the homogeneous group of manual workers that Goldthorpe would later present them as being. They hailed from a wide range of backgrounds: some had been tradesmen in London's East End before moving to Luton for a house or a better paid job; others came from Bedfordshire villages where they had worked as agricultural labourers. They were married to housewives, clerks, factory workers, cleaners and dinner ladies. What they had in common was the short time most of them had lived in Luton: few had been there for more than five years (and would not, therefore, have voted there in the 1959 general election).[9] In their interviews, they made clear that they were often still adjusting to life in a new place, and that this affected their views of community and work, and their experience of both.

Even more seriously, the interviewers had to struggle with the dilemma as to how to allocate these respondents to a social class. They were primarily interested in self-identification, but found that respondents (understandably) struggled with such bland and open-ended questions as: 'What class are you?' and 'Who would you say is upper class?' The researchers decided that most respondents believed class was primarily determined by money, a conclusion published in their study, *The Affluent Worker in the Class Structure*.[10] Yet rereading the interviews highlights that most interviewees resisted the classifications that their interviewers offered them. Instead, they spoke about class in a more historically specific and personal way, and in doing so offer us a valuable and rich account of life in the early 1960s. Fundamentally, however, Goldthorpe's findings have stood the test of time – for his team's central conclusion was that affluence had certainly not destroyed the working class.[11]

The car workers of Luton saw Britain as a two-class society. They and their wives had a strong sense that society was divided into 'the rich' and 'the rest'. 'I think they should do away with the middle and working class,' said Fred Graham.[12] Many of them believed that the upper class was composed of aristocrats: 'Royal family,' said Jim

Falmer when he was asked to define this 'upper class';[13] 'Lords, ladies, the gentry,' replied Harry Harkness.[14] Some thought that the upper class also included a newer group of the richest celebrities: 'film stars and them,' as Ivor Greggs put it.[15]

This upper class possessed wealth and power. Arnold Judd thought the upper class was a 'toffee nosed' bunch whose money and privilege was 'handed down from father to son – rich families marry each other'.[16] Ernest Aldridge agreed; he thought the upper class consisted of 'the gentry, their money has been handed down'.[17] 'Some of those rich people, why are they rich?' asked Joe Nash. 'Because they hold thousands of acres of land that don't belong to them, thieved years ago and handed down.'[18]

By contrast, the working class had to work for whatever they had. 'Most people have to work for their living,' said Anne Baker; she thought car workers like her husband Tony, managers like her son David and clerks like their neighbours were all 'working class'.[19] What separated those who worked from those who did not wasn't simply money, but also the power that came from unearned wealth, aristocratic titles and the right network of influential friends and relations, as well as from governing those who worked for them. 'It's family money and education,' said Geoff Smith, 'which lead to power if you've got them.'[20] 'In my way of thinking the upper class is the type of people who have been born into money . . . and never had to work for it,' said Harry Harkness. 'Whereas the working class have always had to work for their living.' Asked who the power of the upper class affected, Bill Andrews said bluntly, 'Only the working class who are made redundant [by employers].'[21]

Few of these Luton workers saw the 1960s as a golden age of social mobility. Changing social class was hard, and possibly undesirable. They were asked who in their family 'had done well for themselves'. Very few of them could mention anyone who had risen to the professions, or even become solidly middle class. 'He started from the beginning in the plastics trade,' said Irene Peacock of her brother; 'he worked himself up to be a manager at a firm in Walsall,' and he was an exception.[22] Although the men were divided about whether they would want promotion – some did, some thought that going into management would be disloyal to their workmates – most regarded this sort of trajectory as 'doing well'. They also approved of those who'd managed to get 'some letters behind' their names, like Eric Haines's brother, John, who 'studied hard' and had a 'good job' in an office at the Skefco manufacturing firm in Luton.[23] Terry Jameson's cousin, Anne, had also 'got on' through education. 'She's teaching typists,' Terry said. 'She had to go to all the night school classes before she could do it.'[24] The Luton car workers proudly related these as achievements founded on hard work and effort – but they also spoke of them as few and far between. They certainly didn't suggest that post-war Britain was a society in which anyone could get on with talent and hard work.

Those who were seen to have done well had almost all 'worked their way up', but luck played a part too. Women were more likely to be 'lucky' than men, by making a good marriage. Many of the car workers and their wives believed that a woman's choice of husband determined her future – as in most cases it did. Alan Trewick's sister Pam was a nurse. Her profession accrued respect, but she had also 'done well in marrying a doctor. She seems very well set.'[25] Marrying a rich man remained a woman's best guarantee of prosperity. But men could marry well, too. Ralph Hearsall's Uncle Harry 'was lucky, his wife's family left them money' and he had been able to become an insurance agent as a result.[26]

The Luton workers were acutely conscious that they and their relatives had not had the chances available to wealthier people. They pointed out that measuring 'success' depended on where a person had started, indicating they did not believe that equality of opportunity existed. 'He didn't have much of a chance of an education and I think he's done well,' said Amy Cross of her brother Walter, who now worked in a white-collar job for BOAC (the forerunner to British Airways).[27] Others suggested that hard work was a more honest way of achieving success than using family background. Jack Marsden mentioned his brother, Matthew, who 'started as an office boy'. When Matthew did his National Service 'they wanted him to go for a commission but he refused and finished up as a Sergeant Training Instructor.' When he returned to work he got himself a job 'going round the world buying and selling ships'. As well as that, 'he can always get on with people and he will help them out.'[28] Refusing to accept unearned privilege was considered admirable, and a virtue that distinguished ordinary workers from many of 'the rich'.

Goldthorpe's team of researchers was most astonished by the level of dissatisfaction that the Luton workers expressed. They saw only comfortable homes and healthy children, well-fed by hefty wage packets. But while many of the car workers did not live with the fear or insecurity that their parents had experienced, they shared the conviction that their gains depended on never-ending hard work. One anonymous interviewer described his conversation with Mr and Mrs Garret (a car worker and his wife) in the summer of 1963: 'The wife . . . led off before I had my pen out on the lines that everybody had to work far too hard to have any kind of social life, in fact any life at all, and complained greatly about the cost of housing, food, furniture etc.'

Mrs Garrett's interviewer dismissed her complaints. 'In fact,' he said, 'the house was immaculately clean, very well decorated, very tasteful and full of reasonably good and very well maintained furniture.' He was sufficiently reassured of the family's prosperity to disregard Mrs Garrett's concern about the cost of food and engineer himself an invitation to stay for the evening meal. 'Coffee was offered twice as well as biscuits and sandwiches, but I craftily refused the latter and got dinner instead: steak – very good too.' The Garretts, he concluded, were prime examples of affluent workers.[29]

But the Garretts were expressing a deeply felt and widely expressed complaint: that the work needed to create their home comforts was excessive for a so-called 'affluent' society. This was not confined to Luton. In February 1963 a researcher from Liverpool University visited the Jackson family in their council house in Woolton, a leafy southern suburb. Walter Jackson, a telephonist employed by the Post Office, told his interviewer that 'I seem to manage alright', but he also said that his standard of living was 'much the same' as five years earlier; the 'cost of living [was] higher' but there had been 'no rises' in his earnings. His wife, Anne, was responsible for managing the family's budget and with four children she found this a struggle at times. Her oldest daughter was, she explained, now out at work in a factory, 'which makes things easier', but, she said, 'I certainly have to watch my cash, it goes nowhere. Prices are continually rising.'[30]

The grievances that these families expressed were new to sociologists. They were not describing the hunger and insecurity of pre-war poverty, but rather dissatisfaction that the consumer goods to which they were constantly exposed in shop windows and advertisements cost so much. 'We don't go short of food,' said Mrs Jackson, 'but we would like more cash for a few luxuries such as a holiday or better carpets.'[31] Other Woolton women agreed that 'it takes me all my time keeping the family in food'[32] – this from Irene Smith, who worked full-time as a laboratory technician, was married to a clerk, and had just one child.

These grievances were exacerbated by the policies of the Conservative government. The self-congratulatory 'never had it so good' tone of the late 1950s quickly gave way to pay freezes, rising prices and a debate about ending universal state welfare benefits. In the two years that followed the 1959 election, manufacturing firms raised the prices of domestic goods, keen to make a profit out of high consumer demand. In an attempt to reduce inflation, the government imposed a pay freeze on public sector workers, and encouraged employers to reject trade union officials' requests for wage rises. Mrs Garrett and Mrs Jackson were responding to the uncertainty caused by rising prices. Throughout 1962 and 1963 Gallup opinion polls found that people's major concern was the high cost of living, as prices continued to increase.[33]

If rising prices caused women particular concern, many men found that attaining 'affluence' involved loss as well as gain. By the early 1960s, car workers were among the best paid manual workers, and many of them could earn more than white-collar workers if they signed up for overtime. Faced with public sector wage freezes and stagnating wages in skilled occupations, many men felt they had little choice but to opt for the well-paid but boring assembly line.

Alf Chester was one of them. In 1959 he and his wife Mary had moved to Luton from their native north London. By 1963 they were buying their well-kept semi-detached house: 'large gardens front and back, outside painted, net curtains'. Mrs Chester told her interviewer that 'we'd never have been able to afford what we have now ten years ago – a telly and a fridge.' But her husband had mixed feelings about their move. He'd previously been a foreman at the London

Metropolitan Water Board, a responsible job that he'd greatly enjoyed, but which hadn't paid as well as Vauxhall. His interviewer judged Mr Chester to be a 'very intelligent man – who spoilt his answers by nostalgic references to his halcyon days "on the water"'.[34] But Alf Chester's regrets deserve to be taken seriously: they highlight that not everyone experienced home ownership and higher wages as a rise in their 'living standards'.

Alf Chester's regrets help to explain why so many manual workers hankered after being their own boss. Starting your own little business offered a modicum of control that looked attractive in an era of assembly lines, public sector pay freezes and rising prices. Luton workers admired those relatives and friends who were self-employed. Alf Chester himself spoke of his brother Bill, who 'started a business on nothing'.[35] 'He's a butcher,' said Dennis Bell of his younger brother Frank, 'though he has his finger in many pies. He hires out a combine harvester. He also used to do contract ploughing and he does general contract work on farms. He has his own car and his own house.'[36] Frank Bell's labours hinted at the hard work that starting a business from scratch usually entailed. But many of the Luton workers clearly preferred the idea of being beholden to no one to being an employee. Not many people dared take the plunge, feeling they lacked sufficient capital. But their dream testified to a desire for greater control over the work they did and the budget they lived on – and to frustration at their lack of power in the affluent society of 1963.

Factory workers, clerical workers and the least well-paid professional groups – teachers, minor civil servants, nurses and technicians – were the group whose votes Labour needed in order to win the first general election of the 1960s. The Conservatives were obliged to call this in 1964. In fact, most factory workers had voted Labour through the 1950s, discontented at the limited reach of the affluent society. While the Conservatives' promises of increasing affluence had helped to win the election of 1959, many more voters shared the factory workers' disenchantment by the early 1960s – among them many public sector white-collar workers. And far from threatening Labour's chance of government, the migration of blue-collar workers from the industrial heartlands to new towns and suburban estates was helping the party to capture some previously Conservative seats. Luton was one example: a by-election in December 1963 saw these factory workers help turn out the sitting Conservatives and give Labour victory with 48 per cent of the vote.[37] Goldthorpe's team discovered that 'there is no important relationship between affluence and Conservative (or non-Labour) voting with the British working class.'[38]

At the beginning of 1964 serious electioneering began. Labour steered the debate into the tricky terrain of equality. The party turned the election into a contest between the old and the new, the social elite and the popular – presenting their grammar-school-educated leader, Harold Wilson, as being in better touch with ordinary people's needs than the Conservative leader, the aristocratic Alec Douglas-Home. Wilson played down his career as an Oxford don. Instead he emphasized his background as a northern grammar school boy in close touch with the needs of his constituents in working-class Huyton. In 1963 the *Daily Mirror* carried a profile of 'The Man Who May Be the Next Prime Minister' that made much of his background as the 'son of a Huddersfield works chemist'. Wilson spoke of how, as a schoolboy, he 'thought gramophones were very ostentatious . . . mainly because we hadn't got one'. He claimed his favourite sport was 'long distance running' – which among some readers at least would have evoked the recent film adaptation of Alan Sillitoe's short story *The Loneliness of the Long Distance Runner*, starring Tom Courtenay as a working-class Borstal boy and talented runner. Wilson fitted the image Labour wanted to portray of a meritocratic society: here was the northern schoolboy whose father made his living through science and industry, not through inherited privilege, and who had had a 'meteoric' rise from grammar school, to academia and thence into politics.[39]

Wilson had heeded the warnings of Michael Young and Tony Crosland: he was determined not to focus on the evils of affluence. 'We welcome the rise in living standards of so many of our people,' he declared in a speech at the Royal Albert Hall in July 1964. Neither did he focus exclusively on the survival of poverty. Labour, he felt, had tried this in 1955 and again in 1959, and had failed. Throughout the 1950s, both major political parties had spoken of poverty as almost the exclusive preserve of the old and the sick. Ultimately, this had simply reinforced the Conservatives' message that most people had 'never had it so good'. Instead, Wilson returned to Herbert Morrison's older portrayal of 'the useful people' against vested interests, which by 1964 included 'the speculator . . . the tax evader, the land grabber' and those who indulged in 'racketeering', like the slum landlord Peter Rachman.[40]

In this way, Labour addressed the frustrations of those younger workers who were better off than their parents, but disenchanted with their limited opportunities. Wilson's speeches continually referred to the persistence of social and economic inequality. In a speech at Birmingham Town Hall, Wilson denounced the Conservatives as upholding 'a closed society, in which birth and wealth have priority'. He promoted Labour as the party that 'wants to create government of the whole people by the whole people' in a society 'in which brains will take precedence over blue-blood'.[41] Labour's manifesto promised that 'secondary education will be reorganised along comprehensive lines . . . no child will be denied the opportunity of benefiting from [academic education] through arbitrary selection at the age of eleven.' After a comprehensive education, the citizens of this 'New Britain' would be able to enter an expanding range of technical and professional jobs, reliant not on the willingness of employers to create these, but instead guaranteed by the government's 'national plan' for the economy. This was a 'go-ahead' Britain that would benefit from a 'revolution' in education, training and science, bringing about 'equality of opportunity'.[42]

Wilson intended to speak directly to the anxieties and hopes of voters from a wide range of backgrounds, but particularly to the increasing numbers of young wage-earners, to the expanding white-collar workforce, and to women as both mothers and workers.[43] At the Labour Party conference in 1963 – one year before the election – the party's senior officials made skilful use of these groups. The education debate was introduced by Joyce Cope, described by the *Daily Mirror* as 'a slim attractive mother of five sons'. Opposing the eleven-plus, she said that 'There is as much integrity and ability – not to mention morality – in *Coronation Street* as there ever was in Carlton

Terrace.'[44] As her mention of the nation's favourite soap opera suggested, Labour was keen to align the party and its new leader with the fashionable working-class heroes of stage and screen.

In 1964 Wilson developed this notion that working-class people were at least as useful as those higher up the social hierarchy. 'I have found a desire – still rather incoherent but none the less genuine – for a radical new kind of society,' he told a journalist in September 1964, one month before the election. 'There is a very deep indignation about Rachmanism and many people are beginning to wonder whether it is right that the property speculator should rank higher in the material and social scale than people doing a useful productive job.'[45]

Most of Luton's car workers liked Wilson. The majority of them were already committed Labour supporters who – contradicting the theories of Michael Young – saw no reason to change their allegiance simply because they could now afford foreign holidays or a car of their own. 'They are a working man's party,' said Martin Cross; 'their policies are based on the working man.'[46] 'They are the government for the working class,' commented Bernard Harris. 'The Conservatives are just there for their class.' Bernard was an Irishman, who had spent most of the 1950s labouring on building sites and in factories. He was proud of his ability to keep his five young children, but wanted them to have more fulfilling jobs than his own: 'I'd like him to be a draughtsman,' he said of his oldest son.[47] Wilson's emphasis on the 'white heat of technology' and a meritocracy based on planning and science therefore appealed. Older men recalled the 1930s. 'What I've seen before the war, killed me for voting anyway else,' said Bill Allen, who had worked in factories since the depression. Asked to expand, he said shortly, 'Unemployment. [You mean it was the Conservatives' fault?] Definitely.'[48] However well-off these workers were, they knew they lacked the political and economic power of 'the rich', and aligned themselves with the party they saw as representing ordinary people.

Polls in 1964 suggested that the poorest members of society and the elderly were the members of the working class most likely to vote Tory; used to being worse off than the rest of society, many of them believed that the best they could hope for were crumbs from the rich man's table. For Eric Talbot, an unskilled worker from Blackpool, the 1964 election was the second he was eligible to vote in – and he voted Conservative. 'Someone said to me, a farmer, "always remember one thing: when Conservatives are in power, always a bit of money rubs off in tha lap" – it certainly keeps the money flowing.'[49]

Some of Luton's car workers shared Eric Talbot's caution. 'They're used to handling money,' said John Cummings. 'Labour doesn't know what to do, not like the rich man, he's used to it.'[50] Experience counted, but it probably wasn't fair; the working-class Tories didn't suggest their masters were inherently superior or that the social order was entirely satisfactory. These men's attitudes were not new to the 1960s; working-class Conservatives had cited the party's wealth and experience back in the 1930s.[51] And doing so didn't stop men like Eric Talbot and John Cummings from distinguishing unself-consciously between 'them' and 'us'. The Conservative Party's Central Office had in fact found evidence of similar attitudes among voters in 1963, when their researchers revealed that the Tories were widely viewed as being 'supported by business, capable of making the country prosperous, but with little concern for ordinary people'. By contrast, Labour was viewed as 'concerned for ordinary people'.[52] Working-class support for the Conservatives was strong; but it hardly suggested that affluence was destroying class divisions or class identity.

The caution of these voters helped explain why the election of 1964 was closely fought and narrowly won. Polling day came on 15 October. On the eve of the election the *Daily Mirror* was warning its readers that 'it could be close'. The newspaper was right: Labour scraped into government with a majority of just four MPs and a share of the popular vote not much bigger than in 1959. Many middle-class owner-occupiers and those paying the higher rate of tax were content to stick with the Tories. Meanwhile, Wilson's ambitious but vague promises of greater opportunity, and his neglect of concrete policies addressing poverty, did not endear him to the poor or the old. Far from being a resounding Labour victory, the election was really a defeat for the Conservatives, who had failed to recover from the Profumo sex scandal, Rachmanism and the economic inse-curity of the early 1960s.[53]

By October 1964, the sociologists had left Luton. Goldthorpe's research team concluded that despite experiencing rising living standards, most of these affluent workers remained staunchly Labour. The researchers could find no ready explanation for this, but that was because they took 'rising living standards' for granted, without questioning why so many of their interviewees were discontented about their circumstances, and uncertain about the future. Most of the interviewees still felt they were living in circumstances that they had not chosen – that they were 'the rest' as distinct from 'the rich'.[54]

Wilson scored highly with younger wage-earners, many of whom were frustrated with the chasm between the Conservatives' promises of affluence and the reality of everyday life. 'They haven't exactly made it easy for young people to buy houses and furniture,' said Alan Baxter, a worker at Vauxhall; 1964 was the first election in which he was eligible to vote. 'It's necessary to have two wage earners.'[55] His generation had been exhorted to aim high, and they were disillusioned to find themselves working overtime on an assembly line. Pay freezes and price increases led some of them to hope for a different kind of economic management, one over which elected politicians and trade unionists would have more control. 'In this day and age there must be some form of control over things,' believed Baxter's workmate, Stuart Sharples. 'Private enterprise seems to go in fits and starts.'[56] These young workers elected Labour in the hope of realizing their high aspirations. It was largely due to their votes that Labour held Luton in the 1964 election with an increased majority and 50 per cent of the vote.[57]

As thirteen years of Conservative rule came to an end, the worries of some Labour politicians and social scientists that affluence would lead people to consider themselves to be middle class were agreed to be unfounded. Many workers believed that Britain was a two-class society composed of 'them' and 'us', and that 'they' held power unjustly. They identified themselves as being working class not because of the amount of money they earned or the job they did, but because of their relationship to other people in the society in which they lived. The Conservatives' move away from the post-war commitment to full employment and universal welfare provoked widespread frustration, especially among young voters who had begun to take these post-war gains for granted. They were impatient for government to build on this foundation of security by offering them a greater share in the country's profits, and by granting them and their children a wider array of educational, leisure and career opportunities. Under Wilson, Labour promised to deliver a technological revolution, rather than relying on employers to do so; to raise the living standards of everyone, rather than the exceptional few who passed the eleven-plus; to offer true equality of opportunity, rather than nibbling away at the worst excesses of poverty; and to give younger voters the chance of a different sort of life, not simply more consumer goods. In October 1964 Harold Wilson entered Number Ten Downing Street as the first Labour Prime Minister for thirteen years. Whether his party could or would deliver what the Luton workers wanted was, however, another matter.

Interlude VII

On the Make

B Y 1963, VIV realized that money could not buy the life of
liberty she had dreamed of. She and Keith bought a large,
modern, detached house on a new private estate in nearby Garforth:
'that was one of the good moments the money brought'. Although
home ownership was on the rise, most of Castleford's workers were
tenants in 1963, beholden to landlords' rules and regulations. She and
Keith enjoyed having the freedom and largesse to throw raucous
all-night parties for their friends and decorate their home exactly as
they wished. Yet they never felt they belonged in Garforth. Viv's
neighbours were managers and local businessmen; they 'were the
type . . . that would get their car out of the garage, wash it, put it
back, and then get it out again on Saturday and rewash it'. Their
wives didn't work; instead they held coffee mornings, looked after
their quiet, biddable children and tidied their houses. Viv had luxury
and ease, but she felt as cooped up as she had in her old council
house.

To Viv's chagrin, her new neighbours looked down on her; 'not
one of them spoke to us'. They were aggravated by the Nicholsons'
noisy parties, and worried that these brash pools winners would ruin
the neighbourhood's respectable reputation. 'In the end somebody
would say, "Do you want your grass cut?" because things like that
never bothered us.' She contemptuously compared her neighbours'
standoffishness and stuffy conventions with the friendliness of the
streets she and Keith had left behind – forgetting sometimes just
how desperate she had been to escape prying neighbours and peeling
wallpaper. The middle-class lifestyle she appeared to have acquired
was not as attractive as it seemed from the outside. Spending long
hours ostentatiously keeping up appearances and working hard

characterized her neighbours' lives, as they sought to maintain their limited privileges.

The Nicholsons were finding it hard to fill their leisure time. Keith stopped going to the pub. 'I can't talk to them any more about work,' he told Viv; 'I'm sick of it, but I don't know what to do.' They enjoyed exotic holidays to the United States and Europe, but when they returned their lives seemed emptier than ever. Viv had insisted that the children go to boarding school, but found that she missed them badly. 'I found myself needing to be needed,' she said. She was just twenty-seven.

Increasing numbers of men and women shared Viv's feeling of being redundant, though different circumstances explained their enforced leisure. Less than 2 per cent of English workers were unemployed between 1945 and 1962, but in 1963 this figure began to rise. It stalled at about 3 per cent nationally, but in some of England's industrial heartlands the proportion of workers on the dole was far higher.[1]

Jack Ashley, the young BBC reporter who five years earlier had made the documentary *Does Class Matter?*, visited affected families in West Hartlepool. He discovered that hope for the future, so abundant in many other places, had been replaced with fear in those communities hit by unemployment. 'He's just hanging around the house all day, he gets a bit depressed,' one woman said of her husband, 'and so do I.' 'With no money to go out,' Jack Ashley explained, over a scene shot in a working men's club, 'a divide has opened up between those who have work and those who do not.'[2] This division was particularly acute in Britain's traditional industrial heartlands: in the north-east, on Clydeside, across Merseyside and in the South Wales valleys.

Viv Nicholson, like the men and women Jack Ashley spoke to, was slowly realizing that work – whether paid employment or domestic responsibilities – defined who you were. Viv and Keith no longer fitted in with their family and friends, but they didn't conform to the image of hard-working business people that their new neighbours cultivated. They also lacked that sense of entitlement to the good life that Viv had always assumed wealth would bring. Even while they were living it up, Viv and Keith felt 'selfish' and 'guilty' about their good fortune. 'I used to have terrible fears that because we'd won all this money I was going to have to die,' said Viv. 'I really thought I was going to be punished for winning it.' Fear of poverty lurked in the margins of her mind.

In 1965 it seemed to Viv that this punishment had arrived. Keith was killed in a car crash. Not much of his money was left, and most of what did remain was tied up in trust for their children. 'Blonde 29-year-old Mrs Nicholson, a former cinema usherette and factory girl, is looking for a job,' reported the *Mirror*. The unstable circumstances of her life – 'a giant pools win and the dark tragedy of a car crash' as the newspaper put it – struck a chord with many people.[3] Harold Wilson's Labour government was one year old; the age of Merseybeat and mass ownership of motor cars had arrived, but in the same year that Viv lost everything, sociologists reported that poverty, far from disappearing, continued to blight thousands of people's lives. In 1965 Peter Townsend and Brian Abel-Smith of the London School of Economics used Ministry of Labour expenditure surveys – which recorded the consumption patterns of millions of households – to prove that more than 7 million people lived 'substantially below the average earnings of our affluent society', due to low wages and inadequate family allowances.[4]

After a year of grieving, Viv tried to make a new life for herself. She was desperate to preserve some of the glamour and independence that wealth had brought her. By 1967 London's Carnaby Street was a by-word for fashion and celebrity and Viv was keen to become part of the swinging sixties scene. Without money, she fell back on her basic resource: her body. She formed a cabaret act in Soho, a seedy district crammed with brothels and sex shops, whose owners were happy to provide bribes for those officers of the Metropolitan Police willing to turn a blind eye to the porn and prostitution. Still, Soho had its own glamour, fuelled by the celebrities who patronized its clubs and its proximity to the bright lights of Leicester Square and Oxford Street. For a while, this was enough to hold Viv, but the cabaret act didn't last; Viv's performance wasn't as raunchy as that in the more risqué Soho joints, and the club she worked at eventually closed its doors, unable to afford the protection money demanded by police and local gangsters.

In 1968 Viv returned to the north. It was the summer of love on Britain's beaches and university campuses. In Castleford, Viv also found love – with Brian, 'a bouncer at the Crystal Ballroom' who hailed from Manchester. The marriage lasted only three months; Brian broke her jaw in his disappointment at discovering that he hadn't married the millionairess of his dreams. The north, depicted as the centre of cultural change in novels and pop songs, was in some ways little different from the place where Viv had grown up.

Viv needed a new career. She wanted to retrieve the celebrity lifestyle she'd never really had; or find a man to keep her, in a proper, old-fashioned marriage like the one she'd had with Matt, but this time in a more luxurious setting. She didn't want the suburban life that she and Keith had briefly experienced at Garforth; she hankered instead after the bohemian life of adventure being lived by the hippies and the pop stars of Wilson's new, modern Britain. But breaking into the swinging sixties wasn't easy without money and contacts. Viv still had her body, though, and her notoriety could still get her a gig. She sought to break into showbusiness once more, this time by singing 'Big Spender' in a Manchester strip club. Unfortunately, her name was not enough to guarantee her fame – she was soon sacked for refusing to take off her knickers. Sex remained one of the few routes to fortune open to a woman on her own in the sixties.

PART III

The Dispossessed, 1966–2010

13

New Britain

IN 1969 HUW Beynon, a young sociologist at Liverpool University, set out to study relations between workers and employers at Ford's Halewood plant on Merseyside. The workers had a reputation for militancy, and Beynon spent much of his time with the trade union activists among the workforce. They were, he said, united by their youth (most were under thirty) and by having 'little respect for authority': 'They wore sharp clothes; suits with box jackets . . . They walked with a slight swagger . . . They were born and brought up in the city that produced the Beatles and had always known near-full employment . . . They . . . respected tradition but seemed to be less bound by it.'[1]

In the late 1960s the teenagers of the previous decade became militant campaigners in Britain's factories. They fought for more autonomy from politicians and employers and landlords. They wanted greater say over the management of their work.

They instigated the most radical wave of industrial unrest that the country had experienced since the 1920s. Between 1965 and 1975 Britain suffered, on average, 2,885 strikes each year. They were highly disruptive; annually, about 251 working days were lost.[2] The strikes testified to a new assertiveness, which spread beyond male, skilled workers – the traditional constituency of the trade unions – to young and women workers, recent migrants and unskilled wage-earners. They were provoked to strike by the chasm between their high expectations of life in an affluent society, and the reality they experienced on the factory floor.

Three years before Beynon began his researches, many of these young militants had been responsible for returning Labour to government with a resounding majority. On 31 March 1966, after two years in government, Harold Wilson went back to the polls with the slogan 'You *know* Labour government works'. Unemployment had fallen, wages were rising, and the government had increased the level and scope of welfare benefits.[3] 'Since we took office we have started on the long process of modernizing obsolete procedures and institutions,' declared Labour's manifesto, 'ending the dominance of vested interests, liberating the forces of youth and building a New Britain.'[4] Labour was returned to office with an increased majority of ninety-six.

Yet in Britain's factories, anger was brewing. Wilson's promotion of the 'white heat of technology' exacerbated workers' frustration at their primitive working conditions. So too did the discrepancy between the rhetoric of the post-war meritocracy and the meagre rewards that effort and ambition actually brought. Nineteen-year-old Bill Rainford briefly worked at Ford's Halewood plant in 1967. He had left school four years earlier. After spending two years in dead-end manual jobs, he had become an office boy at Automatic Telephones, which advertised in the local press for 'ambitious young men who want to get ahead'.[5] Bill enjoyed his job there sufficiently to stay put for two years: 'We were all eighteen, seventeen, eighteen, nineteen year olds and it was a constant battle of wits between [the supervisor] and us, trying to put one over him.' But he realized that 'getting ahead' wasn't going to be possible however 'ambitious' you were: Automatic Telephones only needed people to do menial work and there were no prospects of promotion. 'So I thought, "I wonder what Fords is like," because the money was meant to be fantastic.' He soon discovered why. 'Someone told me later that the turnover at Fords was amazing . . . The first job I got, it was in the Press Shop. There was a feller banging these panels in and I had to grab them and throw them on the pallet. He had to do so many an hour. By the time I'd finished there were all blisters on the end of my fingers.' Bill Rainford lasted a month.

Meanwhile in Manchester, twenty-eight-year-old Ian White was working at the Metal Box factory where 'the conditions, for the 1960s, for a well-respected firm – they were really bad. The fumes used to come down from the forklifts, the diesel forklifts all day. There was no noise suppression . . . you could hear the clanking when you got home, hear it til about 2 in the morning.'[6] The reality of work compared very poorly with the high-flown 'white heat' rhetoric of government ministers, and the lofty aspirations that these young workers had been encouraged to harbour by teachers, politicians and the press.

These workers' discontent appears incongruous set against the Wilson government's message of modernization and social progress. 'Equality of opportunity' was the government's slogan, but Wilson's government was committed to a different version of this to that promoted by Attlee's administration twenty years earlier. In 1965 Education Minister Tony Crosland requested – though did not oblige – local authorities to submit plans for the reorganization of secondary education in 'schools as socially and intellectually comprehensive as is practicable' to 'give all our children a more ample opportunity', not only to achieve academic qualifications, but to fulfil their social and creative potential in the 'democratic 1960s'.[7]

By 1970, one-third of secondary school pupils attended comprehensive schools.[8] Working-class children who attended comprehensives had as much chance of getting to university as those attending grammar schools. Comprehensives clearly expanded the chances of that majority of children who would otherwise have attended secondary modern schools.[9] At the same time, Labour adopted the recommendations of the 1963 Robbins Report on higher education – chiefly, that university places should be increased by 50 per cent within four years and trebled by 1980.

Most working-class parents supported these reforms. One month after Crosland issued his circular on comprehensive education, a survey of 165 mothers in Essex found that only a minority – described as 'middle-class mothers whose children attended a model primary school' – objected to his proposals. Those women who 'left school at fifteen' and were 'married to a manual worker' were the strongest supporters of change.[10] Odessa Stoute agreed with them. She had moved from Barbados to Leeds in 1960, hoping to make a better life for her children. She and her husband were factory workers, and hoped their children would have better opportunities. 'The authorities just thought children should all be for the factories but I wanted different for my children. I had a great struggle to get them into

277

proper academic schools where they could achieve their GCE [exams].' When the Leeds Education Authority began consultation on Crosland's plan, 'we formed the Chapeltown Parents' Association to fight . . . schools were changing to comprehensive to give the children a better chance.'[11] During the 1970s the proportion and number of working-class university students increased for the first time since the 1930s.[12]

Other changes directly affected adult workers. Between 1964 and 1970 the Labour government built more council houses than the Conservatives had managed in the previous ten years, and reintroduced rent controls into the private sector.[13] People could afford to fill their homes with new domestic appliances. In 1960 less than one-third of British households had possessed a fridge or a washing machine; by 1970 more than half did.[14] Many working-class people experienced something approaching affluence for the first time.

The change was particularly noticeable in the industrial heartlands of northern England, Clydeside and South Wales which had missed out on the prosperity of the 1950s. In 1968 thirty-one-year-old Fred Robson of North Shields, a small industrial town at the mouth of the Tyne, worked as a shipwright at the Swan Hunter shipyard. Asked by sociologists what had changed for him in the last five years he replied that 'industry has given me security. I've got a council house.'[15] 'That was when . . . I got a car,' recalled Terry Rimmer, who worked on the assembly line at Ford's Halewood plant. By the end of the 1960s, the division between working-class people's living standards in the more prosperous south and the industrial north was narrower than it had been since the late 1940s.

For those people who had emigrated from the Caribbean or South Asia to work in Britain during the 1950s and early 1960s, these were also the years when they were able to afford to send for their children and spouses. Odessa Stoute was among them. Leaving her Barbadian home had been 'the most heart-breaking event of my life, leaving my two daughters aged eight and two years old back home with my mother and father'. She got a job at Leeds' Burton's factory making coats. As her wages rose in the mid-1960s, 'my husband and I started saving to buy our house so we could get our two daughters to join us. We managed and in 1965 . . . the girls came.' Agnes Hind had an even longer wait. She and her husband had come to Leeds in 1957, hoping to find work and a better life for their children; but they left their eldest son, David, behind. Not until 1965 did the couple feel secure enough to 'borrow the money to bring him over'.[16]

But these material improvements in people's lives still relied on a great deal of hard work and sacrifice. Many families coped by having two wage-earners. The number of married women in paid work continued to increase during the 1960s. Alan Watkins, by now a fully qualified engineer in Coventry, was initially opposed to his wife, Veronica, returning to work when the elder of their two children began school in 1969, but 'it was just my male pride, I soon got used to it . . . and the money [she earned] came in useful!' But the demands of work and childcare meant that both men and women missed the companionship of their husband or wife. In 1967 Bill Rainford left Ford for Ogden's tobacco works in Liverpool. It was here that he met his wife, Barbara, who worked in the factory's office. By the mid-1970s, they had two young children and were renting a house in the suburb of Norris Green. 'We didn't see much of each other at that time,' said Bill; he would return from work at teatime to care for their daughters, just as Barbara left for an evening 'housewives' shift at the factory.

Men and women of Bill and Barbara's generation were forging new patterns of marriage and parenting. Women's new earning power, together with men's desire to become more involved in home life, precipitated this. In the late 1960s Michael Young and Peter Willmott returned to Greenleigh, the estate where many of Bethnal Green's residents had been rehoused ten years earlier. Young and Willmott discovered that many of the younger married couples there shared domestic duties and financial decisions more equally than their parents had done. '[T]he acquisition of better homes made it more worth-while for husbands to spend money on them,' and to invest time in looking after them. Men were also inclined to look for satisfaction in their homes because they were less likely to find inherent satisfaction in their work, as skilled trades gave way to more lucrative, but stultifying, jobs on the assembly line.[17] Increasingly, too, they worked in jobs that encouraged them to focus on the home as a centre for fulfilment: those who produced domestic appliances, for example, might get a discount on them. In 1966 Ann Turner, a shop assistant in Abingdon, got her first vacuum cleaner via her husband's job. He worked for the Southern Electricity Board. 'He delivered a lady a new [vacuum cleaner] and she said to him, "There's nothing wrong with this old one, would you like it?"' Mr Turner also bought 'a twin tub, he got a discount through SEB'.[18] In 1967 a survey of more than 4,000 households revealed that women were solely responsible for purchasing cookers, fridges or washing machines in only one-third of families; in the majority of cases, husbands or, most typically, the couple together, were present when such a large appliance was bought.[19]

But husbands' and wives' new roles could produce additional strains, for most households still needed to budget carefully. Joint decision-making undermined some women's autonomy. Ron Jones, a bus driver in Liverpool, was proud that in his house, 'it was a case of coming home on payday, throwing your payslip on the table and that was it. No secrets as regards pay and we knew exactly what we could afford.' He and his wife Edna would then plan which appliance or piece of furniture to buy next. Ron believed he was entitled to at least as much say as Edna when it came to deciding between a fridge or a washing machine. But in Edna's view, Ron should have deferred to her a little more because she still shouldered most of the domestic chores. She was keen that their first big purchase should be a washing machine, so that she could stop taking her laundry to Ron's mother, a bus-ride away – something made more desirable when their son was born in 1964. One Saturday Ron went into town to buy a twin-tub on hire purchase, but when he returned, he told Edna that he'd changed his mind. He'd seen what he thought was a real bargain. 'I wanted a washing machine but he went out and bought a fridge,' Edna said; 'I could have thumped him really but we soon bought a washing machine [laughs]' – though the money for that washing machine was earned by Edna, as soon as she was able to return to work.[20]

Policymakers and manufacturers encouraged men to take an important role in these consumption decisions, reinforcing older notions that men were the family breadwinners. Politicians treated husbands as the rightful holders of the household's purse-strings: not until 1974 did a Consumer Credit Act abolish the need for a married woman to acquire her husband's signature on any hire purchase agreement. The manufacturers of vacuum cleaners, washing machines and fridges emphasized the technical wizardry of the appliances, believing this would impress male consumers. Their advertisements encouraged men to view the selection of these goods as a skilled, 'scientific' task.[21] Hazel Wood was a nurse by the mid-1960s, and married to John, a factory worker. 'John's earnings were to live on and mine were for extras' like a washing machine and a television – but it was John's job to choose these: 'he found good models in this secondhand shop' close to their home in Coventry.

Many of these men were proud of being both loving fathers and dependable breadwinners. Bernard Harris, an Irish Catholic who worked at Luton's Vauxhall factory, 'often referred to doing overtime so that he could get the money to buy things for [his five children]', when interviewed by a sociologist in 1963. '[H]e showed me with great pride a frilly, sticky-out yellow nylon party dress he had just bought for the baby.' Mr Harris proudly told his interviewer that 'he did not believe in keeping them down, giving them worse food – they all got the same size helpings as him.' His wife Marjorie 'was in complete accord'.[22] As the sociologist Michael Carter observed in his study of teenagers on a Sheffield housing estate, parents delighted in giving their children a better time of it than they had had.[23] Men like Bernard relished sharing the good things in life with their wives and children, in a way that their own fathers had often been unable to do, or had refused to countenance.

But many men found it difficult to combine being a good bread-winner with being an involved and affectionate spouse and father. Bernard Harris himself was frustrated at his reliance on overtime, which kept him away from home three or four evenings each week. The average working week fell from forty-four hours in 1951 to forty hours by the late 1960s, but most workers did not have any more leisure time, because they ended up working in the evenings and weekends for extra pay.[24] 'It is surprising,' noted Simon Yudkin and Anthea Holme in a study of working mothers published in 1963, 'how society has accepted with strange equanimity the fact that fathers may hardly appear at all as members of their families except in a state of physical exhaustion.'[25] Meanwhile, women continued to bear the brunt of childcare and chores, frequently combining this with part-time work.

Men in unskilled work often faced a particularly difficult choice: earning enough to keep their families often required overtime or working away from home, which meant being absent fathers. John McGuirk – the Bootle boy who had been evacuated to Southport during the war – was among them. After leaving school in 1951 John had a spell in the merchant navy: 'you saw the world and women loved you'. Then, in 1959, he met his wife and settled back on Merseyside. By 1965, the couple had five children, and were renting a badly overcrowded house in north Liverpool. In that year, they were finally given the lease on a new council house, with enough space for all the family to live comfortably. But for John, earning the money necessary to cover the rent meant taking a job with a motorway construction gang, which took him away from home for five or seven days at a time. He felt angry and unhappy at missing so much of his children's lives. 'You had to cut yourself in two,' he said.

More people were renting a council house or flat, but life in public housing was growing harder. Labour had built more council accommodation than the Conservatives, but retained the latter's preference for cheap high-rise flats – a policy that only changed in 1968, with the collapse of a large tower block at Ronan Point in London. Tenants often found themselves marooned in flats that offered little space for the children to play outside, and had few shops or parks nearby. At the same time, local councils appeared increasingly anonymous and high-handed. From 1968, economic growth slowed down in the face of foreign manufacturing competition. In the 1950s Britain had benefited from being one of the European countries least disrupted by war; unlike most of its West European trading rivals, Britain had not suffered occupation. But by the late 1960s West Germany, which had made an excellent recovery after the war, and Japan were becoming serious competitors in several industries on which British workers relied, including car manufacturing, engineering and electronics. The government began to demand public spending cuts to make up for the slowing down of British manufacturing. This meant less money for maintenance, health visitors or rent collectors. In Warrington – an industrial town, but not one noted for particularly high deprivation – the number of health visitors was cut back. By 1970, the town's Medical Officer for Health noted that 'visiting has become highly selective and only the neediest are being seen.'[26] In a pattern repeated across the country, tenants on Norwich's large out-of-town council estates were asked to make long and expensive bus journeys into town if they needed to discuss housing conditions or rent arrears with their landlord, or to telephone – a luxury very few of them could afford.[27]

Frustration could spill into violence. 'I was a hot-head at times,' remembered Ron Jones of his encounters with housing officials at Liverpool Council. By 1968, the Joneses' council flat was too small for their growing family of five, but although Ron repeatedly visited his local housing office he was 'fobbed off' by clerks who told him contradictory tales about how long he would have to wait for a house, and whether he would get one at all. Finally, 'I went down, shouted at the clerk, eventually he could see I was in a right temper, he was scared, he got on the phone, sorted it out.' The Joneses got their house.

Ron Jones was not alone in falling back on physical strength and aggression to overcome the vagaries of bureaucracy. Joe Hastings lived in Norwich; his young family was similarly desperate for a home of their own. Joe 'used to go every lunchtime to the housing office . . . And see this pompous little character'. One day, 'I grabbed him, I pulled him through the hatch . . . within ten days they offered us a house.'[28] The heroic 'little man' who stood up to the bullies has a long history in Britain: Joe Hastings' and Ron Jones's stories are reminiscent of Ernie Benson's account of threatening the means test man back in the 1930s. This story found new relevance in the late 1960s. Whether the details of each man's story are true does not, in one sense, matter; for the stories say much about how they saw themselves in relation to powerful figures of authority, and how limited they understood their control over their lives to be.

★

This was the climate in which anger exploded into militancy in Britain's factories, as workers demanded greater control over the organization of their lives. Labour had done much, but when the government failed to deliver its ambitious promise of a better world of equality and 'white heat' innovation, the workers of the late 1960s determined to create it themselves. They wanted more control over the way their work was organized and paid. Between 1965 and 1970 manual workers enjoyed their longest continuous period of wage rises since the war, and clerical workers also saw their pay increase.[29] But these gains were not handed to workers by a benevolent government; they were won by strikes and walkouts. 'No workman ever got anything at all through the goodness of an employer's heart,' said John McGuirk; 'he got it because of the union or because they went on strike.' The late 1960s was, in his words, 'the time when the unions started to fight'. Trade union membership rose from 10 million members in 1960 to 13 million members by 1979. While 44 per cent of workers were in a union at the beginning of the 1960s, 55 per cent were by the end of the 1970s.[30]

These statistics tell only part of the story. The strikes and walkouts of the late 1960s and early 1970s were often unofficial; they were not orchestrated by trade union leaders, but started on the shopfloor, precipitated by young workers, some of whom were not even union members. These workplace activists framed their claims within an older, working-class struggle for autonomy from employers. Traditionally, having a skill had offered men a degree of autonomy, a set of tools they could take with them from job to job and which could offer negotiating power with employers. But by the late 1960s, employers had succeeded in designating many of the expanding occupations – like assembly-line work – as unskilled and semi-skilled. Often they had done so with the short-sighted collusion of an older generation of trade union officials, who saw staffing the assembly lines as 'women's work' and were happy for it to be defined as low-skilled and low-paid. But by 1967, many men were relying on this kind of work as well as women.

Many employers complacently believed that these workers lacked the political shrewdness of older generations of skilled men. Among them was the Ford Motor Company. Ford's oldest plant in Britain was based at Dagenham in Essex. In the late 1950s the firm opened a plant in South Wales and in 1962 Ford's Halewood works opened on Merseyside. The firm sought to recruit married men with little prior history of trade unionism, and women on work deemed unskilled.[31]

Yet these workers had their own grievances: primarily, their low pay and what this said about the low value attributed to their work. In 1968 Ford's workers walked out on strike over overtime rates – a dispute that provoked Huw Beynon's researches. 'Overtime,' said Terry Rimmer, who was one of these strikers, 'was king.' Terry and his workmates resented the fact that they were not consulted about the allocation of overtime, work on the unpopular but lucrative night shift, or the level of bonus payments.[32]

These were not just demands for better pay. Sustained prosperity and near-full employment encouraged workers like Terry Rimmer to believe that trade unionism could move beyond addressing their immediate material needs – basic pay and working conditions. In the words of the historian Alastair Reid, men like Terry wanted unions to fight for 'the opportunities for creativity, self-expression and participation in everyday working lives'.[33] Terry – a self-described 'Beatnik Teddy Boy' – did not only walk out to dispute the allocation of overtime. His action was provoked, he said, by 'a free spirit inside me that didn't want walls round me': he was tired of being at his employer's beck and call.

Terry Rimmer knew from the leisure scene of the 1960s – in his case enjoyed at Liverpool's dance halls and coffee bars, and in the bands he had performed in – that the world offered more than simply standing on an assembly line. So did those men who formed the rank-and-file strike committee at Merseyside's Pilkington's factory in 1970, most of whom had been in their teens and early twenties in the early 1960s, and were disillusioned with a union they saw as 'hand in glove' with management. They included 'Nick M', who wanted 'to travel and throw off the bonds of convention'; 'George F', who would have liked 'to be a writer about nature'; and 'Arthur G', who regretted his lack of education and 'would like to be the architect of changes whereby people could control their own lives'.[34] Workers like them fused the older labour movement's commitment to workers' collective independence with the sixties ideals of personal autonomy and self-expression that were promoted in pop music, fashion and civil rights campaigns. In doing so, they asserted that greater control over the way they lived their lives should be their human right. But achieving that right would mean workers having an unprecedented level of control over the production process, and over pay.

Car workers provoked many of the strikes. While workers in other sectors were frustrated by the exhausting demands made on them by assembly-line production and overtime, workers in the car plants had three additional motivations. One was the seasonal nature of car production, which meant that overtime dried up at certain times of the year, and temporary lay-offs were common. Another was the strength of the trade unions in many car plants. While increasing numbers of strikes were unofficial – called by workers without first consulting their trade union leaders – the tradition of collective meetings and protest proved influential. But also of importance was workers' fear that car production was unsustainable in the face of increasing foreign competition. When employers argued that they needed to cut costs in order to compete, many workers responded that what was really required was innovation. Terry Rimmer and his workmates were frustrated that their managers

> didn't keep their finger on the pulse, you know. We were doing well, getting contracts, but new machinery was needed because of competitors, especially the Japanese, they had the finger on the pulse, they knew when they needed new plant. I mean some of the plant we had at Ford's when it first started was absolutely dreadful. We had some plant at Halewood that was used to make First World War tanks. So it was only when the unions started shouting a bit that we got started on new stuff.

In 1968 shipbuilding workers on Tyneside were similarly frustrated that they had no opportunity to share their ideas for innovation with their managers. John Ross, a forty-eight-year-old welder at Swan Hunter shipyard, said that the worst thing about his job was 'the regimentation. Time clocking, no scope for individuality in my trade.'[35] Employers, they argued, could learn much from their shopfloor workers' ideas and expertise.

The strikers' demands caused great consternation at the highest levels of government. Concern focused on the car factories. In 1969 Barbara Castle, Labour's Minister of Employment, told a Cabinet meeting that 'the unofficial strike at Standard-Triumph's Liverpool factory gave cause for serious concern.' Castle was most worried at the strength of popular feeling to which it testified, and the lack of authority that trade union leaders could wield over these workers. The strike, she said, was not provoked by a small group of ringleaders: 'it simply reflected a mood of near-anarchy on the shop floor.'[36]

Castle underestimated how reluctant workers were to strike; for most it was a desperate last resort, which spoke of their disillusion with their trade union leaders as well as their bosses. By the end of the 1960s Hazel and John Wood had two young children to support. Hazel was worried when John began working at a Coventry car factory in the late 1960s because 'we'd heard they walked out for nothing'. But Hazel quickly came to sympathize with the strikers when John joined the picket lines: 'it was the only way they could get anything,' she said. Unofficial strikes often erupted in protest at the inaction or indifference of senior trade union officials and managers. Thirty-year-old Ricky Tomlinson – later to become a famous actor – became union organizer of the motorway construction gang of which he was a member. He was surprised to discover that 'some of the other union officials were lazy and corrupt. One in particular would never return my calls . . . One day I rang and said I was [a manager] calling from McAlpine's [a large building firm]. He came to the phone straight away, sounding like a grovelling toad. I don't know if he was in cahoots with the bosses, or just after a quiet life.'[37] Twenty years after strikes had erupted on Britain's docks, more workers than ever were frustrated by the 'top-down' negotiation process established in the 1940s, which in practice gave trade union officials a seat at the managers' table, but offered ordinary workers little say.

These were the kind of men Huw Beynon set out to interview; but by the time he got to Halewood another, even more unexpected constituency, had begun to fight. In 1968, 187 women sewing machinists at Ford's Dagenham plant walked out on strike demanding equal pay with men – to the surprise of both their employer and their trade union. Ford's managers condemned these mostly middle-aged, married woman as 'anarchic and irresponsible'.[38] Lillian Callaghan, one of the machinists, made their position clear: 'Male machinists on night shift receive 1s 4½d an hour more than we do and we think it is grossly unfair. Our claim is a call for equal pay for women at Ford's.' Her managers defended their position by using a long-standing argument – deployed by trade unions as well as employers – that 'women have no right to claim equal pay . . . because they do not do shift work.' A Ford official revealingly dismissed the women's claim for equal pay as 'an emotional issue', thereby suggesting that women's equality was not a matter for serious debate and that female workers were not sufficiently rational to sit at a negotiating table.[39] Amid huge publicity – Callaghan and her workmates were invited to tea by Barbara Castle – the machinists eventually won their battle; though only in part. They were granted 95 per cent of the men's rate, and continued to be classified as 'unskilled' workers rather than attaining the semi-skilled status for which they had fought.[40]

The Ford machinists' fight marked a radical departure from the past. Trade union leaders had been keen to recruit women during the 1960s, but often proved reluctant to take their demands seriously. Only a quarter of women workers were union members between the late 1940s and the early 1960s. Many more joined after 1962, when the Conservatives' pay freeze brought clerical workers into trade unions in large numbers, and as increasing numbers of women found work on the assembly lines. But in 1968, less than one-third of women workers were in a trade union, compared with more than half the male workforce.[41]

Trade union leaders ascribed women's low trade unionism to their apathy. They claimed that women worked 'for "pin money" and couldn't be organised'.[42] The women themselves told a different tale. 'For many of the women workers,' noted a researcher who visited a large food production plant in northern England, 'the shop-stewards were "bosses" men.'[43] The union rarely defended these women's claims for better working conditions and officials resisted demands for equal pay, fearing that this would have a detrimental effect on their male members. At this food processing factory, men who worked the night shift were doing exactly the same work as women did during the day, and were acutely aware that they 'were performing "women's work"'. Only their status within the union distinguished them from the female workforce, and persuaded management to pay them the male rate for the job.[44]

The Dagenham machinists shattered the notion that the unions could get away with ignoring women and survive in the rapidly changing labour market of 1968. Sheila Douglass, one of the Ford machinists who fought for equal pay, recalled that the response of the National Union of Vehicle Builders (NUVB) to the dispute was initially 'what are you doing this for – you only come to work for pin-money'. Going out on strike with little union support was daunting but empowering: 'the mighty Ford Motor Company, right?' said Bernie Passingham, one of Douglass's colleagues. 'Now they've got women in dispute and it's something new. I think it shook them to the core.'[45] Their success led a group of trade unionists to establish the National Joint Action Campaign for Women's Equal Rights (NJACWER). Members called on the TUC to lead a campaign for equal pay and equal employment rights for women. 'After things started up again about equal pay . . . that's when you realized that maybe you'd started something quite big,' said Sheila Douglass.[46] Women's trade union membership continued to rise during the 1970s, not only in the factories but among clerks, nurses and teachers.

The actions of the Dagenham women precipitated some important changes outside the labour movement as well. They contributed to the passing of the Equal Pay Act in 1970. Just as importantly, they demonstrated that unskilled and semi-skilled workers had the commitment to fight for their rights, and possessed powerful strategies for doing so. They proposed that the contribution that a worker made to the finished product should determine pay rates, rather than the technical skill involved in their labour. Clerical trade unions, public service unions and the TGWU had all used this strategy in negotiations through the 1960s, but the Dagenham strike was the first major dispute in which the workers used this rationale to confront their employers – and won.

★

The workers were not always united. Just as women had to stand up to the sexism of trade union officials as well as that of employers, so many black and Asian workers suffered discrimination. In 1961 people from the Caribbean and South Asia composed about 1 per cent of Britain's population. During the 1960s the number of immigrants increased, particularly those coming from India and Pakistan. By 1971, the combined Caribbean and South Asian population constituted 3 per cent of people living in Britain.

Employers often treated black and Asian immigrants as cheap and expendable labour, and trade union leaders frequently viewed them as a threat to white workers. This was the situation into which Sathnam Gill arrived in 1962. He had immigrated to Coventry from the Punjab. The youngest son of a farming family, he could not rely on his father's smallholding for a living, and employment opportunities in India were very limited. In the 1950s British motor companies had staged recruitment drives in Delhi and Sathnam's brother-in-law was one of those who migrated to Britain as a result. But by the time Sathnam arrived to join him in Coventry, work in the car factories was not as abundant as it had been; foreign competition from Japan and Germany meant that demand for cars was no longer growing. Sathnam found that 'you stand in a queue, see the white blokes coming from the back, getting the jobs and you was turned down', an experience that social investigators found was typical.[47]

Trade unions offered little protection to workers like Sathnam Gill. In Bristol in the early 1960s the TGWU's leadership opposed the colour bar introduced by the Bristol Omnibus Company; only to discover that their anti-racist stance was opposed by many of their members.[48] Trade unionists were divided over whether to focus on opposing racial discrimination, or campaigning against immigration on the basis that incomers would undercut British workers' wages.[49] Many groups and individuals held inconsistent attitudes towards immigrants. Coventry Trades Council (an association of local trade unions) vociferously opposed a colour bar instituted by many pub landlords – but was unwilling to admit black and Asian workers into the city's high-paying car factories.[50] Most trade unions neglected, or chose not to recruit, immigrant workers.

But immigrants themselves began to organize. Both trade unions and employers erroneously assumed that migrant workers were, in the words of one trade unionist, 'complete strangers to industrial society'.[51] In reality, many had experience of workplace or community activism, which they drew upon in Britain. The Indian Workers' Association (IWA), for example, had been established by Punjabi migrants in the 1930s, but was revived by a new wave of arrivals during the 1950s. The IWA drew on a Punjabi tradition of direct action, and recruited heavily from former agricultural workers who shared a collective sense of identity which they brought with them to Britain. Then came the 1962 Commonwealth Immigration Act. This restricted immigration and gave priority to migrants with educational and professional qualifications, including clerks, university students, teachers and doctors. 'That's when educated people started coming to this country,' recalled Sathnam Gill. Not all of them could get work commensurate with their qualifications; they ended up on Britain's assembly lines – and in leadership positions within the IWA. Many of them were well-versed in Marxist theory and sympathetic to Communism.[52]

Members of the IWA sought to help each other survive through providing social facilities and friendship, and increasingly they also sought trade union recognition for their work. Sathnam Gill first came into contact with the IWA when 'a few of us decided to organize a Kabbadi [Indian sports] team in Coventry, and they gave us money.' By this stage Sathnam had found work, not at one of the city's car plants but at a small chemical factory where he and his workmates earned meagre wages in filthy conditions working up to ten hours each day. Most of Sathnam's colleagues were from the Indian subcontinent. The Kabbadi team forged bonds of trust and friendship among the group, which included a number of recent, aspirant migrants who had arrived in the mid-1960s. In 1969, with assistance from the IWA, 'we fought and fought and fought', going out on strike and winning the support of the local TGWU branch. The factory became unionized and some of the workers' conditions improved. Sathnam himself became a shop steward and active within the local union branch.

Migrant workers scored similar victories across the country.[53] In 1965 'a remarkable feat of organisation by leaders of the Indian

Workers' Association at Southall' led to a strike of more than 500 Asian workers at a rubber factory. Leading this dispute over wages and union recognition was N.S. Hundal, 'a law graduate of the University of Punjab who is working his way through Gray's Inn'. Despite the TGWU's refusal to pay the workers any strike pay – 'district secretary, Mr F. Howell, said it was a matter of sifting the qualifications of the various strikers before deciding how much they should get' – Hundal and his workmates sustained the strike for six months. They persuaded the local Indian community to make generous donations, and local Indian landlords to forgo rent payments for the duration of the dispute. Their employer eventually agreed to most of their demands.[54] Race and gender relations had always shaped working-class life. At times, migrants' collective ethnic identities – strengthened by being in an unfamiliar and often hostile country – helped forge strong support for their disputes, as among the Indian community in Southall. At the same time, this strong sense of shared interest testified to the racism that these workers experienced from workmates, neighbours, landlords and employers.

By the end of the 1960s, race relations were central to political debate. Throughout the 1960s governments sought to tighten up immigration controls, implicitly suggesting that Britain couldn't cope with more residents. The most infamous attack came in 1968, when the Conservative MP Enoch Powell launched a virulent attack on immigration in his 'Rivers of Blood' speech. Powell's outspoken opposition to racial mixing incurred the disapproval of the Conservative leadership, but hundreds of dock workers demonstrated in his support outside the Houses of Parliament. Less well publicized was that these dockers were non-unionized, and that their demonstration had been provoked by a larger protest against Powell's speech launched by unionized white workers nearby.[55] While black and Asian workers had to endure suspicion and hostility from many of their white workmates, not all white workers were racist. Employers' actions – by using migrants as cheap labour – exacerbated both white workers' hostility to foreign workmates, and the poverty in which many migrants found themselves living.

★

While race and gender relations could cause tension, in other ways the British working class was becoming more homogeneous at the beginning of the 1970s. The division between skilled and unskilled workers was narrowing. In 1968 the sociologist Richard Brown interviewed more than 200 of Tyneside's shipbuilding workers. Most retained 'more specific loyalties to particular groups within this larger whole' – to their gang, workshop, trade or union. Nevertheless, economic security provoked unskilled workers to become more assertive, more willing to join a trade union, and more aware of the concerns they shared with skilled tradesmen. Many of the men Brown interviewed hoped that new educational opportunities would enable their children to enter skilled manual or office work; some of their sons and daughters were already engineers or clerks. These changes meant they were less 'parochial' than their fathers had been. 'They are aware of an "us" as members of the working class and as members of a shipbuilding community,' Brown concluded.[56] This helped explain why so many workers were able to organize around their shared grievances so effectively.

What also united these workers was annoyance at remote and complacent managers. Many of the shipbuilding workers to whom Richard Brown spoke were angry about their managers' unwillingness to accept that workers might have some expertise that professional managers, with no experience of the trade, inevitably lacked. This was not a new grievance among industrial workers, but the 1960s saw the expansion of middle management, together with an increase in the number of graduate managers who had never had any experience of shopfloor working.[57] Older men noticed the change. 'Some of these new chaps that are getting on as managers,' said John Soulsby, a forty-seven-year-old shipyard electrician, 'are getting on people's nerves.'[58]

Younger men, their aspirations raised by education and the political rhetoric of 'white heat', were amazed by the way management treated them. 'It's like going back to the dark ages,' declared twenty-year-old Charles Berry of the relationship between workers and managers at the Swan Hunter shipyard where he worked as an electrician. Charles had stayed on at secondary school until sixteen, before taking an apprenticeship at the yard, assuming that his education and training would lead to a safer job, and a better life, than his father, a miner, had known. But the yard was 'like the old system of barons and serfs. There's too much class distinction.'[59] Post-war welfare and educational reforms, together with near-full employment and Labour's rhetoric of equality and technological innovation, gave young workers a new confidence in their right to be listened to. They were angry to discover that most employers had no intention of consulting them.

Wilson's attitude to the strikers did nothing to assuage their anger. After the election of 1966, the government stopped talking so much about ending social inequality. Changes in the international economic situation were one cause: in the face of foreign manufacturing competition, Wilson fell silent on the issue of full employment, and instead focused on eradicating the most extreme cases of poverty. While this represented a progression from the 1950s, when poverty was rarely a subject for political debate, his approach implied that most workers' lives were entirely satisfactory. The government increasingly negotiated with pressure groups, single-issue organizations like the Child Poverty Action Group (CPAG), established by social scientists and social workers in 1966. Wilson himself attended CPAG's launch. Unlike the trade unions, which were based on the principle of popular participation, CPAG was essentially concerned to speak for the poor, rather than to campaign with them – a direction that led a few leading members to leave the organization in the late 1960s.[60]

Like Macmillan before him, Wilson had become convinced that the labour force needed to become more 'mobile', and that short-term unemployment was going to be an inevitable part of many workers' careers. German and Japanese exports were increasingly threatening the British dominance of engineering and the motor industry. The British economy, Wilson believed, must be leaner; workers must accept lower wages and less job security. Wilson agreed with his Home Secretary, Roy Jenkins, that social security should be targeted at particularly 'vulnerable' groups, especially the short-term unemployed.[61]

At the same time, Wilson encouraged Jenkins to pursue a 'permissive' agenda in home affairs. This included a raft of legislation designed to protect and extend the rights of the individual: in 1967 adult male homosexuality was decriminalized and so was abortion; in 1969 'blameless' divorce became legal for the first time (prior to this, one party had had to accept blame, usually by admitting to cruelty, desertion or adultery). These reforms were accompanied by legislation promoting sexual and racial equality. The 1965 Race Relations Act was the first British law to address race discrimination; the Act made such discrimination illegal in public places. The Equal Pay Act of 1970 prohibited employers from treating a worker less favourably because of their sex.

These hard-won reforms represented important advances in the rights of women, black people and gay men. But they indicated the government's intention that economic and political rights should be attached to individuals rather than to groups. Individual women, for example, would be able to compete for jobs on a level with individual men (at least in theory). This did not address the economic and political subordination that working-class people shared as a result of their relationship to production: their need to labour for a living.

In fact, such legislation went hand in hand with politicians' attempts to undermine the collective economic and political strength of ordinary workers. In 1969 Barbara Castle introduced a white paper, *In Place of Strife*, which was designed to curtail the power of workers to go on strike and of trade unions to initiate industrial disputes. Strikes would only be legal if they were voted for by a large majority of the workforce. The government would have the right to enforce a twenty-eight-day 'cooling off' period in any unofficial dispute, to enable investigation of the strike's motivation. Courts would have the power to fine workers and employers who breached a new code of conduct that would govern disciplinary, dismissal and arbitration matters. In a radical break with post-war arrangements, this code would be enforced not by the trade unions, employers, or the government but instead by an independent Commission of Industrial Relations.

The scope for negotiation between government and organized working people had narrowed. *In Place of Strife*, Castle declared, 'provides the means by which we can reconcile the right to strike, one of the essential freedoms in a democracy, with the need to safeguard the rights of the community – and, above all, to protect the country's economy from the senseless disruption of avoidable strikes'.[62] The anger of backbench Labour MPs and the fury of ordinary workers – leading to the appearance of more picket lines – prevented her white paper from becoming law. Nevertheless, Castle's move marked an important turning point in relations between government and trade unions. From 1969, successive governments would treat the economic and political power of the working class as a threat to social democracy, rather than as a prerequisite for a democratic state. As Castle's defence of her proposals made clear, her government now regarded workers' rights as being distinct from 'the rights of the community'. The people's welfare was no longer of paramount importance: of greater value was 'the country's economy'; and the greatest threat to economic stability was assumed to be workers' militancy.

What had provoked this change of attitude? By the end of 1960s it was clear to business leaders, politicians and many ordinary workers themselves that the needs of big business and the needs of their workers were essentially incompatible. In the 1950s and 1960s both Labour and Conservative governments had struggled to maintain full employment with employers' desire to make a profit, which led to price rises, which in turn caused inflation, a fall in consumer demand, and then unemployment. From the mid-1960s workers' militancy appeared to threaten the ever more delicate equilibrium of Britain's economic state. Partly this was due to foreign competition, such as car manufacture in Germany and Japan. But it was also attributable to the hardening attitude of Britain's industrialists and businessmen towards the country's workers. These employers were keen to see their profits increased rather than reduced, and to see workers' increasingly assertive demands for a share in the spoils of industry jettisoned, in favour of a concentration on increasing shareholders' wealth.

In 1965 a number of British business leaders established the Confederation of British Industries (the CBI). The CBI's lobbying, and more shadowy networks between business leaders and the political elite, put Wilson's government under increasing pressure to undermine the economic and political power of the country's workers. In 1968 Cecil King, chairman of the *Mirror* newspaper group, had secret talks with Lord Mountbatten about establishing 'a national government of businessmen' to avert economic and political 'crisis'.[63] King was sacked and the plot came to nothing, but it was a sign of the increasing frustration that a small but influential group of business leaders, politicians and press magnates felt about the political power of the industrial working class.

While these conservative figures had little sympathy for the Labour government, Harold Wilson was quite prepared to meet them halfway. Indeed, he had offered Cecil King a peerage and a job at the Board of Trade back in 1964, and in 1967 gave Campbell Adamson, a former company director and Conservative supporter, a senior role at the government's new Department for Economic Affairs.[64] Two years later, Adamson became director of the CBI, where he supported Barbara Castle's attempt to have *In Place of Strife* made into law.[65]

Barbara Castle failed. In 1969 the power of the trade unions within the Labour Party was sufficiently strong to prevent her proposals from becoming law. The trade union leaders who opposed her included several who were primarily concerned with maintaining their own small centre of political power. Some of these short-sighted men had done the trade unions no favours by seeking to place the interests of white, male manual workers above those of women, black and migrant workers. But despite this, the organized working class was growing in number and in power at the end of the 1960s. Its ranks were swelled by immigrants, by women, and by white-collar workers. They included clerks and factory workers aged between their teens and early thirties, a generation angry that the promises that teachers and politicians had made them of a more prosperous and more adventurous life than that their parents had known had been broken. They had discovered that it was not true that hard work and initiative were enough to propel you into a better sort of life in the late 1960s.

As 1970 dawned the future looked more uncertain than it had done since 1926. As well as preventing Wilson's government from introducing anti-union laws, these newly militant workers had helped to bring about wage rises that enabled working-class families to enjoy the fruits of affluence they themselves produced on the assembly lines of Britain: fridges, cookers and cars. But the political and economic power they craved – primarily, for more control over how their work was organized, and in whose interests – was not forthcoming. The tension between their demands and the aims of their political and economic leaders grew, rather than lessened, as Britain entered the 1970s.

14

Trouble and Strife

IN 1970 WILSON'S government departed when Edward Heath's Conservative Party won the general election. Heath scored only a narrow victory, testifying to voters' uncertainty about who could best satisfy their desires for greater control over their working and domestic lives. 'Housing' and 'jobs' ranked high in voters' concerns in the opinion polls that preceded the election. Heath's government did nothing to assuage their anxiety. Unemployment grew, and public spending cuts threatened people's livelihoods and their homes. Women played an increasingly important role in campaigns to safeguard the gains they had made during the 1950s and 1960s.

A mythology of the 1970s, as a decade when working-class people's greed caused the economic downfall of the country, has been unquestioningly accepted by many historians and politicians. John Major, Conservative Prime Minister from 1991 until 1997, warned that anti-union legislation was necessary to ensure that there could be no return to the 'political wilderness' and turmoil of the 1970s. On his election to government in 1997, Tony Blair felt it necessary to state that there would be no return to 'beer and sandwiches' at Number Ten; he warned union leaders to expect 'fairness not favours'. Yet the reality of the 1970s is far more curious than this orthodoxy suggests. This was a decade of right-wing plots to stage a coup d'état; government surveillance of labour activists; draconian policing of picket lines and housing estates; and ultimately a dramatic and catastrophic intervention in British domestic policy by a group of international financiers that spelled the end to the post-war relationship between politicians and the people that had brought the latter limited, but important, gains.

★

Edward Heath's government was strongly committed to a 'free market', by which Heath meant one free of government and trade union control. In 1971 he introduced an Industrial Relations Act, which took the recommendations of *In Place of Strife* far further than Barbara Castle had envisaged. Workers' rights to collective bargaining and to strike were sharply constrained. Most controversially, intra-union disputes – which enabled workers from several different trades or industries to mobilize collectively – were made illegal.

The tenor of the Act suggested a return to the labour relations that had characterized the early twentieth century. After 1945, trade unions had held a degree of political power by virtue of representing a large proportion of the workforce; it was through trade unions that these workers participated in the democratic society in which they lived. Heath's Act treated the trade unions as minor players in economic development, which derived their limited power not from the importance of their members, but from the benevolence of the political party in government. Heath's government was determined to curb the existing bargaining rights that trade unionists had wielded since the Second World War.

The years that followed were ones of heightened political tension between the working class and the political establishment. Rumours of coups d'état by military men with aristocratic connections were rife. The most famous came in 1973, when General Sir Walter Walker, NATO Commander of Northern Europe between 1969 and 1972, established a private army to protect Britain against 'Communist' trade unionists – with the covert but strong support of Mountbatten and several senior civil servants, as well as the encouragement of disillusioned businessmen.[1] Ted Heath himself expressed exasperation at the paranoia shown by some senior civil servants, police officers and spies. 'I met people in the security services who talked the most ridiculous nonsense and whose whole philosophy was ridiculous nonsense,' he later recalled. 'If one of them were on a tube and saw someone reading the *Daily Mirror* they would say: "Get after him, that is dangerous. We must find out where he bought it."'[2]

The real threat to working-class people's political and economic rights did not come from these shadowy groups – important though they were – but from the heart of government. During Heath's four years in government he declared five states of emergency, implying that strikers were not to be negotiated with, but should rather be treated as enemies of the state. The strength of the government's determination to crush the political power of ordinary workers was demonstrated by the treatment of the Pentonville Five and the Shrewsbury Two. In the short term, the Industrial Relations Act had been rendered unworkable by the TUC, led by the TGWU, which struck over it. But in 1972 this resulted in the imprisonment of the Pentonville Five, dockers who joined the picket lines in defiance of the Act, which outlawed secondary picketing.

Then, in 1972, came a national strike in the building trade. Thirty-four-year-old Ricky Tomlinson and thirty-six-year-old Des Warren – the Shrewsbury Two – were among the strikers hoping to institute a minimum wage, tighten health and safety regulations and abolish 'the lump'. This was the practice whereby builders could hire casual labourers who undercut union rates and were often employed in highly dangerous conditions, at a time when an average of one building worker died every day in Britain.[3] After visiting picket lines in Shropshire, Tomlinson and Warren were arrested on charges of secondary picketing, unlawful assembly, causing an affray and – most seriously – conspiracy.[4] Tomlinson was incredulous to discover that this conspiracy charge rested on the contention that they had planned their picketing activities in 'a conspiracy hatched in the upstairs room of the Bull and Stirrup pub'. After a three-month trial in 1973, Tomlinson and Warren were found guilty on all counts and sentenced to two and three years in jail respectively.[5]

Meanwhile, many people who would never have considered themselves militants were resorting to drastic actions simply to get by. By 1972, more than 4 per cent of workers were unemployed. Ann Lanchbury and her husband Norman were among those affected. Ann had married Norman, a factory labourer, in 1960. Through the 1960s, Ann worked as a nurse intermittently, fitting this around caring for their two young children. Then, in the early 1970s, Norman was made redundant. With a large mortgage, he and Ann became anxious when he couldn't quickly find a new job.

Ann was unwell at the time and unable to get a full-time or permanent job. She turned to friends for help:

> They told me I must be due some money to help us out. I walked to the Social Security which was miles and miles, and I walked and I was in great pain because I was waiting to go into hospital for an operation. I went up and they said, 'No you're not entitled to anything . . .' and I was mortified. She said, 'If you hadn't paid all your mortgage you'd have had help.' The more you help yourself the worse off you would be.

Strangers, whose circumstances are unknown, invite judgements when help is rationed, and the most conspicuous strangers in 1970s Coventry were Asian immigrants. Ann, who had worked hard to buy a house, 'did resent the fact that there were Indian women who had just come into the country and they were getting money for this and money for that'.

Yet it was Ann herself who felt forced to commit fraud in order to make ends meet. Desperate not to lose her home, she managed to find a part-time cash-in-hand job at the city centre Godiva café. 'I said to Norman, "Right, our lives are in our own hands." He had tried and tried and tried to get a job, now it was my turn. The owner of the Godiva café said, "You can work for us if you keep your mouth shut we won't tell the tax man, cash in hand, you can work for us nine till six."' On Saturdays, when the manager wasn't around, the other waitresses stuffed Ann's bag full of sandwiches and pies for the family 'because they knew it was tough'. Life eventually improved when Norman found a job in Bournemouth – but this meant uprooting the whole family from their home and friends. Ann, like many other women, 'just got by – that was the early seventies.'

Others found hope and relief in organizing together, taking the risk of being branded militants for doing so. Among them were thousands of women who were hit hard by Heath's attempt to reduce council housing drastically. Like Harold Macmillan before him, Heath sought to establish home ownership as the most preferable form of housing tenure, and to turn council housing into residual accommodation for the very poorest by reviving the privately rented sector. His 1972 Housing Act directed councils to prioritize providing

housing for the homeless within a limited space of time. This caused
chaos to the still very long council house waiting lists, and emphasized that council housing was now firmly targeted only at the most
needy. The Act also took control for council rent levels out of the
hands of local authorities by demanding that they set rents at market
rates, meaning that much council accommodation was immediately
made far more expensive that privately rented property. At the same
time, council tenants were given the right to buy their home, although
it was possible for local authorities to delay or veto the implementation
of this right.[6]

In the 1960s the housing expert J.B. Cullingworth had warned
policymakers that 'the dissatisfaction at rising rents may eventually
develop into something more significant.'[7] In the 1970s his prophecy
came true. Council tenants experienced 23 per cent rent rises between
1971 and 1974.[8] Campaigns and rent strikes erupted, many of them
instigated by married women living on council estates. Some of
these women were already involved in organizing the amenities that
their landlords had failed to provide. By the 1970s Betty Ennis of
Coventry's Willenhall estate was working full-time at the city's GEC
factory 'but three nights a week I used to work in the youth club',
which the Residents' Association ran for Willenhall's increasing
number of teenagers. While men were out at work for long hours
each day, women who took chief responsibility for childcare and
household budgeting found themselves drawn together to improve
their neighbourhood. In the early 1970s many tenants, including
Betty, instigated rent strikes. 'The rent kept going up, year after year,'
said Betty. 'We went everywhere, got coaches, demonstrated, to the
council house [town hall] in Coventry, to the Parliament, and we
said, "Not a penny on the rent."'

For women like Betty, rent increases were simply the latest in a
long list of grievances they had against private and council landlords
who refused to listen to their tenants. Betty and her neighbours
couldn't see any tangible reason for these rent increases, since their
council houses were no longer providing an enviable level of comfort.
By 1970, almost a third of British households had central heating; it
was no longer simply the preserve of the rich.[9] However, councils
owned few of these houses. In the early 1970s Betty had to get

special permission from the council before she could have central heating installed – at her own expense – and had to give a guarantee that she'd leave the pipes behind if she moved. 'I said, "Excuse me, who's going to carry the pipes? I don't think so."' It was one example of the lack of trust and petty bureaucracy that council tenants were expected to accept.

The long and bitter dispute over rent ended in failure for the strikers and the Conservatives pressed on with their rent increases. Yet the rent strikes had an unforeseen legacy. Working together for a common purpose, standing up to politicians and the police, and facing the very real prospect of being jailed for their actions profoundly affected many women. One of the longest and bitterest rent strikes occurred on the Tower Hill estate at Kirkby, the overspill district that Liverpool Council had established on the outskirts of the city. Women were instrumental in the dispute.[10] According to one Kirkby tenant:

> If the rent strike hadn't happened, I'd get up, get the kids ready and out to school, have a talk to some of the women about babies and the problems they have, teething. And I still talk to people about that, but it goes deeper, even the kind of conversation about babies, you're no longer discussing the baby's teething problems, you're talking about the kind of clinics that are there for you and when you start talking about what you're going to do for their tea you start talking about prices, which is something I never did before . . . I question every-thing now.[11]

The rent strikes made clear that housekeeping was a political issue, and that housing estates could be centres for campaigns that were just as important as strikes in the factories. As wives and mothers, women took a leading role in these protests.

Having come together to fight rent increases, many of these women began to campaign for greater participation in the way their estates and flats were constructed and controlled. One of them was Judy Walker. Judy had been born in the early 1940s in Coventry. Her father was a factory worker who died of cancer when Judy was just eighteen; her mother was a waitress. Judy had grown up in a small terraced house in the inner-city Hillfields district and attended the local secondary modern school. 'When we left school, you'd always buy a big tin of sweets and go round to the senior boys and pass out your sweets, get all dressed up,' she said. But she'd long seen school as a boring interval before her real life began, and when she turned fifteen in 1955 she was determined not to get caught up with such childish rituals. 'I couldn't be bothered, I just got my tin of sweets, threw 'em over the wall [laughs] . . . and I went through them gates, oh yeah, out into the sunset [laughs] . . . and never looked back.' Life – specifically a job on the cosmetics counter at the city's smart new British Home Stores – beckoned.

By 1960, nineteen-year-old Judy was working in a smart boutique in the centre of Coventry. Her mother had remarried, and together with Judy's stepfather ran a pub, a job that gave them enough to run a car and rent a modern house on a suburban estate. Life was comfortable. Yet Judy sometimes froze with panic at the thought that in ten years she'd wake up to find herself living the same life as them: 'I have a fear of doing the same thing all the time and everything being boring . . . go to work and they come [home], have their dinner, they sit down and have five minutes, they'd have a wash and shave and go down the club, go down the pub, Saturday, Sunday dinner, same thing, go on holiday once a year . . . [I]t was the *sameness* of everything.'

Like many of her generation, Judy felt entitled to things that her parents regarded as privileges – among them, a decent place to live and bring up her children. It was on this foundation that she hoped to build a more adventurous and interesting life than her parents had known.

Ten years later, life was proving harder than Judy and many of her peers had been given to expect. Judy's search for adventure had led her into an early marriage to Roy, a former RAF conscript who became an engineer and took Judy with him when a motor company in South Africa offered him work in the early 1960s. But Judy didn't like Cape Town life: the cost of living was higher than they'd anticipated, they didn't travel as much as she'd hoped and expat life was isolating and 'snobbish'; it was the class hierarchy of Britain all over again but without any family or friends nearby. She returned to Britain in 1969 with her three young children and, by 1972, was divorced and living in a tower block back in Hillfields. Life was difficult.

'There were no after-school clubs or the like, to allow you to work,' no nurseries, and no playground within walking distance.

Judy decided that matters would only change if she took them into her own hands. While Ann and Norman Lanchbury relied on each other, Judy knew that her fight could only be effective if she joined with other local residents. She became instrumental in setting up an informal women's group, initially to help mothers with child-care, but soon the group developed more ambitious aims: 'My place was like a meeting house, we would all sort of meet and talk and have coffee and put ideas together. Things were very hard but we used to have meetings to talk about what we were going to do with the kids in the holidays and everyone would come along – especially the [Warwick University] students that would come and help [with playschemes] in holiday times.'

Similar groups were meeting all over the country. They brought together working- and middle-class women who learned that their experiences of motherhood provided an important common ground. In 1969 Jan Williams was one of the women who met at a 'One O'Clock Club' funded by Peckham Council for local mothers with young children. 'I used to push my kids round and round the duck pond, wishing I could push them in it,' she said. When she joined the group, she discovered that most of the mothers there were working class, though some were middle-class graduates who shared similar grievances. 'We talked about the same things again and again,' she said, 'about children, about sex, about being used.' For Jan and many of the other Peckham women, inequality at work was compounded by their partners' reluctance to help at home. 'I . . . started a part-time job and my husband had said he would look after the kids, but he didn't,' she said, explaining why she became sympathetic to feminism.[12]

Some of these groups brought about lasting changes in their neighbourhoods. In Coventry, Judy's group began an informal nursery and playscheme which they ran voluntarily. Then, spurred on by their success, they began to demand that the local council provide them with funding and with training as nursery nurses, as a means of helping the women to find work for themselves, as well as ensuring that their children were looked after by trained staff. Elsewhere, residents established playgroups, adventure playgrounds and community advice centres. Often these groups were a mix of council tenants, students at the growing number of universities, young middle-class people who were moving into the cheap housing offered by the dilapidated inner cities, and migrants who were unable to find accommodation elsewhere.[13] In Birmingham, for example, twenty-one-year-old Ranjit Sondhi, the son of an Indian doctor, and a former Birmingham University student, joined a housing co-operative in the predominantly working-class district of Handsworth. Ranjit's politics had been changed by his voluntary work at one of the city's adventure playgrounds – 'I never realized, in India, that there was this British working class' – and by his involvement in demonstrations against Enoch Powell's Rivers of Blood speech. 'We were all social workers, teachers,' he said of his Handsworth household, 'and we were united by wanting to do exactly what our training told us not to. Rather than telling people what to do, we wanted to use our training to help the people in our neighbourhood do what they wanted. So at first we just listened, and then people started saying, "Why don't you open a legal rights centre? Why don't we have a women's group?"'[14]

Women's groups like the one that met in Judy Walker's flat were part of the women's liberation movement, broadly defined. Far from simply being a middle-class movement confined to London-based consciousness-raising groups, feminist activism in the 1970s took many forms. Judy Walker's group was one in which working- and middle-class women were able to find common ground for campaigning. But the relationship between class and feminism was never without tension. Many working-class women disagreed with middle-class feminists' belief that male behaviour was primarily to blame for women's exploitation. In Kirkby, Rita, a young mother who worked in a food processing plant, didn't blame her husband for her wearying workload on the production line and in the home: 'What I'd like,' she said, 'is for my husband to earn so much I could stop working. I'd like men paid far more money.'[15] Contradicting the cosy terminology of the 'housewives' shift', which suggested both that women could easily fit work and domestic life together, and that employers were doing them a favour by offering them work in the first place, women like her pointed out that their paid and unpaid work was exhausting and necessary.

Other women felt that feminism didn't deal with the underlying economic injustices that shaped working-class women's lives. Judy Walker refused to describe herself as a feminist, which for her meant 'just talking'. The Warwick University students she met did not have children; they could, she felt, afford the time to sit and discuss sexual and emotional relationships while she had to 'just get on with looking after my kids'. She preferred to describe herself as 'a campaigner' rather than as a feminist. She relished the company and support of the women in her group, but was always aware of the inequalities of class, and the difference between their circumstances. 'Some of them had an education, training in child psychology, so if I was having trouble with one of the kids I might ask them about it.' While Judy found this helpful, she was more ambivalent about her economic position in the group. When she was short of cash, 'Diane [a member of the women's group] needed a cleaner, so she said I could clean for her. I ended up cleaning for a few of them.' As the end of the 1970s approached, some middle-class women's fight for liberation continued to be eased by the labour of less privileged women.[16]

Judy Walker and her allies had some lasting successes. Women's refuges, adventure playgrounds and playschemes survived the 1970s. Nursery provision dramatically increased. In 1965 there had been local authority nursery places available for 21,849 children; almost identical to the number available in 1938. By 1979 there were 28,313, a rise of 30 per cent.[17] Judy herself had acquired a childcare qualification by the end of the 1970s and she became a council employee.

Yet by the mid-1970s, the strikers and community campaigners were as aware of their defeats as their achievements. Internationally, an escalating oil crisis was forcing up fuel prices and threatening the car industry, on which so many British jobs relied. The rent strikes collapsed in the face of government intransigence. Increasing numbers of council tenants chose to buy their homes. Among them was Betty Ennis. She had never aspired to own her house, believing that property 'always causes rows' and being quite content to have the council as her landlord. Yet in 1974, faced with a rising rent and poor council

TROUBLE AND STRIFE

maintenance, Betty 'jumped up and bought my house', becoming one of 46,000 council tenants across Britain who had done so since 1972.[18] A desire to be free of the control of landlords and the vagaries of politicians had provoked many of the tenants' collective campaigns of the early 1970s; the same desire prompted many of these people to seek a more individualistic form of freedom by buying their own home.

By 1974, the living conditions of working-class people looked far more precarious than they had done a decade earlier. Post-war prosperity had proved very short-lived. As the international price of oil increased, Heath's government responded by introducing wage controls. In 1973 Britain's miners struck in protest at these, causing a fuel shortage that led to the government instituting a three-day working week. Heath declared yet another state of emergency – the most serious yet. In January 1974 he announced that commercial and industrial users of electricity would be confined to operating on a three-day week. Yet this move cost the government millions of pounds, since those workers who were subject to the three-day week became eligible for unemployment benefit; 885,000 people registered for this in January 1974.[19] It would have been quicker, less disruptive and cheaper for Heath to settle with the miners, but his government was clearly bent on turning the dispute into a national confrontation. This was a political dispute, not simply an economic one.

When the miners showed no inclination to return to work, Heath called a snap general election, posing voters the question: 'Who Governs Britain?' Unfortunately for Heath, the answer was: not him. Wilson's Labour Party returned to power, with a manifesto more explicitly socialist than that of any previous British government. Labour declared its intention to 'bring about a fundamental and irreversible shift in the balance of power and wealth in favour of working people and their families'. Labour's manifesto was called *Let Us Work Together* and promised to 'make power in industry genuinely accountable to the workers and the community at large'. At the heart of this commitment was the 'social contract', which offered trade unions a central role in policymaking in return for their willingness to curb wage claims in times of austerity. Equality was a

309

central aim: 'economic equality – in income, wealth and living standards' and 'social equality' was to be achieved through 'full employment, housing, education and social benefits'. This was a political programme explicitly directed at the working class – at 'our people'.[20] It appealed sufficiently to secure Labour a narrow victory at the polls.

But Wilson's Labour Party entered government unsure how to achieve its ambitions. In 1975 Wilson's government launched an acrimonious debate about how to deal with the worsening economic crisis. Some left-wingers, like Labour MPs Tony Benn and Stuart Holland, argued that the crisis stemmed from the greed of industrial magnates and financiers. Benn contended that the government should not be distracted from its progressive programme by employers' talk of 'crisis', insisting that people's homes and jobs were more important than safeguarding the large profits of industrial magnates, and calling for the government to create jobs rather than cut them. Like many of the striking workers of the late 1960s and early 1970s, Stuart Holland emphasized that employers were preoccupied with short-term profit margins and thus were failing to innovate. Nationalization, and local workers' control of industries and housing, were the only solutions to the ongoing industrial disputes of the mid-seventies. He called on the government to 'reverse the present dominance of capitalist modes of production . . . into a democratically controlled socialism'.[21]

Wilson, an economist by training, committed to capitalism and convinced that power was best wielded by those with technical and political training, was unwilling to listen. It was not in any case clear how a government committed to private enterprise, and with so many trade links with the rest of the capitalist world, could have delivered the kind of programme that Benn and Holland advocated. Yet neither was it possible for Wilson to fulfil the manifesto promises he had made to the voters. On 16 March 1976 he suddenly resigned; he was over sixty and, according to Geoffrey Goodman, one of his economic advisers, 'tired and ill'.[22] Jim Callaghan became Prime Minister. Eventually, under pressure from the Conservative opposition, senior officials at the Treasury and the CBI, Labour sought the help of the International Monetary Fund (IMF). The Chancellor of the

Exchequer, Denis Healey, agreed to swingeing public spending cuts in return for a huge IMF loan.

Labour's acceptance of IMF assistance suggested that welfare and full employment were luxuries that must be dispensed with in economic crisis. This was a volte-face from the logic of 1945, when Attlee's government had seen providing the people with jobs and public services as essential prerequisites of economic growth. Tony Benn, Callaghan's Minister for Energy, judged the the IMF's demands to be 'a "try-on" by international capital to attack a government it did not like'; capitulating to them 'an act of unilateral economic disarmament from which the government never recovered'.[23]

Labour's agreement with the IMF offered ammunition to right-wing critics of the welfare state, who argued that public spending had led to the current crisis. '[W]e have only got into this humiliating position because of the incontinent expansion of public spending under the very Ministers who are about to call for more sacrifices,' thundered the *Daily Express*.[24] Yet no convincing argument was ever given for how, or why, full employment and welfare expenditure had caused Britain's economic decline. Supporters of the IMF deal argued that without it, employers would have taken their businesses overseas, increasing unemployment in Britain; but these employers were not castigated for their irresponsibility or greed, as striking miners and assembly-line workers so frequently were. The role of the international oil crisis was conveniently overlooked, while the IMF's stance was simply accepted as common sense, rather than as the calculated strategy of those bankers, financiers and right-wing politicians who controlled the IMF, and which promoted a global free market at the expense of workers' welfare.

Labour did oversee some reforms resulting from the campaigns of the past decade. In 1975 the Equal Pay Act of 1970 came into force. In the following year, the government passed the Race Relations Act, which made discrimination on the grounds of race illegal in Britain's workplaces. Yet this equality legislation was a bittersweet victory for the campaigners. It provided a bare minimum of rights that employers and government were meant to respect. The law now officially offered a level playing field for individuals, and the government proved intolerant of the notion that workers' rights should extend beyond equal access to jobs and equal pay. The new laws challenged the need for collective association, and especially the political influence of the unions.

This became clear in the same year that the Race Relations Act was passed, when workers at the Grunwick Film Processing Laboratories in Willesden walked out on strike. They were protesting at their employer's refusal to negotiate with them on pay and conditions and to allow them to join a trade union. Seventy per cent of Grunwick's workers were black or Asian. Most of those who initially went on strike were Asian immigrants, who had settled in Britain from Kenya or Uganda. When the journalist Joe Rogaly went to interview them he found that most were 'very young' or were married women, like Jayaben Desai, the middle-aged Indian woman who had emigrated from Tanzania in 1968 and became the strikers' spokesperson.

The Grunwick strikers challenged the assumption that married women, immigrants and young workers were naïve or apathetic. The Grunwick firm appeared to have recruited migrants in the belief that they were more pliable than white workers. However, as Joe Rogaly observed, the firm had been wrong: 'people of this kind are not easily pushed around for long.' Some of the workers had held leadership roles in their former homelands, and most had a strong sense of community which derived from a shared language and the experience of migration: they looked out for one another. They also shared 'a strongly motivated desire to work, and save'.

There were two other features of their lives that many of the Grunwick workers had in common. Most of them were the wives or children of men who worked in factories with better conditions, and most of them owned their own homes, 'with every able adult in the family working and contributing towards the mortgage'.[25] Trade union leaders had long taken for granted that the wives and children of male workers were less likely to go out on strike, because their wages were of less importance to their home. They also believed that owner-occupiers would be unlikely to risk their mortgage by taking to the picket line. The strikers at Grunwick challenged these assumptions. They used their husbands' and fathers' experience of working elsewhere as an important benchmark against which to

judge their employer, and from which they could learn. Jayaben
Desai's husband worked for the Rank Organisation, and at 'the dining
table we are talking sometimes about my job and his job', she said.
'I was explaining everything that happens in my job and he was
explaining – an exchange of ideas. He once told me: "In your place
if there is a union this type of management cannot behave like this
towards you."'[26] Because Desai and many of her workmates could
rely on some financial support from their husbands or fathers, they
could afford to take the risk of being dismissed for staging an unofficial strike. Not all men were supportive: the picket line also
included some women who had defied their husbands, spurred on
by the friendships and separate identity they had forged at work.[27]

Whatever their motivations, the strikers flatly contradicted their
managers' assumptions about what migrant workers would put up
with. 'What you are running here is not a factory, it is a zoo,' Desai
taunted one of the managers during her first week on the picket
line. 'In a zoo, there are many types of animals. Some are monkeys
who dance on your fingertips, others are lions who can bite your
head off. We are those lions, Mr Manager.'[28]

Grunwick received little publicity until other trade unionists –
among them postmen and miners – showed their support by
appearing on the picket lines in 1977. At this point, the Labour
government and the Conservative opposition united to condemn
this dangerous show of working-class unity. Conservative spokesman
on law and order Keith Joseph declared in the press that 'the
Grunwick rent-a-mob siege is a litmus test, perhaps a turning point,
in our political and constitutional life.'[29] Trade unionists had become,
in the words of the Daily Mirror, 'screaming militants' rather than
representatives of the people.[30]

Politicians' reaction to Grunwick showed how far political and
economic circumstances had changed since 1970. The IMF agreement
had seriously undermined Britain's commitment to the post-war
tenets of full employment and welfare. In the words of Bernard
Donoghue, senior policy adviser to Harold Wilson and his successor,
Jim Callaghan, that particular brand of free market politics known
as Thatcherism was launched 'in primitive form' by the Labour
government and above all by the IMF.[31] Callaghan's government

deployed thousands of police to help strikebreakers get through Grunwick's gates. More than 500 people had been arrested on the picket line in bitter and often violent confrontations. In 1978 the strikers were forced to give up their fight. Most were immediately sacked.

Grunwick was the first major dispute to involve Asian and white workers and men and women, working alongside each other on equal terms. In this sense it marked a radical and hopeful departure in the history of labour protest. But as far as business leaders and politicians were concerned, that new unity was dangerous; it hinted at the emergence of a newly powerful, politically cohesive and potentially militant working class. It was no coincidence that politicians' opposition to the strike grew as the picket line became increasingly diverse.

By the end of the 1970s, the economic and political power of the working class was rapidly declining. Over the preceding decade, governments had accepted that profit-making and the people's welfare were ultimately irreconcilable – a conclusion made more stark by the oil crisis and its repercussions. Faced with the choice, they chose loyalty to those who held economic power in Britain and beyond: to industrialists, businessmen and financiers. The major political parties were united in viewing working-class power as a threat to democracy, rather than being a prerequisite of it. Their decision to govern in favour of capitalists rather than in the interests of the majority of the electorate was to be an important and enduring legacy of the 1970s.

The political attitudes of the people themselves were changing by the end of the decade. Rising unemployment and economic insecurity had exacerbated people's desire to exert more control over their lives, but the collective approach to achieving this – through trade unionism, women's groups and tenants' campaigns – had apparently failed. In 1979 Margaret Thatcher won the general election on a promise to give voters the control over their lives that Labour had failed to deliver. Her brand of Conservatism promised an individualistic freedom, predicated on the myth that everyone could exercise equal choice in a free market. At the end of a troubled decade, this was an alluring message. But the brief, triumphant experience of striking and campaigning would stay with the thousands who had participated in the activism of the late 1960s and 1970s. When times got harder in the 1980s and 1990s, this memory of collective action and what it could achieve would live on in people's minds – a weak riposte to Margaret Thatcher's claim that 'There Is No Alternative' to the free market, perhaps; but a riposte nonetheless.

Interlude VIII

Return to Castleford

IN 1976 JACK Rosenthal, a working-class boy from Lancashire, decided to write a television play about Viv Nicholson's life. *Spend, Spend, Spend* was broadcast the following year. His decision caused immediate controversy on the Garforth estate to which Viv and Keith had moved following their win: the residents got up a petition to prevent the BBC filming there (they failed). Susan Littler, the thirty-year-old actress playing Viv, was furious with them. In playing a scene where Viv returned from holiday to the estate, she 'jumped out of her Chevvy and let rip at "the pale-faced farts" all around', before the film crew decided it 'might be prudent to make a quick getaway'.

The play's success – it attracted millions of viewers and a BAFTA award for Susan Littler – testified to an enduring popular interest in working-class life. Viv Nicholson became heiress to the 'kitchen sink' heroes of the early 1960s. Susan Littler came from Sheffield, and was, the *Guardian* noted, 'the daughter of a Lancashire blacksmith': one of the second generation of working-class actors to benefit from the post-war interest in working-class cultural life. Rosenthal was determined to tell Viv's story from her point of view; Littler said that 'if the play hadn't done justice to Viv', she 'couldn't have done it'.[1] Rather than attempting to understand Viv's story through a middle-class lens, they made Viv's values, appearance and aspirations seem normal and acceptable. The play made an interesting contrast to the very different representations that were beginning to dominate press depictions of working-class life, of dangerous militants, slum estates and greedy trade unionists.

By 1977, when *Spend, Spend, Spend* was broadcast, Viv was back in Castleford for good. Her story was a fable for her generation. The 'jobs for life' to which the teenagers of the 1950s had been advised to apprentice themselves now offered uncertain futures. The car industry, threatened by cheap imports, had begun to decline in the 1960s; other branches of mass manufacturing followed when the oil crisis of 1973 pushed up prices. Viv's own 'dizzy flight from the bottom to the top and back again' (as her autobiography put it) had a bitter contemporary resonance.

Reviewers of *Spend, Spend, Spend* rightly saw the play as dealing with an era that was coming to an end. The *Observer*'s television critic Stephen Gilbert praised the play for interweaving 'the dim rooms and surly faces of the fifties with the bright and brittle glare of sixties affluence'.[2] Back in the 1960s, it had seemed like working-class life was on an upward trajectory: progress was coming, a bit too slowly for many people, perhaps, but their quality of life was gradually getting better. But by 1977 that certainty had been replaced with insecurity, fear and bewilderment about the future – for Viv, for many more of her generation, and for their children.

15

Hard Times

IN 1979 THE bargain that had been struck during the Second World War between the people and their politicians – hard work in exchange for a living wage and a welfare safety net – came to an end. Unemployment increased, while benefits were cut. Once seen as essential pillars of a civilized society, welfare and full employment were now condemned by Margaret Thatcher as obstacles to economic growth. '[T]he relentless growth of the public sector has put a crushing burden on the private wealth-creating sector,' she declared in 1981. '[W]e now have no alternative but to accept a reduction in the standard of living if investment and employment are to recover.'[1] But who was included in that 'we'? The living standards of Britain's wealthiest people did not fall – only those of ordinary workers. For the first time since the 1930s economic inequality grew rapidly; the gap between the rich and the poor expanded in favour of the former.[2] The hard times of pre-war days had returned. People lost both the economic security and political bargaining power that full employment had helped them to achieve.

Yet, initially at least, Thatcher's message proved popular with many working-class people. Among her supporters was Alan Watkins, who had risen from engineering apprentice in the 1960s to production manager of a small Coventry firm by the late 1970s. He voted Conservative in 1979 because 'I liked this message of helping you to help yourself . . . and I felt the unions had got too much power.' For a man like Alan, who had worked hard to buy his own house and car, trade union membership offered little. He agreed with Margaret Thatcher when she proclaimed her intention to liberate Britain from 'vested interests'.[3] Unlike Herbert Morrison in the 1940s, Thatcher did not have in mind profiteering businessmen.

Instead she meant local authorities and trade unions, all of whom her government represented as undemocratic bureaucrats who obstructed the freedom of 'ordinary people'.[4] She proclaimed her intention to create a 'climate in which British people, individuals and industry, can prosper and can build their own independence. They can own their own homes. They have lower taxation on their incomes.'[5] For Howard Blake, another Coventry engineer, Thatcherism in those early days 'was all about standing on your own two feet, and being helped to do that'. He took advantage of the government's new grants for people wishing to start their own small business.

Like Labour in 1945, Margaret Thatcher presented a vision of a society where class background did not matter. Unlike Attlee's Labour Party, she proposed that this would be created by the free market and competition, rather than through co-operation. After the uncertainties and frustrations of the 1970s, her message had appeal for a generation who had grown up aspiring to greater autonomy over their lives, only to find this thwarted by landlords, employers and trade union leaders.

Thatcher's most popular policy was the sale of council accommodation. She wasn't the first Conservative leader to do so. In the 1950s Harold Macmillan had encouraged councils to sell off their housing stock. In 1972 Edward Heath had made it easier for council tenants to buy their homes, by insisting that local authorities considered tenants' requests to do so. But Margaret Thatcher's 1981 Housing Act sought to persuade council tenants to buy their homes, by offering them low mortgages which local councils were obliged to subsidize. At a time when the government was forcing councils to make huge public spending cuts, this was a highly political act.

People took advantage of the Act in large numbers, primarily because it seemed to make economic sense. Ron and Edna Jones of Liverpool were among the first to buy their council house. As Edna explained, they did so because the new, subsidized mortgage available to them was 'cheaper than rent'. Many tenants bought for this reason. The IMF deal of 1976 had led to further cuts in public spending on housing. In the late 1970s and 1980s council tenants were faced with further rent rises, while their neighbourhoods became increasingly socially polarized, and council investment in them fell. Ron and Edna Jones were aware that they might not be able to stand further rent rises. Ron, who had worked as a bus driver in the 1950s and 1960s, had taken a job as a salesman in the 1970s, which felt like a step up – 'white shirt, collar and tie' – but proved insecure. He was made redundant three times as his employers went bust: the last time was in 1979. In 1982, after three years of unemployment, he had managed to get back on the buses. Buying a house looked like a means of getting some security.

The Conservatives encouraged people to use credit and debt (including mortgages) to enjoy the luxuries they had previously been denied. In 1982 the government deregulated financial markets and eliminated credit controls, enabling ordinary people to take on far bigger debts than before. Similarly, banks and building societies encouraged new home owners to take on large loans. When Ron and Edna Jones applied for their mortgage, the Abbey National not only offered them the £5,000 mortgage they needed, but suggested they take out a much bigger loan. The manager knew he was taking no risks: 'He said, "Tell you what, would you like the £11,000?" And we looked at each other. "No," we said, "we'll just take the £5,000" . . . He said, "Let's look at it this way, if you take the £11,000 and you don't pay it, you can't keep your mortgage up, we take the house off you. Simple as that." He said, "Now," he said, "you get a pay rise every year so how come you're not going to be able to afford it?"' But Ron and Edna were taking no chances: 'We stuck at £5,000.'

Far from creating a home-owners' democracy, the early 1980s exacerbated social divisions. The government had no commitment to promoting full employment; it was the first since the Second World War to suggest that this was not even an ideal, let alone a priority. Unemployment rose to 10 per cent by 1982, with young people and adult men being particularly vulnerable.

Discontent at lack of investment, poor housing and rising unemployment exploded into violent confrontations between local residents and the police. In July 1981 residents in Brixton in London, Toxteth in Liverpool, and in Birmingham's Wood Green and Handsworth districts took to the streets to protest about heavy-handed policing. As Lord Scarman commented in a subsequent enquiry into the riots, 'racial disadvantage' was an important provocation. The right of police officers to 'stop and search' people they deemed suspicious – a disproportionate number of whom were black – was an immediate catalyst.[6] Residents' frustration at this blatant racism was heightened by rising unemployment, which meant that more young black people spent their days hanging about on the streets and being harassed by the police for doing so. But the riots of 1981 were not 'race riots' like the disturbances of 1958, when black residents had been attacked by white racists in Nottingham and Notting Hill. In 1981 young white people joined with black protesters to vent their frustration about their lack of jobs and money. Carlton Duncan, who had emigrated from the Caribbean to Birmingham during the 1960s, was living in Handsworth in 1981. He experienced the riots as 'an uprising against deprivation and that deprivation to a very large extent was concentrated on the black community. But white working class [people also] suffered . . . you could see white youths running the streets with blacks and throwing the stones and lighting the fires in the same way.'[7] Rioting was the only form of collective power they were able to exercise. Between 1979 and 1984 trade union membership dropped from 12.6 million to 10.3 million.[8] This reduction was greatest in heavy industry, reflecting massive job losses in those industries that had traditionally been situated in northern England, Scotland and South Wales and which were heavily unionized. For the generation to which the rioters of 1981 belonged, trade unionism was beoming an irrelevance.

New divisions were appearing among the working class of the 1980s. The older distinctions between the skilled and the unskilled, between non-manual and manual workers had already been eroded by the growth of assembly-line work and office jobs in the 1960s. But now a new division emerged between those in work and those on the dole. The sociologist Ray Pahl observed this in a study of people living on the Isle of Sheppey. They included Linda and Jim, a middle-aged couple with three teenage children. Jim, a former labourer, found it impossible to get work after being made redundant, and Linda, a part-time cleaner, was the family's only breadwinner. At the other end of the island lived George, a stevedore in permanent employment, and his wife Beryl who worked part-time as a cook. The couples had similar social and educational backgrounds, yet their lifestyles were entirely different. 'The contrast between the contented, relaxed style of Beryl and George and the tense, anxious and struggling life of Linda and Jim could hardly be greater,' Pahl noted. He argued that unemployment was producing a new form of 'polarisation' within working-class neighbourhoods, citing streets he visited where '[o]ne household has multiple earners and has a surplus of income which poses the pleasant problem of how to spend it in new ways; next door may be a household with growing children under five, who cannot go out because their parents cannot afford to buy them shoes.'[9]

Margaret Thatcher used this polarization to her advantage, scoring a landslide victory in the 1983 general election. Just one year earlier her ratings in the polls had been falling, as voters expressed dissatisfaction at high unemployment and urban unrest. But her government focused on fights it could win. Ignoring the plight of the inner cities (the policy on stop and search was not amended by law until 2007), Thatcher turned instead to promoting patriotism. In 1981 the royal wedding of Prince Charles to Lady Diana Spencer helped; a year later Britain went to war with Argentina over a dispute about the sovereignty of the Falkland Islands, situated about 200 miles off the Argentine coast. The conflict resulted in an important victory, and a surge of nationalistic fervour. The government proved adept at suggesting that the unemployed, the rioters and the poor were marginal groups, whose discontents were of little significance to Britain's national and international interests.

In the wake of her landslide election victory in 1983, Margaret Thatcher's government turned its sights on a far more important enemy than the Argentinians: the organized working class. The Employment Act of 1982 robbed trade unions of much of their political power. Employers no longer had to recognize a trade union unless a majority of their employees voted to join one. While this appeared superficially democratic, many in the union movement asked why workers could not opt out, rather than having to opt in to union membership. Industrial action was now unlawful unless it was preceded by a secret ballot and agreed to by a clear majority.

This denied workers the right to decide quickly when to use this powerful weapon. The 'closed shop', in which all workers in a firm had to join a particular union, was banned. The government presented these as democratic reforms, but the measures diluted the power of those workers who did choose to join trade unions.

In 1984 the government's determination to destroy the labour movement was made starkly clear. In February Ian MacGregor, head of the National Coal Board (NCB), announced plans to close twenty pits with the loss of 20,000 jobs – often in areas that offered little alternative employment. On 12 March 1984 Arthur Scargill, President of the National Union of Mineworkers (NUM) called a national strike against the closures.

When explaining her 'reforms', Margaret Thatcher was fond of invoking the so-called 'TINA' phrase: 'There is no alternative'. But in the case of the miners, there was an alternative. It did not make economic sense to close the mines. The Oxford economist Andrew Glyn convincingly argued that even if the pits were as uneconomic as the NCB suggested (and in fact many still had sufficient resources to merit mining for decades to come), the resulting unemployment would oblige the NCB and the taxpayer funding larger retirement pensions, thousands of redundancy payments and millions of pounds in unemployment benefit. It was cheaper to keep the miners in work.[10]

The decision to close mines was politically motivated, and had a long history. The miners had come close to defeating the government in 1926 and, more recently and more pertinently, they had forced the Conservatives from power just a decade earlier. By the time 1984 arrived, Conservative MP Nicholas Ridley had already drawn up plans to defeat the miners, who he likened to 'Communist disrupters'. The investigative journalist Seamus Milne revealed that the highest echelons of government and the police had authorized the many violent confrontations between miners and police officers, often provoked when police 'invaded' a village on horseback as 5,000 of them did in Orgreave, Yorkshire, on 18 June 1984. Thatcher's government 'showed themselves prepared to encourage any and every method available – from the secret financing of strikebreakers to mass electronic surveillance, from the manipulation of agents provocateurs to attempts to "fit up" miners' officials – in order to undermine or discredit the union and its leaders'.[11]

In the face of this concerted attack it is surprising that the miners struck at all, as 80 per cent of them did.[12] The government and the conservative press represented Arthur Scargill, the NUM's leader, as the 'enemy within' – a dictator to whom the miners were in thrall. But in fact the impetus to strike had come from below. In Yorkshire many miners – angry at the NCB's failure to consult workers on their proposals – had walked out of work before Scargill called the strike. In the months that followed, police violence, press propaganda, and – by December 1984 – the prospect of a long winter without fuel or Christmas presents for the children were powerful incentives for the miners to return to work. Some did, but most stayed out, and they did so because of desperation: they and their communities needed work.

That the strike lasted so long was a testament to the support the miners received from within and outside their communities. Their ardent supporters included many miners' wives, most of whom had not previously been involved in political activism. Before the strike, Margaret Donovan, a young miner's wife in the Rhondda, had a life that 'centred around playgroups, school, [I] certainly didn't go out at all'. She was lonely, having moved to a village where she knew no one except her husband's family. Tied to the house by young children, 'I didn't really get to know anybody.' When the strike began, she started to talk to her neighbours, and then, as the weeks wore on, to become involved in organizing food parcels and a soup kitchen. By the summer of 1984 she knew 'a terrific amount [of people], and we are all good friends'.[13] As in the rent strikes of the 1970s, so the women's role in the 1984 miners' strike often reflected their concerns as wives and mothers: they offered emotional support to their striking husbands, organized soup kitchens and food parcels and Christmas presents for children. But their campaigns sparked a belief that opportunities for their children, sufficient food on the table and decent wages were not luxuries but necessities, the absence of which was not due to a woman's poor housekeeping ability but to the policies of government and employers. From their initial need to look after their children and husbands sprang a desire to intervene in larger political debates.

Meanwhile, strong support came from outside the coalfields. '[I]f you listen to press, and watch TV they say everyone's against us,' said Bob Jackson, a miner at the Armthorpe colliery when he was interviewed in December 1984, 'but there's a hell of a lot of people doing a lot for us.' Local Labour Party branches, Co-operative Societies and community groups organized regular collections of food and clothes for mining communities and holidays for the miners' children. But support also came from more surprising sources. Bob Jackson and his wife were among the hundreds of Labour-supporting mining families who had enthusiastically taken advantage of the right to buy their council house. By 1984 they had a large mortgage, which might have been assumed to be an impediment to striking. But they were astounded at the sympathy they received from their building society. 'I've got to admit they've surprised me,' said Bob. 'I thought they'd be treading on us toes . . . I think I owe them about one and a half grand. They send me a letter every three months just saying, I see there's no change, we'll get in touch again in three months.'[14] At Christmas 1984 donations flooded in from pensioners on inner-city council estates, owner-occupiers in southern suburbs, and retired residents of the Home Counties with addresses like 'the Manor House' and 'the Vicarage'.[15] 'I am sorry my £1.00 is so meagre,' wrote Mary Addey, a pensioner living on London's Wyndham estate. 'My heartfelt hope is that 1985 will be settled according to justice for your cause.'[16] Bill Burke of Portsmouth admitted that he had initially been ambivalent to the miners' cause, but 'the conviction of Mr Arthur Scargill on two charges of obstruction at Orgreave coke depot horrified me. My viewing of the BBC news clearly showed Chief Superintendent Nesbit throwing his weight in a most challenging and unsavoury manner. That type of policing is not condoned by me.' He enclosed £15.00.[17] While Thatcher's emphasis on individual freedom was popular, her encroachment on people's collective entitlements – to a job and to organize in a trade union – was not.

The sentiment of Bill Burke and thousands more like him proved that many people, regardless of social background, rejected the Conservative philosophy that there was 'no alternative' to mass unemployment and welfare cuts. In 1984 the miners had a real chance of winning; Thatcher herself appeared to waver that summer. But the government proved able to mobilize police and much of the press in support of its fight, with little or no opposition from Labour. On 3 March 1985 the NUM capitulated. The miners returned to work. The trade union movement had suffered a huge blow to its political power. But the miners' message – that their living standards, families, villages and towns relied on having work – cut through the Conservative propaganda that presented Britain as divided between affluent workers on the one hand, and unemployed idlers on the other. The miners showed that the real division in 1980s Britain was between the minority of the very rich who could afford private housing, healthcare and education, and the majority who relied on work to get by, and whose security was increasingly precarious.

Life got harder for many people after 1983, and not only for those in mining communities. Thatcher's economic policies failed to deliver recovery, and her welfare reforms exacerbated distress. Between 1984 and 1998 the unemployment rate never fell below 7 per cent and for most of the 1980s more than 10 per cent of the workforce was unemployed.[18] Poverty grew, and at the same time people lost their entitlement to automatic help in times of need. The post-war welfare state had never provided an entirely robust safety net, but it was adequate enough to be missed when the government began to unpick it. In 1988 the Social Security Act reduced the level of some benefits below what the Child Poverty Action Group believed was an acceptable standard of living.[19] For the first time since the 1930s, unemployed people were obliged to show they were 'genuinely seeking work' as a condition of claiming benefit.

Underpinning this was the Conservatives' belief that welfare and full employment had made people lazy and benefit-dependent. Cutting back social security would, claimed John Major, Minister for Social Security, prevent people falling into a 'benefit culture', ignoring the fact that comprehensive welfare provision had not led to high unemployment in the 1950s or 1960s.[20] The government urged the voluntary sector to assist people. In 1989 the Conservative MP Ian Taylor praised 'the caring society that the government has created' by cutting back on state welfare.[21] But charities protested that they couldn't meet demand. Robert Morley, the director of the

Family Welfare Association, pointed out that most charities, including his own, had sufficient funds and expertise to offer 'first-aid', but not to provide the 'day-to-day living expenses' that increasing numbers of people required.[22] He was repeating a truth that had become very clear during the Second World War: that voluntary provision alone could not offer sustained help to large numbers of people.

Some of the Conservatives' voters became uneasy as the economy failed to recover. While Ray Pahl was right to highlight the division between the unemployed and those still in work, the latter were increasingly touched by the stresses and strains of insecurity and limited welfare. As the trade unions' rights were stripped away, Britain became a low-wage economy. Media and politicians' focus on the unemployed neglected the poverty of those in work. 'Whilst Malton, Pickering and Helmsley in North Yorkshire have unemployment rates approximately half the national average, they contain many people living in poverty due to low wages and the inadequacies of the social security system,' warned one Child Poverty Action Group report.[23] Alan Watkins, who had voted Conservative in 1979, faced unemployment in the early 1980s as engineering declined. He was fortunate to get a job as a works manager for Coventry City Council, charged with running a youth training scheme. But Alan was acutely aware that his own job – training young unemployed people – depended on the dole queues. 'I felt quite guilty, because my job was based on unemployment,' he said. 'The fact that people were unemployed had given me employment and you have to think about that for a while. Am I a parasite?' Alan justified this by reminding himself that he was not responsible for their unemployment and 'I was trying to get people back to work, and I did.' Still, he felt 'it's a sad thing that unemployment gives certain people jobs' simply because 'you've got a bit more experience than they have'. As unemployment rose over the decade, thousands more people were faced with Alan's dilemma. Full employment had become a thing of the past; getting into work at all required 'training' and counselling, giving rise to a whole new industry of job centres, trainers and advisers.

By the end of the 1980s, the new generation of home owners

were also feeling the pinch. Right to buy proved disastrous. The policy relied on the assumption that the former tenants would remain in work, but rising unemployment hit the out-of-town estates and the post-war new towns badly. The inhabitants of one of the newest new towns, Skelmersdale, were among them. Since the town's establishment in the late 1960s the residents had relied on Dunlop and Polythene Drums for employment.[24] In the 1970s these firms laid off hundreds of workers. In the 1980s both went bust. The town was full of houses that the residents couldn't afford, but which no one wanted to buy. By 1991 this dismal picture was replicated across the country. By then, 67 per cent of the housing stock in England and Wales was owner-occupied, and just 20 per cent was council housing. In the same year, 75,500 home owners had their homes repossessed for defaulting on their mortgage – almost 1 per cent of all mortgage-holders.[25]

Residents tried to help themselves. Betty Ennis and her neighbours survived the 1980s by helping each other as best they could. A few people moved out of Willenhall, but many more felt trapped; the homes they had bought were worthless. The estate became seen as a 'no-go' area as youth unemployment rocketed – yet this was also the time when neighbourliness became central to estate life. When most of the shops closed down in Willenhall's precinct, Betty and some of her neighbours ran 'a community shop there. People used to bring stuff in, we used to sell it. Because the shops were so, so expensive. And they were closing too. And at the same shop we had a solicitor who used to come there giving advice to the people of the area. Then we had the youth club. You know, it was a really good community.' But self-help was no real alternative to state assistance, and no substitute for a living wage.

Far from giving people independence, Thatcher's reforms robbed them of the little collective power they had had as voters, council tenants and trade unionists. The inhabitants of estates like Betty's found that the privatization of housing and the other services previously offered by their local council did not enable them to take control over their own lives as the government had suggested. Thatcher's governments encouraged local authorities to franchise services like rubbish disposal and gardening to voluntary or private organizations.

In the 1960s white weddings became popular as people had more money to spend, and early marriage became the norm. Pictured are Ann and Norman Lanchbury, just married in Coventry in the early 1960s

By the 1960s more families could afford a washing machine, though most still relied on credit to buy them

Teenagers dancing at a club on Sheffield's Park Hill estate, 1961. Sociologist Michael Carter found that parents wanted their children to 'have a better time of it' than they had had in their youth

Until the late 1960s many children continued to be educated in Victorian 'all-age' schools with poor facilities

By the end of the 1960s a growing number of children were educated in comprehensive schools like this one in Woolwich, London

In 1961 Vivian Nicholson and her husband Keith scooped the largest win on the football pools ever recorded

John Braine's novel *Room at the Top*, published in 1957, was the first of a series to feature working-class young men on the make. It was adapted into a popular film in 1959

Shelagh Delaney's play *A Taste of Honey* became a popular film in 1961, and was a powerful reminder of how little had changed for working-class people

Alan Watkins and his two children enjoying a day out in the family car in the mid-1960s

The changing face of inner-city Britain: a young man weaves his way between washing lines and the occasional car on a cobbled street in Salford, 1962

Increasing numbers of married women were employed on 'housewives' shifts' in post-war factories, like these women at EMI in Middlesex, 1965

In the 1960s some professions expanded, including nursing. This photo shows Hazel Wood and workmates on her first Boxing Day as a nurse in Coventry, *c.*1961

Women workers at Ford's Dagenham plant protest for equal pay, 1968

Grunwick protest at the TUC Congress, 1977. Jayaben Desai is on the right

Many inner-city districts, like Byker in Newcastle, were desolate places by the early 1970s

A woman protests against her husband's arrest during the miners' strike in
Easington, County Durham, August 1984

Picket lines increasingly featured black workers as well as whites, and also
non-industrial wage-earners. Catering staff occupied St Nicholas' Hospital in
Newcastle in 1986 to protest against job cuts

In the 1990s and 2000s residents tried to hold communities
together in the face of rising unemployment and public spending
cuts, like this group on Tyneside's Meadow Well estate

Viv Nicholson back home in Castleford in 2005.
Her fortune was gone but she had 'no regrets'

The removal of these services from the control of elected officials removed much of the limited power that residents had previously exercised. When Betty realized that the grass wasn't being cut in Willenhall's public spaces and the rubbish wasn't being collected 'I rang up, but it's "Oh, it doesn't belong to us, it belongs to the council, it doesn't belong to Whitefriars [Coventry's largest social housing landlord]" or "it belongs to somewhere else".' Studies of council tenants in Norwich and London also found that residents' frustration over rising rents and oblivious councillors was replaced with bewilderment over who was actually responsible for public amenities and the state of people's houses.[26]

The strain of keeping a roof over one's head and holding down a job affected family life. Married women – who were not as vulnerable to unemployment as younger workers or men in industrial work – often struggled to fulfil their roles as wives, mothers and, increasingly, as their family's chief breadwinners. In 1988 sixty-year-old Clare Stevens was living in her home town of Bristol with her husband, their twenty-three-year-old daughter Lynda, her daughter's partner Andy, and Clare's grandchild. Clare had grown up in Bristol during the 1930s; her father had been unemployed until she was ten. In the 1950s she'd got an office job and assumed the bad times had gone for ever, but in the mid-1980s they returned. Clare's husband, Lynda and Andy were all among the 12 per cent of the Bristolian workforce who were unemployed.[27] Clare's earnings kept all of them as well as her young grandchild. 'I felt all the worry was coming onto me,' and when Lynda realized she was expecting her second child, the family were plunged into despair.[28]

Eventually, and with great reluctance, Clare told her daughter she must leave: 'I evicted them.' Clare's house only had two bedrooms. Lynda and Andy had no chance of getting their own place in one of the most expensive cities in Britain. Bristol's council house waiting list was very long, partly because the council had been particularly eager in selling off its property, a policy encouraged by the large prosperous section of the local electorate who worked in banking and finance or lived off independent incomes. In this highly socially polarized city, found a report by the Child Poverty Action Group, this wealthy sector 'enjoy their second homes, live longer . . . benefit from increased house prices, profit from low wages and ensure that their children are provided with selective or private education'. They helped 'to create and conceal the poverty of their deprived neighbours'.[29] Lynda, Andy and their two children 'had to go into bed and breakfast', recalled Clare Stevens, 'and they were living in one room, it wasn't heated and there was no cot provided for the baby'. When they were finally allocated a council house it was in Knowle, miles from anyone they knew and in an area suffering badly from the effects of unemployment and under-investment in council housing. 'I was appalled, I hated leaving them there,' said Clare. She and her husband eventually 'bought them a house' nearer to the rest of the family – a difficult decision, for this meant giving up their own savings, built up gradually over many years so that they could put a bit extra towards the limited state pension.[30] It wasn't the retirement that Clare had planned for herself; no one had imagined, back in the 1960s, that they'd have to support their children and grandchildren just at the stage of life when they were looking forward to enjoying a bit of comfort.

Other women had to renegotiate spousal roles as they found themselves in work while their husbands joined the dole queues. Between 1966 and 1977 the proportion of married couples who were both in waged work rose from 43 per cent to 56 per cent, and continued to increase through the 1980s.[31] Some men adapted well to the changed situation. Betty Ennis's husband, Michael, was made redundant in the 1970s when he was in his forties 'and he never worked again'. Their roles quickly changed: 'He got to like cooking, and he'd look after the kids when they got in from school, I think he quite enjoyed that.' All the same, being out of work was hard: Michael had increasingly frequent bouts of ill-health, and died young in the 1990s.

Jean McLoughlin of Liverpool had a different experience. Her horizons had broadened since 1963, when she'd left school to work at a factory. At the age of seventeen she had 'had to get married' to her boyfriend Freddie when she found herself pregnant, but they were in love and he had prospects as a laboratory technician; they bought their own small bungalow on Liverpool's outskirts, saved hard, took foreign holidays and 'I was trying to make something of my life.' By 1979, she had rented a shop and was running a small carpet business. Her own children were doing well: the oldest, Darren, was aiming for university, and the youngest, Danielle, had won a scholarship to the Royal Ballet School. As home ownership increased in the 1980s, so did demand for Jean's affordable and attractive range of furnishings.

But women like Jean were caught in the double bind of Thatcherite ideology. On the one hand, they were meant to acquire economic independence, as Jean had done; but on the other they were also meant to look after their families. The government's emphasis on 'family values' suggested that prosperity and family welfare went hand in hand, but this was not always the case. Freddie, who had left lab work to help in the shop, still expected Jean to do all the shopping and cooking and to give the shop earnings to him. 'He had no respect for it, it was expected of you.' The journalist Beatrix Campbell discovered that many men reacted to unemployment in a similar manner to Freddie when she retraced George Orwell's steps in *Wigan Pier Revisited*.[32]

In the 1970s a minority of women had found collective support for changing their lives through feminism, but the 1980s offered only the stark alternatives of family life versus individualism. More working-class women were able to be economically independent, yet most of those seeking work did so because of their spouse's unemployment or low wages.[33] The result was often marital tension. When Jean married in 1964, 37,657 petitions for divorce were filed, 58 per cent by women (a similar proportion to the inter-war years). In 1985, 176,969 petitions were filed, 73 per cent by women.[34] In 1989 Jean joined them when she divorced Freddie. 'They put up with it years ago,' she said of her mother's generation; 'but I wasn't going to.' Jean saw herself as one of a pioneering generation whose earning potential gave them greater individual power than her mother had possessed. This power was still very limited: Jean was unable to keep her business, because it was in her married name and belonged to Freddie. However, she was able to find a new job as a saleswoman for WH Smith. But living life alone was challenging, in a society where a woman was still paid less on average than a man, and at a

331

time when single mothers were represented as scroungers. Through the 1970s, the income of households headed by women had increased, but after 1983 this situation was reversed. High unemployment was partly to blame, as these women became their family's only wage-earner, but so were changes to the benefit system that penalized single mothers and divorced women.[35] Women like Jean had to negotiate a minefield of disapproval and potential poverty to achieve anything like independence.

Those with children or grandchildren noted strains in their relationships too. Parents were no longer sure how to prepare their children for adulthood, now that the certainties with which they had grown up – full employment and a welfare state – had disappeared. 'We just thought that if you worked hard, you'd be able to do a bit better than your own parents,' said Carol Hinde, who had married a factory worker in Coventry in the 1960s. When she left school and started courting, she and her family assumed that full employment was here to stay. But by the time Carol's children, Jonathan and Karen, were in their teens times had changed. It was no longer clear that children would be able to look forward to better lives than their parents – or even to the security that their parents had enjoyed. 'If you'd told me, my parents, any of us that by the 1980s it would all have disappeared, we'd have laughed,' said Alan Watkins.

Parents hadn't prepared their children to cope with dole queues and struggling to make ends meet; they'd assumed that they didn't need to. And how did you prepare children for an uncertain future? The old ways of improving one's life, like learning a trade, were fast disappearing as manufacturing declined. 'I'd like to be a plasterer like my dad,' reported one twelve-year-old boy interviewed on a London housing estate in 1983. 'Dad says if you've got a trade you've always got something to fall back on.'[36] But that was no longer true in a decade when skilled work was declining, and skilled workers were likely to suffer unemployment.

Meanwhile, where was Labour? After a brief swing to the left in the early 1980s, Neil Kinnock had taken charge of the party in 1983. Kinnock argued that Labour had to 'adjust to a changing economy' by appealing to 'a changing electorate', including the 'docker . . . who owns his house, a new car, microwave and video, as well as a small place near Marbella'.[37] Labour, argued frontbencher Michael Meacher, needed to recruit 'the technocratic class – the semi-conductor "chip" designers, the computer operators, the industrial research scientists, the high-tech engineers – who hold the key to Britain's future . . . The growing underclass of have-nots, large and desperate though it is, can only in the end come to power through policies that assist, and are seen to assist, the not-so-poor and not-so-powerless.'[38] Unsurprisingly, given such sentiments, the national party offered lukewarm support to the NUM during the miners' strike of 1984–5.

But Labour's change of direction did not impress voters. The proportion who turned out to vote dropped markedly through the 1980s and 1990s, and those who stayed at home included many of Labour's 'traditional' working-class voters.[39] Among them was Chris Colbeck, a teenager in Yorkshire. His parents were factory workers 'but they tend to slate off Kinnock summat awful' and did not vote.[40] In 1987 Margaret Thatcher won her third successive general election. Tony Benn was one of the Labour left-wingers who believed that the party needed to revive its appeal to the working class. 'What the Labour Party has done is to accept the Tory description of class – that there are the employed affluent workers on the one hand and the unemployed no-goods on the other,' Benn argued.

> Actually, the class distinction is between the very, very rich who . . . can afford to buy their house from their dividends, can afford to pay for their children's education, can afford to pay the full cost of medical care and can afford pensions from their own resources – all without working. But the docker from Bermondsey to whom Kinnock referred . . . would be lost completely if he lost his job. So we represent people who depend for their living upon what they earn, and that is a distinction which puts the rich in a minority and labour in a majority.[41]

Even some of those sympathetic to Kinnock's reforms believed that a more progressive programme was necessary to win over voters. Bryan Gould, who was closely involved in designing Labour's general election campaigns in 1987 and 1992, suggested that Labour needed 'a progressive tax policy [imposing] greater increases on a smaller number of people at the top end of the scale. These were, after all, the only people who had enjoyed tax gains under the Tories and there would have been little public sympathy for them if they had been required to pay some of it back.'[42]

The experience of ordinary workers suggested that these dissenting voices had a point. Most of Margaret Thatcher's votes had always been drawn from the wealthiest echelons of society: the richest businessmen and financiers, and also from the affluent, suburban, southern middle class. By the 1989 general election, Conservative support had become increasingly concentrated in England's most prosperous areas: the south-east, and rural pockets elsewhere. There were no Conservative MPs in Scotland after 1987. A small, wealthy minority had benefited from tax cuts and deregulation of financial markets. Meanwhile, the middle-class electorate worried that a Labour government might increase their taxes at a time when they were concerned about large mortgages and job security; hence the call by Labour politicians as diverse as Benn and Gould for the party to focus on the division between the very wealthy and the rest of the population. Far from challenging 'vested interests' and giving ordinary people more power over their lives, the Conservative governments of the 1980s had exacerbated the division between the wealthiest and the rest.

While a wealthy few applauded cuts to public services, working-class people were increasingly ambivalent about Thatcherism. Nineteen-year-old Chris Colbeck, the son of factory workers, was studying for vocational qualifications at a college in the West Midlands. He was typical of the younger generation in believing that 'there's an upper class and a working class and a lower class'. Conservative claims that the idle poor were a social problem made an impact on Chris Colbeck. For him, the lower class were scroungers, who preferred life on the dole to working. But he was adamant that 'the snobby people . . . the country type people' were at least as big a problem – one that no political party was choosing to address.[43] Working-class Conservatives offered negative reasons for supporting Thatcher. Melanie Pilkington was in her twenties, a housewife married to a British Telecom engineer. The daughter of a factory worker who had always voted Tory, she voted Conservative 'because my father does, I suppose', and because she worried about creating further economic and political instability for no obvious reason. 'Give Maggie another couple of years, we might see a difference in the country. Elect anyone else and they'll take four years to find their feet.'[44] A study of Basildon, the Essex town where the Conservatives did very well in the 1980s and early 1990s, revealed that the only consistently popular Conservative policy was home ownership. These voters were less supportive of Thatcher's welfare cuts and very angry about high unemployment, but the researchers who interviewed them observed that 'they can see no alternative . . . there is no political party that speaks to their interests.'[45]

Labour's weak response to Thatcherism only strengthened the Prime Minister's case that there was no alternative to the free market.[46] 'Labour drove Britain bankrupt' was the Conservatives' stark message by 1987. 'You have to give people incentives' was their blunt justification for privatization.[47] 'There is no such thing as society,' Thatcher famously told *Woman's Own* magazine after the 1987 general election. 'It is your neighbour who is supplying [welfare benefits] and if you can earn your own living then you have a duty to do it.'[48] At a time when relatively few people felt financially secure, the Prime Minister's rhetoric stoked fears that raising welfare benefits or giving greater powers to the trade unions would simply take away what little security voters had. Deborah Temple, a shop worker living in Surrey, explained that she voted Conservative because 'I just couldn't understand why two pensioners should be in a three bedroom house – why didn't they just kick them out and put them in a home . . . I've been given nothing as far as housing is concerned. We've done it all ourselves, worked hard for it – paid through the nose really.'[49]

Nevertheless, the unease that people felt about the increase in poverty and in inequality was strong – and ultimately caused Thatcher's downfall. In 1990, 51 per cent of adults thought that the government should redistribute wealth from the rich to the poor; 58 per cent believed that the government should spend more on welfare benefits.[50] In November of that year, just three years after her landslide victory in the general election, Margaret Thatcher was forced to resign in the face of virulent public opposition to her Community Charge, popularly known as the poll tax. This replaced local authority rates – calculated according to the value of a rate-payer's house – with a tax levied on every adult resident, a move that penalized those on lower incomes. Faced with mass demonstrations, rioting in central London, and opinion polls showing that just 12 per cent of voters supported the poll tax, Margaret Thatcher faced a leadership challenge, which led to her resigning from office.

Yet the future remained uncertain and insecure for most people. During the 1980s, being working class had come to mean being poor, or living in fear of poverty. In the 1970s being working class had still meant working hard for a modest reward, but by the end of the 1980s there was no such guarantee. People were less likely to view working-class life as having anything positive to offer in the form of collective support; fewer people had experience of the trade unions or Labour politics. Between 1985 and 1988 a team of researchers led by the social scientist Paul Thompson interviewed members of one hundred families across Britain about how their lives had changed over the twentieth century. They asked each person whether they believed that people belonged to different social classes, and why. Eighteen-year-old Louise Beckwith lived with her parents in Bedlington, a former mining village in Northumberland. She had left school at sixteen, but had only been able to get a temporary, part-time job as a shop assistant. She believed that 'you can always tell people that haven't got money to the people that have got money'.[51] Louise Beckwith's sense that being working class now meant lacking something – in this case, money – was widely shared by her generation. In 1988 Simon Charlesworth, a Cambridge University postgraduate who hailed from Rotherham, returned to his Yorkshire home town – described by CPAG as suffering 'severe hardship and deprivation' – to interview people about working-class life there.[52] 'I'm from a council estate,' was how one man described himself. 'We've got no money, we've got no jobs . . . we've got nowt.' Between 1980 and 1986, 189,000 factory workers had lost their jobs in Yorkshire. Almost half the unemployed men in this region had been out of work for more than a year.[53] Charlesworth spoke to one man who had just lost his job and despaired of ever finding another. 'Thi' [they] walk all ovver everybody nahr [now]. Thi's nowt we can do at all. I mean, if yer working class tha's gorra w'k [work], thi's no other way. We've just gotta w'k, it's ohnny [only] wy [way] we can get a livin'.' When work was taken away, so was that identity. What was left, discovered Charlesworth, was an identity that centred on place rather than on working life or political action: 'Ah'm a Rotherham person,' was how one man put it.[54]

'Thatcher's children' – those who grew up in the 1980s – were conscious that to get on in life they should leave their class background behind. They were also aware that they could not, or should not, rely on politicians or employers to help them do so. In the late 1980s concern about high youth unemployment spurred dozens of social scientists to interview young working-class people about their hopes and expectations for the future. They revealed widespread acceptance that 'qualifications help you to get a good job' – no more walking out of a post on a Friday and into a new one on a Monday as their fathers might have done – and the expectation that they would be unemployed at some point. But more than anything, they wanted – in the words of Shreya, one of the girls interviewed in a survey of Asian and white Glaswegian schoolgirls – to 'make something of myself'. This urgent and individualistic desire, like her classmate Anna's ambition to 'make good money', were typical of their generation.[55] In the early 1960s the car workers of Luton had told sociologists that they wanted enough money to live comfortably and more time with their families and friends. Their children and grandchildren had to worry more about getting work in the first place, but they were also conscious of living in a society where being ordinary was not enough to guarantee security. 'I want to do well, get a good job,' said Chris Colbeck of the 100 Families survey, by which he meant 'well paid'.[56] 'I think the main point is making a name for myself,' explained Lisa, a white English woman in her twenties, when she was asked why establishing her own small business was so important to her. She wanted 'big cars and . . . bigger houses' so that people would 'take a note of you'.[57] But for most of her generation, such 'success' was not an option.

16

A Classless Society

FROM THE 1990s, politicians of both the left and the right heralded the emergence of a 'classless society' – or an exclusively middle-class one. Many academics and journalists agreed that class simply didn't matter any more. And yet in the early twenty-first century polls suggested that more than half of British people still considered themselves working class.[1]

Britain was an increasingly unequal society. In 1979 the Gini index, which measures income inequality, stood at 29 in Britain. By 2010 it had risen to 36. Partly this is because the poorest 10 per cent of people got poorer. But it is also because a tiny elite concentrated greater amounts of wealth in their own hands. During the 1990s and 2000s, the richest 10 per cent – a group of business leaders, corporate professionals, financiers, press barons and aristocrats – enjoyed far bigger rises in their income than any other group. In 1998 they possessed more than a quarter of Britain's income. By 2008 they owned one-third of it. Meanwhile, the least wealthy half of society – millions of pensioners, manual workers, call centre and care home staff, nurses, teaching assistants, cleaners and office workers, as well as those who couldn't find work or were sick – lived on less than one-quarter of the national income.[2]

Rising inequality made people unhealthy and unhappy. In their meticulously researched *The Spirit Level: Why Greater Equality Makes Societies Stronger*, Richard Wilkinson and Kate Pickett reveal that as economic inequality increased, so too did anxiety disorders and depression. These rose most among the poorest, but thousands of other people, including professional, salaried workers and their children, were also suffering. Inequality, as Wilkinson and Pickett show, was bad for everyone outside the wealthiest 10 per cent.[3] Faced with an increasingly insecure labour market, millions of people came to question the political orthodoxy that class was dead and that the working class had disappeared.

In 1990 Conservative Prime Minister John Major declared his intention to create a 'classless society'.[4] Two years later, his victory in the 1992 general election appeared to support his claim that older class allegiances had disappeared. The Conservatives trumpeted their success in 'traditionally' working-class areas like Basildon in Essex. Over the next few years, the Labour Party, led by Tony Blair, came to embrace the idea that class was no longer of political relevance. After Labour's landslide victory in the 1997 general election – ending eighteen years of Tory rule – Deputy Prime Minister John Prescott declared that 'we are all middle class now'. Blair's 'New Labour' project was based on the assumption that class had disappeared with the decline of the old, staple industries on which the manual working class had relied, like steel and coal mining. The new Prime Minister also believed that the globalization of free market capitalism, assisted by Thatcher's 'necessary acts of modernisation', had brought new levels of prosperity to the majority of 'our people'.[5] As Andrew Adonis, one of Blair's closest advisers, put it, rising affluence meant that '[t]he old labels of "working-" and "middle-class" make less and less sense'.[6]

According to this political logic, those who remained outside the affluent mainstream were either feckless scroungers or helpless victims. Conservative politicians favoured the former explanation. In 1993 unemployment rose above 10 per cent. Prime Minister John Major responded by introducing a 'benefits hotline' to combat benefit fraud. Yet Home Office estimates showed that fraudulent benefit claims accounted for less than 0.8 per cent of the social security budget.[7]

When Labour took power in 1997, politicians began to talk of victims rather than scroungers. Yet ministers spoke of ameliorating poverty, rather than of eradicating inequality. The wealthy were praised for their enterprise rather than censured for their monopoly on financial power. 'I have no time for the politics of envy,' declared Tony Blair in Labour's 1997 manifesto.[8] In order to 'encourage work and reward effort', Labour committed 'not to raise the basic or top rates of income tax'. Blair's government focused on tackling the worst poverty. Labour lowered the rate of income tax paid by those people who earned the lowest wages, and focused regeneration strategies — including job training, further education, community centres and policing — on 'extremely deprived' neighbourhoods.[9] Blair's New Labour government continued the older Labour trad-ition of investing more than the Conservatives in public services like education and healthcare, in order to provide voters with a basic standard of living, and to assist people to help themselves.

But attempting to eradicate poverty without tackling economic inequality was fruitless. Tony Blair spoke of his vision for 'equality of opportunity' — another continuity with former Labour govern-ments, but one that none had managed to deliver. Blair's government was far more firmly committed to the free market than its predeces-sors, and even Labour's supporters were dubious that this stance could be combined with egalitarianism. As Labour activist Ken Coates put it, 'How can you talk about equality and assume the permanent continuation of employers and employees? What kind of freedom does an employee have?'[10]

Blair's response was that poverty could be reduced, and social equality improved, by changing the attitudes and behaviour of the poor and 'workless'. His government blamed the Conservatives' lack of welfare provision and investment in working-class neighbourhoods for 'social exclusion' and a 'culture of worklessness'. Firmly committed to a free market, New Labour rejected the notion that job creation schemes would provide a solution. Frank Field, Minister for Welfare Reform, argued that many people out of work were simply not 'employable'.[11] It was their lack of education, training and motivation that had to be addressed, not the behaviour of employers. David Blunkett — Blair's Minister for Education and Employment — argued that Labour must challenge 'anti-social behaviour on the housing estate as well as in the board room'.[12]

In practice, the government was more concerned with addressing and penalizing the behaviour of ordinary people than that of boardroom grandees. In 1998 a Social Exclusion Unit was established to tackle the cultural problems of Britain's 'underclass'. The govern-ment introduced Anti-Social Behaviour Orders, which punished troublemakers in deprived neighbourhoods by imposing curfews and prohibiting them from entering certain areas. Thousands were awarded, testifying to their popularity among working-class residents who had been terrorized by neighbours and forgotten by politicians and the police. But as Betty Ennis had said of her estate, 'people complain about the young people because it's easier than finding the people in power'.

ASBOs reinforced social divisions – not between a feckless under-class and their hard-working neighbours, but between the wealthy elite and those who lacked work, wealth or power. They may have deterred troublemakers, but they also removed young, working-class people from the urban financial centres. In 2008 journalist Anna Minton went to Manchester, where the city's flagship Labour council had awarded more ASBOs than any other local authority. She discovered that while most ASBOs were given to people accused of behaving anti-socially in their neighbourhoods, the most commonly shared characteristic of Manchester's ASBOs was a ban on holders entering the city centre – the most privatized central area of any British conurbation, studded with smart department stores and cafés.[13]

Addressing the needs and concerns of business owners and affluent consumers meant excluding young working-class people from the centre of their city. This did nothing to tackle the lack of opportun-ities for these young people. While working-class communities were encouraged to embrace social 'inclusion', financial inclusion was not a priority. Manchester's largest employers, like those in most other twenty-first-century cities, were fast-food chains, bars and customer service, which employed casual and part-time staff on the minimum wage. These workers could rarely afford to enjoy the services they provided, or to live in the city centre they served.[14]

The government's focus on the 'underclass' suggested that the real social division in Britain was between hard-working consumers and the feckless unemployed. This was a myth. A study that followed hundreds of British families during the 1990s revealed that many people found themselves in poverty at various points in their lives, often as a result of unemployment though sometimes due to low wages. In 1997, 4.5 million people of working age lived in households where no one worked. One in six Britons relied on state benefits to survive, a higher proportion than in any other western European country, and three times that of Germany. Most families who relied on manual work or low-paid office jobs lived in poverty at certain times, being particularly vulnerable to hardship when children were young or if a parent was sick, unemployed or elderly. '[M]any more people are "touched" by poverty and receive short-term help from the benefit system than might at first glance appear,' wrote the social scientist Stephen Jenkins, refuting the political claim that a 'culture of worklessness' and benefit dependency could explain poverty.[15]

At the beginning of the twenty-first century Britain remained a society divided by class: between the wealthy minority who held political and economic power, and the majority who had to earn a decent wage in order to make ends meet. Many of the latter found it harder to keep themselves than their parents had, and the reason was not their own fecklessness, but the increasing insecurity of work. By 1990, Bill Rainford had worked on the production line at Ogden's tobacco factory in Liverpool for twenty years. He'd stayed because the wages were all right and there were other benefits: a staff canteen, a club and a good pension. But by 1990 Bill 'was in a bit of a fuss'. With over 20 per cent of Liverpool's workforce unemployed, and facing stiff international competition, Ogden's reduced wages, and took advantage of anti-union legislation to erode workers' holiday entitlement and to introduce shift work. At the age of forty Bill had to work nights. His managers were able to hold the threat of redundancy over employees who didn't meet demanding new productivity targets. Bill 'was just dreading, dreading going into work'.

Bill tried hard to adapt to the changing situation. Eventually a job as a security guard at Ogden's came up, and he applied and got it: 'it would still be shifts, but I thought I would be in a better frame of mind.' Within months, however, Ogden's was bought by the Hanson Trust, a building company with a reputation for negotiating tough takeovers that made huge profits for them and led to many workers losing their jobs. Such takeovers were routine in British industry by the early 1990s, but times of great anxiety and upheaval for the workers concerned. Within a year 'they told us that the security officers' wages bill was too high, so they laid us all off then brought us back on contract.' Bill recalled that 'we had to do more jobs for less money . . . Apart from being security men we became toilet cleaners as well' – something he found so demeaning at first that he couldn't bring himself to tell his wife Barbara.[16] He consoled himself by looking forward to retirement.

But shift work, insecurity and a lack of control produce stress and ill-health. In 2002 Bill was diagnosed with diabetes and his doctor insisted that he take early retirement. Diabetes, like obesity and heart disease, is increasingly common in wealthy societies – but these conditions tend to affect those outside the wealthiest 10 per cent. These chronic health problems are caused, or exacerbated, by low income and by stress. As Wilkinson and Pickett explain: 'When we experience some kind of acute stress . . . our bodies go into the fight-or-flight response . . . when we go on worrying for weeks or months and stress becomes chronic, then . . . energy in the form of glucose in the bloodstream can lead us to put on weight in the wrong places . . . and even to diabetes.'[17] Shift workers are particularly vulnerable, possibly because irregular sleeping patterns exhaust the body, weaken the immune system, and disrupt a person's family life.[18] Bill retired early, and on a much lower pension than he had expected: Ogden's hadn't mentioned that when they outsourced the security work, Bill's pension rights would disappear.

The country in which Bill Rainford lived was not the resolutely middle-class Britain of political rhetoric. Many people of his generation rejected the notion that their country had become classless. John McGuirk, the labourer's son from Bootle who had made his living in a motorway construction gang, retired in the late 1990s. By the 2000s his wife had died, he lived alone in a condemned council house and enjoyed 'doing the Lottery. I always get my numbers, and I sit here and I dream for hours about what I'd do with the money.' It provided a distraction from 'worrying about the heating bills' which were becoming an increasing burden as fuel costs rose. He relied heavily on his daughter for food and clothing. He was working class, he said, 'because I've less than others', by whom he meant not non-manual workers or home owners, but 'the rich'.

John McGuirk's sense that class sprang from inequality was shared by others in more comfortable circumstances. In retirement, Sathnam Gill hoped to return to his native Punjab, having saved enough money to build a house there. Yet, with his experience of Labour politics and trade unionism, he identified himself as working class: 'I work, I can never be upper class.' Society was divided between 'the five percent of the people who run the country and the ninety-five percent like us'. Carol Hinde agreed. She was a grandmother by 2000; her mother, Christine Elliott, was a widow. Both had worked throughout their adult lives. 'I'm working class,' said Carol Hinde. 'You go to work. And you need to go to work to live. That's what working class means to me.' Alan Watkins, the engineer from Coventry who found himself running a youth training scheme by the 1980s, also said that 'I class myself as working class' because he'd had to work for a living.

Alan Watkins was one of many people who had had to adapt to changing circumstances in ways they hadn't expected. Planning ahead, which had been dinned into the generations who had grown up after the Second World War, did not always lead to the promised results. Hazel Wood was also looking forward to retirement by the 1990s. She and her husband John had both been in paid work since their teens. But in 1999, at the age of fifty-eight, John was diagnosed with non-Hodgkin's lymphoma and told he had only months to live. He took early retirement and Hazel, who'd assumed that she'd continue working into her sixties, did likewise so that she could look after him. John died in 2003 aged sixty-two.

Women's experience of budgeting and their strong family and friendship ties meant that they often found it easier to adapt to the twenty-first-century reality of long retirements than men.[19] Hazel had a close circle of female friends, and relished the fact that their adequate pensions meant they could plan to meet up and see the world together in retirement, after long years of working and bringing up children. All the same, 'losing John was a terrible thing to me because we did so much together . . . it's the fact you work all your life and you're both working full-time and fitting things in and now you've got time to do these things, he's not there . . . It's not fair.' Manual workers' vulnerability to sickness and early death increased after 1979 for the first time in sixty years – the result of stress, unemployment and poverty.[20]

Members of Hazel's generation felt something had been lost since the post-war years. They were clear that the thirty years after 1945 were not perfect: the power of working-class people, such as it was, sprang from employers' need for workers, which in turn gave the workforce and their families unprecedented economic security and new political rights. Job security offered people the ability to plan for the future; so too did the welfare state. Billy and Barbara Rainford explained it this way:

> BARBARA: But they always seemed to be happy times [in their young adult life].
> BILL: Yeah, but don't be putting your rose-tinted spectacles on.
> BARBARA: No no, what I mean to say is people didn't have any money
> – [pauses]
> BILL: The infrastructure of the country seemed to be in place didn't it? . . . I worry more about my grandchildren than worry about [my children].
> BARBARA: Yeah, I was just going to say that, it's just that you're wondering what kind of life they're going to grow into.[21]

For Bill and Barbara Rainford, the dismantling of the welfare state and the disappearance of jobs for life meant that they had no confidence that their grandchildren would enjoy any security in adulthood. They were not alone. In 2011 a survey of thousands of British people conducted by the organization BritainThinks found that the prevailing fear among older working-class people is that 'our children and grandchildren won't be able to afford to get married and have children.'[22] Far from wanting to live on the state, the prevailing fear among this group and their children is that future generations will be denied the independence they prize.

To understand the experiences of these younger generations, I spoke to some of my former classmates about their lives since leaving the large, socially mixed comprehensive school we attended in Newcastle-upon-Tyne.[23] In the early 1990s about 15 per cent of our cohort of 300 students went to university, slightly less than the national average, at a time when a quarter of eighteen-year-olds were entering higher education.[24] My small sample of twenty classmates – all I could trace – reflected this. Two – John and Shelley – had entered higher education at eighteen, but the rest had left school or college to get a job. When I got in touch with them in 2013, we were all in our late thirties. All my former classmates except Shelley were living in north-east England.

Most of my classmates are the children of manual workers, and several watched their fathers struggle with long-term unemployment, or their mothers work in multiple jobs to make ends meet. The importance of hard work to get by was a common theme of their 1980s childhoods. 'My parents worked all hours in order to save up and buy a house,' recalled John, who grew up in a council flat. His parents were office workers. 'I was practically brought up by my grandparents.'[25] Shelley remembered her mother 'doing anything and everything she could to make ends meet and keep two young children', including cleaning and bar work.[26] Jack's mother was a lone parent; she 'had cleaning jobs, sometimes two part-time jobs at a time. She was a very hard worker but didn't earn very much money and would sometimes struggle.'[27] Their emphasis on the necessity of very hard work to make ends meet is reminiscent of the way that children like Christine Elliott described growing up in the 1920s and 1930s. Their stories are a reminder that the 1980s were hard times for many people, and that the memory of those years endures.

Superficially my classmates epitomized Britain's transformation into a middle-class, if not a classless, society. All were in salaried, non-manual positions with impressive titles: they were consultants, administrators and sales executives. Thirty years earlier, 55 per cent of workers had been employed in manual jobs; by the millennium, more than 70 per cent of workers were employed in non-manual work, commonly in sales positions in cafés and call centres, or as data inputters in offices.[28] They dressed in smart suits, sported sharp haircuts and most owned at least one car. None was a senior professional (defined by the Census as doctors, academics, politicians, financiers and barristers), but none was unemployed either. Half of them had grown up in council or privately rented houses or flats, but only one of them now lived in rented accommodation. As Jacqui, a former industrial consultant now studying electronics at university, said of herself and her partner Doug – 'a very hardworking engineer' – 'we look very affluent, because of the big house and the cars.'[29] They apparently lent support to Tony Blair's view that the 'knowledge-based service economy', unfettered by state regulation, 'offers millions of our people the chance to find new jobs, learn new skills, pursue new careers, set up and expand new businesses – in summary, to realize their hopes for a better future.'[30]

But if Jacqui's generation is distinguished from their parents by their non-manual occupations, their lack of security distinguishes them from their grandparents. Those who climbed the career ladder had to take anxiety-inducing risks to do so. Getting a home of one's own involved huge gambles. The dull path of hard work and conformity recalled by post-war grammar school boys like Paul Baker almost appears attractive when contrasted with the uncertainties encountered by ambitious young workers in the 1990s. Shelley had graduated with a degree in fashion and had worked in the industry ever since, eventually becoming executive assistant to one of the world's leading fashion designers. 'The toughest time was being made redundant, while living in London, and needing to fight for a new job in the same company,' she said. Shelley had been in her twenties at the time, 'naïve and miles away from my family!'. She had success-fully hung on to her job, and thought it a 'good life lesson': learning to cope with insecurity was clearly necessary for many of her generation.

The gains could be huge – but the losses were also tremendous. Sandra had been less fortunate than Shelley, though not for want of hard work and determination. In the 2000s she had embraced the 'enterprise culture' lauded by Margaret Thatcher and Tony Blair, by becoming her own boss as a swimming coach. In 2010 Sandra 'voted Tory due to their promise to support small business. I was employing eleven people and felt that the "Big Society" was achievable.' But as recession hit people's pockets, demand for swimming lessons fell, just at the time when Sandra's marriage broke down and she found herself the primary carer for her young children. Her business collapsed, and her eleven employees lost their jobs. Looking back on the vote she cast in 2010 she says only one thing: 'Fool!'[31]

Avoiding risk was not an option in such an uncertain labour market. Since leaving school at eighteen, Jacqui had spent much of her working life employed on temporary contracts, doing routine administrative work. She fought hard to remain in work, having witnessed her father's experience: a former shipbuilder, he left the shipyard for a factory in the 1980s, recognizing that closure was round the corner, only to end up on the dole in the 1990s. As she watched his humiliation and anxiety build up each time he had to sign on, Jacqui 'realized my dad, my hero, was a normal everyday bloke, with worries the same as everyone else'. When he found another job it was 'on one of those bothersome nil hour contracts' – all too common by the mid-1990s. Jacqui learned from her father's experience that you had to look out for yourself: you needed to know when to stay in a job and when to jump.

By the early twenty-first century the kind of casual and temporary work on which Jacqui's father relied had become a way of life for many people. We shouldn't romanticize work in the past – many workers in the 1920s and the 1960s found their jobs boring, and before the Second World War millions of workers suffered insecurity. In the 1930s unemployment had been the primary cause of poverty. In 2000 unemployment was lower, but having a job no longer guaranteed that you could make ends meet. Low wages had become a major cause of poverty. Despite Labour's introduction of a minimum wage in 1998 an increasing number of workers did not earn enough to live on, because the fastest expansion in jobs was in part-time, temporary and casual work.[32]

In 2012 thirty-eight-year-old Jack was among those who had only ever known insecure work. He had left education at eighteen, armed with a BTEC National Diploma in Leisure Studies. He could only find part-time jobs in bars and pubs, working just a few hours each night. 'My first "proper job" was as a shelf stacker in the local Tesco,' he said. 'I worked twenty hours a week and was rewarded with a wage of £4.10 an hour. . . . Then I managed to secure employment as a stockroom manager in a shop,' but this only lasted for two years and its full-time status was a mixed blessing: Jack managed to get a mortgage on the basis of this job, but 'I didn't enjoy my time there.' He managed to get another job, and spent the rest of his twenties working as a shop assistant. In his thirties, he found work that he hopes will last – as an administrative assistant in a large office. But this job can never be entirely secure, for his employer manages mortages; their profits rely on people taking out mortgages, and on the repossession of homes that people can no longer afford. If the economic situation changes, Jack knows he may be laid off. He doesn't like it, but he never expected anything else: 'I think I always knew that I wasn't going to be rich and that I would always have relatively low paid employment, as my mother had before me, and a lot of my friends [have had] too.'

The stories told by Jack's generation share a sense of powerlessness. Employers and politicians defend zero-hour contracts and part-time work by declaring that they are necessary for Britain to compete in a global labour market. They suggest that collective bargaining, promotion structures and tenure of the kind offered by some public service posts – in town halls, or to university academics – breed unproductivity and complacency. In 2002 Tony Blair introduced a new employment structure to the public sector that stressed job flexibility and introduced payment by results. He claimed that 'successful public services have flexible employment and working practices', including 'flexible systems of pay' and 'incentives' like performance-related pay. Job tenure, fixed salaries and promotion structures were 'restrictive practices' that hampered productivity.[33]

Yet no one has ever offered substantive proof that job security and employment rights breed inefficiency. In fact, the reverse appears to be true. In 2011, 131 million working days were lost to sickness – about four and a half for every working adult. The most frequent causes were stress, depression or anxiety.[34] Over the same period of time, employers reported a huge increase in the number of workers coming to work ill, particularly with mental health conditions like depression, suggesting that the sick leave figures grossly underestimate the level of workers' stress, and pointing to employees' fear of losing their jobs through illness during the recession that had begun in 2008.[35]

Even those who 'got on' and 'made it' had a hard time if they lacked private assets to fall back on. Their gains came at the cost of unending hard work and an individualistic orientation that they often disliked. In her twenties, Jacqui set out to conquer the labour market with 'hard work, perserverance, determination and a huge smile'. She worked her way up to a 'full-time market analyst' (by the 2000s, having a 'full-time' job was a major achievement). But in her early thirties, she was asked to leave when her husband resigned to join a rival company. 'My manager thought it was dangerous for me to be in the company as I dealt with confidential information.' As the sociologist Richard Sennett observes of contemporary capitalism, 'a regime which provides human beings no deep reasons to care about one another cannot long preserve its legitimacy'.[36] Today's employers dictate that workers live by two competing and irreconcilable aims: unquestioning loyalty to their bosses, but also self-interest, in a world where employers don't look after their workers. Some employees, like Jacqui's husband, Doug, manage to play the system to their advantage, but they are a minority, and their success is usually limited. For Doug, 'success' meant moving jobs, working long hours, and jeopardizing his wife's career. Getting on in this kind of labour market often necessitates huge social losses, requiring workers to sacrifice time with their families and to relinquish the chance to build up long-term relationships in a local community by regularly moving to new jobs and new places.[37]

But politicians and employers suggest that it is ordinary people's values that are problematic. Despite the fact that the recession that began in 2008 was precipitated by bankers' over-speculation, politicians have blamed the resulting unemployment on workers themselves. They are castigated for failing to work hard enough, or to adapt to the 'global' labour market by accepting wage reductions. In 2010 George Osborne, the Conservative Chancellor of the Exchequer, condemned 'skivers' and 'shirkers' who spent their days 'sleeping off a life on benefits'.[38] In the following year, Prime Minister David Cameron pledged to mend a 'broken Britain' characterized by crime, teenage pregnancy and worklessness – the results of 'reward without effort, crime without punishment, rights without responsibilities'.[39] The media has reflected this tone. In 2007 Britain's tabloid and broadsheet newspapers used the word 'scrounger' 46 times. In 2010 it was mentioned 219 times, and 240 times in 2011.[40]

This narrative proved persuasive. By 2010 most people in Britain believed that fraudsters claimed more than a quarter of the welfare budget and that the Coalition government's benefit cuts would exclusively target the unemployed.[41] Most of my former classmates believed that 'there are those who don't deserve benefits', in Jacqui's words. 'I hate paying for the elective unemployed,' said Maria, who is head of planning for a firm of land agents.[42] In a society where people are told to depend on number one, those in hardship are blamed for their circumstances. In the BritainThinks survey of 2011, respondents believed that working-class people were 'lazy', 'greedy' and 'drug-users'. By contrast, they described middle-class people as 'hardworking' and believed they possessed 'effort' and 'talent'.[43] Yet in fact, the government estimates that less than 1 per cent of the welfare budget is currently fraudulently claimed. As for benefit cuts hitting the unemployed – elective or otherwise – more than 60 per cent of those affected by cuts between 2010 and 2013 were working people.[44]

Resentment at 'scroungers' testifies to people's frustration at the slim rewards their own hard work brings. Ron Jones, the former Liverpool bus driver, is among them. In retirement, he and his wife Edna live in the house in Huyton that they bought from the council in 1982. Ron's neighbours live on welfare benefits; Ron calls them 'scroungers'. He consoles himself that they 'haven't been able to do what we have – the holidays, owning our own home', but resents the fact they are able to 'smoke and drink' – luxuries he had to give up, or cut back, in order to afford the holidays and mortgage payments for which he worked so hard. But anger at those 'on welfare' is often provoked by people's disappointment at their own situation.[45]

If some people blame benefit claimants for their situation, then others resent migrant workers. Politicians and journalists have wrung their hands over the racism of the 'white working class'– a group who appear unable to adapt to multicultural Britain. In 2007 the BBC commissioned a series of dramas and documentaries – the 'White Season' – designed to 'shine the spotlight on the white working-class in Britain today'. As the title hinted, the focus of these programmes was on 'the rise in popularity of far-right politics', and those people on whom the season focused were described as feeling 'under siege'. The programmes were made in the wake of the 2005 local elections, when the far-right British National Party finished fifth in the London mayoral elections and won a clutch of council seats. In 2009 anti-immigration far-right political parties enjoyed great success in the European Parliament: the UK Independence Party polled more than 17 per cent of the vote and the British National Party had two MEPs elected, in the North-West and in Yorkshire and Humber. The BBC journalist Gavin Hewitt concluded that 'the white working class' felt 'ignored and sidelined' by mainstream political parties.[46]

Among my former classmates, Jack, an administrative assistant, was the only one to have joined a political party: the British National Party. He explained: 'my son was five or six years old and I had a mortgage on a three bedroom house. I'd always been in the lower end of the earnings bracket.' Struggling at times to manage, Jack began to take an interest in politics. 'The BNP was in the news at the time because their leader, Nick Griffin, had just been found not guilty of stirring up racial hatred. To me this seemed like the little guy getting picked on by the powers that be.' This was the first political party that had members 'just like me, white, working class', and that explicitly declared its intention of 'getting Britain on the side of people like me'. Jack's concerns were primarily economic; his interest in the BNP was sparked by the party's self-representation as marginalized by the British establishment. The figure of the down-trodden 'little guy' appealed to many voters in Jack's position, but strong support for the BNP's bid for power was less forthcoming. The BNP's electoral successes in 2009 were due to declining voter numbers, as support for the major parties collapsed, rather than to a huge increase in the BNP's vote. This suggests disillusion with the major parties rather than an anti-immigration stance among working-class voters.[47]

Politicians, employers and journalists were partly responsible for the far-right's success. In 1992 and 1997 Basildon's predominantly white working-class residents were asked for their views on immigration. More than half of them believed that the government 'gave too much support' to immigrants, and in 1992 more than one-third believed that immigration should be restricted. But by 1997, fewer than one-fifth thought that immigration should be limited, while over three-quarters expressed support for anti-racist legislation. This change reflected a decline in immigration as a political concern and a news story, as New Labour turned the agenda towards debating unemployment and education in the run-up to the 1997 general election (both of which Basildon's residents cited as key points of concern).[48] But from the early 2000s, politicians once more sought to put race on to the political agenda as they tried to deflect attention from their role in sustaining economic inequality by suggesting that race, not class, was the biggest social division in twenty-first-century Britain. As Owen Jones put it in *Chavs: The Demonization of the Working Class*, those in power ascribed the 'problems of the "white working class" . . . to their whiteness, rather than their class'.[49] At the same time, politicians and employers have willingly used migrant workers as cheap labour – sanctioned by the European Union and the IMF – and then blamed them for unemployment.

This isn't to excuse racism. Many black and Asian Britons and immigrants feel just as disenfranchised as Jack; we need only recall Betty Ennis's anger at the neglect of her council estate in Coventry. Many racists lived in areas where they had nothing to do with black or Asian people, and they were not directly affected by migrant workers. Deborah Temple, who voted Conservative through the 1980s, shared a dislike of 'blacks' with her Labour-supporting father, despite not ever knowing or even seeing a black person in their small Surrey town. 'I know it's wrong,' said Deborah, 'but if a black family moved in next door I'd be out . . . we've not grown up with blacks, we don't know how their lives run.'[50]

But such attitudes were neither inevitable nor universal. Many older, white working-class people, in areas where immigration had been higher than in Deborah's home town, believed that Britain's increasing racial and ethnic diversity could be a change for the better. Alan Watkins talked about having his prejudices overturned:

> I think people do tend to see people in slots, which I think is quite unfortunate really. You don't get that so much in the council, that's good. My boss is an Afro-Caribbean woman – I think twenty-five years ago, I [would have] found that quite hard to handle. I always say to her, 'You and I should not get on because you're an Afro-Caribbean black woman, I'm a fifty-plus white male' – you know, stereotypical, no way can they meet – and of course you can. I think she's a great manager.

James Carroll, a former dock worker, spoke with pride of his home town, Liverpool, as 'a melting pot'. Barbara Rainford, who had worked in Liverpool factories all her life, liked the fact her grandchildren 'play together [with black and Asian children] at school, and it makes no difference to them . . . and that's lovely, that's right'. Like all perspectives, these were selective; Liverpool's neighbourhoods, for example, were strongly segregated by race and religion for much of the twentieth century. Barbara Rainford herself talked of 'feeling like a stranger in my own city centre', a comment on how little Liverpool now offered working-class people in terms of housing, jobs and shopping. But Barbara's attitude – on the one hand, being glad her grandchildren play with a wide ethnic mix of schoolfriends, and on the other, resenting feeling like a 'stranger' – shows that race and immigration have become the only acceptable frames within which white working-class people can talk about inequality. When told by employers and politicians that jobs or homes are scarce, people worry about their children's and grandchildren's chances, against those of migrant workers whom employers are encouraged to use as cheap labour. In a country where no major political party talks of ending economic inequality, but all talk of the need to control immigration, race has become the only legitimate means by which white working-class people can claim their right to some of the goods and services they help to produce.

While the media prefers to shine a scandalized spotlight on selected aspects of 'white working-class' life, bigotry among the middle and upper classes often goes unchallenged – whether aimed at working-class white or black people. On the website Mumsnet, anonymous parents of the early twenty-first century were very open about the correlation they see between class and a good school. Justifying their decision to send their child to a comprehensive school, happy-gardening pointed out that 'we had recently moved to a small exceedingly middle-class market town and the comp was on our doorstep.'[51] In an article for the *Guardian* in 2009, Karen Glaser interviewed atheist, middle-class parents who had chosen to send their children to religious schools. Sian Martin explained that she had moved her son from his local primary to a Jewish school because 'Noah is bookish and he doesn't like football – both things that worked against him in a school where success meant getting everyone to a certain level.'[52] Back on Mumsnet, Lardass, whose children were educated privately, responded to a critic: 'let's face facts – we've all got our snobby inner cores and plenty will pay to avoid having their child speak like the average premier league footballer.'[53] Others talked of wanting to reserve a privilege for their children that may not be open to others. 'In some professions it helps to have the "right" school on your c.v.,' explained amck700.[54] Middle-class parents varied in their views of black and Asian Britons and migrants, just as much as working-class people did. One Mumsnet poster said she had sent her children to a primary school in which white children were the minority because it was more middle class than the other local schools, and 'white working class culture places no value on education', while other parents deliberately choose white schools, often in areas where the local black or Asian population is working class.[55] As the journalist Polly Toynbee notes, 'no [political] party has come up with radical ideas for breaking the class divide concerning who goes to which school' because this would mean 'challenging middle-class interests'.[56]

Yet the motivations of these white middle-class parents were remarkably similar to those of families they would rather avoid. They shared working-class people's fear that, in an era of job insecurity and a shortage of affordable housing, their children will not be able to enjoy the living standards that their parents have experienced. Neither working-class racism nor middle-class bigotry explains why, in 2010, Britain remained the most economically unequal country in the European Union. It is the perpetuation of exploitation, not individual acts of discrimination, that explains inequality. The actions of middle-class people were not responsible for the uneven distribution of wealth and power, from which they have nothing to gain. Just as in 1945, so in 2010 those who had to work for a living had far more in common with each other than they had with those who were able to live off unearned profit.

But by 2010, people were less likely to see class and inequality as a means of making sense of their circumstances. In failing to acknowledge economic inequality as a problem, neoliberal politicians and employers suggest that individuals are responsible for their own unhappiness or poverty, rather than shining a spotlight on broader economic relationships. Some people blame 'scroungers' or immigrants for their difficult circumstances, some blame their middle-class neighbours – but more blame themselves. Looking back on his life, Bill Rainford could point to particular problems with managers, and to the stress and disruption that the economic turbulence of the 1980s and 1990s had caused him, but ultimately he believed that he 'might have done better' if 'I'd not been a dreamer' at school. This idea that people are responsible for their own circumstances is one that Bill's generation imbibed with their free school milk: it was central to the post-war political rhetoric promoting 'meritocracy'. Thinking back to his 'failure' in the eleven-plus examination, Bill said, 'I'm just factory fodder.'

Generations who had grown up in the individualistic 1980s and 1990s were even more convinced that they were entirely responsible for their circumstances. My former classmate John, a junior civil servant, believed that nothing had held him back in life; he had had 'a stable family, plenty of friends and decent educational opportunities. My own fault that I didn't make the best of them!' Women of John's generation offered similarly individualistic explanations for success or failure, but saw their personality as being at least as important as hard work. Shelley was convinced that 'the biggest obstacle' to achieving her ambitions was 'my own personal confidence'. Setbacks were experienced as judgements on their personality: Jacqui felt 'betrayed' when her boss got rid of her, putting paid to her strong conviction that honest hard work, determination and that 'large smile' would lead to success. As the sociologists Bev Skeggs and Valerie Walkerdine have revealed, these attitudes aren't confined to north-east England: women from working-class backgrounds whom they interviewed in southern England similarly saw their appearance and personality as determining their lives, and any failure led to low self-esteem, anxiety and depression.[57]

Yet as my classmates prepared to turn forty, attitudes towards class and inequality did appear to be changing in Britain. The success of *The Spirit Level* provided a clue: this academic study of 'why inequality is bad for all of us', written by two social scientists, became a surprise bestseller when it was published in 2010.[58] Owen Jones's *Chavs* achieved similar success a year later. Increasing numbers of people described themselves as working class. A survey by the thinktank

British Future indicated that more than 60 per cent of Britons identified themselves as being working class.[59]

It was no coincidence that this new interest in class coincided with the first major recession for twenty years. Following the credit crunch of 2008, many workers – regardless of whether they considered themselves working or middle class – felt much less financially secure. In 2011 less than a quarter of those people who described themselves as middle class felt they possessed financial security. This group were retired and they had a corporate or professional career behind them; they were among the 7 per cent of the population wealthy enough to have paid for their children to have a private education.[60] The majority felt far less confident about their circumstances. Regardless of whether people defined themselves as working class or middle class, many recognized that the crucial division in society remained between the richest and most powerful 1 per cent, and the rest of the population who had to earn money to make ends meet.

Those people who considered themselves working class did so, primarily, for the same reason given by earlier generations: they had to work for a living. By 2010, that simple fact seemed very important in a world where work might be taken away. Carol Hinde's son Jonathan was a middle manager for a small business, but Carol wasn't sure he was much better off than her daughter, Karen, a dinner lady at the local primary school. Jonathan and his wife Tash had 'a fabulous car . . . a Mitsubishi, great big black thing' and a 'beautiful' detached house. 'If I didn't know, I'd say they were middle class,' said Carol. But she knew that Jonathan and his wife both had to work long hours to fund their lifestyle, that neither of their jobs was secure, and 'they've got debts, a huge mortgage . . . a lot of debt.' On balance, she didn't think her son's situation was very different from that of her daughter: both had to work for a living, and both would suffer if their jobs disappeared. A younger generation agreed. 'I'm working class because I've had to work hard for everything I've got,' said Jacqui. As thirty-eight-year-old John put it, 'we all have to work for a living, so I'd say I'm still working class. Always will be I suppose.'

People from a wide range of occupations and backgrounds shared John's view that the need to work for a living defined social class.

In 2007 the BBC website publicized the 2006 British Social Attitudes survey, which suggested that almost 60 per cent of British people called themselves working class, though only one-third were employed in manual jobs. Readers and viewers were invited to comment. 'I suppose I'm middle class – being a teacher with a university degree,' said Megan from Cheshire. 'But I go out to work every day . . . so I'm working class really.' Alan Griffiths from London wrote that 'I am working class because I have a job, working for an employer.' 'If you are paid by bosses to work, and you didn't own your business then you are working class,' wrote Lucien from Norwich.[61] Forty years after Goldthorpe's team visited Luton's car workers, these white-collar and professional employees expressed very similar views to those the sociologists had heard on the Vauxhall assembly line. Class was not determined by a person's level of income, but by their power – primarily, their economic power.

Class as a collective political identity was, however, less popular than it had been thirty years earlier. Since the 1980s a political narrative of individualism had been championed by successive governments, and collective manifestations of working-class strength (primarily the trade unions) were berated as selfish or criminal. By the early twenty-first century, sociologists found that many people preferred describing themselves as 'ordinary', seeing 'working class' as a politicized term with connotations of the 1970s. Others viewed 'working class' as a socially stigmatized term that was increasingly interchangeable with 'underclass'.[62] And by 2010 many people viewed class as a collective identity that offered them nothing in such an individualistic society. 'I hope I am of no class,' said Shelley, who had had to fight her way up the career ladder.

But however people described themselves, few, in 2010, felt that an individualistic or unequal society was a good thing. Many questioned the logic of a society that demanded harder and harder work at the expense of family life, friendship and public service. Shelley's daily life revolved around work, her two young children and her husband, and her major worries were 'being a good parent' and 'financial', concerns that coalesced into her anxiety about 'providing a future for my kids so they can have an education and a life with opportunity'. Focusing on children is a means of expressing and finding love, in a society that offers little scope for collective endeavour outside the family. Hayes and Hudson found similar sentiments existed among older people in Basildon, where 'outside the family, there is no way of linking an individual project or set of hopes and aspirations with collective fortunes and endeavours.'[63] Yet among this group, making a medical or scientific discovery that would contribute to the wider social good came top of a list of 'most satisfying personal achievement', suggesting that many people wanted to contribute to society.[64]

Many people believed that collective self-help – facilitated by the state – should be expanded to help those in need. Among the older generation, Judy Walker and Betty Ennis remained involved in housing and community campaigns into the twenty-first century. Looking back over her life, Judy Walker – now a grandmother, a mother of three, shop assistant-turned-nursery worker, one-time expat and twice married – saw her activism as central to all these roles and to who she was: 'I'm a campaigner.' Younger people were less likely to be in trade unions or political parties, reflecting the demise of the unions and the changing direction of the Labour Party. Nevertheless, my classmates overwhelmingly cited 'poverty' as a problem they'd like to eradicate across the globe. Their overriding desire to see those who need it receive state assistance is shared by a majority of British people.[65]

The concerns of people like Jacqui, Shelley and John are grounded in the very real fact that Britain is becoming a more unequal society. In order to ensure that their children and grandchildren can lead fulfilling lives without this fear, we need to create a world committed to economic and social equality. To dismiss this as utopian is to ignore the desires of successive generations, and their experiences of hardship and hard work from which their aspirations spring. In a society as rich in natural resources and as technologically advanced as ours is, they, and we, deserve more.

Epilogue

Vᴵᴠ Nɪᴄʜᴏʟsᴏɴ's sᴛᴏʀʏ, in exaggerated form, echoes the history of the working class from 1910 to 2010. This has been a story of rise and fall (though not destruction or disappearance). At Viv's birth, working-class people were politically subordinate. They still were as she entered her seventies, and she was back where she'd started, too, in a Castleford council house. But in between they'd shared a lot of experiences. These, and the memories they generate, continue to have consequences.

Viv was who she was because of luck – the happenstance of birth determined her starting point in life, and the windfall of the pools gave her notoriety. The same was true for the rest of the working class. They weren't working class because of the way they behaved, whether feckless (as politicians of the 1930s had it) or salt-of-the-earth (as social investigators claimed twenty years later), but because of the circumstances in which they found themselves, and which they hadn't chosen.

Those circumstances were always shaped by a minority of people who held economic and political power, and in whose interests it was to suppress or repress the needs and expectations of the majority of Britain's people. The middle and the upper classes were never entirely united in their aims, and there were always times when working-class people could make their voices heard and achieve at least some of their aspirations. Indeed, the years around Viv's birth were marked by fraught debate about the demise of domestic service, which had previously characterized the relationship between the working class and their employers, and justified the lack of regulation and negotiation within their working lives. But while many of the middle and upper class liked employing servants, increasing numbers came to depend on business and manufacturing for their income; they wanted cheap workers, and former servants provided a plentiful supply. Young working-class people, just a generation older than Viv Nicholson, used this situation to their advantage, deserting domestic service for an industrial or office job where, working alongside tens or hundreds of other wage-earners, they were able collectively to demand better wages and working hours.

Their power grew during the Second World War, thanks to full employment. That didn't lead to social equality, as Viv's own story of deprivation showed, but the working class did become an extremely important economic and political force, whose interests (as represented by trade union and Labour leaders) would shape the political agenda of wartime and peacetime Britain. A growing number of people called themselves working class, or saw their interests as being synonymous with those of working-class people. They included many first-generation white-collar workers, and many public sector employees like teachers, who benefited from the post-war welfare state.

After the Second World War, industrial and office workers became more numerous than servants, their lives shaped by trade unionism, council housing, free education and healthcare. In those exuberant post-war days, Viv experienced the excitement that came from expanding horizons, when she was told that perhaps her ambition of art school was attainable. But she was not alone in feeling the promises of a better life weren't kept; that if poverty was less painful, the need to earn a living wherever you could get work hadn't gone away. Education, like New Look dresses, symbolized a better life tantalizingly out of reach. Working-class people were not as community-spirited or selflessly sacrificial as some of the post-war planners and social investigators liked to suggest: as Viv herself demon-strated, continued social and economic inequality – reinforced by successive Conservative governments – fostered anger, which was as likely to be expressed in envy and avarice as in collective campaigns for better rights.

By the early 1960s, the feeling that affluence only happened to other people was abating; as Viv came into her wealth, so the rest of her generation were realizing their new ambitions – for a home of their own, a television, even a car. Still, poverty wasn't eradicated; women who found themselves without a husband, or childcare, people who were sick or on the dole faced an uncertain future. Politicians liked to present those few who climbed the social ladder as heroes who proved Britain was now a meritocracy; but millions found that their expectations hadn't been met, and many took to the picket lines to protest about it. They did so at a time when many policymakers and employers were deciding that a welfare state and full employment were luxuries that prevented profits from rising as fast as they'd have liked. Militancy in the factories and on the streets made them doubly determined to commit the country to a free market, not only in the interests of economic 'growth' (for a minority), but to destroy the political power of working-class people.

Just as Viv lost her money and her way in the 1970s, so her family and friends back home, and thousands of working people across the country, began to experience a new level of hardship. Politicians and the press blamed the people for their circumstances, which were ascribed to profligacy or to a foolhardy dependence on the state. These critics smoothly ignored that an entire generation had been told by politicians that they should take full employment for granted, embrace new credit opportunities, work hard and buy more in order to provide their children with a comfortable future. Conservative and New Labour governments admonished their voters to look after themselves, rather than relying on the state; to plan for their own and their children's futures. But planning for tomorrow proved hard by the 1990s, as people endured an increasingly insecure job market in a country where profit now clearly came before people's welfare.

Viv preferred Jack Rosenthal's play of her life, broadcast in 1977, to the 1999 musical *Spend, Spend, Spend.* Rosenthal hadn't been afraid to portray Viv as delighting in her good fortune, glamorous and outspoken, grabbing at the good life she hankered after. But by the 1990s, the only acceptable representation of working-class people in politics, the press and on the stage was as either respectable or pathetic. The musical harked back to the early press coverage of Viv and Keith, which sought to portray the pools winners as a naïve yet coarse young couple out of their depth, who secretly longed to be able to return to the humble life they used to lead, or at least to a manageable affluence, in the certainties of suburbia, their horizons limited to a semi-detached house with a car on the drive and a pension at the end of a long working life. 'It was very sad and frustrating to see my life on stage like that,' Viv explained. 'I don't think they really understood the reality of what I went through' – either before or after the win.[1]

If Viv's story reflects a wider history, fantasy explains her ongoing appeal. Viv Nicholson's story offers the radical suggestion that the world is, perhaps, not what it initially appears. In Viv's story, luck and chance explain success, not saving and hard work; the work ethic is subordinated to the pleasure of leisure, present enjoyment takes precedence over planning for the future – and all the scrimping and saving advocated by politicians and social investigators down the decades is shown to be fruitless. There are some who inherit privilege, others who win it through luck or by chance, and then there are the majority of people, who have to fight for everything they get.

Viv Nicholson articulated desires that were, and are, taboo. She refused to be a victim or a martyr, craved the good things in life and dismissed the myth that merit would bring these to her door. She reflected a widespread, deeply felt desire among working-class people for greater control over their lives. An aspiration for autonomy from politicians, employers and landlords shaped many people's actions, whether joining a picket line, buying their council house or filling in a pools coupon or a Lottery ticket. People like Viv did not simply want more money: they wanted the power to shape their circumstances into ones in which they could find fulfilment.

Still, if Viv's story is one of aspiration, it is also a story that demonstrates the limits of fantasy – particularly the fantasy that the contemporary world of short-term work, flexibility, networking and risk is built on: that anyone can reinvent themselves, and must do so at the drop of a hat (or the fall of the pound). For ultimately Viv couldn't: the money drained away and she remained a working-class woman in Castleford. Her experiences before 'the win' were just as important as the thousands she won in defining her place in the world. Viv's story shows that even the largest pools win in history could not make social mobility easy. Once she had reached the private estate of her dreams, she realized that the goal wasn't worth the effort it took her to attain it. For class implicates and confines everyone, and the middle class was, then as now, largely preoccupied with the hard work, effort and self-interest that maintaining and reproducing any degree of privilege in a class society requires.

Some people disapproved and still do. But those who have lived a life touched by some of the economic turbulence of the last four decades are still attracted to Viv's challenge to respectability and the humble life. In 2007 a *Daily Mail* interview with seventy-one-year-old Viv – still living in Castleford – attracted a huge and overwhelmingly positive response from readers to Viv's assertion that, given the chance, 'I'd do exactly the same again'. Katherine of Wakefield simply said: 'I love Viv Nicholson. I was ten when she won her money and have admired her ever since.' 'She did it her way,' was David Luff's approving comment.

Despite the political promotion of a different history of the working class – one in which people knew their place, or strived to get out of it, or at least had the decency to be clean and tidy while living in poverty – many people found in Viv's story something they liked more: ambition, extravagance and a refusal to be cowed into regret and shame for believing that life didn't have to be lived between the tramlines. 'Good luck to Viv,' emailed Katy from Inverness. 'It was a natural thing to do, to brighten your life.'[2]

'Brightening your life' a little was about all that most people could hope for at most points in the twentieth century. The people in this book tell us that we can learn from the past – but that we should not seek to replicate it. The people whose history I have tried to tell offer us stories that contradict those invoked by politicians and journalists. Far from making people idle, welfare benefits, free healthcare and education, and jobs, raised people's aspirations and gave them the security and certainty with which to pursue these. But welfare and jobs were not enough to change their lives entirely. There was always a working class in the twentieth century, because economic inequality was never eradicated. What is hopeful about the stories told here is that they suggest a persistent and shared interest in bringing about a more equal world. The unhappiness, grief, anger and shame that many of these people experienced

– whether as a servant in the early twentieth century, or an unemployed IT consultant one hundred years on – were caused by
inequality. We can learn from the past, and from the memories it
inspires.

The biggest fantasy in twentieth-century Britain, played out time
and again in the tales that we have heard here, is that ordinary people
deserve a better life. This was kept alive before the Second World
War by the labour movement, by parents' hopes for their children,
and by people's determination to have a good time against the odds.
During the Second World War and in the years that followed, the
state gave new hope that the fantasy could be realized, through full
employment and a welfare state.

Unfulfilled this promise may have been, but enough sustenance
was offered – in political rhetoric but also in welfare benefits, employment opportunities, free education and healthcare – for its radical
potential to be fostered. It was given form in parents' ambitions for
their children, and in workplace and community struggles for better
conditions. Sometimes, these struggles turned into demands that
society be reorganized around the needs of its people, and under
their control. The hundreds of people whose stories we have read
here suggest that such a transformation can still be imagined.

Over the last thirty years, the working class has declined as an
economic and political force. Yet the times may be changing. In 2011
the research organization British Future found that a majority of
Britons continued to call themselves working class. This group
included one-third of the country's highest earners. Rachael Jolley,
British Future's editorial director, suggested that being working class
had become 'the trendiest, most prestigious' identity to adopt in
modern Britain.[3]

We have seen that being working class has come to matter once
more because of the return of massive insecurity, for professionals as
well as waged workers, and for home owners as well as tenants. Class
survived for the bleakest of reasons. But Rachael Jolley's words point
to another reason why people choose to call themselves working
class. Despite politicians having demonized the contemporary
working class as feckless and scrounging, many people associate
earlier generations of workers with more laudable virtues: they 'knew

how to have a good time', were 'unpretentious' and created 'community'.[4] The stories of Barbara and Bill Rainford, Betty Ennis and
Paul Baker remind us that it was never that simple: the existence of
class always testified to pervasive inequality. But they also suggest
that some things have been lost: primarily, a vision of life based on
co-operation and camaraderie, rather than on fighting your way to
the top. In learning from their history, we can begin to imagine a
different future.

Acknowledgements

L IKE ALL THE best things in life, this book was a collaborative venture in many ways (though all errors are mine). I would like to thank colleagues at Girton College, Cambridge; the University of Warwick and at Oxford for many fruitful discussions and excellent advice. The unstinting support of the administrative and domestic staff at all of these institutions, and particularly at St Hilda's College, Oxford, made writing this book possible.

That I was able to undertake the research for this project was largely thanks to a grant from the Economic and Social Research Council (RES-061-23-0032-A). I would like to thank the staff at all the archives and libraries I consulted, particularly the archivists at the Modern Records Centre, University of Warwick, and at the Universities of Essex and Liverpool for allowing me access to several social surveys from the 1950s and 1960s, which contain the records of more than one thousand working-class families. Thanks also to staff at the Economic and Social Data Service for help with digitizing these records, and the UK Data Archive for acting as repository for the resulting databases, which any interested researcher may now consult. The Nuffield Foundation provided further small grants which enabled me to benefit from the invaluable research assistance and wisdom of Katie Ankers and Daniel Grey, good friends as well as colleagues.

The ESRC grant enabled me to employ Hilary Young as a research assistant. I owe a particular debt to Hilary. As well as assisting with the digitization of post-war social surveys, she also helped me to uncover some important working-class voices. While hundreds of working-class autobiographies and oral histories were archived by local libraries and archives in the 1970s and 1980s, the generation who grew up after 1945 were rarely represented. Public spending cuts in the 1980s and early 1990s decimated the community groups and small publishing houses that encouraged the collection of working-class people's autobiographies. Hilary Young conducted life history interviews with twenty-two people who self-identified as working class and most of whom were born in the decade after 1938 (we advertised for interviewees in the Coventry and Liverpool press, and asked for people willing to talk about 'ordinary', 'working-class' life after the Second World War). Hilary helped to create an amazingly rich set of interviews, which are now available for consultation via the UK Data Archive. I am extremely grateful to Hilary Young, to her interviewees, and to everyone else who gave up their time to speak to me about their lives and memories: Paul Baker, Howard Blake, James Carroll, Jean Eagles McLoughlin, Christine Elliott, Betty Ennis, Maria Ferguson, Frank Gogerty, Sandra Hastings, John Henderson, Carol Hinde, Edna and Ron Jones, Ann Lanchbury, Shelley Landale-Down, Elaine Leather, Dolly Lloyd, John McGuirk, John Musgrove, Barbara and Bill Rainford, Nellie Rigby, Terry Rimmer, Jacqueline Robinson, Sathnam Singh Gill, Ted Taylor, Judy Walker, Alan Watkins, Hazel Wood, and all the others who preferred to remain anonymous. I would also like to thank Vivian Nicholson and her son Howard for allowing me to place her story at the heart of my book.

Thanks are also due to all those who invited me to discuss this project with them at research seminars and public history events, and in doing so helped refine my ideas. I particularly appreciated visiting fellowships at the University of Sydney (which Chris Hilliard generously hosted) and the Institute of Historical Studies, University of Texas at Austin. In Oxford, Sheila Forbes, Principal of St Hilda's, encouraged me to write for a wider audience than academics, Julia Mannherz read the entire manuscript, and students who opted for my special subject, 'Britain from the Bomb to the Beatles', gave me much food for thought. I also greatly appreciated Lin Harwood's comments on earlier drafts, and her enthusiasm for the book.

That my manuscript became a book owes a great deal to my wonderful agent, Rachel Calder. She helped me to make my ideas readable, and to find a terrific publisher in Georgina Laycock. Both have balanced exacting and perceptive editing with generous enthusiasm. Thanks to them and to the whole team at John Murray for their hard work in producing this book.

I was fortunate to be able to rely on the support, interest and encouragement of many relatives and friends. They include Ruth and Nigel Todd, Lin Harwood, Helen and John Archer, Liz Allen, Manus and Joe Docherty, Margot Finn, Rebecca Liebman, Seria Paseta, Carolyn Steedman and Alex Shepard. The integrity and irreverence of Rob and Carol Lees and Jill Hughes remain invaluable reminders that sometimes you need to change the world, not yourself.

There are three people who are owed special thanks. Mike Savage has been a robust ally, a good friend and an excellent critic. Pat Thane was unstintingly generous with her advice, support, hospitality and critical reading. She also introduced me to Andrew Davies. The last lines of his first book, *Leisure, Gender and Poverty*, suggested that a history of working-class life that advanced beyond 1945 would be worth writing. That spark of inspiration was invaluable, but it has turned out to be the most minor of the contributions that he has made to my life. This book is dedicated to him.

Picture Credits

THE AUTHOR AND publishers would like to thank those inter-viewed in the book who have generously granted permission for their own personal photographs to be reproduced.

Notes

INTRODUCTION

1. E.P. Thompson, *The Making of the English Working Class* (Harmondsworth, 2nd edn, 1968).
2. Figures from A.H. Halsey and J. Webb (eds.), *Twentieth-Century British Social Trends* (Oxford, 2000), pp. 99 and 125.
3. These are drawn from published autobiographies and unpublished oral history and social survey interviews. Full details of where these interviews are located are given in the bibliography. Those undertaken by myself or Hilary Young (noted below) are available from the author. All interviews undertaken by Hilary Young are cited in the endnotes on the first occasion they appear in this book, but not on subsequent occasions. This is to avoid cluttering the text with notes.
4. Andrew O'Hagan, 'What Went Wrong with the Working Class? The Age of Indifference', *Guardian*, Saturday Review (10 January 2009), p. 2.
5. G. Orwell, *The Road to Wigan Pier* (London, 1937), p. 94.
6. 'The Boom Cities', *Daily Mirror* (4 January 1967), p. 5.
7. J.B. Priestley, *English Journey. Being a rambling but truthful account of what one man saw and heard and felt and thought during a journey through England during the autumn of the year 1933* (London, 1934), p. 239.
8. J. Pilger, *Hidden Agendas* (London, 1998), pp. 334–5.
9. V. Nicholson with S. Smith, *Spend, Spend, Spend* (London, 1977). The book was published to capitalize on the publicity surrounding Jack Rosenthal's play of the same name, which dramatized Viv's life. I do not provide page references to the book but I do provide full references to all the other sources cited in the interludes. Information gleaned from the autobiography has been checked against other sources of information, including press interviews with Viv and her family, and housing and education records for Castleford.

CHAPTER 1: DEFIANCE BELOW STAIRS

1. V. Woolf, *Mr Bennett and Mrs Brown* (London, 1924), p. 5.
2. 'Home Politics in 1910', *Manchester Guardian* (31 December 1910), p. 6.
3. 'Industry and Commerce', *The Times* (30 December 1910), p. 7.
4. 'Democracy and its Leaders', *The Times* (30 December 1910), p. 7.
5. There were 1,459,884 servants in 1901 in England, Scotland and Wales, and 1,335,389 in 1921. *Census of England and Wales, 1901: Occupation Tables* (London, 1903); *Census of England and Wales, 1921: Occupations* (London, 1924), table 4; *Eleventh Decennial Census of the Population of Scotland, 1901*, vol. 2 (London, 1903); *Census of Scotland, 1921*, vol. 3: *Occupations and Industries* (Edinburgh, 1924), table 2; *Census, 1951, England and Wales: Occupation Tables* (London, 1956), table 3; *Census, 1951, Scotland*, vol. 4: *Occupations and Industries* (Edinburgh, 1956), table 1.
6. Quoted in G.S. Jones, *Languages of Class* (Cambridge, 1982), p. 244.
7. S.L. Hynes, *The Edwardian Turn of Mind* (London, 1991), p. 4.
8. F. Thompson, *Lark Rise to Candleford* (Harmondsworth, 1973), p. 97.
9. H. Mitchell, *The Hard Way Up: The Autobiography of Hannah Mitchell, Suffragette and Rebel* (London, 1977), p. 33.
10. P. Dale and K. Fisher, 'Implementing the 1902 Midwives Act: Assessing Problems, Developing Services and Creating a New Role for a Variety of Female Practitioners', *Women's History Review*, vol. 18, no. 3 (2009), pp. 427–31.
11. Women's Co-operative Guild, *Working Women and Divorce. An Account of Evidence Given before the Royal Commission on Divorce* (London, 1911), p. 22.
12. 'The Singer Strike', Glasgow Digital Library, University of Strathclyde, http://gdl.cdlr.strath.ac.uk/redclyde/redclyeve01.htm (consulted 3 February 2013).
13. A. Foley, *A Bolton Childhood* (Manchester, 1973), p. 51.
14. 'Dundee Jute Strike', *Scotsman* (21 March 1912), p. 8.
15. Foley, *Bolton Childhood*, p. 57.
16. Much of this paragraph is based on C. Wrigley, 'Mann, Thomas', *Oxford Dictionary of National Biography*.
17. P. Thane, *Foundations of the Welfare State* (London, 1996), pp. 69–90.
18. M. Pember Reeves, *Round about a Pound a Week* (London, 1913), pp. 1–2.
19. Ibid., p. 2.
20. Cited in C.V. Butler, *Domestic Service. An Enquiry by the Women's Industrial Council* (London, 1916) p. 151.

21. Mitchell, *The Hard Way Up*, p. 121.

22. H.W. Fowler, *The Concise Oxford Dictionary of Current English* (Oxford, 1911), p. 1094.

23. See letters page, *Manchester Guardian* (9 March 1914), p. 3.

24. M. Beckwith, *When I Remember* (London, 1936), p. 68.

25. 'Mistress and Maid', *Scotsman* (5 September 1913), p. 7.

26. For a description of the insurance reforms see P. Thane, 'The Making of National Insurance, 1911', *Journal of Poverty and Social Justice*, vol. 19, no. 3 (2011), pp. 214–16.

27. Foley, *Bolton Childhood*, p. 75.

28. 'The Insurance Bill and Domestic Servants', *The Times* (5 June 1911), p. 7.

29. For 'kindly ties' see W. Sighel, 'The Insurance Bill and Domestic Servants', letter to the editor, *The Times* (5 June 1911), p. 7. Sighel went on to say that the Act 'may make for cases of illness'. For 'malingering' see The Writer of Your Special Articles (pseudonym), 'Mistaken Advice to Domestic Servants', letter to the editor, *The Times* (7 December 1911), p. 10. Other letters include: Harold Cox, 'The Insurance Bill', letter to the editor, *The Times* (6 July 1911), p. 6; 'Mistresses' and Servants' Campaign', *The Times* (21 November 1911) p. 14; Lady Portsmouth, Lady Dorothy Nevill et al., 'A Petition of Protest', letter to the editor, *The Times* (21 November 1911), p. 14.

30. J.D. Casswell, *The Law of Domestic Servants: With a Chapter on the National Insurance Act, 1911* (London, 1913), p. 14.

31. Thane, 'National Insurance', pp. 215–16.

32. G. Bernard Shaw, 'National Insurance and Political Tactics', *The Times* (24 October 1911), p. 9.

33. Interview with Mrs M (Margaret is a pseudonym), TS 137, WEA domestic service interview collection, Oxfordshire History Centre (hereafter OHC).

34. Butler, *Domestic Service*, p. 11.

35. Quoted in L. Delap, *Knowing their Place: Domestic Service in Twentieth-century Britain* (Oxford, 2011), p. 49.

36. See, for example, interview with Mrs U3, Stirling women's oral history archive, Scottish Oral History Archive, University of Strathclyde. See also ibid.

37. Interview with Mrs Lockwood, transcript no. 129, Family Life and Work Experience collection (FLWE), ESRC Qualidata Archive, University of Essex.

38. Interview with Mrs Bairnson, transcript no. 156, FLWE.

39. Interview with Mrs Myers, transcript no. 315, FLWE.

40. Margaret Morris, OHC.

41. S. Marshall, *Fenland Chronicle: Recollections of William Henry and Kate Mary Edwards Collected and Edited by her Daughter* (Cambridge, 1967), p. 266.

42. Quoted in Delap, *Knowing Their Place*, p. 28.

43. Interview with Mrs A (Bessie Allan is a pseudonym), TS 137, WEA domestic service interview collection, OHC.

44. Interview with Lily Blenkin, transcript no. 226, FLWE.

45. Ibid.

46. Interview with Walter Blackman, transcript no. 96.

47. Mrs Bairnson, 156, FLWE.

48. Marshall, *Fenland Chronicle*, p. 266.

49. D. Gittins, *Fair Sex* (London, 1982), p. 73.

50. Margaret Morris, OHC.

51. Foley, *Bolton Childhood*, p. 61.

CHAPTER 2: BOBBED-HAIRED BELLIGERENTS

1. R. Roberts, *The Classic Slum* (Hardmondsworth, 1974), p. 222. I have documented the experiences of shop assistants, factory hands and clerks in S. Todd, *Young Women, Work, and Family in England, 1918–1950* (Oxford, 2005), ch. 1.

2. War Cabinet Committee on Women in Industry, *Report* (London, 1919), pp. 241, 99–100.

3. *Census of England and Wales, 1901: Occupation Tables* (London, 1903); *Eleventh Decennial Census of the Population of Scotland, 1901*, vol. 2 (London, 1903); *Census of Scotland, 1911*, vol. 2 (London, 1913), table 2.

4. Membership figures taken from S. Lewenhak, 'Trade Union Membership among Women and Girls in the United Kingdom, 1920–1965', Ph.D. thesis (London, 1972), pp. 32, 45. Density data taken from G.S. Bain and R. Price, *Profiles of Union Growth: A Comparative Statistical Portrait of Eight Countries* (Oxford, 1980), p. 37.

5. Interview with Nellie Andrews (pseudonym), RO11, oral history collection, Bristol Reference Library. Thanks to Josie McLellan for bringing this archive to my attention.

6. 'Industrial Depression and Domestic Service', *Yorkshire Post* (15 September 1920), p. 3; I. Gazeley, 'Manual Work and Pay', in N. Crafts, I. Gazeley and A. Newell (eds.), *Work and Pay in Twentieth Century*

Britain (Oxford, 2007), pp. 66–8; Labour Party, *What's Wrong with Domestic Service?* (London, 1930); D. Caradog Jones, *Social Survey of Merseyside*, vol. 2 (Liverpool, 1934), p. 311, and H.L. Smith, *New Survey of London Life and Labour*, vol. 2 (London, 1934), p. 468.

7. On changes in working hours see Gazeley, 'Manual Work and Pay', pp. 61–2.

8. Quoted in S. Mullins and G. Griffiths, *Cap and Apron: An Oral History of Domestic Service in the Shires, 1880–1950* (Leicester, *c.*1986), p. 15.

9. Lewenhak, 'Trade Union Membership among Women and Girls', p. 45, and Bain and Price, *Profiles of Union Growth*, p. 37.

10. J. Burnett, *A Social History of Housing, 1815–1985* (London, *c.*1986), p. 221.

11. Interview with Percy Wiblin, OT 609, Abingdon Oral History Project, OHC.

12. 'The Luton Riots', *Manchester Guardian* (21 October 1919), p. 8.

13. 'MA Accused in Luton Riots', *Daily Mirror* (1 August 1919), p. 15.

14. J. Smyth, 'Resisting Labour: Unionists, Liberals, and Moderates in Glasgow between the Wars', *Historical Journal*, vol. 46, no. 2 (2003), p. 377.

15. W. Foley, *Child in the Forest* (London, 1974), pp. 18–19.

16. Quoted in Burnett, *Social History of Housing*, p. 222.

17. Ibid., p. 233.

18. 'Domestic Servants and Unemployed Benefit', *The Times* (3 March 1921), p. 11.

19. 'More Servants Soon?', *Daily Express* (9 March 1921), p. 1.

20. No gendered breakdown of unemployment is available for this early period. See B.R. Mitchell, *British Historical Statistics* (Cambridge, 1988), p. 124, table 8.

21. G. Routh, *Occupations and Pay in Great Britain, 1906–1979* (London, 1980), p. 122.

22. 'Unemployed Ex Soldiers', *Manchester Guardian* (2 October 1920), p. 9.

23. 'Pin Money Women. None Employed by the Manchester Corporation', *Manchester Guardian* (27 October 1920), p. 7.

24. 'Slump in Trade', *Observer*, 26 September 1920, p. 16.

25. A. Bingham, *Gender, Modernity and the Popular Press in Interwar Britain* (Oxford, 2004), pp. 68–9.

26. R. Lowe, 'Askwith, George Ranken', *Oxford Dictionary of National Biography*.

27. Ministry of Reconstruction, *Domestic Service* (London, 1917), pp. 2 and 14.

28. 'No Servants', *Daily Mirror* (5 May 1923), p. 5.
29. Interview with Mrs E. Cleary, tape no. 28, Manchester Studies collection, Tameside Local Studies Library (TLSL).
30. Ibid. See also interview with Joan Whitfield, AMS 6416/1/6/13, Lewes in Living Memory collection, East Sussex Records Office (ESRO), Lewes.
31. Quoted in Mullins and Griffiths, *Cap and Apron*, p. 13.
32. Interview with Edith Edwards, tape 36, Manchester Studies collection, TLSL.
33. Ibid.
34. London Advisory Council for Juvenile Employment, *A Guide to Employment for London Boys and Girls* (London, 1928), p. 130.
35. J. Beauchamp, *Working Women in Great Britain* (New York, 1937), p. 24.
36. Interview with Lucy Lees, no. 1999.0335, North West Sound Archive (NWSA), Lancashire Record Office.
37. Interview with Mrs Sandys, tape no. 9, Manchester Studies collection, TLSL.
38. Cited in V. Markham and F. Hancock, *Report on the Postwar Organisation of Private Domestic Employment* (London, 1945), p. 4. On the prevalence of single servants in middle-class households see H. Perkin, *The Rise of Professional Society: England since 1880* (London, 1989), p. 78, and Smith, *London Life and Labour*, vol. 8, part 2 (London, 1934), p. 315.
39. Classified ad., *Manchester Guardian* (1 March 1919), p. 1.
40. W. Foley, *The Forest Trilogy* (Oxford, 1992), p. 140. On middle-class consumers' ability to buy domestic appliances see S. Bowden and A. Offer, 'Household Appliances and the Use of Time: The United States and Britain since the 1920s', *Economic History Review*, vol. XLVIII, no. 4 (1994), p. 745; T. Devine, *The Scottish Nation, 1700–2000* (London, 2000), pp. 243–5.
41. C. Langhamer, *Women's Leisure in England, c.1920–c.1960* (Manchester, 2000), p. 58.
42. D. Beddoe, *Back to Home and Duty: Women between the Wars 1918–1939* (London, 1989), p. 115.
43. http://www.mybrightonandhove.org.uk/page_id__6373_path__0p115p191p980p.aspx
44. H. Harvey, reader's letter, *Manchester Guardian* (18 May 1923), p. 5.
45. Mrs E. Cleary, 28, Manchester Studies collection, TLSL.

CHAPTER 3: ENEMIES WITHIN

1. Interview transcript of interview with Harry Watson by Margaret Morris (1975), TUC Library, London Metropolitan University.
2. http://www.nationalarchives.gov.uk/cabinetpapers/themes/general-strike-cover-papers.htm.
3. Foley, *Child in the Forest*, p. 101.
4. S. Pedersen, 'Triumph of the Poshocracy', *London Review of Books*, vol. 35, no. 15 (8 August 2013), p. 19.
5. P. Williamson, *Stanley Baldwin: Conservative Leadership and National Values* (Cambridge, 1999) and D. Watts, *Stanley Baldwin and the Search for Consensus* (London, 1996).
6. K. Martin, *Father Figures: A First Volume of Autobiography, 1897–1931* (London, 1966), p. 78.
7. Quoted in A. Mason, 'The Government and the General Strike, 1926', *International Review of Social History*, vol. 14, no. 1 (1969), pp. 6–7.
8. Coal Mining Industry Subvention, HC Deb., Hansard, (6 August 1925), vol. 187, col. 1592.
9. 'In Suspense', *Manchester Guardian* (30 April 1926), p. 10.
10. 'Two Days for Peace', *Manchester Guardian* (2 May 1926), p. 16.
11. 'In Suspense', p. 11.
12. Cabinet papers, CAB 23/52 C 21 (26), The National Archives (TNA), p. 1.
13. P. Snowden, *An Autobiography* (London, 1934), p. 151.
14. 'Emergency Plans', *Manchester Guardian* (3 May 1926), p. 13.
15. R. Saltzman, 'Folklore as Politics in Great Britain: Working-class Critiques of Upper-class Strike Breakers in the 1926 General Strike', *Anthropological Quarterly*, vol. 67, no. 3 (1994), p. 105.
16. Ibid., p. 108.
17. Quoted in R. Saltzmann, *A Lark for the Sake of their Country. The 1926 General Strike Volunteers in Folklore and Memory* (Manchester, 2012) p. 110.
18. Interview with Alf Canning (pseudonym), transcript KHP 31, Kingswood History Project, Bristol Reference Library, p. 11.
19. A. Davies, *City of Gangs. Glasgow and the Rise of the British Gangster* (London, 2013), p. 45.
20. Quoted in Saltzman, *A Lark*, p. 66.
21. Saltzman, 'Folklore as Politics', p. 110.
22. Both quotes from ibid., p. 105.

23. J. Mitford, *Hons and Rebels* (London, 1996), p. 20.

24. Ibid.

25. For an account see Beckwith, *When I Remember*, p. 86.

26. Saltzman, 'Folklore as Politics', p. 111.

27. D. Athill, *Life Class: The Selected Memoirs of Diana Athill* (London, 2009), pp. 166–7.

28. Stanley Baldwin, quoted in *British Gazette* (7 May 1926), p. 1.

29. Interview with Harry Wicks, in Harry Wicks's papers, MSS. 102, Modern Records Centre (MRC), University of Warwick.

30. *Birmingham Post* (7 May 1926), p. 1.

31. Interview with Harry Watson.

32. 'Rioters Jailed', *Birmingham Post* (12 May 1926), p. 1.

33. 'Disorder', *Birmingham Post* (11 May 1926), p. 1.

34. H. Barron, *The Miners' Lockout: Meanings of Community in the Durham Coalfield* (Oxford, 2009), pp. 104–5.

35. Quoted in ibid., p. 105.

36. Quoted in ibid., p. 136.

37. Interview with Edith Holt (pseudonym), transcript R02, oral history collection, Bristol Reference Library, pp. 13–14.

38. 'The End of the Strike', *Birmingham Post* (13 May 1926), p. 1.

39. Interview with Harry Wicks.

40. K. Middlemas, *Politics in Industrial Society: The Experience of the British System since 1911* (London, 1979), p. 195.

41. Ibid., p. 18.

42. C. Wrigley, '1926: Social Costs of the Mining Dispute', *History Today*, vol. 34, no. 11 (1984); Saltzman, *A Lark*, ch. 9; http://ethelsmith. hubpages.com/hub/Welsh-Coal-Mining-A-thriving-business-in-the-past; http://aswanseavalleyman.wordpress.com/

43. Smyth, 'Resisting Labour', p. 384.

44. Interview with Alf Canning, p. 31.

45. W. Foley, *Child in the Forest*, p. 141.

46. Ibid., p. 230.

CHAPTER 4: DOLE

1. W. Holtby, *Women and a Changing Civilisation* (London, 1934), p. 118.

2. N. Crafts, 'Living Standards', in Crafts et al. (eds.), *Work and Pay*, p. 21.

3. I. Gazeley, *Poverty in Britain, 1900–1965* (Basingstoke, 2004), p. 108.

4. C. Steedman, *Landscape for a Good Woman* (London, 1986), p. 35.

5. P. Thane, 'The "Welfare State" and the Labour Market', in Crafts et al. (eds.), *Work and Pay*, p. 187.

6. A. Bingham, 'Stop the Flapper Vote Folly', *Twentieth Century British History*, vol. 13, no. 1 (2002).

7. P. Thane, 'What Difference did the Vote Make?', *Historical Research*, vol. 76, no. 192 (2003), pp. 268–85.

8. *Census of England and Wales, 1921: Occupation Tables* (London, 1924), table 4; *Census of England and Wales, 1931: Occupation Tables* (London, 1934), table 3; *Census of Scotland, 1921*, vol. 3 (London, 1924), table 2; *Census of Scotland, 1931*, vol. 3 (London, 1934), table 1.

9. Report of the Ministry of Labour for the Year 1938, xii (PP 1938–9), Cmd. 6016.

10. Priestley, *English Journey*, pp. 13 and 16–17.

11. Ibid., p. 68.

12. Ibid., p. 74.

13. C. Burge, 'A Flaw in the National Housing Scheme', *Daily Mirror* (19 April 1934), p. 12.

14. M. Clapson, *Invincible Green Suburbs, Brave New Towns* (Manchester, 1998), ch. 2; P. Scott, 'Mr Drage, Mr Everyman, and the Mass Market for Domestic Furniture in Interwar Britain', *Economic History Review*, vol. 62, no. 4 (2009), pp. 802–27.

15. Unpublished minute to the Secretary of State, 1937, ED 11/278, TNA.

16. 'Work, Wages and the Dole', *The Times* (12 June 1931), p. 17.

17. 'Iron and Steel', letter to *The Times* (22 August 1931), p. 6.

18. 'The Means Test', letter to the *Scotsman* (19 December 1931), p. 9.

19. Ibid. See also 'Tomorrow's Elections', *The Times* (31 October 1933), p. 15.

20. A.L. Bowley and M. Hogg, *Has Poverty Diminished?* (London, 1925), p. 197.

21. Smith, *New Survey of London Life and Labour*, vol. 3, p. 83.

22. B.S. Rowntree, *Poverty and Progress. A Second Social Survey of York* (London, 1941), p. 51.

23. H. Tout, *The Standard of Living in Bristol: A Preliminary Report of the Work of the University of Bristol Social Survey* (Bristol, 1938), p. 46.

24. Interview with Jack Bell (pseudonym), KHP 50, Bristol Reference Library.

25. C. Cameron, A. Lush and G. Meara, *Disinherited Youth: A Report on the 18+ Age Group Enquiry Prepared for the Trustees of the Carnegie United Kingdom Trust* (Edinburgh, 1943), pp. 70, 75; Rowntree, *Poverty and Progress,*

pp. 188–9; H.L. Beales and R.S. Lambert (eds.), *Memoirs of the Unemployed* (London, 1934), pp. 20, 40–41, 82–7; W. Temple and the Pilgrim Trust, *Men Without Work* (Cambridge, 1938), pp. 147–8.

26. A.D. Lindsay, 'Means Test', letter to *The Times* (14 February 1935), p. 8.

27. Interview with Stanley Iveson, tape no. 898, Manchester Studies collection, TLSL.

28. 'The Means Test', letter to *The Times* (18 February 1935), p. 8.

29. Cameron, Lush and Meara, *Disinherited Youth*.

30. Rowntree, *Poverty and Progress*, p. 8.

31. E. Benson, *To Struggle is to Live. Vol. 2: Starve or Rebel* (Newcastle, 1980), pp. 47–9.

32. Interview with Frank Haynes, OT555, TS227, Abingdon Oral History Project, OHC.

33. Emily Swankie in I. MacDougall (ed.), *Voices from the Hunger Marches* (Edinburgh, 1991), pp. 227–8.

34. Ibid.

35. Benson, *To Struggle is to Live*, p. 46.

36. E. MacColl, *Journeyman: An Autobiography* (London, 1990), p. 122.

37. Ibid., p. 201.

38. Ibid., p. 29.

39. L. Lee, *As I Walked Out One Midsummer Morning* (Harmondsworth, 1971), p. 20.

40. A.D.K. Owen et al., *A Survey of Juvenile Employment and Welfare in Sheffield* (Sheffield, 1933), p. 18; Caradog Jones, *Social Survey of Merseyside*, vol. 3 (Liverpool, 1934), p. 203; Caradog Jones, *Social Survey of Merseyside*, vol. 2, p. 33; J. and S. Jewkes, *The Juvenile Labour Market* (London, 1938), pp. 12–13.

41. W. Greenwood, *Love on the Dole* (London, 1933).

42. This is calculated from Digitization of R. Brown, Orientation to Work and Industrial Behaviour of Shipbuilding Workers 1968–1969: Manual Workers' Questionnaires, Study Number (SN) 6586, UK Data Archive (UKDA).

43. Interview with Mr Savage, transcript no. 477, Manchester Studies collection, TLSL.

44. Interview with Peggy, transcript no. A66/a, Making Ends Meet oral history collection, Nottingham Local Studies Library (NLSL).

45. K. Whitehorn, *Selective Memory* (London, 2007), p. 3.

46. Lindsay, 'Means Test'.

47. Pilgrim Trust, *Men without Work*, p. 200.

48. 'The Running Sore', *The Times* (25 March 1931), p. 15.

49. 'An Unemployed Business Man', in Beales and Lambert, *Memoirs of the Unemployed*, p. 57.
50. Ibid., p. 61.
51. 'A South Wales Miner', in ibid, p. 69.
52. 'A Scottish Hotel Servant', in ibid., pp. 260–61.
53. This information is taken from the webpages of the Left Book Club Archive, which is held at the University of Sheffield. See http://librarysupport.shef.ac.uk/leftbook.pdf
54. *Left Review*, no. 1 (October 1934), p. 1.
55. C. Hilliard, *To Exercise Our Talents: The Democratization of Writing in Britain* (Cambridge, Mass, 2006).
56. S. Constantine, '"Love on the Dole" and its Reception in the 1930s', *Literature and History*, no. 8 (1982), pp. 232–47.
57. Benson, *To Struggle is to Live*, p. 56.
58. Quoted in J. Stevenson and C. Cook, *Britain in the Depression: Society and Politics, 1929–39* (London, 1994), p. 228.
59. Quoted in L. Tabili, *Global Migrants, Local Culture: Natives and Newcomers in Provincial England, 1841–1939* (Basingstoke, 2011), p. 147.
60. D.S. Lewis, *Illusions of Grandeur: Mosley, Fascism and British Society, 1931–81* (Manchester, 1987), pp. 71–2.
61. Questionnaires to District Labour Parties on Fascist Activity in their Region, 1934–5, Labour Party Archive, Labour History Archive, Manchester.
62. Interview with Arthur Rogers, OT 404, TS 225, Abingdon Oral History Project, OHC.
63. Quoted in S. Rawnsley, 'The Membership of the British Union of Fascists', in K. Lunn and R. Thurlow (eds.), *British Fascism. Essays on the Radical Right in Interwar Britain* (London, 1980), p. 154.
64. Quoted in Stevenson and Cook, *Britain in the Depression*, p. 227. On Mosley's influential support see D. Cannadine, *The Decline and Fall of the British Aristocracy* (New Haven, 1992), pp. 547–51; N. Todd, *In Excited Times: The People against the Blackshirts* (Newcastle, 1990), p. 20; R. Skidelsky, *Oswald Mosley* (London, 1975), pp. 325–26.
65. Skidelsky, *Oswald Mosley*, pp. 325–6.
66. Viscount Rothermere, 'Give the Blackshirts a Helping Hand', *Daily Mirror* (22 January 1934), p. 12.
67. 'Daughter of Peer Nazi Guest of Honour', *Daily Mirror* (11 September 1935), p. 3; Mitford, *Hons and Rebels*, pp. 62–3.
68. W. Goldman, *East End My Cradle* (London, 1988), p. 20.
69. Oral history recording with Charlie Goodman, no. 16612/4, Imperial War Museum (IWM).

70. B. Alexander, *British Volunteers for Liberty: Spain, 1936–1939* (London, 1986), p. 29.

71. 'Death in Spain', *Yorkshire Post* (10 December 1938), p. 9.

72. 'He Fought in Spain War, Brought Spanish Wife to Fight Here', *Daily Mirror* (27 January 1938), p. 1.

73. Quoted in MacDougall, *Voices from the Hunger Marches*, p. 133.

74. Quoted in Alexander, *British Volunteers for Liberty*, pp. 25–6.

75. Oral history recording with Charlie Goodman, no. 16612/4, Imperial War Museum.

76. On the *Mirror's* popularity see A. Bingham, *Family Newspapers? Sex, Private Life and the British Popular Press 1918–1978* (Oxford, 2010), pp. 1, 8, 17 and 19.

77. Quoted in J. Pilger, *Hidden Agendas* (London, 1998) p. 382.

78. C. Webster, 'Healthy or Hungry Thirties?', *History Workshop Journal*, vol. 13, no. 1 (1982), p. 117.

79. P. Thane, 'Visions of Gender in the British Welfare State', in G. Bock and P. Thane (eds.), *Maternity and Gender Policies. Women and the Rise of the European Welfare States 1880s–1950s* (London, 1991), p. 105.

80. 'Maternal Mortality', *The Times* (23 June 1934), p. 13.

81. Ministry of Health, *Report on Maternal Mortality in Wales* (London, 1937), pp. 93–4, 115.

82. Ministry of Health, HC Deb., Hansard (17 July 1935), vol. 304, col. 1118.

83. Midwives Bill, HC Deb., Hansard (30 April 1936), vol. 311, col. 1169.

84. M. Spring Rice, *Working Class Wives: Their Health and Conditions* (Harmondsworth, 1939), pp. 77, 79.

85. Ibid., p. 94.

86. Ibid., p. 103.

87. 'A Wealthier Britain', *The Times* (19 July 1937), p. 9.

88. Midwives Bill, HC Deb., Hansard, (30 April 1936), vol. 311, col. 1160.

89. 'Maternal Mortality', HC Deb., Hansard (27 May 1937), vol. 324, col. 417.

90. Ministry of Health, HC Deb., Hansard (17 July 1935), vol. 304, col. 1064.

91. Ministry of Health, HC Deb., Hansard (17 July 1935), vol. 304, col. 1072. See also M. Mitchell, 'The Effects of Unemployment on the Social Condition of Women and Children in the 1930s', *History Workshop Journal*, vol. 19, no. 1 (1985), p. 117.

92. J. Harris, 'War and Social History: Britain and the Home Front during the Second World War', *Contemporary European History*, vol. 1, no. 1 (1992), p. 30.

93. 'Jarrow Marchers at Bedford', *The Times* (27 October 1936), p. 11.
94. 'Jarrow's Petition', *The Times* (5 November 1936), p. 15.
95. Spring Rice, *Working Class Wives*, pp. 205–6.
96. V. Woolf, 'Introductory Letter', in M.L Davies (ed.), *Life as We Have Known It* (London, 1984), pp. xxix, xxxi.

INTERLUDE I: A STAR IS BORN

1. Orwell, *Road to Wigan Pier*, p. 31.
2. N. Dennis, F. Henriques and C. Slaughter, *Coal is Our Life: An Analysis of a Yorkshire Mining Community* (London, 1956), p. 41.
3. Priestley, *English Journey*, pp. 198–9.
4. Hoggart, *Uses of Literacy*, pp. 35, 68.
5. Ibid., pp. 35–6.

CHAPTER 5: POLITICS AT THE PALAIS

1. C. Madge and T. Harrisson, *Britain by Mass Observation* (Harmondsworth, 1939), p. 139.
2. 'Harry, Toffee Apple Prince, Shows 'em How', *Daily Express* (21 October 1938), p. 5.
3. Priestley, *English Journey*, pp. 130–31, 133, 148–9.
4. P. Bailey, 'Fats Waller meets Harry Champion: Americanization, National Identity and Sexual Politics in Inter-war Music Hall', *Cultural and Social History*, vol. 4, no. 4 (2007), pp. 495–510; R. Fagge, 'J.B. Priestley, the "Modern" and America', *Cultural and Social History*, vol. 4, no. 4 (2007), pp. 481–94.
5. L. MacNeice, *The Strings Are False: An Unfinished Autobiography* (London, 1965), p. 132.
6. W. Holtby, *The Land of Green Ginger* (London, 1927), p. 36.
7. 'Girls We All Know: The Adding Machine', *Manchester Evening News* (1 April 1930), p. 3.
8. Quoted in R. Sennett, *The Corrosion of Character: The Personal Consequences of Work in the New Capitalism* (New York, 1998), p. 40.
9. J. Christy, *The Price of Power: A Biography of Charles Eugene Bedaux* (London, 1984).
10. Quoted in 'Strike at Wolsey Works', *Leicester Evening Mail* (10 December 1931), p. 2.
11. Internal Wolsey Management Report on Meeting of Workers and the

Trade Union, 8 February 1932, DE 4823, Leicestershire Records Office (Leics RO).

12. 'Wolsey Strike', *Leicester Evening Mail* (12 December 1931), p. 1.

13. Lewenhak, 'Trade Union Membership', pp. 32, 45; Bain and Price, *Profiles of Union Growth*, p. 37.

14. Quoted in Beauchamp, *Women*, p. 25.

15. E. Balderson with D. Goodlad, *Backstairs Life in a Country House* (Newton Abbott, 1982), p. 13.

16. Foley, *Child in the Forest*, p. 101.

17. London Trades Council, *Annual Report for the Year 1932* (London, 1933), p. 9.

18. Interview with Mary Abbott, tape no. 671, Manchester Studies collection, TLSL.

19. Transport and General Workers' Union, *Delegate Conference of 1935* (London, 1936), pp. 7–9.

20. Quoted in S. Alexander, 'A New Civilization? London Surveyed 1928–1940s', *History Workshop Journal*, vol. 64, no. 1 (2007), p. 298.

21. S. O'Connell, *The Car and British Society: Class, Gender and Motoring 1896–1939* (Manchester, 1998).

22. Interview with Frank Gogerty by Hilary Young (2006).

23. Interview with Alf Canning, Bristol Reference Library, pp. 27–8.

24. A. Cameron, *In Pursuit of Justice* (London, 1946), p. 30.

25. Ibid., pp. 29–31.

26. R. Croucher, *Engineers at War* (London, 1982), pp. 24–8.

27. B. Jones, 'Slum Clearance, Privatization and Residualization: The Practices and Politics of Council Housing in Mid-twentieth Century England', *Twentieth Century British History*, vol. 21, no. 4 (2010), pp. 510–39.

28. Quoted in M. McKenna, 'The Suburbanization of the Working-Class Population of Liverpool between the Wars', *Social History*, vol. 16, no. 2 (1991), p. 178.

29. Interview with Mr N2L, Elizabeth Roberts Archive, University of Lancaster.

30. Burnett, *Social History of Housing*, p. 248.

31. Interview with Clare Stevens (pseudonym), transcript KHP01, Bristol Reference Library, p. 4.

32. Interview with Percy Wiblin, OT 609, OHC.

33. Lifetimes Group, *A Couple from Manchester* (Manchester, 1975), p. 40.

34. L. Whitworth, 'Men, Women, Shops and "Little Shiny Homes": The Consuming of Coventry, 1930–39', Ph.D. thesis (University of Warwick, 1997), pp. 74–6.

35. Interview with Mrs Hughson, tape no. 26, Manchester Studies collection, TLSL.

36. Ernest Brown, Holidays with Pay Bill, HC Deb., Hansard (14 July 1938), vol. 338, col. 1553.

37. S. Dawson, 'Working-Class Consumers and the Campaign for Holidays with Pay', *Twentieth Century British History*, vol. 18, no. 3 (2007), pp. 277–305.

38. Shorter Hours of Labour, HC Deb., Hansard (11 November 1936), vol. 317, col. 896.

39. Interview with M. Sharp, 1994.0128, NWSA.

40. Consultative Committee on Secondary Education, *Report of the Consultative Committee on Secondary Education with Special Reference to Grammar Schools and Technical High Schools* (Spens Report) (London, 1938), p. 88, table 1 and p. 93, table 4.

41. I. Gazeley and A. Newell, 'Unemployment', in Crafts et al. (eds.), *Work and Pay*, p. 235.

42. Thane, 'The "Welfare State"', p. 188.

43. Interview with Jack Bell, KHP 50, Bristol Reference Library, p. 18.

44. Lifetimes Group, *Something in Common* (Manchester, 1976), p. 35.

45. Ibid., p. 16. See also J. White, *The Worst Street in North London: Campbell Bunk between the Wars* (London, 1986), pp. 216–17.

46. White, *The Worst Street in North London*, p. 190.

47. Madge and Harrisson, *Britain by Mass Observation*, p. 169.

CHAPTER 6: THE PEOPLE'S WAR

1. Quoted in A. Calder, *The People's War: Britain 1939–45* (London, 1969), p. 126.

2. File Report (FR) no. 159, 'Morale Today' (1 June 1940), Mass-Observation Archive (MOA), University of Sussex, p. 6.

3. MOA: FR 167, 'Atmosphere in Dover' (3 June 1940), p. 3.

4. MOA: FR 124, 'Morale Today' (18 May 1940), p. 1.

5. T. Harrisson, *Living Through the Blitz* (Harmondsworth, 1978), p. 22.

6. MOA: FR 159, 'Morale Today', p. 10.

7. Topic Collection (TC) 51/2/C, 'Attitudes to Jobs – Young Women and Girls', 1940, MOA.

8. Emergency Powers (Defence) Bill, HC Deb., Hansard (22 May 1940), vol. 361, col. 154–85.

9. 'Leader', *The Times* (1 July 1940).

10. Middlemas, *Politics in Industrial Society*, p. 276.
11. A. Bullock, *The Life and Times of Ernest Bevin. Vol. 2, Minister of Labour, 1940–1945* (London,1966), p. 63.
12. Middlemas, *Politics in Industrial Society*, p. 277.
13. G. Field, *Blood, Sweat and Toil: Remaking the British Working Class, 1939–1945* (Oxford, 2011), p. 79.
14. Bullock, *Life and Times of Ernest Bevin*, p. 63.
15. Middlemas, *Politics in Industrial Society*, p. 275.
16. Membership figures taken from Lewenhak, 'Trade Union Membership among Women and Girls', pp. 32, 45. Density data taken from Bain and Price, *Profiles of Union Growth*, p. 37.
17. Quoted in J. Hinton, *Nine Wartime Lives* (Oxford, 2010), pp. 101 and 105.
18. Quoted in M. Allen, 'The Domestic Ideal and the Mobilization of Womanpower in World War Two', *Women's Studies International Forum*, vol. 6, no. 4 (1983), p. 410.
19. *Ministry of Labour Gazette* (March 1942), p. 98; see also J. Hinton, *Women, Social Leadership, and the Second World War: Continuities of Class* (Oxford, 2002), p. 29, n. 57.
20. Hinton, *Women, Social Leadership, and the Second World War*, p. 29.
21. Quoted in H.L. Smith, *War and Social Change. British Society in the Second World War* (Manchester, 1986), p. 44.
22. Quoted in Allen, 'The Domestic Ideal', p. 409.
23. Ibid., p. 411.
24. R. Titmuss, *Problems of Social Policy* (London, 1950), p. 420.
25. E.C. Bailey, 'Strikes and Lockouts. Accounts of Individual Lockouts', 1946, LAB 76/29, TNA, pp. 53–6.
26. W. Hamilton Whyte, Report of Enquiry into the Bath Co-operative Society Strike, 1942, LAB 10/164, TNA.
27. Letter from 'Bath Co-op Employee', *Bath and Wiltshire Chronicle and Herald* (29 December 1941), p. 5.
28. 'Bath Co-operative Society Strike', LAB 10/164, TNA, pp. 5–6.
29. Ibid., p. 4.
30. Ibid.
31. Ibid., p. 8.
32. Field, *Blood, Sweat and Toil*, p. 121.
33. 'Bath Co-operative Society Strike', p. 3.
34. Editorial, *Daily Express* (13 November 1939), p. 3.
35. Titmuss, *Problems of Social Policy*, pp. 522–4, provides a summary of the data and the sources from which it derives, including the reports of medical officers.

36. Quoted in J. Gaffin and D. Thoms, *Caring and Sharing: The Centenary History of the Co-operative Women's Guild* (Manchester, 1993), p. 132.
37. T. Harrisson, *Living Through the Blitz*, p. 24.
38. V. Brittain, *Testament of Experience* (London, 1980).
39. Figures from J. Welshman, *Churchill's Children: The Evacuee Experience in Wartime Britain* (Oxford, 2010), p. 5.
40. Ibid., p. 32.
41. Interview with John McGuirk by Hilary Young (2006).
42. See T. Harrisson and C. Madge, *War Begins at Home* (London, 1940), pp. 299–300.
43. Quoted in H.L. Smith, *Britain in the Second World War: A Social History* (Manchester, 1996), p. 41.
44. Mass Observation, *War Begins at Home*, p. 323.
45. Quoted in 'Wesker, Arnold', *Current Biography*, vol. 23, no. 2 (1962), p. 43.
46. H. Pickles, *Crooked Sixpences Among the Chalk* (Hawes, 1993), pp. 85–6.
47. W. Utting, 'Cooper, Joan Davies', *Oxford Dictionary of National Biography*.
48. Calder, *The People's War*, p. 189.
49. Quoted in ibid., p. 207.
50. Harrisson, *Living Through the Blitz*, p. 136.
51. See also MOA: FR 503, 'Air Raid on Leicester' (26 November 1940), p. 5.
52. Interview with Bert Sheard, TWC 26, Barton Hill History Group interview, Bristol Reference Library.
53. Harrisson, *Living Through the Blitz*, p. 38.
54. Ibid., p. 219; 'Manchester's Rest Centres', *Manchester Guardian* (2 January 1941), p. 6.
55. R. Davison, 'Britain Abolishes the Household Means Test', *Social Service Review*, vol. 15, no. 3 (1942), pp. 533–41. See also Bullock, *Ernest Bevin*, p. 65.
56. MOA: FR 497 'Coventry' (November 1940); FR 502 'Local Morale Reports' (November 1940) and FR 503 'Leicester'.
57. Emily Swankie, in MacDougall, *Voices from the Hunger Marches*, p. 228.
58. Field, *Blood, Sweat and Toil*, p. 229.
59. Quoted in Calder, *People's War*, p. 383.
60. Board of Trade, *Patriotic Patches* (London, 1943), p. 1.
61. 'Army Frustration', *Tribune* (31 July 1942), p. 16.
62. Interview with Margaret Amosu, no. 16704, oral history collection, IWM.

63. Titmuss, *Problems of Social Policy*.
64. J. Harris, 'Political Ideas and Social Change', in Smith, *War and Social Change*, pp. 247–9.
65. MOA: FR 1568, 'Public Reaction to the Beveridge Report' (January 1943), p. 3.
66. Bullock, *Ernest Bevin*, p. 202.
67. Quoted in K. Jeffreys, *War and Reform: British Politics during the Second World War* (Manchester, 1994), p. 98.
68. 'The Government and the Beveridge Report', Home Intelligence report, 11 March 1943, INF 1/292, TNA.
69. MOA: FR 1568, 'Beveridge', p. 4.
70. MOA: FR 1606, 'What are People in Britain Thinking and Talking About?' (February 1943), p. 7.
71. Quoted in Jeffreys, *War and Reform*, p. 95.
72. MOA: FR 1606, 'What are People in Britain Thinking and Talking About?', p. 5.
73. Field, *Blood, Sweat and Toil*, p. 236.
74. *Millions Like Us*, dir. S. Gilliat (1943).
75. Quoted in Smith, *Britain in the Second World War*, pp. 129–30.
76. L. Beers, *Your Britain: Media and the Making of the Labour Party* (Cambridge, Mass., 2010), p. 173.
77. Labour Party, *Labour. Cross Here!*, General Secretary's papers, 1945, Labour Party Archive (LPA), People's History Museum, Manchester.
78. MOA: FR 2059, 'Will the Factory Girls Want to Stay Put or Go Home?' (March 1944), p. 2.
79. Ibid., p. 7.
80. Jeffreys, *War and Reform*, p. 81.
81. Quoted in S. Brooke, *Labour's War: The Labour Party during the Second World War* (Oxford, 1992), p. 309.
82. Field, *Blood, Sweat and Toil*, p. 372.
83. Interview with Kitty Murphy, no. 11849, oral history collection, Imperial War Museum (IWM).
84. N. Tiratsoo, 'Labour and the Electorate' in D. Tanner, P. Thane and N. Tiratsoo (eds.), *Labour's First Century* (Cambridge, 2000), p. 283.

CHAPTER 7: NEW JERUSALEMS

1. Interview with Hazel Wood by Hilary Young (2006).
2. Crafts, 'Living Standards', p. 21.

3. D. Lessing, *Walking in the Shade: Volume Two of my Autobiography* (London, 1998), pp. 4–5.

4. Economic Situation, HC Deb., Hansard (26 October 1949), vol. 468, cols 1387–8.

5. Interview with Nellie Rigby by Hilary Young (2007).

6. G. Routh, *Occupations and Pay*, p. 157.

7. Interview with Mr N2L, Elizabeth Roberts Archive.

8. MOA: FR 3075, 'A Report on the Present-Day Cost of Living' (January 1949), p. 20. This conclusion was based on a sample of 2,040 people. See also C. Schenk, 'Austerity and Boom' in P. Johnson (ed.), *Twentieth-Century Britain: Economic, Social and Cultural Change* (London, 1994), p. 302.

9. F. Zweig, *Labour Life and Poverty* (London, 1949), p. 49.

10. K. Box, 'The Cinema and the Public', Government Social Survey (1946), held at Nuffield College, Oxford, pp. 1–2.

11. Interview with Carol Blackburn, 2001.0424, NWSA.

12. Zweig, *Labour Life and Poverty*, pp. 48–9.

13. I. Zweiniger-Bargielowska, *Austerity in Britain: Rationing, Controls, and Consumption: 1939–1955* (Oxford, 2000), p. 45, table 1.5.

14. 'Queue-Arm? Housewives Tell of Queue-legs Too', *Manchester Evening News* (14 March 1947), p. 3; 'You have been Warned! Manchester Enforcement Officers tell Black Market Hawkers', *Manchester Evening News* (7 March 1947), p. 8.

15. Interview with Brian Thresh, 1998.0035, NWSA. See also 'Stole Bedspreads', *Liverpool Echo* (15 November 1955), p. 10.

16. MOA: FR 2580 'Women and Industry' (March 1948); FR 3036 'Queuing' (September 1948); FR 3055 'Shopping' (November 1948).

17. MOA: FR 2461B 'Who are the Fuel Wasters?' (February 1948).

18. 'Stop Week-End Veg Ramp', *Daily Mirror* (16 February 1951), p. 6.

19. Zweiniger-Bargielowska, *Austerity in Britain*, p. 45, table 1.5.

20. MOA: FR 3109, 'Some Comments on the National Health Survey' (April 1949), p. 6.

21. Interview with Beryl Gottfried, OT 549, Abingdon Oral History Project, OHC.

22. Interview with Mrs B4.1, Stirling Oral History Archive, Scottish Oral History Archive, University of Strathclyde.

23. R. Fitzpatrick and T. Chandola, 'Health', in Halsey with Webb (eds.), *Twentieth-Century British Social Trends*, p. 97, table 3.3.

24. A. Bevan, *In Place of Fear* (London, 1952), pp. 102–3.

25. Family Allowances Bill, HC Deb., Hansard (8 March 1945), vol. 408, col. 2261.

26. A.J. Reid, *United We Stand: A History of Britain's Trade Unions* (London, 2010), p. 339.
27. MOA: FR 2999, 'Trade Unions' (May–June 1948), p. 3.
28. P. Thane, 'Labour and Welfare', in Tanner et al., *Labour's First Century*. Criticisms of the indices used in the post-war years, and a suggestion for adopting a different measurement of poverty, were offered in B. Abel-Smith and P. Townsend, *The Poor and the Poorest: A New Analysis of the Ministry of Labour's Family Expenditure Surveys of 1953–54 and 1960* (London, 1965).
29. P. Thane and T. Evans, *Sinners? Scroungers? Saints?: Unmarried Motherhood in Twentieth-century England* (Oxford, 2012).
30. Interview with Mr N2L, Elizabeth Roberts Archive.
31. 'Widow's Plight', *Liverpool Echo* (5 July 1948), p. 3.
32. P. Thane, 'Unmarried Motherhood in Twentieth-Century England', *Women's History Review*, vol. 20, no. 1 (2011), p. 21.
33. A. Bevan, quoted in *The Times* (15 August 1947), p. 2.
34. MOA: FR 2059, 'Will the Factory Girls Want to Stay Put or Go Home?'
35. 'Women Workers', *Manchester Guardian* (2 June 1947), p. 3. See also G. Isaacs, Economic Situation, HC Deb., Hansard (11 March 1947), vol. 434, col. 1149.
36. Central Advisory Council for Education (England), *Children and their Primary Schools* (London, 1967), p. 108, table 4.
37. 'Isaacs Tells Women: We Need You', *Daily Mirror* (2 June 1947), p. 1.
38. Ibid.
39. Central Office of Information, *The Battle for Output: Economic Survey for 1947* (London, 1947).
40. Ministry of Labour, 'Average Earnings and Hours Enquiry, October 1948', *Ministry of Labour Gazette* (January 1949).
41. Calculated from A. Holmans, 'Housing', in Halsey with Webb (eds.), *Twentieth-Century British Social Trends*, pp. 469–510.
42. Aneurin Bevan, HC Deb., Hansard (16 March 1949), vol. 462, cols 2121–231.
43. 'Must have Middle Class to be a Real Town, Planners Warn', *Daily Mirror* (10 May 1949), p. 7.
44. 'First Tenants are now in Luxury Flats', *Manchester Evening News* (4 July 1948), p. 4.
45. Interview with Bill Rainford by Hilary Young (2007).
46. The waiting list in Birmingham, December 1950, HLG 117/415, TNA, p. 3; see also Birmingham Trades Council, 'Report on the Methods of Allocating Council Houses' (1951), MSS 292/835/6, MRC.

47. Interview with Philip Gilbert, OT 740, Seven Roads Community Oral History Project, OHC.

48. Interview with Alan Watkins by Hilary Young (2007).

49. Interview with Mr N2L, Elizabeth Roberts Archive.

50. Confidential Summary Report on the General Election of 1950, November 1950, General Election Departmental Records, CCO 500/24/1, Conservative Party Archive, Bodleian Library, University of Oxford, p. 41.

51. 'Tory Victory in a Winter of Discontent', *Manchester Guardian* (22 September 1951), p. 6.

52. http://news.bbc.co.uk/onthisday/hi/dates/stories/october/26/newsid_3687000/3687425.stm.

53. K.O. Morgan, *The People's Peace* (Oxford, 1990), p. 81.

54. MOA: FR 3073 'Middle Class – Why?' (December 1948), p. 27.

55. MOA: FR 2461B 'Who are the Fuel Wasters?' (February 1947), p. 3.

56. Field, *Blood, Sweat and Toil*, p. 378. See also ibid., pp. 23–4.

57. M. Savage, *Identities and Social Change in Britain since 1940: The Politics of Method* (Oxford, 2010), ch. 4.

58. M. Savage, 'Affluence and Social Change in the Making of Techno-cratic Middle-Class Identities: Britain, 1939–55', *Contemporary British History*, vol. 22, no. 4 (2008), pp. 471–2.

59. MOA: FR 3152 'Non-Medical Aspects of the National Health Service' (August 1949); FR 3025 'Present Day Education' (August 1948). R. Lowe, 'Modernizing Britain's Welfare State', in L. Black and H. Pemberton (eds.), *An Affluent Society? Britain's Post-War 'Golden Age' Revisited* (Aldershot, 2004), p. 45.

60. N. Last, P. and R. Malcolmson, *Nella Last in the 1950s* (London, 2010), pp. 17, 65.

61. MOA: FR 3170 'Defects in Modern Education' (October 1949), p. 5.

62. Quoted in 'Easing the Middle Class Burden', *Daily Mirror* (24 January 1950), p. 2.

63. On the nature of middle-class distinction, see P. Bourdieu, *Distinction: A Social Critique of the Judgement of Taste* (London, 1984).

64. Morgan, *Britain since 1945*, p. 62. See also Housing Managers' file, 1946, HLG 104/5, TNA.

INTERLUDE III: SETTING THE PEOPLE FREE

1. 'The Tennis Girl goes Feminine', *Picture Post*, vol. 51, no. 11 (16 June 1951), pp. 20–21.

2. 'The Princess goes to a Tennis Party', ibid., vol. 52, no. 8 (25 August 1951), p. 25.
3. C. Harding and B. Lewis (eds.), *Talking Pictures: The Popular Experience of the Cinema* (Castleford, 1993), p. 78.
4. 'Winning the Pools – and Losing her Clothes', *Guardian* (15 March 1977), p. 9.
5. Anonymous usherette quoted in Harding and Lewis, *Talking Pictures*, p. 81.
6. Whitehorn, *Selective Memory*, p. 43.
7. M. Broady, 'The Organisation of Coronation Street Parties', *Sociological Review*, vol. 4, no. 2 (1956), p. 228.
8. On love and marriage in post-war England see C. Langhamer, *The English in Love: The Intimate Story of an Emotional Revolution* (Oxford, 2013).
9. Burnett, *Social History of Housing*, p. 277.

CHAPTER 8: COMMUNITIES

1. Interview with Betty Ennis by Hilary Young (2007).
2. Figure from Burnett, *Social History of Housing*, p. 274.
3. A. Holmans, 'Housing', in Halsey with Webb (eds.), *Twentieth-Century British Social Trends*, p. 487, table 14.12.
4. Quoted in 'Doorstep Wives Set Planners a Standard', *Daily Mirror* (9 September 1953), p. 6.
5. M. Young and P. Willmott, *Family and Kinship in East London* (Harmondsworth, 1957), p. 187. See also C. Vereker and J.B. Mays, *Urban Redevelopment and Social Change: A Study of Social Conditions in Central Liverpool, 1955–56* (Liverpool, 1961), which was based on the Crown Street interviews archived at the University of Liverpool Archives and Special Collections, and undertaken in 1954–6; E.I. Black and T.S. Simey, *Neighbourhood and Community: An Enquiry into Social Relationships on Housing Estates in Liverpool and Sheffield* (Liverpool, 1954); J.M. Mogey, *Family and Neighbourhood: Two Studies of Oxford* (London, 1956); M. Stacey, *Tradition and Change: A Study of Banbury* (London, 1960).
6. Interview with Ann Lanchbury by Hilary Young (2007).
7. Shelagh Delaney, quoted in *Shelagh Delaney's Salford*, dir. Ken Russell (London, 1960).
8. Interview with Terry Rimmer by Hilary Young (2007).

9. Crown Street Survey, Merseyside Social Survey Archive, D416/1/23/230, University of Liverpool Archives and Special Collections (ULASC).

10. P. Thane, *Old Age in Britain* (Oxford, 2000), p. 421.

11. D.V. Donnison, 'The Movement of Households in England', *Journal of the Royal Statistical Society*, Series A, vol. 124, no. 1 (1961), p. 60; D416/23/198, ULASC.

12. A study of the kinds of people who wanted to move was made by Vereker and Mays, *Urban Redeveloment and Social Change*. The conclusions drawn here also rely on the fieldnotes held at D416/1/23-24, ULASC.

13. Holmans, 'Housing', p. 487.

14. D416/1/23/207, ULASC.

15. Donnison, 'The Movement of Households in England', p. 60.

16. M. Woolf, *The Housing Survey in England and Wales* (London, 1964), p. 78, table 4.22.

17. Quoted in R. Forrest and A. Murie, *Selling the Welfare State: The Privatisation of Public Housing* (London, 1991), p. 26; H. Macmillan, HC Deb., Hansard (4 December 1951), vol. 494, cols 2227–354. See also memorandum cited in S. Ball, *The Conservative Party since 1945* (Manchester, 1998), p. 107.

18. Interview with Christine Elliott by Hilary Young (2007).

19. Ibid.

20. Committee on Housing in Greater London (Milner Holland Committee), *Report* (London, 1965), p. 156.

21. Interview with Vera Goldsmith by Hilary Young (2007).

22. D. Kelly in Belle Vale Prefab Project, *Prefab Days: A Community Remembers* (Liverpool, 2008), p. 16.

23. Black and Simey, *Neighbourhood and Community*, p. 80.

24. Sage, *Bad Blood*, p. 102.

25. Ministry of Housing and Local Government, *The New Towns* (London, 1965), p. 2.

26. H. Beynon, *Working for Ford* (Harmondsworth, 1973), and H. Beynon and R. Blackburn, *Perceptions of Work* (Cambridge, 1972). See also D416/1/23/182, ULASC.

27. D416/1/23/190, ULASC.

28. Young and Willmott, *Family and Kinship*, p. 135.

29. H.B. Rodgers, 'Employment and the Journey to Work in an Overspill Community', *Sociological Review*, vol. 7, no. 2 (1959), pp. 213–29.

30. Young and Willmott, *Family and Kinship*, p. 187. See also Vereker and Mays, *Urban Redevelopment and Social Change*; Mogey, *Family and Neighbourhood*; and Stacey, *Tradition and Change*.

31. D719/4/W10, ULASC.

32. Holmans, 'Housing', pp. 494–5; Black and Simey, *Neighbourhood and Community*, p. 103.

33. F. Devine, *Affluent Workers Revisited: Privatism and the Working Class* (Edinburgh, 1992), p. 6; M. Clapson, 'The Suburban Aspiration in England since 1919', *Contemporary British History*, vol. 14, no. 1 (2000), pp. 151–74.

34. P. Mandler, 'New Towns for Old: The Fate of the Town Centre', in B. Conekin, F. Mort and C. Waters (eds.), *Moments of Modernity: Reconstructing Britain, 1945–1964* (London, 1999).

35. Forrest and Murie, *Selling the Welfare State*, p. 26. See also Jones, 'Slum Clearance'.

36. Conservative Party Central Office, *United for Peace and Progress. The 1955 Conservative Party General Election Manifesto* (London, 1955), p. 3.

37. 'Problem Families and Homeless Families, 1960–64', LCC/CL.HSG, London Metropolitan Archives. See also B. Rogaly and B. Taylor, *Moving Histories of Class and Community: Identity, Place and Belonging in Contemporary England* (Basingstoke, 2009), p. 49 on Norwich, and Jones, 'Slum Clearance', p. 526, for an account of a similar policy in Brighton.

38. Interview with Elaine Leather by Hilary Young (2006).

39. Interview with Leo Jones, The Immigrants Project, http://theimmigrantsproject.org/people/jones/, consulted 11 March 2013.

40. Interview with Esme Lancaster, Birmingham Black Oral History Archive (BBOHP), Birmingham City Library.

41. Vereker and Mays, *Urban Redevelopment and Social Change*, pp. 79–80.

42. Second Chance to Learn Women's History Group, *No One Ever Mentions Love* (Liverpool, 1997), pp. 6–7.

43. S. Patterson, *Dark Strangers: A Sociological Study of the Absorption of a Recent West Indian Migrant Group in Brixton, South London* (London, 1963), pp. 278–92.

44. On Rachman see J. Drake, 'From "Colour Blind" to "Colour Bar": Residential Separation in Brixton and Notting Hill', in L. Black et al., *Consensus or Coercion? The State, the People and Social Cohesion in Post-war Britain* (Cheltenham, 2001).

45. J. Davis, 'Rents and Race in 1960s London', *Twentieth Century British History* vol. 12, no. 1 (2001), pp. 69–92.

46. K.H. Perry, '"Little Rock" in Britain: Jim Crow's Transatlantic Topographies', *Journal of British Studies*, vol. 51, no. 1 (2012) ; M. Collins, *Modern Love: An Intimate History of Men and Women in Twentieth-century Britain* (London, 2003), p. 265, n. 23.

47. Quoted in Drake, 'Residential Separation in Brixton and Notting Hill', p. 89.
48. 'LCC Comment', *Cambridge Evening News* (26 February 1965), p. 19.
49. 'Council Ban Coloured Workers from Scheme', *Cambridge News* (24 February 1965), p. 4.
50. 'LCC Comment', ibid., (26 February 1965), p. 19.
51. Interview with Clare Stevens, Bristol Reference Library, pp. 20–21.
52. R. Colls, 'When we Lived in Communities', in Colls and R. Rodger (eds.), *Cities of Ideas. Governance and Citizenship in Urban Britain 1800–2000* (Aldershot, 2005), p. 4.
53. A. Richmond, *Migration and Race Relations in an English City*, pp. 148–60.
54. Interview with Carol Hinde by Hilary Young (2006),
55. P. Collison, *The Cutteslowe Walls: A Study in Social Class* (London, 1963).
56. An argument convincingly made in Jones, 'Slum Clearance', pp. 510–39.
57. Record no. 008, SN 4871, UKDA.
58. Jones, 'Slum Clearance', p. 528. See also 'Babies Born to Get Houses', *Cambridge News* (22 February 1963), p. 5.
59. C.H. Butler, 'Development of New Towns. Shaping a Balanced Community', letter to the editor, *The Times* (29 June 1953), p. 9. See also Hemel Hempstead Development Corporation, *The Development of Hemel Hempstead* (Hemel Hempstead, 1952), p. 3.
60. Report on Speke Township by City Architect and Director of Housing, 19 September 1946, D416/1/15, ULASC, p. 601. See also 'All Mod Con', *Manchester Evening News* (12 March 1947), p. 4.
61. A. Simmonds, 'Conservative Governments and the New Town Housing Question in the 1950s', *Urban History*, vol. 28, no. 1 (2001), pp. 65–83.
62. J. Madge, 'Some Aspects of Social Mixing in Worcester', in L. Kuper (ed.), *Living in Towns: Selected Research Papers in Urban Sociology of the Faculty of Commerce and Social Science, University of Birmingham* (London, 1953).
63. 'Town in the Making', *Liverpool Echo* (30 May 1962).
64. P. Willmott, *Evolution of a Community* (London, 1963), p. 109.
65. Ibid., pp. ix, 109, 111.
66. Quoted in J. Pilger, *Hidden Agendas* (London, 1998) p. 399.

INTERLUDE IV: LOVE AND MARRIAGE

1. K. Fisher, *Birth Control, Sex and Marriage in Britain 1918–1960* (Oxford, 2006), p. 108.

CHAPTER 9: NEVER HAVING IT SO GOOD

1. B.S. Rowntree and G. Lavers, *Poverty and the Welfare State* (London, 1951), pp. 30–31.
2. Quoted in Thane, 'Labour and Welfare', p. 104.
3. Harold Macmillan, speech at Bedford, 20 July 1957, quoted in 'More Production "the Only Answer to Inflation"', *The Times* (22 July 1957), p. 4.
4. A.B. Atkinson and A. Brandolini, 'On Data: A Case Study of the Evolution of Income Inequality across Time and across Countries', *Cambridge Journal of Economics*, vol. 33, no. 3 (2006), fig. 1, p. 383. While Atkinson and Brandolini make the point that the Gini index of income inequality continued to fall during the 1950s before tax, it is clear that after tax the gap between the income groups widened. This was due to Conservative taxation policies which benefited the middle and upper classes, as I discuss later in this chapter. I thank Warren Oliver for bringing this article to my attention.
5. F. Zweig, *The Worker in an Affluent Society: Family Life and Industry* (London, 1961), p. 5.
6. Routh, *Occupations and Pay*, p. 159.
7. Beynon, *Working for Ford*, p. 65.
8. 'Now the Boys Interview the Bosses!', *Daily Mirror* (16 September 1955), p. 8.
9. Interview with James Carroll by Hilary Young (2007). See also B. Reed, *Eighty Thousand Adolescents* (London, 1950), ch. 2. Thanks to Hera Cook for bringing the latter source to my attention.
10. Calculated from SN 6567, Crown Street, 1955–1963, UKDA.
11. V. Raitz, *Flight to the Sun: The Story of the Holiday Revolution* (London, 2001), p. 229.
12. 'They Even Get Married on Tick!', *Daily Mirror* (6 March, 1953) p. 2.
13. Calculated from SN 6567.
14. D719/3/9, SN 6567.
15. S. O'Connell, *Credit and Community: Working-Class Debt in the UK since 1880* (Oxford, 2009), p. 16.
16. Raitz, *Flight to the Sun*, p. 228.
17. 'Tories Hit the Housewife', *Daily Mirror* (27 October 1955), p. 1.
18. E.H.H. Green, *Ideologies of Conservatism. Conservative Political Ideas in the Twentieth Century* (Oxford, 2002), p. 175.
19. Routh, *Occupations and Pay*, p. 159.

20. Ibid.

21. Quoted in S. Ball, *The Conservative Party since 1945* (Manchester, 1998), pp. 111–12.

22. Reid, *United we Stand*, pp. 290–91.

23. Ibid.

24. Interview with Howard Blake by Hilary Young (2007). See also Field, *Blood, Sweat and Toil*, ch. 3.

25. P. Thane, 'Family Life and "Normality" in Post-War British Culture', in R. Bessel and D. Schumann (eds.), *Life after Death: Approaches to a Cultural and Social History of Europe during the 1940s and 1950s* (Cambridge, 2003).

26. D. Kynaston, *Family Britain, 1951–57* (London, 2010).

27. M. Young, 'Distribution of Income within the Family', *British Journal of Sociology*, vol. 3, no. 4 (1952).

28. See for example 'An Investigation into Problem Families', 1950, D495 (LI), R1, pp. 45–6, ULASC.

29. P. Ayers, 'Work, Culture and Gender: The Making of Masculinities in Post-war Liverpool', *Labour History Review*, vol. 69, no. 2 (2004).

30. Rowntree and Lavers, *Poverty and the Welfare State*, pp. 36–8.

31. On opinion polls see R. Lowe, 'Modernizing Britain's Welfare State', in L. Black and H. Pemberton (eds.), *An Affluent Society? Britain's Post-War 'Golden Age' Revisited* (Aldershot, 2004), p. 37.

32. Conservative Party, *General Election Manifesto 1959* (London, 1959).

33. Rowntree and Lavers put the figure at 3 per cent but this was due to a miscalculation of their own data, as later researchers convincingly proved: Abel-Smith and Townsend, *The Poor and the Poorest*; T. Hatton and R. Bailey, 'Seebohm Rowntree and the Postwar Poverty Puzzle', *Economic History Review*, vol. 53, no. 3 (2000), pp. 517–43.

34. C. Cockburn, *Brothers: Male Dominance and Technological Change* (London, 1983), pp. 52–60 and Reid, *United We Stand*, pp. 294–329.

35. S. Bowden, 'The New Consumerism', in P. Johnson (ed.), *Twentieth Century Britain* (London, 1992).

36. Calculated from *Census of England and Wales, 1951: Occupation Tables* (London, 1954), table 3 and *Census of England and Wales, 1961: Occupation Tables* (London, 1964), table 3.

37. A. Hunt, *A Survey of Women's Employment. Vol. I, Report*, Government Social Survey 379 (London, 1968), pp. 115–17.

38. Rowntree and Lavers, *Poverty and the Welfare State*, p. 57.

39. S. Yudkin and A. Holme, *Working Mothers and their Children. A Study for the Council for Children's Welfare* (London, 1963), p. 168.

40. P. Jephcott et al., *Married Women Working* (London, 1963), p. 11.

41. Yudkin and Holme, *Working Mothers and their Children*, p. 27.
42. Jephcott et al., *Married Women Working*, p. 171.
43. LUA, D719/4/16, ULASC.
44. Interview with Jean Eagles McLoughlin by Hilary Young (2007).

INTERLUDE V: THE AFFLUENT SOCIETY

1. Readers' letters in 'Andy Capp Comes Alive!', *Daily Mirror* (19 June 1958), pp. 12–13.

CHAPTER 10: THE GOLDEN AGE OF THE GRAMMAR SCHOOL

1. Consultative Committee on Secondary Education, *Report of the Committee with Special Reference to Secondary Schools and Technical High Schools* (London, 1938), p. 93, table 4.
2. R.D. Anderson, 'Education and Society in Modern Scotland: A Comparative Perspective', *History of Education Quarterly*, no. 25 (1985); A. McPherson, 'Schooling' in A. Dickson and J.H. Treble (eds.), *People and Society in Scotland, vol. 3, 1914–1999* (Edinburgh, 1992), pp. 80–107; the middle-class bias evident in inter-war school selection in Scotland is documented by J.C. Stocks, 'The People versus the Department: The Case of Circular 44', *Scottish Educational Review*, vol. 27, no. 1 (1995).
3. L. Moss, *Education and the People*, NS 46, Government Social Survey (London, 1945), p. 2.
4. Interview with Ian White, 2000.0341, NWSA.
5. E. Wilkinson, quoted in Labour Party, *Annual Conference Report* (Manchester, 1946), p. 22.
6. Board of Education, *Educational Reconstruction* (London, 1943), pp. 24–5.
7. Wilkinson, quoted in Labour Party, *Annual Conference Report*, p. 22.
8. G. Smith, 'Schools', in Halsey with Webb (eds.), *Twentieth-Century British Social Trends*, p. 209; McPherson, 'Schooling'.
9. R. McKibbin, *Classes and Cultures* (Oxford, 1997), p. 262. The proportion of children educated in academic secondary schools was higher in Scotland, but a child's education was just as dependent on class background as in England and Wales; see L. Patterson, A. Pattie and I.J. Deary, 'Social Class, Gender and Secondary Education in the 1950s', *Oxford Review of Education*, vol. 37, no. 3 (2011), pp. 383–401, and McPherson, 'Schooling'.

10. Mr A.J. Irvine (Lab., Liverpool Edge Hill) Parliamentary Question, House of Commons, Thursday 29 November 1951, ED 34/165, TNA.

11. School Inspectors' Reports, Lancashire, 'L', ED 156/129, TNA.

12. Ministry of Education, *Secondary Education for All. A New Drive* (London, 1958), p. 2.

13. Quoted in D. Sandbrook, *Never Had It So Good: A History of Britain from Suez to the Beatles* (London, 2005), p. 424.

14. McKibbin, *Classes and Cultures*, p. 262; A.H. Halsey, A.F. Heath and J.M. Ridge, *Origins and Destinations: Family, Class and Education in Modern Britain* (Oxford, 1980), p. 61, table 4.8, and p. 140, table 8.11.

15. 'Keep Class Warfare out of the Classrooms', *Liverpool Daily Post* (4 January 1962).

16. 'Golden Gate or Prison Wall?', *Economist* (30 January 1951), p. 125.

17. J.W.B. Douglas, J.M. Ross and H.R. Simpson, *All Our Future: A Longitudinal Study of Secondary Education* (London, 1971).

18. Richard Hoggart recalls this in *The Uses of Literacy*, and working-class families continued to buy encyclopedias after the Second World War. See, for example, the account of one of the sociologists who visited Luton in the early 1960s to talk to car workers about their affluence. Their interviewees included Bernard Harris, in whose living room the sociologist noted 'a glass-fronted book shelf in the corner full of books, including encyclopedia': record no. 023, SN 4871, UKDA. When asked how they helped their children with schoolwork, Martin and Amy Cross replied, 'Well we've bought a set of encyclopedias': record no. 007, SN 4871, UKDA.

19. J.G. Ballard, *Miracles of Life. An Autobiography* (London, 2008), p. 160.

20. Committee of Higher Education, *Report of the Committee appointed by the Prime Minister under the Chairmanship of Lord Robbins 1961–63* (Robbins Report) (London, 1963), p. 11.

21. Interview with Paul Baker by Hilary Young (2007).

22. For example F1102 and T04, SN 6586, UKDA.

23. Mr N2L, Elizabeth Roberts Archive.

24. *Census 1951, England and Wales: General Report* (London, 1956), table 59; *Census, 1951, Scotland: Occupations*, table 1; *Census, 1961, England and Wales: Occupation Tables*, table 1; *Census, 1961, Scotland: Terminal Education Age* (Edinburgh, 1966). On the expansion of nursing see R. White, *The Effects of the NHS on the Nursing Profession 1948–1961* (London, 1985).

25. Young and Willmott, *Family and Kinship in East London*, p. 29.

26. Record 023, SN 4871, UKDA.

27. B. Jackson and D. Marsden, *Education and the Working Class: Some General*

Themes Raised by a Study of 88 Children in a Northern Industrial City (Harmondsworth, 1966), pp. 161 and 97.

28. On working-class mothers' educational aspirations see also F. Musgrove, 'Parents' Expectations of the Junior School', *Sociological Review*, vol. 9, no. 2 (1961), pp. 167–80.
29. 'Spotlight on Education', *Daily Mirror* (16 January 1954), p. 2.
30. Report by HM Inspectors on Cheylesmore Secondary School, Coventry, 21 April 1959, ED 162/2205, TNA.
31. Central Advisory Council for Education (England), *15 to 18* (Crowther Report) (London, 1959), p. 64.
32. J.E. Floud (ed.), A.H. Halsey and F.M. Martin, *Social Class and Educational Opportunity* (London, 1956), p. 77.
33. J.M. Bynner, Department of Education and Science, *Parents' Attitudes to Education* (London, 1971), p. 21.
34. Central Advisory Council for Education (England), *Early Leaving* (Gurney-Dixon Report) (London, 1954), p. 36. See also M. Forster, *Hidden Lives: A Family Memoir* (London, 1996), p. 180.
35. Floud et al., *Social Class and Educational Opportunity*, pp. 44–8; J.E. Floud and A.H. Halsey, 'Intelligence Tests, Social Class and Selection for Secondary Schools', *British Journal of Sociology*, vol. 8, no. 1 (1957).
36. 'These Bright Children are NOT Held Back', *Daily Mirror* (3 January 1955), p. 7.
37. H.G. Harvey, 'Development Plan Minute', GORE, 1948, ED 152/135, TNA.
38. J. Brothers, *Church and School. A Study of the Impact of Education on Religion* (Liverpool, 1964), pp. 83–4, 97.
39. Sage, *Bad Blood*, p. 148.
40. Ibid.
41. Jackson and Marsden, *Education and the Working Class*, p. 47.
42. Ibid., pp. 106, 112; Douglas et al., *All Our Future*, p. 50.
43. Jackson and Marsden, *Education and the Working Class*, p. 134.
44. Ibid., p.126.
45. Bablake School, *Prospectus 1956*, at www.chascook.com/bablake/prospectusitems (consulted 10 April 2012), p. 4.
46. Jackson and Marsden, *Education and the Working Class*, p. 124; P. Bailey, 'Foreword' in M. Bailey and M. Eagleton (eds.), *Richard Hoggart: Culture and Critique* (Nottingham, 2011), p. 10.
47. Forster, *Hidden Lives*, p. 181.
48. P. Townsend, *Adolescent Boys of East London*, pp. 92–3.
49. Forster, *Hidden Lives*, pp.93–4.

50. Crowther, *15–18*, pp. 62–3.

51. Jackson and Marsden, *Education and the Working Class*, p. 163; D. Reay, 'Surviving in Dangerous Places: Working-class Women, Women's Studies and Higher Education', *Women's Studies International Forum*, vol. 21, no. 1 (1998), pp. 11–14.

52. Robbins Report, p. 52; see also A.H. Halsey, 'Further and Higher Education', in Halsey with Webb (eds.), *Twentieth-Century British Social Trends*, pp. 226–7.

53. Robbins Report, p. 1.

54. On this see C. Mills, 'Managerial and Professional Work-histories', in T. Butler and M. Savage (eds.), *Social Change and the Middle Classes* (London, 1995), pp. 95–115, and J.H. Goldthorpe with C. Payne, 'Class Structure and the Pattern of Intergenerational Fluidity', in J.H. Goldthorpe with C. Llewellyn and C. Payne, *Social Mobility and Class Structure in Modern Britain* (Oxford, 1987), pp. 115–16.

55. Goldthorpe with Payne, 'Class Structure and the Pattern of Intergenerational Fluidity', in Goldthorpe et al., *Social Mobility and Class Structure in Modern Britain*; and J.M. Goldthorpe, 'Problems of "Meritocracy"', in A.H. Halsey et al. (eds.), *Education. Culture, Economy and Society* (Oxford, 1997).

56. Goldthorpe, 'Problems of "Meritocracy"', in Halsey et al. (eds.), *Education. Culture, Economy and Society*.

57. *Robbins Report*, p. 80.

58. Jackson and Marsden, *Education and the Working Class*, p. 175. See also T. Bottomore, *Classes in Modern Society* (London, 1965), pp. 38, 40.

59. Jackson and Marsden, *Education and the Working Class*, ch. 5.

60. T. Courtenay, *Dear Tom: Letters from Home* (London, 2001), p. 191.

61. Jackson and Marsden, *Education and the Working Class*, ch. 5.

62. 'Brown's Social Mobility "Crusade"', BBC News (23 June 2008), accessed at news.bbc.co.uk/1/hi/uk/7468506.stm (consulted 13 September 2013). See also 'Alan Milburn: "Threat to New Era of Social Mobility"', *Observer* (26 May 2012), p. 5; Social Mobility, HL Deb., Hansard (20 June 2013), vol. 746, col. 139; Richard Bilton, 'Social Mobility', BBC News (2 February 2011), www.bbc.co.uk/news/uk-12339401 (consulted 12 September 2013); G. Hinsliff, 'Middle-class Grip on Professions "Must End"', *Observer* (11 January 2009), www.theguardian.com/politics/2009/jan/11/labour-government-education-social-mobility (consulted 13 September 2013).

63. A point also made by Goldthorpe, 'Problems of "Meritocracy"' pp. 664–5, 675.

64. Quoted in H. Carpenter, *Dennis Potter: The Authorised Biography* (London, 1998), pp. 58 and 80–81.

CHAPTER 11: WORKING-CLASS HEROES

1. Quoted in Carpenter, *Dennis Potter*, pp. 92–3.
2. K. Tynan, 'Backwards and Forwards', *Observer* (30 December 1956), p. 8.
3. T. Warren, *I Was Ena Sharples' Father* (London, 1969), p. 61.
4. Review from 1959 quoted in C. McInnes, *England, Half-English* (London, 1986), p. 206.
5. Quoted in S. Laing, *Representations of Working-Class Life, 1957–1964* (Basingstoke, 1986), p. 96.
6. S. Barstow, *In My Own Good Time* (Otley, 2001), p. 85.
7. Quoted in H. Ritchie, *Success Stories: Literature and the Media in England, 1950–1959* (London, 1988), p. 191.
8. K. Waterhouse, 'Beanstalkers are Big Business!', *Daily Mirror* (4 November 1959), p. 9.
9. M. Abrams, *The Teenage Consumer* (London, 1958), p. 13.
10. Waterhouse, 'Beanstalkers are Big Business!', p. 9.
11. 'Hope in Teddy-Boy Trend', *Manchester Guardian* (5 May 1958), p. 5.
12. B. Davies, *From Voluntaryism to Welfare State. A History of the Youth Service in England. Vol. I: 1939–1979* (Leicester, 1999), ch. 2.
13. Courtenay, *Dear Tom*, p. 190.
14. Interviewed by Andrew Martin on *1960: Year of the North*, dir. R. Whyte, BBC 4, 14 September 2010.
15. Rita Tushingham, speaking at Liverpool FACT Centre, 10 October 2008.
16. R. Hoggart, *Uses of Literacy*.
17. H. Davies, *The Beatles, Football, and Me. A Memoir* (London, 2006), p. 150.
18. Rita Tushingham, 2008.
19. S. Cohen, *Decline, Renewal and the City in Popular Music Culture: Beyond the Beatles* (Aldershot, 2007), pp. 168–9.
20. 'Miss Asher Falls in Love', *Daily Mirror* (29 June 1964), p. 14.
21. 'I've Got That No. 1 Feeling all Over!', *Daily Express* (18 February 1964), p. 5.
22. On working-class parents' attitudes to their children's leisure see M.P. Carter, *Home, School and Work: A Study of the Education and Employment of Young People in Britain* (Oxford, 1962), p. 280.

23. Interview with Judy Walker by Hilary Young (2007).
24. P. Willmott, *Adolescent Boys of East London* (London, 1966), pp. 163–4.
25. Courtenay, *Dear Tom*, p. 189.
26. R. Colls, 'When We Lived in Communities: Working-class Culture and its Critics', in Colls and R. Rodger (eds.), *Cities of Ideas. Governance and Citizenship in Urban Britain 1800–2000: Essays in Honour of David Reeder* (Aldershot, 2004), pp. 286 and 284.
27. 'Books Teenagers Really Enjoy', *Observer* (13 January 1963), p. 27.
28. 'What *Coronation Street* Means to Me', *Manchester Evening News* (24 October 1961), p. 10.
29. Pilger, *Hidden Agendas*, p. 401.

INTERLUDE VI: SPEND, SPEND, SPEND

1. Routh, *Occupations and Pay*, pp. 164–6.
2. Quoted in 'Opinion of Others', *Torrance Herald* (3 January 1960), p. 1.
3. Dennis et al., *Coal is Our Life*, p. 196.
4. PEP, *Family Needs and the Social Services*, pp. 82–3.
5. 'She Just Loved Signing Men's Cheques', *Daily Mirror* (Friday, 13 June 1958), p. 10.
6. 'A Fourpenny Bus Ride to Mum', *Daily Mirror* (30 September 1961), p. 7.
7. Readers' letters, *Daily Mirror* (4 October 1961), p. 8.

CHAPTER 12: A NEW MIDDLE CLASS?

1. 'Political Sixties', *Guardian* (1 January 1960), p. 3.
2. Routh, *Occupations and Pay*, p. 164; A. Cairncross, 'Economic Policy and Performance, 1964–1990', in R. Floud and D. McCloskey (eds.), *Economic History of Britain since 1700. Vol. 3: 1939–1992* (Cambridge, 1994), p. 67.
3. T. Harrisson, *Britain Revisited* (London, 1961), pp. 32–5.
4. Interview with Brain Thresh, NWSA.
5. Interview with Edna and Ron Jones by Hilary Young (2007).
6. M. Young, *The Chipped White Cups of Dover* (London, 1960), p. 11.
7. J.H. Goldthorpe et al., *The Affluent Worker in the Class Structure* (Cambridge, 1969), p. 21.
8. Ibid., p. 22.
9. Devine, *Affluent Workers Revisited*, p. 1.

10. Goldthorpe et al., *Affluent Worker in the Class Structure*.

11. Ibid., pp. 151–6.

12. Record no. 109, SN 4871, Digitized Sample of *The Affluent Worker in the Class Structure*, 1961–1962, UKDA. All names are pseudonyms.

13. Record no. 031, SN 4871, UKDA.

14. Record no. 081, SN 4871, UKDA.

15. Record no. 033, SN 4871, UKDA.

16. Record no. 049, SN 4871, UKDA.

17. Record no. 056, SN 4871, UKDA.

18. Record no. 034, SN 4871, UKDA.

19. Record no. 005, SN 4871, UKDA.

20. Record no. 043, SN 4871, UKDA.

21. Record no. 082, SN 4871, UKDA.

22. Record no. 021, SN 4871, UKDA.

23. Record no. 047, SN 4871, UKDA.

24. Record no. 018, SN 4871, UKDA.

25. Record no. 048, SN 4871, UKDA.

26. Record no. 079, SN 4871, UKDA.

27. Record no. 007, SN 4871, UKDA.

28. Record no. 009, SN 4871, UKDA.

29. Record no. 037, SN 4871, UKDA.

30. Record no. W402, SN 6567, Crown Street, 1955–1963, UKDA.

31. Record no. W40, SN 6567, UKDA.

32. Record no. W5702, SN 6567, UKDA.

33. J. Tomlinson, 'It's the Economy, Stupid! Labour and the Economy, c.1964', *Contemporary British History*, vol. 21, no. 3 (2007).

34. Record no. 030, SN 4871, UKDA.

35. Ibid.

36. Record no. 006, SN 4871, UKDA.

37. Luton by-election November 1963, British Elections Ephemera Archive, http://by-elections.co.uk/63.html#luton (consulted 20 April 2012).

38. Goldthorpe et al., *The Affluent Worker in the Class Structure*, pp. 164–7.

39. Tony Miles, 'The Man Who May Be The Next Prime Minister', *Daily Mirror* (15 February 1963), p. 12.

40. H. Wilson and the Labour Party, *The New Britain. Labour's Plan. Selected Speeches 1964* (Harmondsworth, 1964), pp. 126–7.

41. Ibid., pp. 9–10.

42. Ibid., p. 2.

43. S. Fielding, 'Rethinking Labour's 1964 Campaign', *Contemporary British History* vol. 21, no. 3 (2007), pp. 310–15.

44. 'Cheers for Mum and her Five Boys', *Daily Mirror* (2 October 1963), p. 4.
45. 'Mr Harold Wilson Replies', *Guardian* (22 September 1964), p. 10.
46. Record no. 007, SN 4871, UKDA.
47. Record no. 023, SN 4871, UKDA.
48. Record no. 071, SN 4871, UKDA.
49. Interview with Eric Talbot, tape no. 2001.0724, NWSA.
50. Record no. 003, SN 4871, UKDA.
51. C. Steedman, *Landscape for a Good Woman*, pp. 119–21.
52. Quoted in S. Ball, *The Conservative Party since 1945* (Manchester, 1998), pp. 113–14.
53. P. Barberis, 'The 1964 General Election – the "Not Quite, But" and "But Only Just" Election', *Contemporary British History*, vol. 21, no. 3 (2007), pp. 283–94.
54. Goldthorpe et al., *Affluent Worker in the Class Structure*, p. 172.
55. Record no. 025, SN 4871, UKDA.
56. Record no. 063, SN 4871, UKDA.
57. Political Science Resources, http://www.politicsresources.net/area/uk/ge64/i13.htm (consulted 12 April 2012). This archive has subsequently been deleted from the web, but can still be consulted via the UK Web Archive: www.webarchive.org.uk.

INTERLUDE VII: ON THE MAKE

1. Gazeley and Newell, 'Unemployment', p. 234.
2. *Waiting for Work*, dir. J. Ashley (1963).
3. 'The "Spend, Spend" Widow Weds Again', *Daily Mirror* (14 March, 1969), p. 5.
4. Abel-Smith and Townsend, *The Poor and the Poorest*.

CHAPTER 13: NEW BRITAIN

1. Beynon, *Working for Ford*, pp. 70–71, 191. See also 'Interview with Chaplain, Wallsend Yard', unpublished ms, 1968, Box 1, Informal Interviews, Brown: Shipbuilding Workers (MSS 371), Modern Records Centre, University of Warwick.
2. W. Brown, 'Industrial Relations and the Economy', in Floud and Johnson (eds.), *Cambridge Economic History of Modern Britain*, vol. 3, p. 403.

3. On Labour's success see P. Thane, 'Labour and Welfare', p. 107.

4. Labour Party, *Time for Decision. The 1966 Labour Party Manifesto* (London, 1966), p. 2.

5. Advertisement, *Liverpool Echo* (1 June 1965), p. 9.

6. Ian White, 2000.0341, NWSA.

7. A. Crosland, *Comprehensive Education. Speech by the Secretary of State for Education and Science, at the North of England Education Conference, January 7th, 1966* (London, 1966).

8. G. Smith, 'Schools', in Halsey with Webb (eds.), *Twentieth-Century British Social Trends,* p. 199.

9. A. McPherson and J. Douglas Willms, 'Equalization and Improvement: Some Effects of Comprehensive Reorganisation in Scotland', in Halsey et al., *Education. Culture, Economy and Society*, pp. 683–702.

10. 'Comprehensive Issue a Damp Squib?', *Guardian* (18 June 1965), p. 5.

11. Chapeltown Black Women Writers' Group, *When our Ship Comes In: Black Women Talk* (Castleford, 1992), p. 29.

12. M. Sanderson, 'Education and the Labour Market', in Crafts et al. (eds.), *Work and Pay*, p. 281; A.H. Halsey, 'Higher Education', in Halsey (ed.), *British Social Trends since 1900: A Guide to the Changing Social Structure of Britain* (Basingstoke, 1988), p. 235, table 6.2.

13. P. Thane, 'Labour and Welfare', p. 108.

14. S. Bowden and A. Offer, 'Household Appliances and the Use of Time in the USA and Britain since the 1920s', *Economic History Review*, second series, vol. 47, no. 4 (1994), pp. 745–6.

15. SW20, SN 6586, UKDA.

16. Chapeltown Black Women Writers' Group, *When our Ship Comes In*, pp. 24 and 27.

17. M. Young and P. Willmott, *The Symmetrical Family. A Study of Work and Leisure in the London Region* (London, 1973), pp. 82 and 100.

18. Interview with Ann Turner, OT 603–604, Abingdon Oral History Project, OHC.

19. IPC Surveys Division, *Domestic Appliances* (London, 1967), p. 72, table 45.

20. For other examples see E. Roberts, *Women and Families: An Oral History, 1940–1970* (Oxford, 1995), p. 104.

21. H. Beynon et al., *The Rise and Transformation of the UK Domestic Appliances Industry* (Cardiff, 2003), p. 8.

22. Record no. 023, SN 4871, UKDA. See also record no. 074, SN 4871, UKDA.

23. Carter, *Home, School and Work*, p. 180.

24. Reid, *United We Stand*, pp. 291–2.

25. Yudkin and Holme, *Working Mothers and their Children*, p. 165.

26. County Borough of Warrington, Medical Officer of Health, *Annual Report of the Medical Officer of Health for the Year 1970* (Warrington, 1970), p. 5.

27. Rogaly and Taylor, *Moving Histories*, p. 119.

28. Ibid., p. 160.

29. Cairncross, 'Economic Policy and Performance, 1964–1990', p. 67.

30. J. McIlroy, N. Fishman, A. Campbell, (eds.), *British Trade Unions and Industrial Politics*, vol. 1 (Aldershot, 1999), p. 103, and A. Campbell, N. Fishman and J. McIlroy (eds.), *British Trade Unions and Industrial Politics*, vol. 2 (Ashgate, 1999), p. 120.

31. Beynon, *Working for Ford*, p. 65.

32. Reid, *United We Stand*, pp. 286–8.

33. Ibid., p. 287; see also M. Savage 'Class and Manual Workers, 1945–1979', in J. McIlroy, N. Fishman and A. Campbell (eds.), *The High Tide of British Trade Unionism: Trade Unions and Industrial Politics, 1964–79* (Monmouth, 2007).

34. Quoted in T. Lane and K. Roberts, *Strike at Pilkingtons* (London, 1971), pp. 164–5.

35. EW08, SN 6586, UKDA.

36. Cabinet Office, Cabinet conclusion on industrial relations, CAB 128/44 CC51 (69) 3, TNA.

37. R. Tomlinson, *Ricky* (London, 2003), p. 143.

38. 'This is Anarchy, Ford Girls Told', *Daily Mirror* (19 June 1968), p. 1.

39. 'Hope in "Sex War" Strike', *Daily Mirror* (15 June 1968), p. 1.

40. A. Coote and B. Campbell, *Sweet Freedom: The Struggle for Women's Liberation* (London, 1982), p. 10.

41. Department of Employment, *British Labour Statistics: Historical Abstract: 1886–1968* (London, 1982), table 2.1.

42. H. Beynon and R. Blackburn, *Perceptions of Work: Variations within a Factory* (Cambridge, 1972) p. 142.

43. Ibid.

44. Ibid., pp. 22, 115.

45. 'This is Anarchy, Ford Girls Told', p. 1.

46. 'A Woman's Worth: The Story of the Ford Sewing Machinists', Recording Women's Voices Collection, transcript available at http://www.unionhistory.info/equalpay/display.php?irn=619 (consulted 3 July 2012).

47. Interview with Sathnam Singh Gill by Hilary Young (2006). See also A. Richmond, *Migration and Race Relations in an English City: A Study of Bristol* (London, 1973), pp. 50–54.

48. Correspondence, Bristol Omnibus Company Ltd, MSS. 126/TG/RES/P/7/D, MRC, University of Warwick.
49. For a review of the mixed responses to the riots see S. Patterson, *Dark Strangers*, pp. 143–68.
50. Coventry Trades Council: correspondence, MSS.5/3/2/42,44, MRC, University of Warwick.
51. 'Immigrant Solidarity Shown in Strike by Indian Workers', *Guardian* (21 December 1965), p. 4.
52. J. DeWitt, *Indian Workers' Associations in Britain* (Oxford, 1969), pp. 15–18.
53. Ibid.
54. 'Immigrant Solidarity Shown in Strike by Indian Workers'.
55. G. Field, 'Social Patriotism and the Working Class: Appearance and Disappearance of a Tradition', *International Labor and Working-Class History*, no. 42 (1992).
56. R. Brown and P. Brannen, 'Social Relations and Social Perspectives amongst Shipbuilding Workers – A Preliminary Statement: Part Two', *Sociology*, vol. 4, no. 197 (1970), p. 207.
57. M. Roper, *Masculinity and the British Organization Man since 1945* (Oxford, 1994).
58. Record no. E11, SN6586, UKDA. See also J05, SN 6586, UKDA.
59. Record no. E07, SN 6586, UKDA.
60. R. Lowe and P. Nicholson, 'The Rediscovery of Poverty and the Creation of the Child Poverty Action Group', *Contemporary Record*, vol. 9, no. 3 (1995), pp. 602–11. On the government's relationship with CPAG see 'Child Poverty Action Group: Request to PM to Receive Manifesto December 1969', memorandum briefing ministers on CPAG, in Correspondence with CPAG, 1965–69, BN 89/142, TNA.
61. J. Tomlinson, 'The 1964 Labour Government, Poverty and Social Justice', *Benefits*, vol. 16, no. 2 (2008), pp. 135–45.
62. Barbara Castle quoted in 'Law for the Jungle', *Daily Mirror* (18 January 1969), p. 9.
63. Pilger, *Hidden Agendas*, pp. 407–8; J.W. Young, 'The Diary of Michael Stewart as British Foreign Secretary, April–May 1968', *Contemporary British History*, vol. 19, no. 4 (2005), pp. 481–510.
64. Pilger, *Hidden Agendas*, pp. 407–8.
65. 'Safari, then Steel', *The Times* (28 April 1969), p. 23; 'CBI Election Call for Curb on Wage Claims', *The Times* (21 May 1970), p. 19.

CHAPTER 14: TROUBLE AND STRIFE

1. *The Plot Against Harold Wilson*, dir. P. Dwyer, BBC 2 (2006). For years talk of these plots has been downplayed as paranoia and conspiracy theorizing, although commentators and those close to the actors have long acknowledged that conversations about coups did take place (see, for example, Young, 'Diary of Michael Stewart'). This documentary offered robust evidence that these plots did exist and were taken seriously by both Edward Heath's government and the Wilson government that succeeded him in 1974 (and which attracted far greater right-wing ire than Heath did). See also J. Freedland, 'Enough of this Cover-up: The Wilson Plot was our Watergate', *Guardian* (15 March 2006), p. 30; 'Britain's Reluctant Colonels', *Observer* (18 August 1973), p. 9.

2. Quoted in S. Milne, *The Enemy Within: The Secret War against the Miners* (London, 1995), p. 302.

3. Tomlinson, *Ricky*, p. 131.

4. 'Why They Were Jailed', *Daily Mirror* (15 January 1975), p. 5.

5. Tomlinson, *Ricky*, p. 154.

6. In fact they had only briefly been unable to buy their home. The Conservatives had enshrined the 'right to buy' in the 1936 Housing Act. This was revoked by Bevan's 1948 Housing Act, but Harold Macmillan reinstated the right to buy just six years later. That said, this remained a theoretical right for most tenants until the 1970s. Prior to 1972, local authorities had great autonomy over whether or not to sell council houses. Heath's government changed this by demanding that councils give a robust justification of why they could not sell off their council housing stock to tenants. They also provided an incentive, by allowing councils to use some of the profits to build new houses for their poorest residents. See Forrest and Murie, *Selling the Welfare State*, pp. 43–8.

7. J.B. Cullingworth, *Housing in Transition* (London, 1963), p. 197.

8. P. Thane, 'Labour and Welfare', p. 108.

9. Holmans, 'Housing', pp. 474 and 479.

10. J. Murden, 'The 1972 Kirkby Rent Strike: Dockland Solidarity in a New Setting?', paper presented to Economic History Society Annual Conference, University of Reading (2006).

11. Quoted in *Behind the Rent Strike*, dir. N. Broomfield (1974).

12. Quoted in Coote and Campbell, *Sweet Freedom*, p. 9.

13. V. Karn, 'The Financing of Owner-Occupation and its Impact on Ethnic Minorities', *New Community*, vol. 1, no. 1 (1977), pp. 49–50.

14. Interview with Ranjit Sondhi, BOHP.
15. Quoted in *Behind the Rent Strike*.
16. For an excellent discussion of the continued importance of private domestic service see Delap, *Knowing Their Place*.
17. Central Advisory Council for Education (England), *Children and their Primary Schools* (Plowden Report) (London, 1967) p. 108, table 4; and A. Rumbold et al., *Starting with Quality. The Report of the Committee of Inquiry into the Quality of the Educational Experience Offered to 3- and 4-Year-Olds* (Rumbold Report) (London, 1990), p. 54.
18. A. Murie, *The Sale of Council Houses: A Study in Social Policy* (Birmingham, 1975).
19. This figure and much of the subsequent information comes from documents held at TNA. The TNA has now provided a helpful summary: see 'British Economics and Trade Union politics 1973–1974', TNA, http://www.nationalarchives.gov.uk/releases/2005/nyo/politics. htm (consulted 16 September 2013).
20. Labour Party, *Let Us Work Together. Labour's Way out of the Crisis. The Labour Party Manifesto 1974* (London, 1974), pp. 14–15.
21. S. Holland, *The Socialist Challenge* (London, 1975), pp. 36–8.
22. T. Benn, *Against the Tide. Diaries 1973–76* (London, 1990), p. 627.
23. Ibid., p. 551.
24. 'Opinion', *Daily Express* (24 November 1976), p. 10.
25. J. Rogaly, *Grunwick* (Harmondsworth, 1977), p. 27.
26. Quoted in ibid., pp. 15–16.
27. Ibid.
28. Quoted in 'Jayaben Desai', Obituary, *Guardian* (27 December 2010), p. 18.
29. Quoted in 'Mob Rule Challenge to the Cabinet', *Daily Express* (19 June 1977), p. 1.
30. 'Madness and the Martyrs', *Daily Mirror* (24 June 1977), p. 1.
31. Quoted in Morgan, *People's Peace*, p. 385.

INTERLUDE VIII: RETURN TO CASTLEFORD

1. 'Winning the Pools – and Losing her Clothes', *Guardian* (15 March 1977), p. 9.
2. 'The Week in View', *Observer* (13 March 1977), p. 32.

CHAPTER 15: HARD TIMES

1. M. Thatcher, speech at the Lord Mayor's Banquet (10 November 1980), Margaret Thatcher Foundation, http://www.margaretthatcher.org/document/104442 (consulted 27 February 2013).

2. Atkinson and Brandolini, 'On Data', p. 384; P. Johnson, 'The Welfare State, Income and Living Standards', pp. 228–32.

3. M. Thatcher, 'Speech to Confederation of British Industry Annual Dinner' (19 April 1983), Margaret Thatcher Foundation, http://www.margaretthatcher.org/document/105295 (consulted 17 September 2011); Thatcher, 'Speech to Journalists Commemorating 5th Anniversary in Office' (27 April 1984), Margaret Thatcher Fundation, http://www.margaretthatcher.org/document/105671 (consulted 20 September 2011).

4. Quoted in B. Harrison, *Finding a Role?: The United Kingdom, 1970–1990* (Oxford, 2010), p. 149.

5. M. Thatcher, speech at general election press conference launching manifesto (international press) (18 May 1983), Margaret Thatcher Foundation, http://www.margaretthatcher.org/document/105320 (consulted 20 February 2013).

6. L. Scarman, *The Scarman Report: The Brixton Disorders 10–12 April 1981: Report of an Inquiry* (London, 1982). This is still an under-researched area of recent history. For an important survey see S.J. Lee, *Aspects of British Political History, 1914–1995* (London, 1996), p. 358.

7. Interview with Carlton Duncan, BOHP. See http://bbohp.org.uk/node/45 (consulted 16 September 2013). See also Lee, *Aspects of British Political History*, p. 358.

8. Harrison, *Finding a Role?*, p. 149.

9. R. Pahl, *Divisions of Labour* (Oxford, 1984), p. 309. See also P. Townsend et al., *Inequalities in the Northern Region. An Interim Report* (Bristol, c. 1985), p. 11.

10. A. Glyn, *The Economic Case against Pit Closures* (Sheffield, 1985).

11. Milne, *Enemy Within*, p. 5. Quotes from Ridley and Lawson also from this source, p. 7.

12. Ibid., p. 14.

13. Interview with Margaret Donovan, AUD/503, South Wales Miners' Library, Swansea.

14. B. Bloomfield, G. Boanas and R. Samuel, *The Enemy Within: Pit*

Villages and the Miners' Strike of 1984–85 (London, 1986), p. 169. See also p. 25.

15. See letters in WAIN 1/1-2, Hilary Wainwright collection, Labour History Archive, Manchester (LHA).

16. Letter from Mary Addey, 4 December 1984, WAIN 1/1, Wainwright collection, LHA.

17. Letter from Bill Burke, 4 December 1984, WAIN 1/1, Wainwright collection, LHA.

18. D. Gallie, 'The Labour Force', in Halsey with Webb (eds.), *Twentieth-Century British Social Trends*, p. 316.

19. C. Oppenheim and Child Poverty Action Group, *Poverty: The Facts* (London, 1988).

20. Social Security, HC Deb., Hansard (2 April 1987), vol. 113, col. 1250.

21. Child Poverty, HC Deb., Hansard (19 December 1989), vol. 158, cols 259–60.

22. Quoted in Family Welfare Association and Child Poverty Action Group, *Carrying the Can: Charities and the Welfare State* (London, 1984).

23. S. Winyard, *Poverty and Deprivation in Yorkshire and Humberside* (London, 1987), p. 1.

24. 'Town Centre Parking for 14,000 in Skelmersdale's Master Plan, Women Workers Will be Able to Live Near Jobs', *Liverpool Echo* (2 June 1965), p. 19.

25. Holmans, *Housing*, pp. 487–9.

26. C. Peach and M. Byron, 'Council House Sales, Residualisation and Afro Caribbean Tenants', *Journal of Social Policy*, vol. 23, no. 3 (1994), pp. 363–83; Taylor and Rogaly, *Moving Histories*, pp. 79–91.

27. B. Deacon, *Poverty and Deprivation in the South West* (London, 1987), p. 6.

28. Interview with Clare Stevens, Bristol Reference Library.

29. Deacon, *Poverty and Deprivation*, p. 14.

30. Ibid.

31. H. Joshi, 'The Changing Form of Women's Economic Dependency', in H. Joshi (ed.), *The Changing Population of Britain* (Oxford, 1989); and Joshi, 'The Opportunity Costs of Childbearing: More than Mothers' Business', *Journal of Population Economics*, vol. 11, no. 2 (1998).

32. B. Campbell, *Wigan Pier Revisited: Poverty and Politics in the Eighties* (London, 1984).

33. L. Harker, *A Secure Future? Social Security and the Family in a Changing World* (London, 1996), p. 6.

34. D. Coleman, 'Population and Family', in Halsey with Webb (eds.), *Twentieth-Century British Social Trends*, p. 62.

35. Joshi, 'Women's Economic Dependency'.

36. Quoted in T. Parker, *The People of Providence: A Housing Estate and Some of its Inhabitants* (London, 1983), p. 56.

37. Kinnock's speech was reported around the world; see 'Kinnock Fights Copycat-party Image', *New York Times* (30 September 1987), p. 12.

38. Quoted in S. Fielding, *The Labour Party: Continuity and Change in the Making of 'New' Labour* (Basingstoke, 2003), p. 134.

39. R. Hefferman and M. Marqusee, *Defeat from the Jaws of Victory: Inside Kinnock's Labour Party* (London, 1992).

40. Interview with Chris Colbeck, interview no. 035, 100 Families study, SN 4938, UKDA.

41. Quoted in Fielding, *Labour Party*, p. 137.

42. Quoted in ibid., p. 141.

43. Chris Colbeck, 035, SN4938, UKDA.

44. Interview with Melanie Pilkington, interview no. 107, SN 4938, UKDA.

45. D. Hayes and A. Hudson, *Basildon: The Mood of the Nation* (London, 2001), p. 50. See also Devine, *Affluent Workers Revisited*, p. 7.

46. Quoted in J. Lawrence and F. Sutcliffe-Braithwaite, 'Margaret Thatcher and the Decline of Class Politics', in B. Jackson and R. Saunders (eds.), *Making Thatcher's Britain* (Cambridge, 2013), p. 146. Thanks to Jon Lawrence for sending me a copy of this chapter in proof.

47. Margaret Thatcher, speech to Conservative Central Council (18 March 1987), Margaret Thatcher Foundation, http://www.margaretthatcher. org/document/107605 (consulted 10 April 2012).

48. Margaret Thatcher, interview for *Woman's Own* (23 September 1987), Margaret Thatcher Foundation, http://www.margaretthatcher.org/ document/106689 (consulted 10 April 2012).

49. Deborah Temple, interview no. 139, SN 4938, UKDA.

50. A. Park and P. Surridge, 'Charting Change in British Values', in Park et al., *British Social Attitudes. The Twentieth Report*, p.152.

51. Interview with Louise Beckwith, interview no. 10, SN 4938, UKDA.

52. Winyard, *Poverty*, p. 1.

53. Ibid., p. 3.

54. S. Charlesworth, *A Phenomenology of Working-Class Experience* (Cambridge, 2000), pp. 171, 259, 269.

55. E.P. Thornley and S.G. Siann, 'The Career Aspirations of South Asian Girls in Glasgow', *Gender and Education*, vol. 3, no. 3 (1991), pp. 237–48.

56. Chris Colbeck, 035, SN 4938, UKDA.

57. V. Walkerdine, 'Reclassifying Upward Mobility: Femininity and the Neo-liberal Subject', *Gender and Education*, vol. 15, no. 3 (2003), p. 243.

CHAPTER 16: A CLASSLESS SOCIETY

1. For example, *Guardian*/ICM poll, 2007, reported in 'Riven by Class and No Social Mobility', *Guardian* (20 October 2007), p. 3; A. Park et al. (eds.), *British Social Attitudes: The 23rd Report. Perspectives on a Changing Society* (London, 2007); Gallup/MORI, 'Class and the British', 2006; A Park et al. (eds.), *British Social Attitudes: The 27th Report* (London, 2010).

2. Figures taken from http://www.poverty.org.uk/09/index.shtml (consulted 18 January 2013) and R. Wilkinson and K. Pickett, *The Spirit Level. Why Greater Equality Makes Societies Stronger* (London, 2010), pp. 17–18.

3. Wilkinson and Pickett, *Spirit Level*, pp. 63–72 and 129–44.

4. Quoted in *Today* (24 November 1990).

5. Tony Blair quoted in Fielding, *The Labour Party. Continuity and Change*, p. 80.

6. Quoted in Hayes and Hudson, *Basildon*, p. 30.

7. Department for Work and Pensions, *The Results of the Area Benefit Review and the Quality Support Team from April 2000 to March 2001: Fraud and Error in Claims for Income Support and Jobseeker's Allowance* (London, 2002). See also K.A. Grove, 'Understanding Benefit Fraud: A Qualitative Analysis', Ph.D. thesis, University of Leeds (2002); S. Brand and R. Price, *The Economic and Social Costs of Crime*, Home Office Research Study no. 217 (London, 2000), table 4.6.

8. Labour Party, *New Labour because Britain Deserves Better* (London, 1997), p. 2.

9. Social Exclusion Unit (SEU), *Bringing Britain Together: A National Strategy for Neighbourhood Renewal* (London, 1998), p. 2.

10. Quoted in S. Fielding, *Labour: Decline and Renewal* (Manchester, 1999), p. 148.

11. Quoted in ibid., p. 106.

12. David Blunkett, quoted in ibid., p. 146.

13. A. Minton, *Ground Control: Fear and Happiness in the Twenty-first-century City* (London, 2012).

14. S. Griffiths, *A Profile of Poverty and Health in Manchester* (Manchester, 1998).

15. S.P. Jenkins, 'Dynamics of Household Incomes', in R. Berthoud et al. (eds.), *Seven Years in the Lives of British Families: Evidence on the Dynamics of Social Change from the British Household Panel Survey* (Bristol, 2000), p. 127. See also C. Pantazis, D. Gordon and R. Levitas,

Poverty and Social Exclusion in Britain: The Millennium Survey (Bristol, 2006), p. 21.

16. See also ibid.

17. Wilkinson and Pickett, *The Spirit Level*, pp. 85–6.

18. Health and Safety Executive, *Managing Shiftwork* (London, 2006), p. 10.

19. P. Thane, *Old Age in English History. Past Experiences, Present Issues* (Oxford, 2000), p. 491.

20. R. Fitzpatrick and T. Chandola, 'Health', in Halsey with Webb (eds.), *Twentieth-Century British Social Trends*, pp. 110–13.

21. Interview with Bill and Barbara Rainford by Hilary Young (2007).

22. BritainThinks, *What about the Workers? A New Study on the Working Class* (London, 2011), p. 6.

23. I contacted twenty former classmates using social networking sites. We either spoke in person or corresponded by email. What follows is also supported by contemporary sociological work including R. Sennett, *The Corrosion of Character. The Personal Consequences of Work in the New Capitalism* (London, 1998).

24. Halsey, 'Further and Higher Education', p. 226.

25. John Henderson to the author (2013).

26. Shelley Landale-Down to the author (2013).

27. Jack M (pseudonym) to the author (2012).

28. D. Gallie, 'The Labour Force', in Halsey with Webb (eds.), *Twentieth-Century British Social Trends*, p. 288.

29. Jacqueline Robinson to the author (2013).

30. Tony Blair, quoted in Fielding, *Continuity and Change*, p. 80.

31. Sandra Hastings to the author (2013).

32. R. Dickens, P. Gregg and J. Wadsworth (eds.), *The Labour Market under New Labour* (Basingstoke, 2003); Harker, *A Secure Future?*, pp. 4–5.

33. Prime Minister's Office of Public Services Reform, *Principles into Practice* (London, 2002).

34. Office of National Statistics, 'Working Days Lost', http://www.hse.gov.uk/statistics/dayslost.htm (consulted 23 January 2013).

35. Chartered Institute for Personnel and Development, 'Absence Management Annual Survey', http://www.cipd.co.uk/research/_absence-management (consulted 23 January 2013); S. Bevan, 'Sickness Presence Makes the Heart Grow Weaker?', Work Foundation, http://www.theworkfoundation.com/blog/920/Sickness-presence-makes-the-heart-grow-weaker (consulted 23 January 2013).

36. Sennett, *Corrosion of Character*, p. 148.

37. Ibid., ch. 2.

38. George Osborne, speech at the Conservative Party Annual Conference (8 October 2012), quoted on http://www.channel4.com/news/osborne-unveils-10bn-benefits-cut-package (consulted 18 January 2013).

39. David Cameron quoted in 'Broken Society is Top Priority – Cameron', www.bbc.co.uk/news.15/08/2011 (consulted 13 January 2013).

40. A. Chakrabortty, 'To Understand the Deepening Mess We are in Now, it's Worth Looking at the Words of a Polish Economist in 1944', *Guardian: G2* (15 January 2013), p. 4.

41. S. Milne, 'There is a Problem with Welfare, but it's not "Shirkers"', *Guardian*, http://www.guardian.co.uk/commentisfree/2013/jan/08/welfare-problem-real-scroungers-greedy (consulted 18 January 2013).

42. Maria Ferguson to the author (2013).

43. 'Deborah Mattinson: From Cloth Caps to Cafetieres', *Independent on Sunday* (20 March 2011), p. 5; BritainThinks, *Speaking Middle English. A Study on the Middle Classes* (London, 2011).

44. Milne, 'There is a Problem with Welfare'; 'Voters "Brainwashed by Tory Welfare Myths"', *Independent*, http://www.independent.co.uk/news/uk/politics/voters-brainwashed-by-tory-welfare-myths-shows-new-poll-8437872.html (consulted 22 January 2013).

45. For a brilliant account of this attitude among American blue-collar workers see R. Sennett and J. Cobb, *The Hidden Injuries of Class* (New York, 1972) pp. 138–40.

46. G. Hewitt, 'The BNP and the White Working Class', http://www.bbc.co.uk/blogs/thereporters/gavinhewitt/2009/10/the_bnp_and_the_white_working.html, 22 October 2009 (consulted 24 January 2013); R. Klein, 'White and Working Class', *Daily Mail* (29 February 2008). Klein commissioned the BBC's 'White Season'.

47. A conclusion also reached by Hayes and Hudson, *Basildon*, pp. 39, 50–51.

48. Ibid., pp. 50–52.

49. O. Jones, *Chavs: The Demonization of the Working Class* (London, 2012), p. xv.

50. Interview with Deborah Temple, 100 Families.

51. Happygardening, post on thread 'boarding prep to local comp', Mumsnet, 16 May 2011, http://www.mumsnet.com/Talk/education/1214948-boarding-prep-to-local-comp/AllOnOnePage (consulted 26 April 2013).

52. 'The Meaning of Life in School', *Guardian: Education* (6 September 2009), p. 1.

53. Lardass, post on thread 'Cheltenham Ladies College or Wycombe

Abbey?', Mumsnet, 19 March 2012, http://www.mumsnet.com/Talk/secondary/a1419346-Cheltenham-Ladies-College-or-Wycombe-Abbey, (consulted 26 April 2013).

54. Amck700 post on thread 'Why on Earth would you go State if you could Afford Private?', Mumsnet, 20 February 2013, http://www.mumsnet.com/Talk/education/a1688558-Why-on-earth-would-you-go-state-if-you-could-afford-private (consulted 26 April 2013).

55. Shagmundfreud, post on thread 'Schools and their Ethnic Make-up', Mumsnet, 12 March 2012, http://www.mumsnet.com/Talk/education/a1703982-Schools-and-their-ethnic-makeup (consulted 26 April 2013). On parents choosing schools for their social and ethnic composition see M. Benn, *School Wars: The Battle for Britain's Education* (London, 2011) and D. Reay, *White Middle-class Identities and Urban Schooling* (Basingstoke, 2011).

56. P. Toynbee, 'This Bold Equality Push is Just What we Needed. In 1997', *Guardian* (28 April 2009), p. 9.

57. B. Skeggs, 'Haunted by the Spectre of Judgement: Respectability, Value and Affect in Class Relations', in K.P. Sveinsson (ed.) and Runnymede Trust, *Who Cares about the White Working Class?* (London, 2009), pp. 36–44; Walkerdine, 'Reclassifying Upward Mobility'.

58. 'The Spirit Level', *Guardian* (14 August 2010), http://www.guardian.co.uk/books/2010/aug/14/the-spirit-level-equality-thinktanks?intcmp=239, (consulted 21 January 2013).

59. British Future, *State of the Nation* (London, 2013), p. 3.

60. BritainThinks, *Middle English*, p. 37.

61. 'What is Working Class?', *BBC Magazine*, http://news.bbc.co.uk/1/hi/magazine/6295743.stm (consulted 20 September 2013).

62. B. Skeggs, *Formations of Class and Gender: Becoming Respectable* (London, 1997); M. Savage, G. Bagnall and B. Longhurst, 'Ordinary, Ambivalent and Defensive: Class Identities in North-west England', *Sociology*, vol. 35, no. 4 (2001), pp. 875–92. On the negative connotations of being working class, see also T. Woodin, 'Muddying the Waters: Changes in Class and Identity in a Working-class Cultural Organisation', *Sociology*, vol. 39, no. 5 (2005), pp. 1001–18.

63. Hayes and Hudson, *Basildon*, p. 35.

64. D. Hayes and A. Hudson, 'Basildon Man: Beyond the Shell-suits', *Spikedonline*, http://www.spiked-online.com/newsite/article/11735#.UimUWhwug9A (consulted 3 March 2012).

65. A. Park et al. (eds.), *British Social Attitudes: The 29th Report* (London, 2013), pp. vi–vii.

EPILOGUE

1. 'What happened next?', *Observer* (6 July 2003), accessed online at http://www.guardian.co.uk/theobserver/2003/jul/06/features.magazine67 (4 January 2013); S. Browne and J. Greene, *Spend, Spend, Spend*, dir. J. Sams (1999).

2. 'Spend, Spend, Spent', *Daily Mail* (22 April 2007); website http://www.dailymail.co.uk/femail/article-449820/Spent-spent-spent--pools-winner-living-87-week.html (consulted 20 September 2010).

3. British Future, *State of the Nation*, p. 3.

4. BritainThinks, *What About the Workers?*, p. 26.

Select Bibliography

The date given in each entry is that of the edition used, rather than of first publication.

UNPUBLISHED MATERIAL

Birmingham City Library: Birmingham Black Oral History Archive
Bodleian Library, University of Oxford: Conservative Party Archive
Brighton Museum, My Brighton and Hove archive, http://www.mybrightonandhove.org.uk
Bristol City Library: Bristol oral history collections
East Sussex Record Office: Lewes in Living Memory oral history collection
The Immigrants Project: http://theimmigrantsproject.org
Imperial War Museum: oral history collection
Labour History Archive, People's History Museum, Manchester: Labour Party Archive and Hilary Wainwright Archive
Lancashire Record Office: North West Sound Archive
Leicestershire Record Office: Wolsey strike papers
Liverpool Central Library: Liverpool Corporation Archives
London Metropolitan University: TUC Archive
Margaret Thatcher Foundation: Margaret Thatcher's speeches
Modern Records Centre, University of Warwick: TUC Archive
Nottingham Local Studies Library: Making Ends Meet oral history collection
Nuffield College, Oxford: Great Britain Social Survey
Oxfordshire History Centre: oral history collections
South Wales Miners' Library: oral history collections
Tameside Local Studies Library: Manchester Studies oral history collection

The National Archives: Cabinet Office, Ministry of Education, Ministry of Housing and Ministry of Labour papers

UK Data Archive: SN 2000, Family Life and Work Experience Before 1918; SN 4871, Digitized sample of The Affluent Worker in the Class Structure, 1961–1962; SN 4938, 100 Families; SN 6567, Crown Street, 1955–1963 and SN 6586, Digitization of Richard Brown, Orientation to Work and Industrial Behaviour of Shipbuilding Workers 1968–1969: manual workers' questionnaires

University of Essex: the National Social Policy and Social Change Archive

University of Lancaster: the Elizabeth Roberts Archive

University of Liverpool: Family Service Units Archive and Merseyside Social Surveys Archive

University of Sheffield: Left Book Club Archive

University of Strathclyde: Scottish Oral History Archive

University of Sussex: Mass-Observation Archive

BIOGRAPHICAL MATERIAL

Athill, D., *Life Class: The Selected Memoirs of Diana Athill* (London: Granta, 2009)

Balderson, E. with D. Goodlad, *Backstairs Life in a Country House* (Newton Abbott: David and Charles, 1982)

Ballard, J., *Miracles of Life: An Autobiography* (London: Fourth Estate, 2008)

Barstow, S., *In My Own Good Time* (Otley: Smith Settle, 2001)

Beckwith, M., *When I Remember* (London: Nicholson and Watson, 1936)

Belle Vale Prefab Project, *Prefab Days: A Community Remembers* (Liverpool: Enterprise, 2008)

Benn, T., *Against the Tide: Diaries 1973–76* (London: Arrow, 1990)

Benson, E., *To Struggle is to Live*, 2 vols. (Newcastle: People's Publications, 1980)

Brittain, V., *Testament of Youth: An Autobiographical Study of the Years 1900–1925* (London: V. Gollancz, 1978)

——*Testament of Experience: An Autobiographical Study of the Years 1925–1950* (London: Virago, 1979)

Bryan, B., S. Dadzie and S. Scafe, *The Heart of the Race: Black Women's Lives in Britain* (London: Virago, 1985)

Burnett, J., *Useful Toil: Autobiographies of Working People from the 1820s to the 1920s* (London: Allen Lane, 1974)

——*Idle Hands: The Experience of Unemployment, 1790–1990* (London: Routledge, 1994)

Castle, B., *Fighting All the Way* (London: Macmillan, 1993)

Chapeltown Black Women Writers' Group, *When Our Ship Comes In: Black Women Talk* (Castleford: Yorkshire Art Circus, 1992)

Colls, R., 'When We Lived in Communities', in Colls and R. Rodger (eds.), *Cities of Ideas. Governance and Citizenship in Urban Britain 1800–2000: Essays in Honour of David Reeder* (Aldershot: Ashgate, 2005)

Courtenay, T., *Dear Tom: Letters from Home* (London: Black Swan, 2001)

Davies, H., *The Beatles, Football, and Me: A Memoir* (London: Headline, 2006)

Foley, A., *A Bolton Childhood* (Manchester: WEA, 1973)

Foley, W., *Child in the Forest* (London: BBC, 1974)

——*The Forest Trilogy* (Oxford: Blackwell, 1992)

Forster, M., *Hidden Lives: A Family Memoir* (London: Penguin, 1996)

Goldman, W., *East End My Cradle* (London: Robson, 1988)

Halsey, A.H., *No Discouragement: An Autobiography* (Basingstoke: Macmillan, 1996)

Heron, L. (ed.), *Truth, Dare or Promise: Girls Growing Up in the 50s* (London: Virago, 1985)

Hoggart, R., *The Uses of Literacy* (Harmondsworth: Penguin, 1957)

Last, N., R. Broad and S. Fleming, *Nella Last's War: The Second World War Diaries of Housewife, 49* (London: Profile, 2006)

Last, N., P. and R. Malcolmson, *Nella Last's Peace: The Second World War Diaries of Housewife, 49* (London: Profile, 2008)

——*Nella Last in the 1950s* (London: Profile, 2010)

Lee, L., *As I Walked Out One Midsummer Morning* (Harmondsworth: Penguin, 1971)

Lessing, D., *Walking in the Shade: Volume Two of my Autobiography, 1949–1962* (London: HarperCollins, 1998)

Lifetimes Group, *A Couple from Manchester* (Manchester: Manchester Polytechnic, 1975)

——*Something in Common* (Manchester: Manchester Polytechnic, 1975)

MacColl, E., *Journeyman* (London: Sidgwick and Jackson, 1990)

MacDougall, I. (ed.), *Voices from the Hunger Marches* (Edinburgh: Polygon, 1991)

Marshall, S., *Fenland Chronicle: Recollections of William Henry and Kate Mary Edwards Collected and Edited by Her Daughter* (Cambridge: Cambridge University Press, 1967)

Mitchell, H., *The Hard Way Up: The Autobiography of Hannah Mitchell, Suffragette and Rebel* (London: Virago, 1977)

Mitford, J., *Hons and Rebels* (London: Indigo, 1996)

Mullins, S. and G. Griffiths, *Cap and Apron: An Oral History of Domestic Service in the Shires, 1880–1950* (Leicester: Leicestershire Museums, c.1986)

Nicholson, V. with S. Smith, *Spend, Spend, Spend* (London: Jonathan Cape, 1977)

Pickles, H., *Crooked Sixpences Among the Chalk* (Hawes: Leading Edge, 1993)

Roberts, R., *The Classic Slum* (Hardmondsworth: Penguin, 1974)

Sage, L., *Bad Blood: A Memoir* (London: Fourth Estate, 2000)

Second Chance to Learn Women's History Group, *No One Ever Mentions Love: An Inside View of Black and White Relationships* (Liverpool: Liverpool Community College, 1997)

Snowden, P., *An Autobiography* (London: Nicholson and Watson, 1934)

Steedman, C., *Landscape for a Good Woman* (London: Virago, 1986)

Thompson, F., *Lark Rise to Candleford* (Harmondsworth: Penguin, 1973)

Tomlinson, R., *Ricky* (London: Time Warner, 2003)

Warren, T., *I Was Ena Sharples' Father* (London: Duckworth, 1969)

Whitehorn, K., *Selective Memory* (London: Virago, 2007)

CONTEMPORARY BOOKS

Abel-Smith, B. and P. Townsend, *The Poor and the Poorest: A New Analysis of the Ministry of Labour's Family Expenditure Surveys of 1953–54 and 1960* (London: Bell, 1965)

Beales, H.L. and R.S. Lambert (eds.), *Memoirs of the Unemployed* (London: V. Gollancz, 1934)

Berthoud, R. et al. (eds.), *Seven Years in the Lives of British Families: Evidence on the Dynamics of Social Change from the British Household Panel Survey* (Bristol: Policy, 2000)

Beynon, H., *Working for Ford* (Harmondsworth: Penguin, 1975)

Beynon, H. and R.M. Blackburn, *Perceptions of Work: Variations Within a Factory* (Cambridge: Cambridge University Press, 1972)

Black, E.I. and T.S. Simey, *Neighbourhood and Community: An Enquiry into Social Relationships on Housing Estates in Liverpool and Sheffield* (Liverpool: Liverpool University Press, 1954)

Bott, E., *Family and Social Networks: Roles, Norms, and External Relationships in Ordinary Urban Families* (London: Tavistock, 1957)

Bowley, A.L. and M. Hogg, *Has Poverty Diminished?* (London: P.S. King, 1925)

BritainThinks, *Speaking Middle English: A Study on the Middle Classes* (London: BritainThinks, 2011)

—*What About the Workers? A New Study on the Working Class* (London: BritainThinks, 2011)

British Future, *State of the Nation* (London: British Future, 2013)

Brothers, J., *Church and School: A Study of the Impact of Education on Religion* (Liverpool: Liverpool University Press, 1964)

Butler, C.V., *Domestic Service. An Enquiry by the Women's Industrial Council* (London: G. Bell, 1916)

Cameron, C., A. Lush and G. Meara, *Disinherited Youth: A Report on the 18+ Age Group Enquiry Prepared for the Trustees of the Carnegie United Kingdom Trust* (Edinburgh: Constable, 1943)

Campbell, B., *Wigan Pier Revisited: Poverty and Politics in the Eighties* (London: Virago, 1984)

Caradog Jones, D., *Social Survey of Merseyside*, 3 vols. (Liverpool: Liverpool University Press, 1934)

Carter, M.P., *Home, School and Work: A Study of the Education and Employment of Young People in Britain* (Oxford: Pergamon Press, 1962)

Casswell, J., *The Law of Domestic Servants: With a chapter on the National Insurance Act, 1911* (London: Jordan, 1913)

Charlesworth, A., *A Phenomenology of Working-Class Experience* (Cambridge: Cambridge University Press, 2000)

Coates, K. and R. Silburn, *Poverty. The Forgotten Englishman* (Harmondsworth: Penguin, 1970)

Collison, P., *The Cutteslowe Walls: A Study in Social Class* (London: Faber and Faber, 1963)

Crosland, A., *Comprehensive Education. Speech by the Secretary of State for Education and Science, at the North of England Education Conference, January 7th, 1966* (London: Labour Party, 1966)

Cullingworth, J.B., *Housing in Greater London* (London: LSE, 1961)

—*Housing in Transition: A Case Study in the City of Lancaster, 1958–1962* (London: Heinemann, 1963)

Davies, M.L. (ed.), *Life as We Have Known It* (London: Virago, 1984)

Dennis, N., F. Henriques and C. Slaughter, *Coal Is Our Life. An Analysis of a Yorkshire Mining Community* (London: Eyre and Spottiswoode, 1956)

Douglas, J.W.B. and H.R. Simpson, *All our Future: A Longitudinal Study of Secondary Education* (London: P. Davies, 1971)

Family Welfare Association and Child Poverty Action Group, *Carrying the Can: Charities and the Welfare State* (London: CPAG, 1984)

Floud, J.E. (ed.), with A.H. Halsey and F.M. Martin, *Social Class and Educational Opportunity* (London: Heinemann, 1956)

Gavron, H., *The Captive Wife: Conflicts of Housebound Mothers* (Harmondsworth: Penguin, 1968)

Glass, D. (ed.), *Social Mobility in Britain* (London: Routledge, 1954)

Glyn, A., *The Economic Case against Pit Closures* (Sheffield: National Union of Mineworkers, 1985)

Goldthorpe, J.H., D. Lockwood, F. Bechofer and J. Platt, *The Affluent Worker: Industrial Attitudes and Behaviour* (Cambridge: Cambridge University Press, 1968)

——*The Affluent Worker in the Class Structure* (Cambridge: Cambridge University Press, 1969)

Gordon, D. and C. Pantazis, *Breadline Britain in the 1990s* (Aldershot: Ashgate, 1997)

Harrisson, T., *Britain Revisited* (London: V. Gollancz, 1961)

——*Living Through the Blitz* (London: Collins, 1976)

Harrisson, T. and C. Madge, *War Begins at Home* (London: Chatto and Windus, 1940)

Hayes, D. and A. Hudson, *Basildon: The Mood of the Nation* (London: Demos, 2001)

Hemel Hempstead Development Corporation, *The Development of Hemel Hempstead* (Hemel Hempstead: Hemel Hempstead Corporation, 1952)

Holland, S., *The Socialist Challenge* (London: Quartet, 1975)

Jackson, B. and D. Marsden, *Education and the Working Class: Some General Themes Raised by a Study of 88 Children in a Northern Industrial City* (Harmondsworth: Penguin, 1966)

Jephcott, P., *Rising Twenty: Notes on Some Ordinary Girls* (London: Faber and Faber, 1948)

——*Some Young People* (London: Allen and Unwin, 1954)

Jephcott, P., N. Seear and J. Smith, *Married Women Working* (London: Allen and Unwin, 1962)

Jones, O., *Chavs: The Demonization of the Working Class* (London: Verso, 2012)

Kerr, M., *The People of Ship Street* (London: Routledge and Kegan Paul, 1958)

Kuper, L. (ed.), *Living in Towns: Selected Research Papers in Urban Sociology of the Faculty of Commerce and Social Science, University of Birmingham* (London: Cresset Press, 1953)

Madge, C., *War-time Patterns of Saving and Spending* (Cambridge: Cambridge University Press, 1943)

Madge, C., and T. Harrisson, *Britain by Mass Observation* (Harmondsworth: Penguin, 1939)

Marsden, D., *Mothers Alone: Poverty and the Fatherless Family* (London: Allen Lane, 1969)

Mogey, J.M., *Family and Neighbourhood: Two Studies in Oxford* (London: Oxford University Press, 1956)

Muchnick, D.M., *Urban Renewal in Liverpool: A Study of the Politics of Redevelopment* (London: Bell, 1970)

Orwell, G., *The Road to Wigan Pier* (London: V. Gollancz, 1937)

Pantazis, C., D. Gordon and R. Levitas, *Poverty and Social Exclusion in Britain: The Millennium Survey* (Bristol: Policy, 2006)

Park, A. et al. (eds.), *British Social Attitudes: The 20th Report* (London: Sage, 2003).

——*British Social Attitudes: The 22nd Report. Two Terms of New Labour: The Public's Reaction* (London: Sage, 2005)

——*British Social Attitudes: The 23rd Report. Perspectives on a Changing Society* (London: Sage, 2007)

——*British Social Attitudes: The 26th Report* (London: Sage, 2010)

——*British Social Attitudes: The 27th Report* (London: Sage, 2010)

——*British Social Attitudes: The 29th Report* (London: Sage, 2013)

Parker, T., *The People of Providence: A Housing Estate and Some of its Inhabitants* (London: Hutchinson, 1983)

Patterson, S., *Dark Strangers: A Sociological Study of the Absorption of a Recent West Indian Migrant Group in Brixton, South London* (London: Tavistock, 1963)

Pember Reeves, M., *Round About a Pound a Week* (London: G. Bell, 1913)

Pickett, K.G., *Migration and Social Adjustment: Kirkby and Maghull* (Liverpool: Liverpool University Press, 1974)

Political and Economic Planning, *Family Needs and the Social Services* (London: Allen and Unwin, 1961)

Priestley, J.B., *English Journey. Being a rambling but truthful account of what one man saw and heard and felt and thought during a journey through England during the autumn of the year 1933* (London: Heinemann and V. Gollancz, 1934)

Richmond, A.A., *The Colour Problem* (Harmondsworth: Penguin, 1955)

——*Migration and Race Relations in an English City: A Study in Bristol* (London: Oxford University Press, 1973)

Rogaly, J., *Grunwick* (Harmondsworth: Penguin, 1977)

Rosser, C. and C. Harris, *The Family and Social Change: A Study of Family and Kinship in a South Wales Town* (London: Routledge and Kegan Paul, 1965)

Rowntree, B.S., *Poverty and Progress: A Second Social Survey of York* (London: Longman, 1941)

Rowntree, B.S. and G.R. Lavers, *Poverty and the Welfare State: A Third Social Survey of York Dealing only with Economic Questions* (London: Longman Green, 1951)

Scarman, L., *The Scarman Report: The Brixton Disorders 10–12 April 1981: Report of an Inquiry* (London: HMSO, 1982)

Smith, H.L., *New Survey of London Life and Labour*, 9 vols. (London: P.S. King, 1934–5)

Spence, J., *A Thousand Families in Newcastle-upon-Tyne: An Approach to the Study of Health and Illness in Children* (London: Oxford University Press, 1954)

Spring Rice, M., *Working-Class Wives: Their Health and Conditions* (Harmondsworth: Penguin, 1939)

Stacey, M., *Tradition and Change: A Study of Banbury* (London: Oxford University Press, 1960)

——*Power, Persistence and Change: A Second Study of Banbury* (London: Routledge and Kegan Paul, 1975)

Sveinsson, K.P. (ed.) and Runnymede Trust, *Who Cares about the White Working Class?* (London: Runnymede Trust, 2009)

Temple, W. and the Pilgrim Trust, *Men without Work* (Cambridge: Cambridge University Press, 1938)

Titmuss, R.M., *Birth, Poverty and Wealth: A Study of Infant Mortality* (London: Hamish Hamilton, 1943)

——*Problems of Social Policy* (London: HMSO, 1950)

——*Essays on the Welfare State* (London: Allen and Unwin, 1959)

Tout, H., *The Standard of Living in Bristol: A Preliminary Report of the Work of the University of Bristol Social Survey* (Bristol: Arrowsmith, 1938)

Townsend, P., *The Family Life of Old People: An Inquiry in East London* (London: Institute of Community Studies, 1957)

——*Poverty in the United Kingdom* (Harmondsworth: Penguin, 1979)

Townsend, P. and N. Davidson, *Inequalities in Health: The Black Report* (Harmondsworth: Penguin, 1982)

Vereker, C. and J.B. Mays, *Urban Redeveloment and Social Change: A Study of Social Conditions in Central Liverpool, 1955–56* (Liverpool: Liverpool University Press, 1961)

Wilkinson, R. and K. Pickett, *The Spirit Level: Why Greater Equality Makes Societies Stronger* (London: Penguin, 2010)

Williams, R., *The Long Revolution* (Harmondsworth: Penguin, 1965)

Willmott, P., *Evolution of a Community. A Study of Dagenham After Forty Years* (London: Institute of Community Studies, 1963)

——*Adolescent Boys of East London* (London: Institute of Community Studies, 1966)

Women's Group on Public Welfare, *Our Towns: A Close-Up* (Oxford: Oxford University Press, 1944)

Young, M., and P. Willmott, *Family and Kinship in East London* (London: Routledge and Kegan Paul, 1957)

——*Family and Class in a London Suburb* (London: Routledge and Kegan Paul, 1960)

——*The Symmetrical Family: A Study of Work and Leisure in the London Region* (Harmondsworth: Penguin, 1973)

Yudkin, S. and A. Holme, *Working Mothers and Their Children: A Study for the Council for Children's Welfare* (London: Sphere, 1963)

Zweig, F., *Labour, Life and Poverty* (London: V. Gollancz, 1948)

——*Women's Life and Labour* (London: V. Gollancz, 1952)

——*The Worker in an Affluent Society: Family Life and Industry* (London: Heinemann, 1961)

CONTEMPORARY ARTICLES

Broady, M., 'The Organisation of Coronation Street Parties', *Sociological Review*, vol. 4, no. 2 (1956)

Brown, R. and P. Brannen, 'Social Relations and Social Perspectives amongst Shipbuilding Workers – A Preliminary Statement' parts 1 and 2, *Sociology*, vol. 4, no. 197 (1970)

Davison, R., 'Britain Abolishes the Household Means Test', *Social Service Review*, vol. 15, no. 3 (1942)

Donnison, D.V., 'The Movement of Households in England', *Journal of the Royal Statistical Society*, Series A, vol. 124, no. 1 (1961)

Floud, J.E. and A.H. Halsey, 'Intelligence Tests, Social Class and Selection for Secondary Schools', *British Journal of Sociology*, vol. 8, no. 1 (March 1957)

Mildon, I. and I. Wallis, 'West Indian Home Owners in Croydon', *New Community*, vol. 6, nos. 1 and 2 (1977–8)

Mogey, J.M., 'Changes in Family Life Experienced by English Workers Moving from Slums to Council Estates', *Marriage and Family Living*, vol. 17, no. 2 (1955)

Rodgers, H.B., 'Employment and the Journey to Work in an Overspill Community', *Sociological Review*, vol. 7, no. 2 (1959)

Young, M., 'Distribution of Income within the Family', *British Journal of Sociology*, vol. 3, no. 4 (1952)

HISTORIES AND COMMENTARIES (BOOKS)

Addison, P., *Now the War Is Over: A Social History of Britain, 1945–51* (London: BBC, 1985)

Alexander, B., *British Volunteers for Liberty: Spain, 1936–1939* (London: Lawrence and Wishart, 1986)

Alexander, S., *Becoming a Woman and Other Essays in Nineteenth and Twentieth Century Feminist History* (London: Virago, 1992)

Bain, G.S. and R. Price, *Profiles of Union Growth: A Comparative Statistical Portrait of Eight Countries* (Oxford: Blackwell, 1980)

Barron, H., *The Miners' Lockout: Meanings of Community in the Durham Coalfield* (Oxford: Clarendon, 2009)

Bingham, A., *Gender, Modernity and the Popular Press in Interwar Britain* (Oxford: Clarendon, 2004)

Black, L. and H. Pemberton (eds.), *An Affluent Society? Britain's Post-War 'Golden Age' Revisited* (Aldershot: Ashgate, 2004)

Bloomfield, B., G. Boanas and R. Samuel, *The Enemy Within: Pit Villages and the Miners' Strike of 1984–85* (London: Routledge, 1986)

Bullock, A., *The Life and Times of Ernest Bevin*, 3 vols. (London: Heinemann, 1966–83)

Burnett, J., *A Social History of Housing, 1815–1970* (Newton Abbot: David and Charles, 1978)

Calder, P., *The People's War: Britain 1939–45* (London: Cape, 1969)

Cannadine, D., *The Decline and Fall of the British Aristocracy* (New Haven: Yale University Press, 1992)

Clapson, M., *Invincible Green Suburbs, Brave New Towns* (Manchester: Manchester University Press, 1998)

Conekin, B., F. Mort and C. Waters (eds.), *Moments of Modernity: Reconstructing Britain, 1945–1964* (London: Rivers Oram, 1999)

Crafts, N., I. Gazeley and A. Newell (eds.), *Work and Pay in Twentieth Century Britain* (Oxford: Oxford University Press, 2007)

Davies, A., *Leisure, Gender and Poverty: Working-Class Culture in Salford and Manchester, 1900–1939* (Buckingham: Open University Press, 1992)

——*City of Gangs: Glasgow and the Rise of the British Gangster* (London: Hodder, 2013)

Davies, A. and S. Fielding, (eds.), *Workers' Worlds: Cultures and Communities in Manchester and Salford, 1880–1939* (Manchester: Manchester University Press, 1992)

Delap, L., *Knowing their Place: Domestic Service in Twentieth-Century Britain* (Oxford: Oxford University Press, 2011)

Devine, F., *Affluent Workers Revisited: Privatism and the Working Class* (Edinburgh: Edinburgh University Press, 1992)

DeWitt, J., *Indian Workers' Associations in Britain* (Oxford: Oxford University Press, 1969)

Dickens, R., P. Gregg and J. Wadsworth (eds.), *The Labour Market under New Labour* (Basingstoke: Palgrave, 2003)

Field, G., *Blood, Sweat and Toil: Remaking the British Working Class, 1939–1945* (Oxford: Oxford University Press, 2011)

Fielding, S., *Labour: Decline and Renewal* (Manchester: Baseline, 1995)

——*The Labour Party: Continuity and Change in the Making of 'New' Labour* (Basingstoke: Palgrave, 2003)

Forrest, R. and A. Murie, *Selling the Welfare State: The Privatization of Public Housing* (London: Routledge, 1991)

Gallie, D., C. March and C. Vogler (eds.), *Social Change and the Experience of Unemployment* (Oxford: Clarendon, 1994)

Gazeley, I., *Poverty in Britain, 1900–1965* (Basingstoke: Palgrave, 2003)

Gilroy, P., *There Ain't No Black in the Union Jack: Cultural Politics of Race and Nation* (London: Unwin Hyman, 1987)

Gittins, D., *Fair Sex: Family Size and Structure, 1900–39* (London: Hutchinson, 1982)

Glennerster, H., *British Social Policy since 1945* (Oxford: Oxford University Press, 2000)

Goldthorpe, J.H., with C. Llewellyn and C. Payne, *Social Mobility and Class Structure in Modern Britain*, 2nd edn (Oxford: Oxford University Press, 1987)

Gorst, A., L. Johnman and W.S. Lucas (eds.), *Post-War Britain, 1945–64: Themes and Perspectives* (London: Pinter, 1989)

Halsey, A.H. (ed.), *British Social Trends since 1900: A Guide to the Changing Social Structure of Britain* (Basingstoke: Macmillan, 1988)

Halsey, A.H., A.F. Heath and J.M. Ridge, *Origins and Destinations: Family, Class and Education in Modern Britain* (Oxford: Oxford University Press, 1980)

Halsey, A.H. with J. Webb (eds.), *Twentieth-Century British Social Trends* (Oxford: Oxford University Press, 2000)

Holmes, C., *John Bull's Island: Immigration and British Society, 1871–1971* (Basingstoke: Macmillan, 1988)

Jeffreys, K., *War and Reform: British Politics During the Second World War* (Manchester: Manchester University Press, 1994)

Johnson, P., *Saving and Spending: The Working-Class Economy in Britain 1870–1939* (Oxford: Clarendon Press, 1985)

——(ed.), *Twentieth-Century Britain: Economic, Social and Cultural Change* (London: Longman, 1994)

Jones, B., *The Working Class in Mid Twentieth-Century England: Community, Identity and Social Memory* (Manchester: Manchester University Press, 2012)

Joyce, P., *Visions of the People: Industrial England and the Question of Class, 1848–1914* (Cambridge: Cambridge University Press, 1990)

Kynaston, D., *Family Britain, 1951–57* (London: Bloomsbury, 2010)

Laing, S., *Representations of Working-Class Life 1957–1964* (Basingstoke: Macmillan, 1986)

Langhamer, C., *Women's Leisure in England, c.1920–c.1960* (Manchester: Manchester University Press, 2000)

McKibbin, J., *The Ideologies of Class: Social Relations in Britain, 1880–1950* (Oxford: Clarendon Press, 1991)

——*Classes and Cultures: England 1918–1951* (Oxford: Oxford University Press, 1998)

——*Parties and People: England 1914–1951* (Oxford: Oxford University Press, 2010)

Mahoney, P. and C. Zmroczek (eds.), *Class Matters: 'Working Class' Women's Perspectives on Social Class* (London: Taylor and Francis, 1997)

Middlemas, K., *Politics in Industrial Society: The Experience of the British System since 1911* (London: André Deutsch, 1979)

Milne, S., *The Enemy Within: The Secret War Against the Miners* (London: Pan, 1995)

Minton, A., *Ground Control: Fear and Happiness in the Twenty-First-Century City* (London: Penguin, 2012)

Morgan, K.O., *The People's Peace: Britain since 1945* (Oxford: Oxford University Press, 1990)

O'Connell, S., *The Car and British Society: Class, Gender and Motoring 1896–1939* (Manchester: Manchester University Press, 1998)

——*Credit and Community: Working-Class Debt in the UK since 1880* (Oxford: Oxford University Press, 2009)

Pilger, J., *Hidden Agendas* (London: Vintage, 1998)

Reid, A.J., *United We Stand: A History of Britain's Trade Unions* (London: Penguin, 2010)

Roberts, E., *A Woman's Place: An Oral History of Working Class Women 1890–1940* (Oxford: Blackwell, 1984)

——*Women and Families: An Oral History, 1940–1970* (Oxford: Blackwell, 1995)

Rogaly, B. and B. Taylor, *Moving Histories of Class and Community: Identity, Place and Belonging in Contemporary England* (Basingstoke: Palgrave, 2009)

Routh, G., *Occupations and Pay in Great Britain, 1906–1979* (London: Macmillan, 1980)

Saltzman, R., *A Lark for the Sake of their Country: The 1926 General Strike Volunteers in Folklore and Memory* (Manchester: Manchester University Press, 2012)

Samuel, R. and P. Thompson, *The Myths We Live By* (London: Routledge, 1990)

Savage, M., *The Dynamics of Working-Class Politics: The Labour Movement in Preston 1880–1940* (Cambridge: Cambridge University Press, 1987)

——*Identities and Social Change in Britain since 1940: The Politics of Method* (Oxford: Oxford University Press, 2010)

Savage, M., and A. Miles, *The Remaking of the British Working Class, 1840–1940* (London: Routledge, 1994)

Sennett, R., *The Corrosion of Character: The Personal Consequences of Work in the New Capitalism* (London: Norton, 1998)

Sennett, R., and J. Cobb, *The Hidden Injuries of Class* (London: Fontana, 1971)

Skeggs, B., *Formations of Class and Gender: Becoming Respectable* (London: Sage, 1997)

Smith, H.L., *War and Social Change: British Society in the Second World War* (Manchester: Manchester University Press, 1986)

——*Britain in the Second World War: A Social History* (Manchester: Manchester University Press, 1996)

Stevenson, J. and C. Cook, *Britain in the Depression: Society and Politics, 1929–39* (London: Longman, 1994)

Tabili, L., *Global Migrants, Local Culture: Natives and Newcomers in Provincial England, 1841–1939* (Basingstoke: Palgrave, 2011)

Tanner, D., P. Thane and N. Tiratsoo (eds.), *Labour's First Century* (Cambridge: Cambridge University Press, 2000)

Thane, P., *Foundations of the Welfare State* (London: Longman, 1996)

——*Old Age in English History: Past Experiences, Present Issues* (Oxford: Oxford University Press, 2000)

Thompson, E.P., *The Making of the English Working Class* (Harmondsworth: Penguin, 1968).

Todd, S., *Young Women, Work, and Family in England, 1918–1950* (Oxford: Oxford University Press, 2005)

White, J., *Rothschild Buildings: Life in an East End Tenement Block, 1887–1920* (London: Routledge and Kegan Paul, 1980)

——*The Worst Street in North London: Campbell Bunk, Islington, Between the Wars* (London: Routledge, 1986)

Zweiniger-Bargielowska, I., *Austerity in Britain: Rationing, Controls, and Consumption: 1939–1955* (Oxford: Oxford University Press, 2000)

HISTORIES AND COMMENTARIES (ARTICLES)

Abrams, L., '"There was Nobody like my Daddy": Fathers, the Family and the Marginalisation of Men in Modern Scotland', *Scottish Historical Review*, vol. 78, no. 206 (1999)

Alexander, S., 'A New Civilization? London Surveyed 1928–1940s', *History Workshop Journal*, vol. 64, no. 1 (2007)

Ayers, P., 'Work, Culture and Gender: The Making of Masculinities in Post-war Liverpool', *Labour History Review*, vol. 69, no. 2 (2004)

Bowden, S. and A. Offer, 'Household Appliances and the Use of Time: The United States and Britain since the 1920s', *Economic History Review*, vol. 48, no. 4 (1994)

Clapson, M., 'The Suburban Aspiration in England since 1919', *Contemporary British History*, vol. 14, no. 1 (2000)

Dale, P. and K. Fisher, 'Implementing the 1902 Midwives Act: Assessing Problems, Developing Services and Creating a New Role for a Variety of Female Practitioners', *Women's History Review*, vol. 18, no. 3 (2009)

Davis, J., 'Rents and Race in 1960s London: New Left on Rachmanism', *Twentieth Century British History*, vol. 12, no. 1 (2001)

Dawson, S., 'Working-Class Consumers and the Campaign for Holidays with Pay', *Twentieth Century British History*, vol. 18, no. 3 (2007)

Gazeley, I. and C. Langhamer, 'The Meanings of Happiness in Mass Observation's Bolton', *History Workshop Journal*, vol. 75, no. 1 (2012)

Hatton, T.J. and R.E. Bailey, 'Seebohm Rowntree and the Post-war Poverty Puzzle', *Economic History Review*, vol. 53, no. 2 (2000)

Jones, B. 'Slum Clearance, Privatization and Residualization: The Practices and Politics of Council Housing in Mid-twentieth-century England', *Twentieth Century British History*, vol. 21, no. 4 (2010)

——'The Uses of Nostalgia: Autobiography, Community Publishing and Working Class Neighbourhoods in Post-war England', *Cultural and Social History*, vol. 7, no. 3 (2010)

Joshi, H., 'The Opportunity Costs of Childbearing: More than Mothers' Business', *Journal of Population Economics*, vol. 11, no. 2 (1998)

Karn, V., 'The Financing of Owner-Occupation and its Impact on Ethnic Minorities', *New Community*, vol. 1, no. 1 (1977)

Langhamer, C., 'The Meanings of Home in Postwar Britain', *Journal of Contemporary History*, vol. 40, no. 2 (2005)

Lowe, R. and P. Nicholson, 'The Rediscovery of Poverty and the Creation of the Child Poverty Action Group', *Contemporary Record*, vol. 9, no. 3 (1995)

Lucey, H., J. Melody and V. Walkerdine, 'Uneasy Hybrids: Psychosocial Aspects of becoming Educationally Successful for Working Class Young Women', *Gender and Education*, vol. 15, no. 3 (2003)

Mitchell, M., 'The Effects of Unemployment on the Social Condition of Women and Children in the 1930s', *History Workshop Journal*, vol. 19, no. 1 (1985)

Pedersen, S., 'Triumph of the Poshocracy', *London Review of Books*, vol. 35, no. 15 (8 August 2013)

Rawnsley, S., 'The Membership of the British Union of Fascists', in K. Lunn and R. Thurlow (eds.), *British Fascism. Essays on the Radical Right in Interwar Britain* (London: Croom Helm, 1980)

Reay, D., 'Surviving in Dangerous Places: Working-class Women, Women's Studies and Higher Education', *Women's Studies International Forum*, vol. 21, no. 1 (1998)

——'A Useful Extension of Bourdieu's Conceptual Framework? Emotional Capital as a Way of Understanding Mothers' Involvement in Children's Schooling', *Sociological Review*, vol. 48, no. 4 (2000)

Saltzman, R., 'Folklore as Politics in Great Britain: Working-class Critiques of Upper-class Strike Breakers in the 1926 General Strike', *Anthropological Quarterly*, vol. 67, no. 3 (1994)

Savage, M., 'Affluence and Social Change in the Making of Technocratic Middle-Class Identities: Britain, 1939–55', *Contemporary British History*, vol. 22, no. 4 (2008)

Smyth, J., 'Resisting Labour: Unionists, Liberals, and Moderates in Glasgow between the Wars', *Historical Journal*, vol. 46, no. 2 (2003)

Thane, P., 'What Difference Did the Vote Make?', *Historical Research*, vol. 76, no. 192 (2003)

——'Michael Young and Welfare', *Contemporary British History*, vol. 19, no. 3 (2005)

——'The Making of National Insurance, 1911', *Journal of Poverty and Social Justice*, vol. 19, no. 3 (2011)

——'Unmarried Motherhood in Twentieth-Century England', *Women's History Review*, vol. 20, no. 1 (2011)

Thompson, E.P., 'The Peculiarities of the English', *Socialist Register*, no. 2 (1965)

Thornley, E.P. and S.G. Siann, 'The Career Aspirations of South Asian Girls in Glasgow', *Gender and Education*, vol. 3, no. 3 (1991)

Tiratsoo, N., 'Popular Politics, Affluence and the Labour Party', in A. Gorst, L. Johnman and W.S. Lucas (eds.), *Contemporary British History, 1931–61: Politics and the Limits of Policy* (London: Pinter, 1991)

Tomlinson, J., 'It's the Economy, Stupid! Labour and the Economy, *c.*1964', *Contemporary British History*, vol. 21, no. 3 (2007)

Webster, C., 'Healthy or Hungry Thirties?', *History Workshop Journal*, vol. 13, no. 1 (1982)

UNPUBLISHED THESES

Grove, K.A., 'Understanding Benefit Fraud: A Qualitative Analysis', Ph.D. (Leeds, 2002)

Lewenhak, S., 'Trade Union Membership among Women and Girls in the United Kingdom, 1920–1965', Ph.D. (London, 1972)

Whitworth, L., 'Men, Women, Shops and "Little Shiny Homes": The Consuming of Coventry, 1930–39', Ph.D. (Warwick, 1997)

Index

Barstow, Stan: *A Kind of Loving*,
238–9
Basildon, Essex, 335, 339, 352, 359
Bath Co-operative Society: strike
(1941), 129–31
*Bath and Wiltshire Chronicle and
Herald*, 130
Baxendales (Manchester store), 43
Baxter, Alan, 266
Beales, H.L. and R.S. Lambert:
Memoirs of the Unemployed, 75–6
Beatles, the (pop group), 242
Beckwith, Louise, 336
Beckwith, Lady Muriel, 22
Bedaux, Charles: factory system,
102–4, 128
Beers, Laura, 145
Bell, Dennis and Frank, 261
Bell, Jack, 68, 113
benefit culture, 326; *see also* welfare
(social)
Benn, Tony, 310–11, 333–4
Benson, Eileen, 69
Benson, Ernie, 69–71, 79, 283
Berry, Charles, 293
Bethnal Green: community life, 175;
residents rehoused in Essex, 183
Bevan, Aneurin: on workers'
independence, 158; housing
programme, 162–3, 166, 174–5,
179, 185; on housing differences,
168; condemns affluent society,
247
Beveridge, Sir William, 141; Report
(*Social Insurance and Allied Services*,
1942), 140, 142–5, 150
Bevin, Ernest: as trade unionist, 106;
as Minister of Labour in wartime
government, 124–5, 128, 130; and
wartime strikes, 130–1; argues for
increased rations for manual
workers, 132; promotes abolition

of means test, 138; and wartime
radio broadcasts, 139; advocates
healthy workforce, 141; post-war
welfare plans, 142–4; on the
people, 148; guarantees jobs for
returning servicemen, 154;
reforms dock labour, 159; pleads
for prioritizing welfare, 161
Beynon, Huw, 275, 285, 287
bicycles, 106–7
Billy Boys (Glasgow gang), 52
Birmingham: riots (1981), 320
Birmingham Post, 55
birth control: advice on, 85;
availability, 196–7
Black, Cilla, 242
Blackburn, Carol, 156
Blair, Tony, 299, 339–40, 346–7, 349
Blake, Howard, 206, 227–8, 319
Bland, G.M., 133
Blenkin, Lily, 27
Blitz (wartime), 136–8
Blunkett, David, 340
Board of Guardians: attitude to poor,
20–1; and means tests, 62–3
Board of Guardians (Default) Act
(1927), 63
Bolton, Lancashire ('Worktown'),
253
Bosanquet, Helen, 17
Boscawen, Arthur Griffith- *see*
Griffith-Boscawen, Arthur
Bowley, A.L., 68
Braine, John: *Room at the Top*, 238
Bridport, Dorset, 119, 121
Brierley, Walter: *Means Test Man*, 78
Bright Young People, 53–4
Brind, Bill, 34
Bristol: unemployment and poverty,
68, 329–30; race relations, 190
BritainThinks (organization), 345,
351